THE ORGANIZATIONAL FRONTIERS SERIES

The Organizational Frontiers Series is sponsored by the Society for Industrial and Organizational Psychology (SIOP). Launched in 1983 to make scientific contributions to the field, the series has attempted to publish books that are on the cutting edge of theory, research, and theory-driven practice in industrial/organizational psychology and related organizational science disciplines.

Our overall objective is to inform and to stimulate research for SIOP members (students, practitioners, and researchers) and people in related disciplines, including the other subdisciplines of psychology, organizational behavior, human resource management, and labor and industrial relations. The volumes in the Organizational Frontiers Series have the following goals:

1. Focus on research and theory in organizational science, and the implications for practice
2. Inform readers of significant advances in theory and research in psychology and related disciplines that are relevant to our research and practice
3. Challenge the research and practice community to develop and adapt new ideas and to conduct research on these developments
4. Promote the use of scientific knowledge in the solution of public policy issues and increased organizational effectiveness

The volumes originated in the hope that they would facilitate continuous learning and a continuing research curiosity about organizational phenomena on the part of both scientists and practitioners.

Previous Organizational Frontiers Series volumes, all published by Jossey-Bass, include:

Health and Safety in Organizations
David A. Hofmann and Lois E. Tetrick, Editors

Managing Knowledge for Sustained Competitive Advantage
Susan E. Jackson, Michael A. Hitt, and Angelo S. DeNisi, Editors

Personality and Work: Reconsidering the Role of Personality in Organizations
Murray R. Barrick and Ann Marie Ryan, Editors

Emotions in the Workplace
Robert G. Lord, Richard J. Klimoski, and Ruth Kanfer, Editors

Measuring and Analyzing Behavior in Organizations: Advances in Measurement and Data Analysis
Fritz Drasgow and Neal Schmitt, Editors

Work Careers: A Developmental Perspective
Daniel C. Feldman, Editor

The Nature of Organizational Leadership: Understanding the Performance Imperatives Confronting Today's Leaders
Stephen J. Zaccaro and Richard J. Klimoski, Editors

Multilevel Theory, Research, and Methods in Organizations: Foundations, Extensions, and New Directions
Katherine J. Klein and Steve W. J. Kozlowski, Editors

Compensation in Organizations: Current Research and Practice
Sara L. Rynes and Barry Gerhart, Editors

The Changing Nature of Performance: Implications for Staffing, Motivation, and Development
Daniel R. Ilgen and Elaine D. Pulakos, Editors

New Perspectives on International I-O Psychology
P. Christopher Earley and Miriam Erez, Editors

Individual Differences and Behavior in Organizations
Kevin R. Murphy, Editor

The Changing Nature of Work
Ann Howard, Editor

Team Effectiveness and Decision Making in Organizations
Richard A. Guzzo and Eduardo Salas, Editors

The Dark Side of Organizational Behavior

Ricky W. Griffin and

Anne M. O'Leary-Kelly

Editors

Foreword by Robert D. Pritchard

JOSSEY-BASS
A Wiley Imprint
www.josseybass.com

Published by Jossey-Bass
A Wiley Imprint
989 Market Street, San Francisco, CA 94103-1741   www.josseybass.com

Jossey-Bass books and products are available through most bookstores. To contact
Jossey-Bass directly, call our Customer Care Department within the U.S. at 800-956-7739,
outside the U.S. at 317-572-3986, or fax 317-572-4002.

Jossey-Bass also publishes its books in a variety of electronic formats. Some content that
appears in print may not be available in electronic books.

Library of Congress Cataloging-in-Publication Data

Griffin, Ricky W.
  The dark side of organizational behavior / Ricky W. Griffin and Anne M.
O'Leary-Kelly.
      p. cm.
Includes bibliographical references and index.
  ISBN 0-7879-6223-6 (alk. paper)
  1. Quality of work life. 2. Work environment. I. O'Leary-Kelly,
Anne. II. Title.
  HD6955.G72 2004
  302.3'5—dc22

                                                        2003025428

Printed in the United States of America
FIRST EDITION
HB Printing 10 9 8 7 6 5 4 3 2 1

The Organizational Frontiers Series

Contents

Foreword

This is the twenty-first book in the Organizational Frontiers series of books initiated by the Society for Industrial and Organizational Psychology (SIOP). The overall purpose of the series is to promote the scientific status of the field. Ray Katzell first edited the series, followed by Irwin Goldstein, Sheldon Zedeck, and Neal Schmitt. The editors and topics for the volumes are chosen by the editorial board, or individuals propose topics for the volumes to the editorial board. The series editor and the editorial board then work with the volume editor(s) in planning the volume. During the writing of the volume, the series editor often works with the volume editor and the publisher to bring the book to completion.

The success of the series is evident in the high number of sales (now over forty-five thousand). Volumes have received excellent reviews, and individual chapters as well as entire volumes have been cited very frequently. A recent symposium at the SIOP annual meeting examined the impact of the series on research and theory in industrial and organizational psychology. Although such influence is difficult to track and volumes are varied in intent and perceived centrality to the discipline, the conclusion of most participants was that the volumes have exerted a significant impact on research and theory in the field and are regarded as being representative of the best the field has to offer.

This volume, edited by Ricky Griffin and Anne O'Leary-Kelly, reflects new thinking and research on a series of issues that reflect negative behaviors in organizations, hence the name *The Dark Side of Organizational Behavior.* There is a clear need for attention to these topics. Most research in industrial and organizational psychology and organizational behavior has focused on the positive contributions people make to organizations. Although the positive side is clearly important, there is a growing awareness of the impact of more negative aspects of behavior, such as theft, harassment, alcohol and drug abuse, and retaliatory behavior. This volume pulls together the research and thinking of some of the strongest scholars in these areas. We all hope this volume will energize researchers in this important topic of our discipline and stimulate new ideas about how to understand and deal with negative behaviors.

The volume has a number of important strengths. First, it covers a broad range of topics, including workplace aggression and violence; injustice, stress and aggression; intimate partner violence and the workplace; discrimination; sexual harassment; sexual orientation discrimination; the dark side of organizational politics; under-the-table deals; extreme careerism; psychological contract breach violations; alcohol and drug abuse; organizational retaliatory behavior; incivility; and employee theft.

The volume also focuses on the antecedents, processes, and consequences of behaviors in organizations that have a negative impact on the organization, the people in them, or the people in their environments. It also considers all levels of analysis from the individual to the organizational to, in some cases, the societal level as well. It considers the practical issues of how organizations do or could deal with such negative behaviors.

Another major strength of the volume is how it identifies the research needs and agenda for each area, including the appropriate research methodologies. This strength is particularly important because we want the volume to stimulate research. The more the questions and methodologies are presented by these experts, the better other researchers can use the information to do new research. Future research ideas are presented in each chapter and covered extensively in the concluding chapter, where the editors present a valuable summary of the conceptual issues and research needs in this area. For scholars who are interested in the dark side topics, this concluding chapter presents an excellent summary of the important issues and a road map for guiding future research.

An interesting point the editors make in the concluding chapter is that each of these dark side behaviors is actually quite distinct from the others. The editors argue the importance of this issue in noting that earlier work in this area tended to combine negative behaviors into categories such as "workplace aggression" or "organizational deviance." Such grouping offered little discriminant validity between the behaviors, and the concern was that identifying antecedents and consequences for separate behaviors was not really feasible. By breaking down these general behaviors more specifically, the editors show that studying them separately is not only possible but also highly desirable.

The target audiences for the Organizational Frontiers Series include graduate students in industrial and organizational psychology and organizational behavior, as well as doctoral-level researchers and practitioners who want to gain knowledge on the most up-to-date data and theory regarding these dark side behaviors. I believe that this book represents a significant advance in our thinking about such negative behaviors. It broadens our perspective on important dark side behaviors, combines current theory and empirical work, and integrates these in a way that should have a major impact on the scholarship and practice in our field for years to come.

The editors and chapter authors deserve our gratitude for pursuing the goal of clearly communicating the nature, application, and implications of the theory and research described in this book. Production of a volume such as this involves the hard work and cooperative effort of many individuals. The editors, the chapter authors, and the editorial board all played important roles in this endeavor. Because all royalties from the series are used to help support SIOP financially, none of the participants received any remuneration. They deserve our appreciation for engaging in a difficult task for the sole purpose of furthering our understanding of organizational science. We also express our sincere gratitude to Cedric Crocker, Matt Davis, Nina Kreiden, and the entire staff at Jossey-Bass/Pfeiffer. Over many years and several volumes, they have provided support during the planning, development, and production of the series.

January 2004   Robert D. Pritchard
                                                University of Central Florida
                                                Series Editor, 2003–2008

Preface

George Lucas has made numerous contributions to American popular culture, none more ubiquitous than the concept of "the dark side." Indeed, there are not many people today who cannot readily see or hear Darth Vader beckoning young Luke Skywalker to "give in and turn to the dark side of the force." And more than a few no doubt secretly think that perhaps once, just once, the noble hero should consider using his adversary's own methods against him. After all, wouldn't it be just the sweetest justice of all to see Luke embrace the dark side but then use it to smite down both Lord Vader and the evil emperor and his minions before returning to the light and again becoming the noble hero?

But when the concept of the dark side is taken off the movie screen and applied to a real world context such as an organization it quickly loses its allure. Indeed, there is nothing lighthearted about the real dark side—situations in which people hurt other people, injustices are perpetuated and magnified, and the pursuits of wealth, power, or revenge lead people to behaviors that others can only see as unethical, illegal, despicable, or reprehensible.

This book represents a collective effort by an array of organizational scholars to explore and reveal the true nature of the dark side as applied to organizational behavior. The contributors were selected because of their past and current work in areas that reflect the dark side. Each was invited to tackle a specific part of the dark side of organizational behavior, charged with reviewing existing theory and research about that behavior, and challenged to outline and propose avenues for future research.

We would like to thank these contributors for agreeing to join us and for working diligently to achieve the goals set out before them. We would also like to thank Robert Pritchard. It was Bob who first proposed this volume to us and who then provided encouragement and support in many different ways as we moved through the process of creating this book. We would also like to acknowledge numerous reviewers who helped us and the other authors sharpen our thinking and refine our ideas. These reviewers include Vikas Anand, University of Arkansas; Allen Bluedorn, University of Missouri; Wendy Boswell, Texas A&M University; Lynn Bowes-Sperry, Western New England College; Dan Ganster, University of Arkansas; David Glew, Tulsa; Michelle Duffy, University of Kentucky; Deborah Knapp, Kent State University; Ramona Paetzold, Texas A&M University; Christine Pearson, Thunderbird; Robert Pritchard, University of Central Florida; Daniel Skarlicki, University of British Columbia; Bennett Tepper, University of North Carolina at Charlotte; Lois Tetrick, University of Houston; Bill Turnley, Kansas State University; Michael Wesson, Texas A&M University; Richard Woodman, Texas A&M University; Stuart Youngblood, Texas Christian University; and Jing Zhou, Rice University.

January 2004

Ricky W. Griffin
College Station, Texas

Anne M. O'Leary-Kelly
Fayetteville, Arkansas

The Contributors

Ricky W. Griffin is Distinguished Professor of Management and Blocker Chair in Business at Mays Business School at Texas A&M University. His research interests include workplace aggression and violence, organizational security, and leadership. Griffin's work has been published in such journals as the *Academy of Management Review, Academy of Management Journal, Administrative Science Quarterly,* and *Journal of Management.* He has also served as editor of the *Journal of Management.* Griffin has served the Academy of Management as chair of the Organizational Behavior Division. He has also served as president of the Southwest Division of the Academy of Management and on the board of directors of the Southern Management Association. Ricky is a Fellow of both the Academy of Management and the Southern Management Association. He currently serves as executive associate dean at the Mays Business School.

Anne M. O'Leary-Kelly is a professor in the Department of Management at the University of Arkansas. She received her Ph.D. in organizational behavior and human resources management from Michigan State University in 1990. Her research interests include the study of aggressive work behavior (violence and sexual harassment) and individual attachments to organizations (psychological contracts and identification). Her work has appeared in the *Academy of Management Review, Academy of Management Journal, Journal of Applied Psychology, Journal of Management,* and *Journal of Organizational Behavior,* as well as other publications. She has been a corecipient of the Outstanding Publication in Organizational Behavior Award and the Dorothy Harlow Outstanding Paper Award given by the Academy of Management; a corecipient of the Richard A. Swanson Award for Excellence in Research from the American Society for Training and Development; and a corecipient of the Ralph C. Hoeber Award for Excellence in Research for work published in the *American Business Law Journal*. She currently serves on the executive committee of the Organizational Behavior Division of the Academy of Management.

Robert A. Baron is Dean R. Wellington Professor of Management and professor of psychology at Rensselaer Polytechnic Institute. He received his Ph.D. from the University of Iowa in 1968, and has held faculty appointments at Purdue University, the University of Minnesota, University of Texas, University of South Carolina, University of Washington, and Princeton University. He has been a Fellow of the American Psychological Association since 1978, and is also a Charter Fellow of the American Psychological Society. Baron has published more than one hundred articles in professional journals and thirty-five chapters in edited volumes. He is the author or co-author of forty books in the fields of management and psychology, including *Behavior in Organizations* (8th ed.) and *Social Psychology* (10th ed.). His new book, *Entrepreneurship: A Process Perspective*, was published in January 2004. Baron's research and consulting activities focus primarily on social and cognitive factors in entrepreneurship, workplace aggression and violence, and the impact of the physical environment (for example, lighting, air quality, and temperature) on productivity.

Michael G. Bowen is a visiting professor at the University of South Florida. He received a Ph.D. in business administration from the University of Illinois at Urbana-Champaign. He previously served on the faculty of the University of Notre Dame. Bowen has published scholarly papers and case studies on the escalation phenomenon, business ethics, leadership, organizational culture, political behavior, and decision making. His articles have appeared in such journals as the *Academy of Management Review, Business Ethics Quarterly,* and *System Dynamics Review.* Bowen is a co-founder of the Leadership Development Center at the University of South Florida.

Virginia K. Bratton is a doctoral candidate in organizational behavior at Florida State University. She received her M.A. in arts administration at Florida State University. Prior to her doctoral candidacy, Bratton was an assistant director for a multidisciplinary arts festival in the Southeast. Her research interests include impression management, business ethics, and organizational identity. Virginia coauthored a paper that recently received a best paper award at the Academy of Management annual meeting and has articles under review and forthcoming in the *Journal of Organizational Behavior* and *Journal of Vocational Behavior.*

Arthur P. Brief is the Lawrence Martin Chair of Business at Tulane University with a courtesy appointment in the Department of Psychology. He received his Ph.D. from the University of Wisconsin, Madison in 1974. He also is director of the William B. and Evelyn Burkenroad Institute for the Study of Ethics and Leadership in Management. Prior to his move to Tulane in 1989, Brief was on the faculties of several other schools, including, most recently, New York University's Stern School of Business. He is a recipient of the Freeman School's most prized award for teaching, the Wissner Award, and the Academic Leadership Award from the Aspen Institute's Initiative for Social Innovation Through Business and the World Resources Institute for integrating social and environmental concerns into business education. In January 2003, Brief became the editor of the *Academy of Management Review.* He is a Fellow of the Academy of Management, the American Psychological Association, and the American Psychological Society. He has also served as the chair of the Academy of Management's Organizational Behavior Division.

Graham Brown is a doctoral candidate at the University of British Columbia. He is a student in organizational behavior at the Sauder School of Business, University of British Columbia. His research interests focus primarily on territoriality. As a master's student at the University of Utah he studied the positive impact of territoriality in reducing crime in urban neighborhoods. His recent work involves studying the role of territoriality in organizations. This includes the positive side, such as increasing organizational commitment of those who engage in territoriality, and the "dark" side, such as the preoccupation with claiming and defending territories.

Rebecca M. Butz is a doctoral candidate in organizational behavior at the A. B. Freeman School of Business at Tulane University. Her primary research interests are diversity in organizations and worker well-being.

Elizabeth Ann Deitch is a professor at Loyola University, New Orleans. She earned her doctorate from Tulane University in 2002. Her research interests include prejudice, stereotyping, and discrimination in the workplace, with an emphasis on the well-being of those who are targets of workplace discrimination. She has done work focusing on racial and gender discrimination, and is now turning her efforts to the emerging issue of sexual orientation discrimination on the job.

Robert L. Dipboye is the Herbert S. Autrey Professor of Psychology and Management and director of the industrial and organizational psychology Ph.D. program at Rice University. He graduated from Purdue University with a Ph.D. in industrial and organizational psychology in 1973. He has held faculty positions in the business schools at the University of Tennessee and Purdue University, and was department chair at Rice University for six years. His research interests include employee staffing, recruiting, and other issues of human resource management, as well as discrimination and diversity in organizations. He published articles on these and other topics in a variety of journals, including the *Journal of Applied Psychology, Personnel Psychology, Organizational Behavior and Human Decision Processes, Academy of Management Review,* and *Academy of Management Journal.* He is the author of three books: *Selection Interviews: Process Perspectives, Understanding Industrial and Organizational Psychology: An Integrated Approach,* and *Essentials of Industrial and Organizational Psychology.* He is a Fellow of the American Psychological Association, the American Psychological Society, and the Society of Industrial and Organizational Psychology. He is also an elected member of the Society of Organizational Behavior and has been an associate editor of the *Journal of Applied Psychology* and on the editorial boards of the *Academy of Management Review, Journal of Organizational Behavior,* and the *SIOP Frontiers Series.*

Gerald R. Ferris is Francis Eppes Professor of Management and professor of psychology at Florida State University. He held the Robert M. Hearin Chair of Business Administration and was professor of management and acting associate dean for faculty and research in the School of Business Administration at the University of Mississippi from 1999 to 2000. Before that, he served as professor of labor and industrial relations, business administration, and psychology at the University of Illinois at Urbana-Champaign from 1989 to 1999, and as the director of the Center for Human Resource Management at the University of Illinois from 1991 to 1996. Ferris received a Ph.D. in business administration from the University of Illinois at Urbana-Champaign. He has research interests in the social influence processes in human resource systems and the role of reputation in organizations. Ferris is the author of articles published in such journals as the *Journal of Applied Psychology, Organizational Behavior and Human Decision Processes, Personnel Psychology, Academy of Management Journal,* and *Academy of Management Review.* He served as editor of the annual series *Research in Personnel and Human Resources Management,* from 1981 to 2003.

Robert Folger is a professor at the University of Central Florida. He received his Ph.D. in 1975 from the University of North Carolina at Chapel Hill. He is a Fellow of the American Psychological Association, the Society of Industrial and Organizational Psychology, and the Society for Personality and Social Psychology. He has also been a member-at-large on the executive board of the Conflict Management Division of the Academy of Management, and he is currently member-at-large for the Organizational Behavior Division. His honors and awards include the New Concept Award from the Organizational Behavior Division of the Academy of Management. His research funding includes grants from the National Science Foundation and the National Institute of Mental Health. Folger has authored over a hundred publications, including articles in the *Academy of Management Journal, Academy of Management Review, Organizational Behavior and Human Decision Processes, Journal of Applied Psychology, Psychological Bulletin, Psychological Review,* and *Research in Organizational Behavior.* He is currently on the editorial boards of *Organizational Behavior and Human Decision Processes* and *Social Justice Research.* He edited *The Sense of Injustice* and coauthored *Controversial Issues in Social Research Method.* Another of his coauthored books, *Organizational Justice and Human Resources Management,* was judged "Book of the Year" in 1998 by the International Association for Conflict Management. Folger has also served as a consultant with the U.S. Department of Justice, the U.S. Postal Service, the IRS, and with companies in industries such as manufacturing, wholesale distribution, public utilities, transportation, state government, health care, and computer software. This work has included several Fortune 500 firms.

Jerald Greenberg is the Abramowitz Professor of Business Ethics and professor of organizational behavior at the Ohio State University's Fisher College of Business. He is best known for his pioneering work on organizational justice. He has published extensively on this topic, with over 140 professional journal articles and twenty books to his credit. From the Organizational Behavior Division of the Academy of Management, Professor Greenberg has won the New Concept Award and twice has won the Best Paper Award. Greenberg is coauthor of the forthcoming volume *Organizational Justice: A Primer,* and coeditor of the forthcoming *Handbook of Organizational Justice.* Greenberg has been inducted as a Fellow of the American Psychological Association, the American Psychological Society, and the Academy of Management. He also is past-chair of the Organizational Behavior Division of the Academy of Management.

Angela T. Hall is a doctoral candidate at Florida State University. She received a Juris Doctor degree from Florida State University in 1993, and has been a member in good standing of the Florida Bar since her admittance in 1994. Her research interests include accountability, ethics, workplace accommodations, and organizational politics. She has coauthored several book chapters, including a chapter on work-family conflict and family-friendly policies that appeared in *Individual and Organizational Health* (SIOP Organizational Frontiers Series).

Stefanie K. Halverson is a graduate student at Rice University. She received her M.A. and is working toward her Ph.D. in industrial and organizational psychology. Her research interests include various aspects of organizational behavior, including leadership, selection, teams, and organizational citizenship behavior. Her dissertation, for which she received a National Academies of Sciences Ford Foundation Dissertation Fellowship, focuses on the impact of emotions on leadership behavior and leader-follower interactions.

Michael M. Harris is professor of management and holds a fellowship in the International Business Institute of the University of Missouri, St. Louis College of Business Administration, and is a Fellow in the University of Missouri, St. Louis Center for International Studies. His research interests include staffing and selection, performance management, compensation, and substance use in the workplace, and he has examined these topics in both domestic and international settings. He has also consulted with a variety of organizations in these areas and has served as an expert witness regarding employment discrimination. He is coeditor of the *Employment Interview Handbook* and is currently editing a volume entitled *The Handbook of Research in International Human Resource*

Management. Harris has served on seven editorial boards, including the *Journal of Applied Psychology, Journal of Health and Social Behavior, Journal of Organizational Behavior,* and *Personnel Psychology.*

Wayne A. Hochwarter is currently associate professor of management at Florida State University. Prior to this appointment, he held similar positions at Mississippi State University and the University of Alabama. Hochwarter received his Ph.D. from Florida State University. His research interests lie in the areas of social influence, accountability, workplace politics, and organizational cynicism. He has published articles in the *Journal of Applied Psychology, Journal of Management, Journal of Vocational Behavior, Educational and Psychological Measurement,* and *Journal of Applied Social Psychology.*

K. Michele (Micki) Kacmar is Charles A. Rovetta Professor of Management and the director of the Center for Human Resource Management at Florida State University. She received her Ph.D. in human resource management from Texas A&M University. Her general research interests fall in the area of organizational entry. Of particular interest to Kacmar is how impression management and organizational politics can be applied to these areas. She has published over fifty articles in journals such as the *Journal of Applied Psychology, Organizational Behavior and Human Decision Processes,* and *Human Relations.* Kacmar served as editor of the *Journal of Management* from 2000 to 2003 and on the board of directors of the Society for Human Resource Management Foundation from 1993 to 2000.

Joel H. Neuman is associate professor of management and organizational behavior and director of the Center for Applied Management in the School of Business at the State University of New York at New Paltz. His research and consulting activities involve interpersonal relations and group process in organizational settings. More specifically, his work focuses on interpersonal conflict, workplace aggression and violence, and, most recently, the use of collaborative inquiry within the action research process. His work has appeared in the *Journal of Management, Public Administration Quarterly, Aggressive Behavior, Antisocial Behavior in Organizations,* and *Bullying and Emotional Abuse in the Workplace: International Perspectives in Research and Practice.* In recognition of his research in the area of workplace aggression and violence, he received the 2001

Chancellor's Award for Excellence in Research from the Research Foundation of the State University of New York.

Ramona L. Paetzold is professor and Mays Faculty Fellow in the Management Department at Texas A&M University. She holds a doctoral degree from Indiana University in statistics and a J.D. from the University of Nebraska, specializing in the field of employment law. Her research interests involve the legal and psychological aspects of discrimination, particularly with regard to sexual harassment and mental disabilities. Her work has appeared in major journals such as *Academy of Management Review, Personnel Psychology, American Business Law Journal,* and *North Carolina Law Review.* She has served as editor of the *American Business Law Journal* and currently serves on the editorial board of *Academy of Management Review.* Her research has received awards from both the Academy of Management and the Academy of Legal Studies in Business.

Christine M. Pearson is associate professor of management at Thunderbird, American Graduate School of International Management. She holds a Ph.D. in business from the Marshall School, University of Southern California. Her research focuses on workplace incivility, aggression, and violence, as well as global organizational crisis management. Pearson's work has appeared in publications such as *Academy of Management Review, Harvard Business Review, Human Relations, Academy of Management Executive,* and *Organizational Dynamics.* She is currently writing her fourth book on international organizational crisis management.

Christine L. Porath is a professor of management and organizational behavior at the Marshall School of Business, University of Southern California. She received her Ph.D. from Kenan-Flagler Business School at the University of North Carolina at Chapel Hill. She is interested in situated, motivated, interpersonal behavior. Specifically, her research focuses on two types: individual self-regulation and (in)civility in the workplace. Her research has been published in *Harvard Business Review, Organizational Dynamics, Academy of Management Executive,* as well as in several books.

Carol Anne Reeves is a professor of management in the Sam M. Walton College of Business at the University of Arkansas. She received her Ph.D. in strategic management from the University of Georgia. Her research interests include strategic management, entrepreneurship, and corporate social responsibility, with a particular interest in the relationship between family conflict and the workplace. Her work has appeared in journals such as the *Academy of Management Review, Quality Management Journal, Cornell H.R.A. Quarterly,* and *Journal of Small Business Management.* She is on the case editorial board for *Entrepreneurship Theory and Practice.*

Sandra L. Robinson is an associate professor of organizational behavior at the Sauder School of Business, University of British Columbia. Her research focuses primarily on the "dark side" of organizational behavior. She has studied psychological contract breach and trust betrayal, workplace deviance and aggression, and, most recently, territorial behavior in organizations. Her publications have appeared in various journals, such as *Administrative Science Quarterly, Academy of Management Journal,* and *Journal of Applied Psychology.* She has received a number of awards, including the Ascendant Scholar Award from the Western Academy of Management, and the Cummings Scholar Award from the Academy of Management. Currently, Dr. Robinson serves on the editorial boards of *Academy of Management Journal, Journal of Organizational Behavior,* and *Journal of Engineering and Technology Management* and is an associate editor at the *Journal of Management Inquiry.* She has served as a board member of the Western Academy of Management as well as the Organizational Behavior Division of the Academy of Management.

Denise M. Rousseau is the H. J. Heinz II Professor of Organizational Behavior at Carnegie Mellon University, jointly in the Heinz School of Public Policy and Management and in the Graduate School of Industrial Administration. She has been a faculty member at Northwestern University, the University of Michigan, and the Naval Postgraduate School (Monterey). Her research addresses the employment relationship and organizational change. Her books include *Relational Wealth: Advantages of Stability in a Changing Economy,* with Carrie Leana; *Psychological Contracts in Employment: Cross-National Perspectives,* with Rene Schalk, which won the Academy of Management's best book award in 1996; the *Trends in Organizational Behavior Series,* with Cary Cooper; *Developing an Interdisciplinary Science of Organizations,* with Karlene Roberts and Charles Hulin; and *The Boundaryless Career,* with Michael Arthur. Dr. Rousseau is a Fellow in the Academy of Management, American Psychological Association, and Society for Industrial/Organizational Psychology, and is editor-in-chief of the *Journal of Organizational Behavior.* She is president-elect of the Academy of Management. Rousseau has a B.A. in psychology and anthropology, an M.A. in psychology, and a Ph.D. in psychology from the University of California, Berkeley.

Daniel P. Skarlicki is an associate professor at the Sauder School of Business at the University of British Columbia. Daniel received his Ph.D. from the University of Toronto. His general research area is in organizational behavior and human resource management. His research interests focus on the antecedents and consequences of organizational justice, in particular, organizational citizenship behavior and retaliation in the workplace. His research has appeared in *Academy of Management Journal, Administrative Sciences Quarterly, Journal of Applied Psychology,* and *Personnel Psychology.* He is the coeditor of *Research on Social Issues in Management,* consulting editor of *Journal of Organizational Behavior,* and serves on the editorial board of *Journal of Management.* In 2000 he received the Ascendant Scholar Award from the Western Academy of Management.

Edward C. Tomlinson is a doctoral candidate at Ohio State University. He holds an undergraduate degree in economics and business from Virginia Military Institute, an MBA from Lynchburg College, and a master's in labor and human resources from Ohio State University. His primary research interests within organizational behavior include the role of trust in professional relationships, negotiation and dispute resolution, and employee deviance.

The Dark Side of
Organizational Behavior

CHAPTER 1

An Introduction to the Dark Side

Ricky W. Griffin, Anne M. O'Leary-Kelly

Organizational behavior is the study of human behavior in organizational settings. It is also a relatively young field of study, one that is still seeking to define its boundaries and determine its fundamental concepts and processes. In some ways, organizational behavior emerged as a counterpoint to the widespread popularity of Frederick Taylor's scientific management, an industrial engineering-based approach to management that emerged in the early 1900s (cf., Taylor, 1911). Scientific management was primarily focused on how managers could boost the productivity of workers through efficiency and standardization techniques such as time-and-motion study and piece-rate pay systems. In Taylor's view, the roles of individuals and groups in organizations were either ignored altogether or given only minimal attention.

First There Was the Light . . .

A few early writers and managers, however, did begin to recognize the importance of individual and social processes in organizations. The noted German psychologist Hugo Munsterberg, for instance, was one of the pioneers of industrial psychology and argued that the field of psychology could provide important insights into areas such as motivation and the hiring of new employees. And in some ways his approach to human behavior in organizations set the tone for what would follow. At the end of his seminal book *Psychology and Industrial Efficiency,* published in 1913, Munsterberg argues that it is in the best interests of both employers and employees to improve industrial efficiency and the psychological conditions of work. He goes on to suggest that if managers can find the right blend of efficiency (for organizations) and psychological fulfillment (for workers), then "mental dissatisfaction at work may be replaced in our social community by overflowing joy and perfect social harmony." (One can almost hear the birds singing, feel the breeze gently blowing, and see the flowers blooming!)

In later years, during the so-called human relations era of management, these same basic ideas were reflected (albeit with much more restraint) in the popular writings of Douglas McGregor and Abraham Maslow (cf., McGregor, 1960; Maslow, 1943). McGregor is best known for his classic book *The Human Side of Enterprise,* in which he identified two countervailing perspectives that he believed to typify managerial views of employees. Some managers, McGregor said, subscribed to what he labeled Theory X. Theory X takes a pessimistic view of human nature and employee behavior and is in many ways consistent with the original premises of scientific management. But a much more optimistic and positive view of employees is found in Theory Y, which suggests that workers are internally motivated and committed and can be led to enjoy working. McGregor argues that managers who adopt a Theory X mentality are wrong—that the Theory Y perspective is really more consistent with human nature and is thus the perspective that enlightened managers should adopt.

Abraham Maslow's famous hierarchy of needs, arguably the best-known theory of human motivation, also takes a similarly optimistic and positive view of human behavior. Maslow argued that human beings are "wanting" animals: they have innate desires to satisfy a given set of needs. Furthermore, Maslow believed that these needs are arranged in a hierarchy of importance, with the most basic needs at the foundation of the hierarchy. The three sets of needs at the bottom of the hierarchy are deficiency needs, because they must be satisfied for the individual to be fundamentally comfortable. The top two sets of needs are growth needs, because they focus on personal growth and development. One basic implication is that managers can motivate people to work if they (1) understand where on the hierarchy an individual is currently functioning and (2) provide performance-contingent opportunities for the individual to satisfy needs associated with the next level of the hierarchy.

Since these early pioneering contributions to the field, organizational behavior theorists and researchers have continued to direct most of their attention on how various behaviors benefit organizations and the antecedent conditions associated with those beneficial behaviors. For example, most theories and models of individual behavior have concentrated on how processes within organizations affect such variables as job satisfaction, employee motivation, performance, organizational commitment, and so forth. Theories and models of leadership and decision making examine how the organization might improve leadership effectiveness or decision-making quality and the leader's ability to motivate workers. At the group level, the dependent variables of interest are usually things like cohesiveness, performance norms, communication patterns, and group-level performance, as well as individual responses to a group or team context.

Implicit in these theories and models is the assumption that if we can learn more about cause-and-effect linkages among key variables, managers and organizations would thus be in a position to enhance these outcome variables by manipulating their causes. For example, a basic implicit assumption of job characteristics research is that if researchers can identify specific job attributes that cause employees to be motivated and to perform at a higher level, managers can then redesign jobs to enhance those attributes, thereby also enhancing motivation and performance.

In general, the common themes of these dependent variables are functionality enhancement. That is, they are presumed to be phenomena that can serve to improve and enhance the organization in one or more beneficial ways—to boost productivity, improve morale, or make the organization more effective. These functional variables thus serve, at least in theory, to boost an organization's revenues or lower its costs (through improved performance or productivity, for example) or improve the internal climate (through improved morale, for example) or all of these. Indeed, employee turnover and absenteeism are perhaps the only historically common dependent variables that have a negative connotation. But even these variables are seen as things that are

(1) caused by specific events and attributes in the organization, (2) accompanied by various replacement costs, and (3) thus manageable in the sense of changing organizational events and attributes so as to reduce those costs.

. . . Then Came the Dark

But just as other social sciences have continued to evolve in the level of sophistication and complexity in their theories and models, however, so too has organizational behavior moved from a relatively simplistic and narrowly focused discipline to a much richer and more encompassing field with a broader array of concepts and variables. As part of this evolution, new types of dependent variables have emerged in theory and research. Although some of these newly defined types of behaviors are also functional in nature, others are considerably less functional in that they relate to negative consequences or involve direct costs to the individuals who make up organizations and to the organizations themselves. Representative of this new type of dependent variable, for example, is workplace violence. Violent behavior in no way benefits the organization and, if acknowledged at all in an organization, is seen as something to be controlled, minimized, or eliminated altogether (O'Leary-Kelly, Griffin & Glew, 1996).

This book was conceived to provide an opportunity for scholars interested in these kinds of behaviors to have a forum to present, expand, and further develop their thinking about what we are calling the "dark side" of organizational behavior. We consider dark side behavior to be motivated behavior by an employee or group of employees that has negative consequences for an individual within the organization, another group of individuals within the organization, or the organization itself. Several elements of this framing warrant additional discussion and will be explored in the following paragraphs.

First, dark side behaviors result in negative outcomes. These outcomes, in turn, are perhaps best conceptualized as costs. The costs resulting from dark side behaviors may take a variety of forms. For example, they might be real and measurable costs (for example, theft of company property) or indirect and subjective costs (suboptimal organizational decision making to promote a personal agenda). They may also relate more to public relations or reputation than to bottom-line performance, or be insidious costs involving such things as neglect or sabotage. Finally, they might also take more than one form (reputational damage [subjective costs] from a media scandal concomitant with legal fines [direct costs] resulting from a widely publicized sexual harassment case).

Second, dark side behaviors are motivated in some way. That is, there is intention or awareness on the part of the individual(s) exhibiting the behavior as to the potential ramifications of that behavior. Thus, the behaviors of a manager who makes an incorrect decision, a clerk who inadvertently offends a client, or a production worker who accidentally causes a fire in a factory do not fit into the dark side arena. Although they may indeed result in real costs for the organization, they are not intentional. Moreover, individuals exhibiting the behaviors have not intended to incur costs or other damages for the organization, but, rather, are victims of simple human error. The organization will also presumably have systems in place for controlling such behaviors over time. For example, if the clerk repeatedly offends customers, the firm's performance appraisal system should identify this problem and have the individual trained in customer relations, reassigned to a different job, or terminated. Intent, then, is key to distinguishing dark side behavior from accidents, errors, or mistakes.

Our conceptualization of dark side behavior is similar to—but subtly different from—other emerging frameworks that seek to capture a richer and more complete array of work behaviors. Notable among these are antisocial behaviors (Giacalone & Greenberg, 1997) and deviance (Robinson & Bennett, 1995). Both of these approaches seek to describe a set of negative behaviors that are separate and distinct from other behaviors. For example, antisocial behaviors are intended to be the theoretical opposite of a different set of behaviors called prosocial behaviors. Likewise, deviance is conceptualized as a distinct set of behaviors falling outside of normatively acceptable behaviors.

Our viewpoint, however, recognizes that in some cases the same behavior can be either functional or dysfunctional, depending on intent, motive, context, and consequences. For example consider the behavior of a supervisor firing an employee. If the employee is a poor performer who has been given ample opportunity to improve but who is obviously unable or unwilling to do so, the supervisor has given the employee several prior warnings, and the supervisor follows established organizational procedures, this behavior is functional in that it is appropriately undertaken in the best interests of the organization. Although there are obvious negative consequences to the employee, they are nevertheless acceptable in that most observers would agree that the behavior was undertaken for functional reasons. However, if the supervisor is firing a high-performing worker as a result of a personal vendetta or to achieve some ulterior outcome (such as freeing up a position for hiring a friend), this behavior—exactly the same as the former at a surface level—is clearly dysfunctional in that the organization is losing the contributions of a valued employee and the individual is being treated in an unfair and inappropriate manner. Thus, this perspective avoids having to separate behaviors into one of two discrete categories, instead allowing us to more realistically include at least some behaviors that can vary in terms of their functionality.

In planning this volume, we first acknowledged that there are a number of antecedent factors that may contribute to the incidence of dark side behavior. Some of these antecedents reside at the individual level. Examples include an individual's ethics, values, and morals, pathological characteristics such as alienation, depression, and hostility, and extra-work phenomena such as family context and personal stress. Other antecedents exist more at the group or organizational level and include things such as norms, the organization's culture, and reward and control systems.

These antecedents increase or decrease the potential for the incidence of dark side behaviors in an organization. For example, an individual with a weak value system and a history of unethical behavior, who is generally hostile toward others and is experiencing personal problems, is more likely to engage in dark side behaviors at work than is an individual with strong values and a commitment to ethical conduct, who is also emotionally healthy and has a strong social support network outside of work. Likewise, an organization with norms and a culture that foster dark side behaviors, that actually rewards such behaviors, and that has weak control systems is more likely to experience dark side behaviors than is an organization with norms and a culture that discourage dark side behaviors, that does not reward such behaviors, and that has a stronger control system.

Behaviors, of course, may manifest themselves at the individual or group levels. In most cases these behaviors reflect choices by those individuals or groups. That is, an individual will choose whether to enact a behavior known to be positive (working hard, being honest, treating others fairly) or negative (performing far below one's capabilities, being dishonest, treating others unfairly). Similarly, the members of a group will work together in ways known to be positive (making effective decisions, working collaboratively with other groups) or negative (making suboptimal decisions, working against other groups). Finally, when dark side behaviors do occur, as already noted, they result in negative consequences for the individual, the group, and the organization.

Kinds of Dark Side Behaviors in Organizations

Given the wide array of dark side behaviors that have been explicitly and implicitly suggested, we might find it useful to first categorize them in terms of whether the costs of a particular dark side behavior are incurred primarily by individual people in particular or the organization in general. For instance, if the behavior being examined involves sexual harassment, virtually everyone would agree that the first and foremost concerns regarding the negative consequences of that behavior are for the individual or individuals being harassed. Although the organization may also suffer negative consequences in terms of damaged morale or bad publicity, the individual(s) being harassed bears the major costs.

But suppose an individual intentionally and knowingly reveals proprietary information about a new product breakthrough to someone outside the organization. If that information finds its way to a competitor that is then able to react in a preemptive fashion, it is the first organization itself that incurs the primary costs of this behavior through the loss of a competitive advantage. Although individuals may also suffer as a result of this set of dark side behaviors, it is the organization itself that is most directly affected.

When the costs of dark side behaviors reside primarily with individuals or groups of individuals, we consider these as *behaviors injurious to human welfare*. It then becomes useful to provide one further subclassification in terms of whether the costs of an individual's dysfunctional behavior are borne primarily by others or by that individual him- or herself. For instance, the costs of sexual harassment, as already noted, are incurred first and foremost by the individual(s) being harassed. But if an individual's dysfunctional behavior is drug abuse in the workplace, it is that person who is likely to bear the greatest costs. Obviously, of course, there are also potential secondary effects from both types of behaviors. For example, the individual engaging in the harassing behaviors may also suffer job loss if the victim files a complaint, thereby also experiencing negative consequences. Similarly, erratic behaviors by the drug abuser may cause accidents that harm others. Thus, although some classifications are clearly arbitrary, we group behaviors injurious to human welfare according to who generally bears the initial and major costs while acknowledging that second-level effects are also not only possible but also quite probable.

The other major category of dark side behaviors consists of *behaviors injurious to the organization*. These behaviors are those that result in negative consequences that are primarily borne by the organization itself, rather than by any given individual. Again, there are two levels of this category as well. In some instances, for example, dark side behaviors may result in specific and measurable costs. If an employee steals a computer from her employer, the organization has thus incurred specific initial costs associated with the actual purchase of the computer, as well as the costs of investigating the theft and replacing the stolen property.

Other forms of dark side behavior can also result in negative consequences for the organization, albeit of a form that is subjective, ambiguous, and difficult—if not impossible—to measure. For example, consider the case of a manager with average performance-related skills but with exceptionally strong impression management skills. By adroitly using the impression management skills, this manager may be promoted ahead of others with stronger performance-related skills, even to the point of eventually reaching a high-level position in the organization. As a result, the overall performance of the unit or department under this person's control may be less than it would have been had a different, more qualified manager been given the position. But this assessment, while highly plausible, cannot generally be demonstrated in an empirical fashion.

Dark Side Behaviors Injurious to Human Welfare

As already noted, behaviors that are injurious to others are those that result first and foremost in costs that are borne by individuals. As also noted above, certain of these behaviors result most directly in harm to others, whereas other behaviors result more immediately in harm to the individual enacting the dark side behavior.

Dark Side Behaviors That Harm Others

There are several forms of dark side behaviors injurious to human welfare that primarily and most directly harm others. These are verbal and psychological violence, physical violence, sexual harassment, and general unsafe work practices.

Verbal and Psychological Violence

Given the interpersonal nature of organizations, interactions among people in organizational settings can obviously take many different forms, some very positive and constructive, others relatively benign and of negligible impact, and still others quite negative and destructive. Managers and supervisors may, of course, occasionally find it necessary to reprimand or discipline employees, offer constructive criticism, or use their formal authority to control or coerce the behaviors from others. When handled appropriately, these actions help shape future behaviors, improve performance, and even protect the individual from more severe sanctions.

But in other cases the verbal interactions among people may constitute verbal or psychological abuse. For example, one survey found that during a one-year period as many as six million U.S. workers are likely to be threatened and another sixteen million the target of some form of harassment (Northwestern National Life Insurance Company, 1993). These behaviors are, of course, quite dysfunctional and can result in a wide array of undesirable outcomes, especially for the targets of such abuse. For example, these individuals may suffer from fear, insecurity, and higher levels of stress. They may also suffer from damaged self-esteem or self-concepts. In addition, verbal and psychological violence may also result in turnover among the targets, a climate in the workplace of hostility and fear, or retaliation from these individuals against their abusers.

Physical Violence

Even more troubling are instances in which an employee is the victim of actual physical violence. Again, the statistics are alarming. In any given year, for example, murders in the workplace are generally among the major causes of death for all employees. In general, women are often affected to a greater degree than are men. Workplace homicide is also the fastest growing form of murder in the United States (Filipczak, 1993). One recent survey found that among those organizations responding, almost 25 percent had had at least one employee murdered in the workplace during a four-year period.

Of course, homicides are only the extreme form of physical violence in the workplace. In addition, individuals may be physically assaulted through such actions as being pushed or shoved, slapped or hit, or raped—all without being killed. The authors of one study estimated more than two million U.S. workers may be physically attacked each year (Northwestern National Life Insurance Company, 1993). In the case of physical violence, the individual victim obviously incurs the greatest costs—physical pain and suffering, lost work time, medical expenses, psychological damage, or death. Other costs are also borne by witnesses and observers, coworkers, family members, and others. Assuming the perpetrator of the violence is known, even that person suffers costs in the form of social ostracization, termination from work, financial sanctions, or incarceration. And the organization may incur medical and legal expenses, lost work time, and a damaged culture and public image.

Sexual Harassment

Sexual harassment is another dark side behavior resulting primarily in costs for the victim. Of course, sexual harassment can be seen as a form of verbal, psychological, or physical violence. But given the special attention accorded this problem by researchers, managers, and even the media, it makes sense to highlight it as a separate category of dark side behavior in organizations. The costs of sexual harassment to the victim or victims are similar to those of the other forms of violence: damaged self-esteem or self-concept, stress, or physical damage. Similarly, there may also be corresponding costs to the organization and even to the perpetrator.

General Unsafe Work Practices

A final category of dark side behaviors primarily injurious to others is what might be termed general unsafe work practices. Examples include using equipment or machinery in ways that deviate from normal practice (such as driving a fork-lift through a crowded work area without warning), breaking traffic laws while driving on organizational business (such as exceeding the speed limit while traveling between sales calls), using chemicals or other toxic materials without following normal safety practices (such as pouring dangerous materials into an open trash receptacle), and not following standard security rules or procedures (such as allowing an unauthorized person to enter company premises or leaving doors unlocked). The potential costs of behaviors such as these to other individuals include serious injury or death. Costs to the organization include medical and legal fees, lost production time, government intervention and control, damaged public relations, and the intrusive effects of unauthorized individuals into sensitive work areas.

Dark Side Behaviors That Harm Self

Other dark side behaviors injurious to human welfare take their primary toll on the individual perpetrating the behavior. Representative examples of these kinds of behaviors include alcohol or drug abuse, smoking, specific unsafe work practices, and suicide.

Alcohol and Illicit Drug Abuse

Although illicit drug and alcohol abuse is an organizational problem often discussed in the popular media, it has received relatively little attention among organizational scholars (Harris & Trusty, 1997). The potential effects of alcohol and illicit drug abuse on the individual abuser include physiological damage to the body, financial hardship due to the costs of acquiring alcohol and illicit drugs, social and interpersonal difficulties, marital and family difficulties, and impaired judgment and decision making. Legal sanctions may also be incurred in some cases. And, of course, many of these outcomes may have consequences for others as well. From the organization's perspective, alcohol and illicit drug abuse at work can result in lower performance and higher accident rates, absenteeism, turnover, and insurance premiums.

Smoking

In general, the dysfunctional character of smoking behaviors mirrors that of alcohol and illicit drug abuse, but it also differs in some important ways. For example, drinking too much can result in legal consequences, whereas by definition the simple possession of illicit drugs is also illegal. But there are no legal consequences for adults possessing tobacco products, nor is smoking "too much" punishable by law. As a result, although organizations generally ban alcohol use during work and have strict rules about both intoxication and drug abuse, smoking is a perfectly legal activity.

Thus, while most organizations today prohibit smoking inside some or all facilities, most also provide designated smoking areas for employees. The costs to the individual smoker are well documented and can be reviewed simply by examining the warning labels on a package of cigarettes—respiratory problems, lung cancer, and so forth. Likewise, the effects of secondary smoke on others are also widely known and accepted. For the organization, the costs of smoking by employees include higher insurance premiums, lost productivity as workers move to and from their smoking areas, and the expense of monitoring compliance with no smoking rules.

Specific Unsafe Work Practices

We have already noted the dark side nature of general unsafe work practices and their potential for causing harm to others. There may also be a variety of specific unsafe work practices that are most likely to result in harm to the individual. For example, an employee who uses heavy equipment without wearing proper safety equipment—gloves, goggles, or ear protection—is risking injury. Similarly, improperly lifting heavy boxes, not wearing a seat belt when driving on company business, and carelessly handling dangerous chemicals can all result in serious injury to the individual. Additional costs to the organization include lost productivity, medical and legal expenses, and property damage.

Suicide

A final form of dark side work behavior with primary injurious consequences for self is suicide. Though relatively rare, there are documented cases in which individuals have chosen to end their lives in their office or elsewhere on the premises of their employer. And when suicide does occur at work, it is the individual whose life has ended who bore the primary costs. But the effects of suicide on survivors are also widely recognized. Aside from the obvious grief of the person's family, his or her coworkers, colleagues, and other business associates will suffer as well.

Dark Side Behaviors Injurious to the Organization

Several of the dark side behaviors described above are likely to result in costs to the organization, but as also noted earlier, these costs will usually be of secondary concern to those incurred by one or more individuals. A second broad category of dark side behaviors, meanwhile, has costs that are more directly related to the organization itself, whereas the costs to human welfare may be either of secondary importance or at least one step removed from those incurred by the organization. That is, the behavior in question may result in costs for the organization; the organizational costs, meanwhile, may then result in subsequent costs to the organization. Some of these costs are specific, while others are more general.

Dark Side Behaviors That Have Specific Financial Costs

Some dark side behaviors result in specific costs to the organization that, at least in theory, can be objectively measured and related to their associated financial impact on the organization. These behaviors include inappropriate absenteeism or tardiness, theft of organization assets or property, destruction of organization assets or property, and violations of laws, codes or regulations.

Inappropriate Absenteeism or Tardiness

Virtually every employee in an organization will occasionally be absent from work due to personal illness, family emergencies, and similar appropriate reasons. Likewise, an employee may occasionally be late reporting to work due to car trouble, traffic jams, and so forth. And any given employee may be absent from work for an extended period of time due to a serious illness or injury. None of these behaviors is considered to fall into the dark side arena. Although they all have financial costs for the organization, they are also known to be a routine and necessary part of doing business and their associated costs are implicitly or explicitly accounted for through mechanisms such as sick leave allocations.

But some employees abuse their employers' sick leave privileges. For example, they may report illness simply because they want to stay home from work on a given day. Some employees routinely use sick days to extend their employers' vacation or personal time allocation. Or they may exaggerate a minor ailment to get extra time off. Likewise, some employees may frequently be tardy or late for work simply because they don't get out of bed early enough in the morning or make minimal effort to meet their employers' work schedule start times. In each of these instances, the organization incurs specific financial costs in the form of lost productivity. Other costs include those associated with developing and monitoring an attendance policy, training replacement workers, and so forth.

Theft of Organization Assets or Property

Another potentially significant dark side behavior with direct costs to the organization is the theft of organization assets or property. Examples of assets or property that might be targets for theft include office supplies, equipment, computers and printers, and so forth. The embezzlement or direct theft of cash is also a serious cost to the organization. Each of these types of theft can be assessed in terms of its financial impact—the cost of supplies taken or the amount of cash stolen, for example. In addition, more subtle forms of theft can also be identified. These usually take the form of inappropriate or unauthorized use of organization property. For example, using the company's copier for personal copies, driving a company vehicle on personal errands, and personal long-distance telephone calls at work also constitute theft (Greenberg & Barling, 1996).

Destruction of Organization Assets or Property

Employees also sometimes engage in dark side behaviors intended to damage or destroy assets and property of the organization. These behaviors are similar to verbal or psychological and physical violence, as discussed previously, but the target of the behavior is inanimate. Examples of these kinds of behaviors might include breaking machinery, destroying valuable archival information, inserting viruses into computers, and so forth. In some cases these behaviors might arise spontaneously—and be quite public—in response to a specific stimulus (such as being fired), whereas in other cases the emergence of the behaviors might be more gradual—and be relatively clandestine—as the individual seeks to damage or harm the organization over time and without being caught. Regardless of the circumstances, however, the organization bears the costs of the destruction.

Violation of Laws, Codes, or Regulations

Finally, yet another category of dark side behavior resulting in costs to the organization is the intentional or knowing violation of laws, codes, or regulations. For example, an employee who improperly disposes of toxic wastes, a manager who knowingly discriminates in hiring practices, and a construction supervisor who intentionally violates local building codes are all behaving in ways that can result in costs for the organization. These costs will usually come in the form of legal penalties and reparations.

Dark Side Behaviors That Have Nonspecific Financial Costs

Although the costs of the dark side behaviors described above can be calculated with some degree of precision, there also exists yet another category of dark side behaviors that result in real costs, albeit costs that cannot readily be measured. That is, the costs of the behaviors are real, but are also of sufficient ambiguity and subtlety as to defy quantification. Examples of these behaviors include destructive political behaviors, excessive impression management behaviors, breach of confidentiality, and sustained suboptimal performance.

Destructive Political Behaviors

Political behaviors in organizations refer to intentional efforts by people to use power in order to advance preferred courses of action. In some cases, of course, political behaviors can result in positive benefits to the organization. In others, the consequences of political behavior are negligible, neutral, or of indeterminate effect. But in some situations political behaviors will result in real costs for the organization. For example, if a manager uses political behavior to further a particular course of action that will benefit his own department and career, but which is suboptimal for the organization, this behavior is dysfunctional and results in costs for the organization. Likewise, if a manager uses political behavior to achieve a promotion for a friend who is less qualified than other candidates, this behavior also qualifies as dysfunctional and results in costs for the organization.

Inappropriate Impression Management Behaviors

A similar situation can occur as a result of inappropriate impression management behavior. Impression management is a common strategy used by individuals in organizations to further their own careers. As with political behaviors, the results of impression management are often positive or neutral. But occasionally someone may use impression management to such an extreme that a completely artificial image is created. If this image results in that person getting promoted or given job assignments in lieu of more qualified individuals, the organization may incur costs as a result of the subsequent performance of that individual.

Breach of Confidentiality

Members of organizations sometimes possess information that is proprietary and that may have value to entities outside the organization. Examples include planned competitive strategies, impending technological breakthroughs, bargaining and negotiating positions, and similar sensitive details. If these individuals divulge the information in ways that benefit the external entities to the detriment of the organization, the organization incurs costs as a result. To the extent that the information is divulged intentionally or through carelessness, as opposed to through a genuine and honest mistake or error, the behavior can be seen as dysfunctional.

Sustained Suboptimal Performance

A final form of dark side behavior with general costs to the organization is sustained suboptimal performance. For more than a hundred years, at least, managers have known that employees may not always produce up to their potential. Frederick Taylor, for example, called this *soldiering*. But this behavior is frequently unavoidable and thus not truly dysfunctional. Few people can sustain peak performance on a continuous basis. Over time, therefore, the performance of any given individual is likely to rise and fall within a range bounded by that individual's maximum peak performance level and some minimum level defined by a variety of factors. At any given time the individual's energy, emotions, attitudes, motivation, environment, and a host of other factors interact to determine where within the range that individual's performance will occur.

But some individuals may intentionally restrict their performance levels toward the lower areas of the range, doing just enough to get by without attracting attention or triggering some response from their supervisor. For example, suppose a given worker is really capable of occasionally assembling a hundred units of a particular product per day while maintaining an average of eighty units and never falling below seventy units. But instead of actually working at this level over time, the person instead chooses to do just enough to get by. Thus, assuming that the supervisor will accept seventy units per day without question, the worker might choose to produce between seventy-two and seventy-eight units per day, never making the potential average, much less attaining the peak level of a hundred.

Organization of the Book

The book is organized into four sections plus this opening chapter and the closing chapter, both written by the editors. Part One deals with the general issues of workplace aggression and violence. In Chapter Two, "Workplace Aggression and Violence: Insights from Basic Research," Robert Baron provides an excellent overview of existing knowledge concerning human aggression. Joel Neuman explores similar themes but also introduces two related concepts as they relate to aggression in Chapter Three, "Injustice, Stress, and Aggression in Organizations." Chapter Four, "When the Dark Side of Families Enters the Workplace: The Case of Intimate Partner Violence," by Carol Reeves, explores another important but relatively neglected perspective on violence in organizations—situations in which outsiders enter an organization seeking to enact violence against an employee.

Part Two of the book focuses on one special category of dark side behaviors related to discrimination. Robert Dipboye and Stefanie Halverson set the stage in Chapter Five, "Subtle (and Not So Subtle) Discrimination in Organizations." Ramona Paetzold then focuses the issue even more precisely in Chapter Six, entitled "Sexual Harassment as Dysfunctional Behavior in Organizations." Last in Part Two, the special case of discrimination based on sexual orientation is the subject of Chapter Seven, "Out of the Closet and Out of a Job? The Nature, Import, and Causes of Sexual Orientation Discrimination in the Workplace," by Elizabeth Deitch, Rebecca Butz, and Arthur Brief.

Next, Part Three addresses a variety of dark side issues that generally involve interpersonal influence, including attempts and tactics. Angela Hall, Wayne Hochwarter, Gerald Ferris, and Michael Bowen set the stage in Chapter Eight, "The Dark Side of Politics in Organizations." Denise Rousseau then explores a different perspective in Chapter Nine, "Under the Table Deals: Preferential, Unauthorized, or Idiosyncratic?" Virginia Bratton and Michele Kacmar then examine impression management issues in Chapter Ten, "Extreme Careerism: The Dark Side of Impression Management." Finally, the role of psychological contracts in the dark side is discussed in Chapter Eleven, "Psychological Contract Breach and Violation in Organizations," by Sandra Robinson and Graham Brown.

Finally, Part Four addresses a variety of dark side behaviors and issues. Michael Harris, for example, examines substance abuse issues in Chapter Twelve, "Alcohol and Drug Use in the Workplace." Similarly, retaliation behaviors are described in detail by Daniel Skarlicki and Robert Folger in Chapter Thirteen, "Broadening Our Understanding of Organizational Retaliatory Behavior." What might appear on the surface to be a relatively benign element of the dark side, incivility is discussed by Christine Pearson and Christine Porath in Chapter Fourteen, "On Incivility, Its Impact, and Directions for Future Research." Finally, in a chapter that addresses both methodological issues as well as the dark side, Jerald Greenberg and Ed Tomlinson describe "The Methodological Evolution of Employee Theft Research: The DATA Cycle."

As noted earlier, we also then present a concluding chapter that seeks to identify common themes and issues across the various chapters and outlines some future directions for this increasingly important area of work. And now, to paraphrase Stephen King (who has spent much of his professional life in another part of the dark side), let's lock the doors, turn on the lights, and dive in!

References

Filipczak, B. (1993). Armed and dangerous at work. *Training,* July, 39–43.

Giacalone, R. A., & Greenberg, J. (1997). *Antisocial behavior in organizations.* Thousand Oaks, CA: Sage.

Greenberg, J., & Barling, L. (1996). Employee theft. In C. L. Cooper and D. M. Rousseau (Eds.), *Trends in organizational behavior* (Vol. 3, pp. 49–64). Chicester, UK: John Wiley.

Harris, M. M., & Trusty, M. L. (1997). Drug and alcohol programs in the workplace: A review of recent literature. In I. Robertson and C. L. Cooper (Eds.), *International review of industrial and organizational psychology* (pp. 289, 315). Chicester, UK: John Wiley.

Maslow, A. (1943). A theory of human motivation. *Psychological Review,* July, 370–396.

McGregor, D. (1960). *The human side of enterprise.* New York: McGraw-Hill.

Munsterberg, H. (1913). *Psychology and industrial efficiency.* Boston: Houghton Mifflin.

Northwestern National Life Insurance Company (1993). *Fear and violence in the workplace: A survey documenting the experience of American workers.* Minneapolis: Northwestern National Life Insurance Company.

O'Leary-Kelly, A. M., Griffin, R. W., & Glew, D. J. (1996). Organization-motivated aggression: A research framework. *Academy of Management Review,* 21, 225–253.

Robinson, S. L., & Bennett, R. B. (1995). A typology of deviant workplace behavior: A multi-dimensional scaling study. *Academy of Management Journal,* 38, 555–572.

Taylor, F. W. (1911). *Principles of scientific management.* New York: Harper.

PART 1

Workplace Aggression and Violence: Truly Dark Places

CHAPTER 2

Workplace Aggression and Violence

Insights from Basic Research

Robert A. Baron

Abstract: In a key sense, workplace aggression and violence can be viewed as instances of human aggression occurring in work settings. To the extent this is so, the findings of basic research on aggression can provide important insights into the nature, causes, and reduction of workplace aggression and violence. This chapter is designed to provide researchers with an overview of existing knowledge concerning human aggression. An initial section considers definitional issues (for example, the distinction between aggression and violence). Subsequent sections examine modern theories of human aggression (as well as extensions of these to workplaces), antecedents of aggression (personal, situational, and social factors that play a role in the occurrence of such behavior). A final section considers various techniques for reducing aggression and their applicability in workplaces. Throughout the chapter, efforts are made to explicate links between the findings of basic research on aggression and current research on workplace aggression and violence.

The purpose of education is to keep a culture from being drowned in senseless repetitions, each of which claims to offer a new insight.
    —HAROLD ROSENBERG, 1972

Every time history repeats itself, the price goes up.
    —ANONYMOUS

In recent years, researchers have focused increasing attention on the topics of workplace aggression and violence (Baron, Neuman, & Geddes, 1999; Neuman & Baron, 1998; Skarlicki & Folger, 1997). These investigations have provided much information concerning the potential causes (Dietz et al., 2003) and effects (Catalano, Novaco, & McConnell, 2002) of workplace aggression, and have already begun to inform management practice with respect to techniques for reducing these and other forms of counterproductive (that is, deviant) workplace behavior (Lee & Allen, 2002; Robinson & Bennett, 1995). It is a basic premise of this chapter, however, that progress toward full understanding of workplace aggression and violence can be measurably enhanced by the establishment of closer conceptual links between this active area of research and the large, existing body of knowledge concerning human aggression generally (Baron & Richardson, 1994; Berkowitz, 2001; Moeller, 2001). Without such links, there is considerable risk of experiencing the kind of wasted effort and "senseless repetitions" described in the two quotations above.

This is not to say, of course, that information concerning human aggression gathered in basic investigations of such behavior is automatically or universally useful for answering important questions about workplace aggression; on the contrary, important differences exist between work settings and the contexts in which aggression has been studied in the past (for example, short-term encounters between strangers; see Baron & Richardson, 1994). Further, most basic research on human aggression has been performed in laboratory settings; as a result, the extent to which the findings can be generalized to other contexts remains uncertain. However, it also seems reasonable to suggest that many of the principles and findings uncovered in basic research on human aggression can at least inform current efforts to identify the causes, forms, targets, and effects of workplace aggression and violence. The primary goal of this chapter, therefore, is simply that of facilitating "cross-fertilization" between these active areas of research by providing a summary of key findings of basic research on aggression. It is hoped that the overview of this work in the present book will make these findings more readily available to researchers currently studying aggression in workplaces.

In order to present a succinct but relatively comprehensive overview of the findings of basic research on aggression, this chapter is organized into four discrete sections. The first deals with important *definitional issues* (for example, What actions constitute aggression? What is the distinction between aggression and violence?). Researchers studying human aggression largely resolved these issues several decades ago, so it seems useful for investigators studying workplace aggression to consider these conclusions carefully. The second section briefly reviews *modern theories of human aggression*. These theories adopt a sophisticated perspective that goes far beyond earlier—and less complete—theoretical frameworks such as the famous "frustration and aggression" theory (Dollard, Doob, Miller, Mowrer, & Sears, 1939). In contrast to earlier views that tended to focus on a single aspect of aggression, modern theories trace the roots of such behavior to a complex interplay among physiological, cognitive, social, environmental, and possibly even genetic factors (Buss, 1999). Basic knowledge of these frameworks may well prove useful to researchers seeking to investigate various aspects of workplace aggression. This section also considers the extension of such theories to aggression that occurs in workplaces.

The third section examines various *antecedents of aggression*—personal, social, and situational or environmental variables that have been found, in empirical research, to affect the occurrence and intensity of human aggression. Finally, a concluding section examines techniques for the *reduction of aggression* and their potential applicability in workplaces.

Definitional Issues: Defining Aggression and Violence

Consider the following scenarios:

1. A drug addict, desperate for money to buy drugs, robs a convenience store; when the clerk is slow to empty the cash register, the addict shoots and kills him.
2. At a meeting, one employee viciously belittles another employee's presentation, greatly embarrassing her and thus interfering with her further performance at the meeting.

3. An individual working the graveyard shift is so fatigued that he fails to operate a dangerous piece of equipment properly, thus causing serious injury to another worker.
4. A manager sends a scathing, negative performance review to a subordinate toward whom she has a grudge. However, the review is lost in internal mail, so the subordinate never receives it, and it is not made part of his permanent record.
5. An executive decides not to recommend a subordinate for a new position that the subordinate greatly desires because the executive honestly believes that the subordinate needs further training before she will be ready to assume this position.

Which of these events constitute *aggression?* Most persons would agree that the first and second fall into this category, but what about the third? The individual who injured a coworker did not intend to produce such harm and may be very sorry that this happened. Similarly, consider the fourth incident, in which harm was intended but did not occur. Was this aggression? Finally, what about the fifth incident? Here, harm was produced—the employee did not gain the promotion she wanted—but the executive acted out of what appear to be beneficial motives: he wanted to protect the employee from almost certain failure.

Whether each of these incidents does or does not constitute aggression clearly depends on two factors: (1) whether harm was or was not produced, and (2) whether the outcomes were or were not intended. In the first and second incidents, both factors are present: harm was produced and was clearly intended. In the third, in contrast, harm was produced but was not intended. In the fourth, harm was intended but was not produced. And in the fifth, harm was produced from the point of view of the employee but was *not* intended or produced from the point of view of the executive. In the 1960s and 1970s, researchers studying human aggression wrestled long and hard with these issues in order to formulate a useful and accurate definition of aggression (Berkowitz, 2001; Buss, 1961; Zillmann, 1979). The overall result of these discussions was clear: a consensus emerged that both factors were required for a useful definition of human aggression. The definition that was— and still is—widely adopted is as follows: *Aggression is any form of behavior directed toward the goal of harming or injuring another living being who is motivated to avoid such treatment* (Baron, 1977). This definition suggests that actions that produce harm without intention are *not* aggressive in nature, whereas actions that fail to produce harm, but that intend to do so, *do* constitute aggression. Further, the definition suggests that only actions that have as their goal harming a living recipient (for example, another person) constitute aggression. As noted below, this can be accomplished through harm to inanimate objects (for example, by damaging or destroying another's prized possessions), but even in such cases the intended victim must always be another person (or some other living being, such as an animal or pet). Finally, this definition requires that the intended victim desire to avoid the harm produced. For instance, an individual who enjoys being hurt or humiliated is *not* the victim of aggression when such acts are directed at that person by others (for example, a lover, a boss). Only when actions produce harm that the victim wishes to avoid does it make sense to describe such action as aggression.

In sum, decades of heated debate produced a consensus concerning the criteria for describing specific actions as *aggression*; since workplace aggression, too, involves efforts to inflict harm on various victims (specific persons, an entire organization), the definition stated above appears to provide an appropriate and useful basis for defining workplace aggression. Specifically, workplace aggression can be viewed as *any form of behavior directed by one or more persons in a workplace toward the goal of harming one or more others in that workplace (or the entire organization) in ways the intended targets are motivated to avoid.*

Having offered this definition, it is important to clarify two points relating to it. First, including "intention" as a key element certainly introduces an element of ambiguity into the equation. Intentions are private events, not directly observable by others. Moreover, they can be exceedingly complex and, in many cases, are unclear even to the persons involved (Anderson & Bushman, 2002). For instance, consider instances of sexual harassment—an all too common event in many work settings. When questioned, the persons who have perpetrated such actions often deny any intention of causing harm; they maintain, instead, that they viewed their words or actions as totally innocuous, and express surprise over the fact that these words or actions have generated negative reactions from coworkers. Are they reporting their true beliefs? Or are they simply attempting to minimize any repercussions by protesting their innocence? Clearly, in this and many other situations, determining the precise intentions behind the actions in question is a difficult task—and one that often leaves juries deadlocked or at least confused. Clearly, then, including "intention" in the definition of aggression opens a veritable Pandora's box of complexities.

But—and here is the second key point—excluding it creates problems that seem to many researchers who have studied human aggression to be even more problematic. Accidental harm to another person is clearly different in important ways from harm that was fully intended; this, in fact, is why legal systems attempt to differentiate clearly between crimes such as manslaughter, accidental homicide, and murder. Whether they are able to do so effectively remains controversial, but there has been general agreement in legal circles that the effort is required. Largely for this reason—the logical paradoxes that emerge if intention is omitted from consideration—the definition presented above became fairly standard more than thirty years ago (Baron, 1977). However, I am well aware of the ambiguities it involves, and I offer it with the proviso that intention can only be inferred, never established in a direct and certain manner.

Forms of Aggression: Differentiating Between Aggression and Violence

If aggression is defined as any form of behavior designed to inflict some kind of harm (physical, psychological) on one or more unwilling victims, another issue immediately arises: what forms can such behavior take? This question, too, was widely debated during the 1960s and 1970s, mainly from the point of view of devising a classification scheme to describe the tremendously wide range of actions that can constitute aggression. One valuable framework in this respect was provided by Buss (1961), who suggested that aggression varies along three key dimensions: *physical-verbal, active-passive,* and *direct-indirect.* The physical-verbal dimension refers to harm through actions or words, and requires no further comment. The active-passive dimension refers to the fact that harm can be produced by acting or, alternatively, failing to act. For instance, if one employee needs information from another to complete a project and the first person purposely withholds this information, this individual may be demonstrating a form of passive aggression. Finally, the direct-indirect dimension relates to the fact that harm can be produced by actions directed at the intended victim or by actions that harm the victim indirectly. Table 2.1 provides examples of the eight combinations of aggression yielded by these three dimensions. As will be noted below, these dimensions of aggression have been found to be useful in classifying instances of workplace aggression (Baron, Neuman, & Geddes, 1999; Kaukiainen et al., 2001).

Table 2.1. Buss's Major Categories of Aggression.

Type of Aggression	Examples
Physical-active-direct	Punching, kicking, stabbing, shooting another person
Physical-active-indirect	Sabotaging a piece of equipment so that another person will be hurt when using it; hiring a paid assassin to kill another person
Physical-passive-direct	Physically preventing another person from obtaining a desired goal or performing a desired act (e.g., by failing to move out of the person's way when asked to do so)
Physical-passive-indirect	Refusing to perform necessary tasks (e.g., refusing to provide information or help needed by a coworker)
Verbal-active-direct	Insulting or derogating another person in some manner
Verbal-active-indirect	Spreading malicious rumors or gossip about another person
Verbal-passive-direct	Refusing to speak to another person or refusing to answer questions posed by this person
Verbal-passive-indirect	Failing to speak up in another person's defense when he or she is unfairly criticized

Note: The examples above were developed by the author.

The framework proposed by Buss (1961) is very useful from another perspective, too: it helps distinguish clearly between the terms *aggression* and *violence,* which have sometimes been used interchangeably in the literature on workplace aggression. As noted above, *aggression* is the more general term—it refers to *all* forms of intentional harm-doing behavior. In contrast, the term *violence* refers primarily to intense instances of aggression that are physical, active, and direct in nature (Baron & Richardson, 1994). Thus, describing less intense actions or ones that are indirect or verbal in nature (for example, spreading negative rumors, intercepting important information) as "violence" is not consistent with general usage of this term in the study of human aggression and is, potentially, an important source of confusion. I suggest that the terms *aggression* and *violence* be used by researchers studying workplace aggression in the same way that investigators of human aggression have used them. Doing so would help create closer links between the two literatures and, moreover, help avoid a potentially damaging source of confusion.

Another important distinction concerning forms of aggression focuses on the primary motive behind such behavior. One form of aggression—known as *hostile aggression*—involves actions for which producing harm is the central goal: the person or persons acting aggressively chiefly wish to harm the victim in some way. In contrast, a second form of aggression—known as *instrumental aggression*—refers to harm-doing that is performed in pursuit of other goals; in such behavior, harming the victim is *instrumental* to some other purpose or motive. For example, an executive who wants a promotion may seek to sabotage the career of a rival not because he or she wants to harm this person, but primarily to gain the promotion; harm to the victim is incidental to obtaining another, more important goal (Buss, 1971; Dodge & Coie, 1987).

In sum, researchers studying human aggression gradually reached consensus on a working definition of aggression—one that includes not only the criterion of *harm* but also the criterion of *intention to harm.* In addition, they developed several useful frameworks for describing and classifying the many forms that aggression can take. Researchers investigating various aspects of workplace aggression may benefit in several important respects from taking careful note of this earlier work. Doing so may help them to avoid potential sources of confusion that once plagued basic research on aggression and may also provide shared definitions and perspectives that can facilitate communication and the exchange of new ideas.

Modern Theories of Human Aggression: Beyond "Frustration and Aggression"

Early efforts to trace the roots of human aggression focused either on biological factors (for example, the view that tendencies to aggress are part of our basic human or genetic nature; Lorenz, 1966) or on the role of internal motives (drives) that are produced by external, environmental factors (for example, the famous frustration-aggression theory; Dollard et al., 1939). Neither view fared well when subjected to logical and empirical scrutiny, although the biological perspective has recently reemerged in the field of *evolutionary psychology*; for example, Buss, 1999). Both perspectives will now be briefly reviewed, primarily as background for a discussion of more modern theories that follows directly.

Biological Theories of Human Aggression: From Instincts to Evolved Psychological Mechanisms

Theoretical frameworks of human aggression based on the concept of *instincts*—inherited and universal tendencies shared by all members of a species—were strongly criticized by psychologists on several grounds, but perhaps the most important were that these views were largely circular in nature and ignored huge differences in the rates and forms of aggression across different human societies (Fry, 1998). Circularity of reasoning is apparent in the fact that in many instinct theories of aggression, the existence of aggressive instincts was deduced from the widespread occurrence of aggression between members of a given species (for example, during mating seasons) and then these instincts were proposed as the major cause of such behavior (see Baron & Richardson, 1994). Instinct theories also tended to ignore the fact that the rate, intensity, and form of human aggression varies greatly across human societies—a finding very difficult to explain if, in fact, aggression stems from universally inherited proclivities to harm others.

More recently, however, the view that genetic factors play a role in human aggression has reemerged within the context of *evolutionary psychology* (Buss, 1999). This perspective suggests that through the process of evolution, all species acquire *evolved psychological mechanisms* that help (or once helped) them to deal with important problems relating to survival. Since aggression can help increase males' access to females (by eliminating rivals) and in this way can enhance their chances of contributing their genes to the next generation, a tendency toward such behavior may well be part of our biological heritage (Hilton, Harris, & Rice, 2000). Some findings offer support for this reasoning. For instance, males appear to have weaker tendencies to aggress against females than against other males; this makes sense from an evolutionary perspective, since it is primarily males who are sexual rivals. Females, in contrast, seem to have equally strong tendencies to aggress against both sexes. This, too, is compatible with a perspective suggesting that aggression may have a genetic basis even in humans. However, even staunch supporters of the evolutionary perspective note that such tendencies are only a small part of the total picture, so such theories offer only partial explanations of human aggression at best.

Drive Theories of Aggression: Is Frustration the Primary Cause of Aggression?

A somewhat more compelling theoretical perspective on human aggression involves the operation of *aggressive drives*—externally elicited motives to harm others. The most famous example of this approach is the well-known *frustration-aggression hypothesis* (Dollard et al., 1939). In its original form, this theory offered two sweeping propositions: (1) all forms of aggression stem from *frustration* (defined as interference with ongoing, goal-directed behavior), and (2) frustration *always* leads to some form of aggression. In fact, both proposals are highly questionable. Human aggression appears to stem from many sources other than frustration; for instance, as noted earlier, it may be a form of *instrumental behavior,* directed toward attaining other ends quite distinct from inflicting harm on another person. Consider, for example, a salesperson who seeks to "derail" a rival not because she dislikes this person or wants to harm him, but simply to eliminate an obstacle to obtaining an important sale and a large commission.

Similarly, frustration does *not* always result in aggression. When frustrated, human beings react in many different ways, including strong feelings of sadness or depression; assaults on the perceived source of frustration are, in fact, relatively rare (Geen, 1998; Neuman & Baron, 1998). In view of these facts, which were established by a large body of empirical studies, most researchers on aggression concluded that frustration is only one potential cause of aggression, and perhaps not the most important cause (Baron & Richardson, 1994). Indeed, modern theories of aggression that include frustration as one potential cause of such behavior assign it a much weaker role than the original frustration-aggression hypothesis. For instance, Berkowitz (1989, 1993) has proposed that frustration is an unpleasant experience that may lead to aggression largely because of the unpleasant feelings associated with it. Further, he proposes, along with many other researchers, that frustration leads to aggression only under specific conditions (for example, when it is viewed as unjustified and illegitimate). Given the limited role assigned to frustration by modern theorists, it would seem useful for researchers investigating workplace aggression to take careful note of this work and to look elsewhere for the strongest antecedents of such behavior. Unfortunately, this has not always been the case and efforts to interpret a wide range of variables ranging from unemployment (Catalano, Novaco, & McConnell, 2002) through mistreatment by abrasive supervisors as instances of frustration may be counterproductive from the point of view of understanding the actual nature of such factors. (Please refer to the discussion of antecedents of aggression below for further clarification of this point.)

Modern Theories of Aggression: The Joint Role of Learning, Cognition, Mood, and Arousal

If aggression does not stem primarily from instincts, genetic factors, or frustration, then how can it be understood? Modern theories of aggression (Anderson, 1997; Zillmann, 1994) answer this question by drawing heavily on advances in many fields of behavioral science. The result is that such frameworks view aggression as stemming from a wide range of variables and experiences rather than from one primary or central cause. For instance, consider the view proposed by Anderson (1997), known as the general affective aggression model (GAAM). This theory suggests that aggression is triggered by a wide range of *input variables,* which, in turn, fall into two major categories: aspects of a current situation, or tendencies individuals bring with them to that situation. Variables falling into the first category include frustration, provocation from another person (for example, an insult), exposure to others behaving aggressively, the presence of stimuli associated with aggression (for example, guns or other weapons), and virtually anything that causes individuals to experience discomfort—everything from uncomfortably high temperatures to unpleasant noise or crowding in a workplace. Variables in the second category *(individual difference factors)* include traits that predispose individuals toward aggression (for example, high irritability), attitudes and beliefs about violence (for example, believing that it is acceptable or even appropriate), and specific skills related to aggressiveness (for example, knowing how to fight or use various weapons; familiarity with various forms of organizational politics).

According to the GAAM, these situational and individual difference variables then lead to overt aggression through their impact on several psychological processes—*arousal, affective states* (negative feelings and emotions), and *cognitions* (for example, they can induce individuals to think hostile thoughts or bring hostile memories to mind). Depending on how the persons involved interpret various events in a given situation, the strength of restraining factors (for example, fear of retaliation), and other variables, aggression then occurs or does not occur and takes a particular form and level of intensity. In short, modern theories such as the GAAM (which is presented here merely as an example of such views) note that aggression derives from a wealth of variables and conditions, and can only be understood within the context of a complex interplay among cognitive, affective, and physiological processes, plus the impact of past experience and cultural influences (see Figure 2.1). Certainly, such views are more complex than simpler frameworks such as the frustration-aggression hypothesis, but a large body of empirical findings suggest that they are also much more

Figure 2.1. The General Affective Aggression Model.

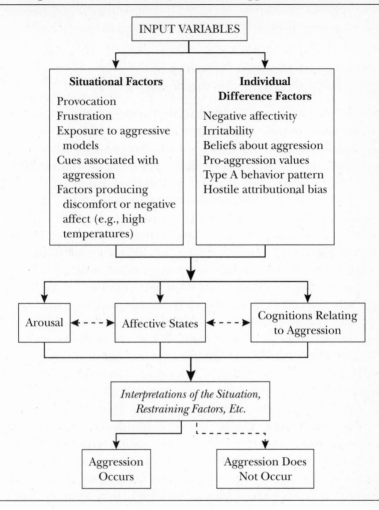

accurate. Thus, it seems useful for researchers investigating workplace aggression to take note of such factors in planning their own studies and in interpreting their results.

Extension of Modern Theories to Aggression Occurring in Workplaces

Although theories such as the GAAM provide a valuable framework for understanding human aggression generally, they were not specifically designed to address such behavior as it occurs in workplaces. All of the variables identified by the GAAM almost certainly play a role in workplace aggression. But workplaces are different, in several respects, from many other settings in which aggression occurs. For instance, in contrast to public places in which aggression is relatively frequent (bars, parks, sports arenas, beaches) and in which acts of violence often occur between strangers, the people in workplaces usually know each other well. Further, they are part of an existing organization with a culture that, in some ways, may differ from that of society at large. In short, whereas the same basic processes are at work, these occur against a background of *contextual* factors that are relatively specific to workplaces, or at least loom larger in them than in other settings. For this reason, it seems reasonable to extend the GAAM as shown in Figure 2.2. The proposed model, which for consistence is termed the GWAAM (General, Workplace Affective Aggressive Model), divides situational factors into two categories—organization-related situational factors and general situational factors. Similarly, it divides individual difference factors into organization-related and general categories. For instance, included under organization-related situational factors are organizational culture, abusive supervision, organizational politics, and reward systems. Included under organization-related individual difference factors are variables that seem directly relevant to workplaces, such as stress tolerance, Machiavellianism, and sensitivity to unfairness. The GWAAM also takes note of the fact that aggression, when it occurs, can be directed against other individuals within the organization, individuals outside the organizations, or against the organization itself. It should be emphasized that the GWAAM represents an extension and adaptation of the GAAM to workplaces; it in no way suggests

Figure 2.2. The General Workplace Affective Aggressive Model.

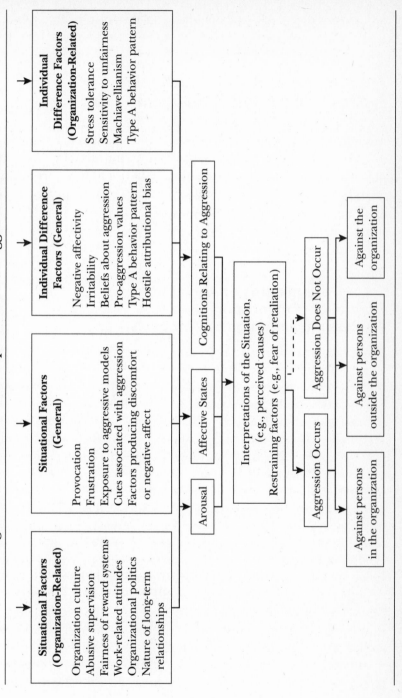

that workplace aggression is different in its basic nature from aggression in other contexts.

Antecedents of Human Aggression: Personal, Social, and Situational Causes

As noted above, modern theories of aggression suggest that it stems from a wide range of factors and conditions. Although literally scores of variables have been found to play a role in the occurrence, form, and intensity of aggressive behavior, most of these fall under one of three broad headings: social determinants of aggression, situational and environmental determinants of aggression, and personal determinants of aggression. Variables included in each of these categories will now be reviewed.

Social Determinants of Aggression: Frustration, Provocation, Displaced Aggression, and Aggressive Models

Many factors that play a role in human aggression involve the actions of other persons—their words and deeds. Among these, *frustration*—interference with goal-directed behavior by another person—is perhaps the factor that has received the greatest attention. A large body of evidence suggests that when individuals conclude that their efforts to attain various goals have been blocked by others, they may, indeed, respond with anger, irritation, and overt aggression (Baron & Richardson, 1994; Berkowitz, 1993). However, this is most likely to occur when they perceive such frustration as illegitimate or unjustified (Folger & Baron, 1996). When, in contrast, frustration is viewed as legitimate, it has been found to be much weaker as a precursor of aggression (Baron & Richardson, 1994). For example, consider the case of an employee who requests assignment to a specific project; after considering the request, this person's supervisor refuses. How will the employee react to the blocking of this goal? This depends, to an important extent, on how she or he interprets the supervisor's action. If the refusal is viewed as illegitimate (for example, the employee is clearly the best person in the work group for this task), then intense anger and some form of aggression may occur. However, if the refusal is viewed as legitimate (the employee is not the best person for this job, or it is simply not her or his turn for a desirable assignment), little anger will follow, and aggression is unlikely. In short, the effects of frustration on subsequent aggression are moderated by several factors, so it is misleading to conclude that frustration is always, or even usually, a powerful antecedent of aggressive behavior.

In contrast, another variable—*direct provocation* from another— has been found to be a much stronger and consistent determinant of human aggression (Chermack, Berman, & Taylor, 1997). Provocation involves physical or verbal assaults from other people—acts that are identified by the recipient as aggressive in nature. Many studies on the effects of provocation suggest that in general, we rarely "turn the other cheek" when subjected to such treatment. On the contrary, most people tend to reciprocate in one way or another, returning aggression for aggression received. Indeed, there is a strong tendency to retaliate at a higher level than that received—one reason that aggressive encounters often show an alarming tendency to spiral upward (Ohbuchi & Kambara, 1985). Several studies designed to compare the relative impact of provocation and frustration on subsequent aggression reported consistent results: at equivalent levels of perceived intensity, provocation was the stronger elicitor of subsequent aggression, perhaps in part because retaliation is viewed as more appropriate or even necessary in response to provocation, whereas a wider range of reactions are perceived as appropriate to frustration (Berkowitz, 1989).

Closely related to this discussion of the effects of provocation is the topic of *displaced aggression*—aggression against someone other than the source of a given provocation or perceived frustration (Dollard et al., 1939). That displaced aggression occurs is apparent; almost all readers have either witnessed or experienced situations in which an individual is provoked by someone else toward whom retaliation is inappropriate or dangerous (for example, a boss). As a result, the person involved aggresses against a safer target, such as a subordinate or family member. Perhaps more interesting from the point of view of workplace aggression is the existence of *triggered displaced aggression*—instances in which an individual responds explosively to a mild current provocation by one person because he or she has recently been more strongly provoked by another person (Marcus-Newhall et al., 2000). For example, after a severe "dressing-down" by a supervisor concerning one issue, an individual may aggress strongly against a coworker who offers a mild criticism on a totally unrelated matter.

Such effects have been observed in carefully conducted laboratory studies. For instance, in one such investigation, Pederson, Gonzales, and Miller (2000) arranged for participants to work on a series of anagrams. In one experimental condition (no provocation), the anagrams were fairly easy and participants in the study were treated in a neutral manner by the experimenter. In the second condition (strong prior provocation), the anagrams were difficult and participants were treated very rudely by the experimenter. Following these events, participants received an evaluation of their work from another, unrelated person. This evaluation was either slightly negative, thus serving as a trivial triggering event for displaced aggression, or neutral in nature. Finally, participants rated the person who had evaluated their work. Results were clear: in the no-provocation condition, the triggering event produced little or no aggression toward the rater. In the strong prior-provocation condition, in contrast, the same mild criticism generated very harsh ratings of the evaluator. In short, prior provocation by another person produced strong aggression against a currently available target. This aspect of displaced aggression appears to be highly relevant to many instances of workplace aggression, in which individuals seem to overreact to mild provocations from others. In a sense, they have been "set up" for outbursts of aggression by recent unpleasant experiences.

An additional factor that has been found to play a strong role in the occurrence of aggression is exposure to other people behaving in an aggressive manner either in person or, symbolically, on television and in films (Anderson, 1997; Baron & Richardson, 1994). A very large body of evidence indicates that exposure to such *aggressive models* facilitates aggression by persons who observe them for several reasons (Huesmann & Eron, 1986). First, individuals often acquire new means of aggressing by observing others engage in such behavior. This is especially true of relatively subtle and disguised modes of aggression, such as those that are part of organizational politics (Kacmar & Baron, 1999). Second, exposure to aggressive models may serve to "prime" hostile thoughts, so that individuals think about real or imagined wrongs they themselves have suffered at the hands of others; such cognitions, in turn, can facilitate various forms of aggression (Anderson, 1997). Third, exposure to aggressive models may suggest that such behavior is an appropriate response to provocation or frustration, thus creating an organizational culture of aggression. Such effects have recently been observed by Dietz et al. (2003) with respect to workplace aggression. These researchers found that aggression in branches of a large government organization well known for high levels of workplace aggression was related to the level of violence present in the communities in which branches of the organization were located: the higher the level of violence in the surrounding communities, the higher the level of aggression within the organization. One mechanism that may have contributed to these findings is that the higher the levels of violence in the surrounding communities, the greater the exposure of employees to aggressive models in their personal lives.

In sum, a large number of variables related to the actions of other persons have been found to play an important role in the occurrence of workplace aggression. Close examination of these factors suggests that they almost certainly operate in workplaces, as well as many other contexts. Thus, important insights into the causes of workplace aggression may be gained by careful attention to the potential impact of these and related variables.

Situational and Environmental Determinants of Aggression

Although social factors (other persons' words or deeds) have been found to exert powerful effects on aggression, they are not the only determinants of such behavior. External conditions relating to the situations in which aggression occurs can also be important. For purposes of efficiency, these factors will be examined under two major headings: situational causes of aggression (for example, the presence of specific stimuli related to aggression, such as weapons), and aspects of the physical environmental (for example, high temperature, noise, poor air quality).

Situational Elicitors of Aggression: The Effects of Alcohol and Aggressive Cues

It is widely believed that some persons become more aggressive when they consume alcohol. This idea is supported by the fact that bars and nightclubs are frequently the scene of violence. Systematic research on this topic has tended to confirm the existence of a link between alcohol consumption and aggression. In several experiments, participants who consumed substantial doses of alcohol—enough to make them legally drunk—have been found to behave more aggressively and to respond to provocations more strongly than those who did not consume alcohol (Bushman & Cooper, 1990; Gustafson, 1990; Pihl, Lau, & Assaad, 1997). (Needless to state, participants in such research are always warned, in advance, that they may be receiving alcoholic beverages and only those who consent to such procedures actually take part.)

What accounts for such effects? One possibility is that alcohol acts directly on the brain, stimulating areas that govern emotion and rage and releasing them from control by the cerebral cortex. If this is the case, then people who consume alcohol may find it extremely difficult, if not impossible, to control their tempers and refrain from aggressive outbursts (Zeichner & Phil, 1980). Another, less disturbing, possibility is that alcohol does indeed weaken restraints against aggressive behavior but leaves people able to monitor and regulate their own actions to some degree.

Research findings offer support for the latter conclusion. For instance, individuals who are intoxicated are still capable of responding to social cues in their environment; if they are urged by others to show restraint, they generally do, but if they are urged to aggress, they engage in such behavior (Taylor & Sears, 1988). Such findings indicate that intoxicated persons do indeed still have voluntary control over their own behavior. Perhaps the most unsettling finding in research on the effects of alcohol on aggression is that this drug sometimes increases the tendency to attack helpless victims—persons who have no means of protecting themselves or retaliating (Gantner & Taylor, 1992).

Overall, these findings appear to have relevance to workplace aggression. Employees often consume alcohol at work, in ways ranging from the "two-martini lunch" through swigs taken surreptitiously out of a thermos or other container. If alcohol does indeed increase the chances that individuals will respond more strongly to provocation, frustration of other aggression-eliciting conditions than would otherwise be the case, then this is a factor well worth considering in efforts to understand and reduce the incidence of aggressive behavior at work.

Another potentially important situational elicitor of aggression in work settings is the presence of what have been termed *aggressive cues*—stimuli that are somehow associated with or linked to aggression or prior anger arousal. A substantial body of findings indicates that the presence of such cues can sometimes "tip the balance" in favor of overt aggression (Berkowitz & Frodi, 1979; Carlson, Marcus-Newall, & Miller, 1990). Specific persons can become associated with aggression because of their reputations in an organization (for example, as being abrasive or confrontational) or as a result of their occupational role (for example, prize fighter, police officer, military personnel). Such persons, because they are linked in memory with anger or aggression, may elicit aggressive thoughts and increased arousal, and these factors, in turn, may intensify negative reactions to their actions, especially if these are at all provocative in nature.

Perhaps even more interesting is the finding that physical objects, too, can serve as aggressive cues, increasing the likelihood of aggressive actions on the part of persons who are exposed to their presence. The most obvious example of such objects is weapons, which are clearly linked to aggressive behaviors. It has been noted in several studies that the mere presence of such objects on the scene may increase aggression on the part of persons who have been provoked or frustrated (Caprara et al., 1984). In contrast, weapons do *not* exert such effects on individuals who have not been annoyed or frustrated. Why does the presence of weapons or other objects associated with aggression (for example, military insignia) increase such behavior by persons already predisposed to aggress? Perhaps because these objects trigger aggression-related cognitions (thoughts, memories) and emotions (anger, annoyance), and these internal states facilitate subsequent aggressive actions. Whatever the precise mechanisms involved, it seems clear that the presence of aggression-related objects in a workplace may be a factor in at least some instances of aggression. Perhaps this is one reason behind the controversy over allowing pilots of commercial jet planes to carry weapons in the cockpit: many people realize, even if they are unfamiliar with the "weapons effect," that the presence of weapons can facilitate aggression even if the weapons themselves are not used for this purpose. In any case, workplaces in which weapons and other objects associated with aggression are present (for example, factories that produce weapons or some kinds of sports equipment) would appear to be at greater risk for various forms of workplace aggression than workplaces in which such objects are absent.

Environmental Determinants of Aggression: Effects of Heat, Crowding, and Noise

At one point in my career, I worked for the federal government in Washington, D.C. The heating, ventilation, and air conditioning system of the building (which was leased by a federal agency) was primitive, to say the least. In the summer, temperatures approaching ninety degrees Fahrenheit were regularly recorded in many offices, while in the winter, the same rooms were generally in the low sixties or even high fifties Fahrenheit. The air was stale and dusty, and noise from a construction project across the street was both loud and irritating. The effects of these unpleasant environmental conditions on productivity were obvious: many people found it hard to concentrate and often spent more time complaining about the miserable work environment than actually doing their jobs. From the point of view of the present discussion, however, another observation is even more relevant: on days when the environmental conditions were especially bad, instances of workplace aggression seemed to rise. In other words, the negative feelings and emotions produced by working under uncomfortable conditions put everyone in a bad mood, and this, in turn, generated increased interpersonal friction.

Although the above observations are informal, they are consistent with a very large body of evidence suggesting that unpleasant environmental conditions do indeed increase aggression. Many studies conducted both in laboratory and in field settings indicate that unpleasantly high temperatures increase anger, irritability, and aggression (Anderson, Bushman, & Groom, 1997; Baron & Bell, 1975). There may be some limits to such effects, so that at very high temperatures, aggression actually declines as a result of fatigue or debilitation (Rotton & Cohn, 2000). But in general, and within the limits generally encountered in most work settings, uncomfortably high temperatures seem to be one precursor to increased aggression.

Similar effects have been uncovered for other environmental variables, including noise (Geen & McCown, 1984) and unpleasant air quality (Rotton, Frey, Barry, Milligan, & Fitzpatrick, 1979; Zillmann, Baron, & Tamborini, 1981). Overall, these findings suggest that one potential cause of heightened aggression in many workplaces may involve unpleasant physical working conditions. This relationship seems especially relevant at a time when many organizations view continuous cost-cutting as a central goal. Unfortunately, one of the first things cut in such efforts to reduce costs is the quality of the physical environment; this is often viewed as an expendable "frill" or unnecessary "nicety," which can be reduced with no ill effects. In fact, however, a large body of research findings suggests that savings in energy costs produced by such efforts may incur nasty side effects relating to reduced productivity and increased workplace aggression (Baron, 1994). This would seem to be a potentially important area for future research on the causes of workplace aggression.

Personal Determinants of Aggression

Informal observation suggests that some persons are much more prone to aggressive encounters than others: they are more likely to initiate aggressive actions and more likely to respond aggressively to even mild provocations. These observations have been confirmed by basic research, which suggests that several personal characteristics do indeed play a role in human aggression. The most important of these dimensions are as follows.

The Type A Behavior Pattern

Most people have acquaintances who can be described as (1) extremely competitive, (2) always in a hurry, and (3) highly irritable and aggressive. Such persons show the characteristics of what psychologists term the type A behavior pattern (Glass, 1977; Strube, 1989). At the opposite end of the continuum are persons who do not show these characteristics—individuals who are not highly competitive, who are not always fighting the clock, and who do not readily lose their temper; such persons are described as showing the type B behavior pattern. Given the characteristics mentioned above, it seems reasonable to expect that type A's would tend to be more aggressive than type B's in many situations. In fact, the results of several experiments indicate that this is actually the case (Baron, Russell, & Arms, 1985; Carver & Glass, 1978).

Additional findings indicate that type A's are truly hostile people: they don't merely aggress against others because this is a useful means for attaining other goals such as winning athletic contests or furthering their own careers (instrumental aggression, as described previously). Rather, they are more likely than type B's to engage in *hostile aggression*—aggression in which the prime objective is inflicting some kind of harm on the victim (Strube et al., 1984). In view of this fact, it is not surprising to learn that type A's are more likely than type B's to engage in actions such as child abuse or spouse abuse (Strube et al., 1984). Additional evidence suggests that type A's are more likely to become involved in conflict and workplace aggression (e.g., Baron, 1989; Baron, Neuman, & Geddes, 1999). Thus, persons showing this pattern may add more than their proportionate share to the total level of aggression occurring in the organizations in which they work.

Perception of Evil Intent in Others: Hostile Attributional Bias

Many actions that other persons perform are somewhat inscrutable: the actions and their consequences are open to direct observation, but the *motives* behind these actions are unknown. This is true with respect to behaviors by others that produce some kind of harm. Was the harm intended? If so, the action can reasonably be viewed as aggressive in nature. If the harm was unintended, however, the action itself does not meet the key criteria for being described as aggressive in nature.

Many actions that produce some form of harm pose precisely this kind of puzzle: it is difficult to determine whether they were intended to yield harmful consequences. The causes of such actions are, in a word, ambiguous. In such cases, attributional processes come into play: the persons involved must try to determine *why* others have acted as they did. In this respect, research findings indicate that individuals differ greatly in terms of the conclusions they characteristically reach about the causes of such ambiguous, harm-producing actions. Some tend to perceive such actions as stemming primarily from hostile intentions, whereas others show much less tendency in this direction. In other words, people differ greatly with respect to what has been termed the *hostile attributional bias* (Dodge et al., 1986)—the tendency to perceive hostile intentions or motives as causes of others' actions, even when these actions are ambiguous. In other words, persons high in hostile attributional bias rarely give others the benefit of the doubt: they simply *assume* that any provocative actions by others are intentional, and they react accordingly. The results of many studies offer support for the potential impact of this factor (Dodge & Coie, 1987), so it seems to be another important personal (individual difference) factor in the occurrence of aggression.

Clearly, hostile attributional bias may play an important role in workplace aggression. Persons who perceive negative outcomes such as setbacks in their work, failure to obtain a promotion, or even an unfavorable vacation schedule as the result of hostile intentions and actions by others will be more likely to seek to retaliate for such real or imagined wrongs than persons who do not attribute negative outcomes to others' hostile intentions (Skarlicki & Folger, 1997). Thus, such persons may be more likely than others to contribute to the overall level of aggression in their workplaces.

Narcissism, Ego-Threat, and Aggression: On the Dangers of Wanting to Be Superior

Narcissus was a character in Greek mythology who fell in love with his own reflection in the water of a fountain and drowned trying to reach it. His name has now become a synonym for excessive self-esteem—for holding an overinflated view of one's own virtues or accomplishments. Research findings indicate that this trait may be linked to aggression in important ways. Specifically, studies by Bushman and Baumeister (1998) suggest that persons high in *narcissism* (ones who agree with statements such as "If I ruled the world it would be a much better place" and "I am more capable than other people") react with exceptionally high levels of aggression to "slights" from others—feedback that threatens their inflated self-image. Why? Perhaps because such persons have nagging doubts about the accuracy of their inflated egos, and so react with intense anger toward anyone who threatens to undermine them.

Can excessive, inflated self-esteem play a role in workplace aggression? It seems possible that it can. Criticism is a normal part of organizational life (Baron, 1990), so virtually everyone receives it at one time or another. Individuals who possess a tendency to over-react to even mild negative feedback because it is inconsistent with their inflated sense of worth may be especially likely to react with intense anger in such situations and to nurse grudges that they express, at later times, in various forms of workplace aggression. In sum, this characteristic may be one worth investigating in future research.

To summarize: basic research on human aggression has determined that several personal factors—dimensions along which individuals differ greatly—play an important role in such behavior. Including these factors within the scope of ongoing research on workplace aggression may provide important insights into the nature, causes, form, and targets of this important form of organizational behavior.

Management of Human Aggression: Techniques Suggested by Basic Research

A key question in research on workplace aggression is, How can this, and other deviant forms of organizational behavior, be managed—reduced or prevented? Much of this work has been focused on preventing extreme forms of workplace aggression (that is, workplace violence; see Braverman, 1999). But as noted earlier, and as demonstrated in many recent studies (Baron, Neuman, & Geddes, 1999; Kaukiainen et al., 2001), aggression takes a wide variety of forms in workplaces, and preventing these, too, is important from the point of view of making organizations safer and more productive places in which to work. Basic research on human aggression has also focused on the issue of prevention or control. This section reviews several techniques that have been found to be useful in this regard. If, as has been assumed throughout the chapter, workplace aggression can be reasonably viewed as human aggression occurring in a particular environment (workplaces), these techniques should, with suitable adjustments, prove useful for managing workplace aggression.

Actual or Threatened Punishment

The pendulum of scientific opinion regarding the potential value of punishment in reducing human aggression has swung widely over the decades. It is interesting that the scholars who first proposed the famous "frustration-aggression" hypothesis viewed punishment as *the* technique for preventing aggressive outbursts (Dollard et al., 1939). Research on the effects of punishment, which can be defined as the delivery of aversive consequences to decrease the frequency or intensity of some behavior, soon revealed, however, that punishment can often have unintended consequences. For instance, parents who punish their children physically for aggressive actions may succeed in temporarily suppressing such behavior. At the same time, however, they may be teaching their offspring that one appropriate response to annoyance or provocation is physical aggression. Moreover, punishment is often viewed as arbitrary or illegitimate by the persons who receive it and, as such, may generate resentment and a desire for vengeance rather than any genuine desire to change or "reform" in the future (Zechmeister & Romero, 2002).

In view of such considerations, psychologists and other behavioral scientists concluded, during the 1960s and 1970s, that punishment was not an effective means for controlling human aggression or other undesirable forms of behavior. More recent findings, however, point to a somewhat different conclusion (Baron & Richardson, 1994). Systematic research suggests that punishment can, indeed, be effective in reducing subsequent aggression but only when it is delivered in accordance with certain principles. The most important of these are as follows: (1) punishment must be *prompt*— it must quickly follow aggressive actions; (2) it must be *certain*—the probability that it will occur must be very high; (3) it must be *strong*— of sufficient magnitude to be highly unpleasant to the persons who receive it; and (4) it must be perceived as *justified* or *legitimate*. When punishment is delivered under these conditions, it can be highly effective in deterring subsequent aggressive actions by the persons who receive it.

Unfortunately, of course, these conditions often are not met. Consider, for instance, the criminal justice system in the United States. Punishment for aggressive actions, even very serious ones such as murder, is often delayed for months or years as one appeal follows another. Further, even if perpetrators of harmful aggressive actions are convicted, the magnitude of punishment they receive for specific crimes varies greatly from one jurisdiction to another. Perpetrators of aggressive actions are well aware of these variations, and this often leads them to perceive the punishments they receive as unjust.

Unfortunately, similar problems exist with respect to the use of punishment in most organizations. Employees who engage in various forms of aggression against coworkers are occasionally punished through reprimands, suspensions, or other actions, but often they are not. Further, punishment is not always administered in an impartial and evenhanded manner, so that again, it is perceived as unjust or illegitimate by many recipients. If these flaws in the use of punishment could be corrected, it might well provide a useful means for preventing or reducing the occurrence of many forms of workplace aggression. Whether this can actually be accomplished, however, is an empirical question deserving of further research. One conclusion does seem justified, however: under present conditions, punishment is *not* being effectively used as a means of deterring workplace aggression.

Cognitive Interventions: Apologies and Countering Cognitive Deficits

As noted earlier, direct provocation appears to be a powerful elicitor of aggressive behavior: when provoked by another person, either physically or verbally, most individuals form the intention of repaying the perceived source of provocation in kind. Aggression may be delayed and may take a form very different from the original provocation, but few persons "turn the other cheek" and forgive the people who provoke them. That is the general rule; an important exception involves the use of *apologies*. If persons who provoke another quickly apologize for their actions, or provide an explanation suggesting that their past provocative actions did not stem from an intention to harm a victim, subsequent aggression may be greatly reduced (Ohbuchi, Kameda & Agarie, 1989). Why is this so? Primarily because aggression, like many other forms of

WORKPLACE AGGRESSION AND VIOLENCE

human behavior, is strongly influenced by cognitive factors. This is an important point, worthy of further comment.

Although "commonsense" views of aggression tend to emphasize the emotional nature of such behavior (for example, the view that people lash out at others when they are angry or uncomfortable), modern theories of human aggression (Anderson, 1997) suggest that, in fact, it is far from an entirely emotional reaction. On the contrary, in many cases individuals employ cognitive mechanisms to control their anger and refrain from immediate acts of aggression. Apologies can strengthen restraining processes and for this reason can be highly effective in reducing overt aggression.

In contrast, factors that produce *cognitive deficits*—reductions in the ability to think clearly or carefully—have the opposite effect. Cognitive deficits may make it difficult for individuals to control their anger or annoyance and difficult for them to carefully weigh the consequences of various actions. Many factors can produce such deficits, including information overload (placing individuals in a situation where they are exposed to more information than they can process at one time), intense emotional arousal (not necessarily arousal relating to anger or annoyance), and high levels of stress or fatigue (Zillmann, 1993). Basic research on aggression suggests that any steps useful in preventing such deficits may ultimately help reduce the incidence of overt acts of aggression. One such technique involves *preattribution*—attributing provocative actions by others to factors other than an intentional desire on their part to harm the potential victim *before* such actions occur. For instance, an individual might reason that another person is in a very bad mood because of factors beyond her or his control, and therefore is not fully responsible for any provocation behaviors in which she or he engages. Another involves efforts to avoid pondering prior provocations; doing so tends to generate negative emotions, including intense anger.

Applying these findings to workplace aggression, it seems possible that training employees in the use of such techniques (for example, preattribution, avoiding rumination over past "wrongs" at the hands of others) might provide them with cognitive techniques useful in restraining their own aggression. This, in turn, might reduce the incidence and intensity of various forms of workplace aggression. Another, more general implication of basic research is that organizations should avoid exposing employees to information overload, excessive levels of stress, or extremely uncomfortable working conditions. Such exposure may reduce employees' ability to think clearly and systematically and contribute to emotionally driven "lashing out" at others—precisely the kind of behavior most organizations strongly prefer to minimize. (Needless to add, there are many other reasons for assuring that employees are not exposed to such conditions.)

Additional Techniques

Several other techniques for reducing aggression have been identified by basic research. A brief description of the most important of these follows below, as well as comments on the potential usefulness of these and other techniques for reducing workplace aggression.

Exposure to Nonaggressive Models

As noted earlier, exposure to other persons behaving in an aggressive manner (either in person or in media representations) has been found to be an important elicitor of aggression. Conversely, exposure to other persons who demonstrate restraint in the face of strong provocation has been found to significantly reduce the likelihood of aggression among persons who observe such self-control (Baron, 1972; Donnerstein & Donnerstein, 1976). Apparently, exposure to such nonaggressive models suggests strongly that aggression is inappropriate and strengthens observers' restraints against engaging in such behavior.

Training in Social Skills

One reason many persons become involved in aggressive encounters is that they are lacking in basic social skills. They don't know how to make requests to others in a nonprovocative manner; they don't know how to refuse requests from others in a way that will not anger them; and in general, they are insensitive to the effects of their words or deeds on other persons. As a result, they often produce negative feelings in others that they do not intend and of which they may be only dimly aware. Fortunately, these and many other social skills can be readily learned and improved, so providing such training for perpetual "troublemakers" in an organization may be a useful means for reducing the overall incidence of aggression in work settings.

Incompatible Responses

One intriguing finding of basic research on aggression germane to the present discussion is that when people who are angry are exposed to events or stimuli that induce affective states incompatible with such negative reactions, they are less likely to engage in overt aggression than would otherwise be the case. Several types of events or stimuli appear to be highly effective in this respect, including humor, feelings of empathy toward potential victims, and even mild sexual arousal (Baron, 1993). Apparently, the positive affect produced by such stimuli counters the negative feelings generated by previous provocation, frustration, or other sources, and so reduces the likelihood that the persons involved will aggress against others. Of course, this technique does not always operate successfully: trying to induce someone who is very angry to laugh may backfire and annoy them still further. But if used early in the process—before the persons involved have become truly infuriated—efforts to replace negative internal states with positive ones can be quite successful.

Applicability of Techniques Identified by Basic Research to the Reduction of Workplace Aggression

At this point, it is important to note that all of the techniques described above have been investigated primarily in the context of aggressive actions between persons who do not know each other well and who do not anticipate long-term, continued contacts. Since aggression in workplaces often occurs between persons who have known each other for months or even years and who are in contact with one another several hours each day, the applicability of these techniques to workplaces is uncertain. However, it appears that with appropriate modifications, several of the techniques can be employed to reduce the frequency or intensity of aggression in workplaces.

Turning first to punishment, it is clear that because workplace aggression often takes subtle forms (for example, spreading damaging rumors about a particular person, withholding information or resources they need; Baron, Neuman, & Geddes, 1999), it is less amenable to punishment than other, more obvious forms of unacceptable behavior (for example, chronic tardiness, chronic unwillingness to adhere to organizational work rules). However, when workplace aggression takes more direct verbal or physical forms, punishment can be used to deter repetitions of these actions. Because these instances of workplace aggression are dangerous, the kind of progressive discipline used to deter other forms of unacceptable behavior in organizations may not be appropriate (Arvey & Jones, 1985). Instead, it is important that the punishment be delivered immediately and that it be of at least moderate intensity. This might involve actions such as putting the employee on probation or withholding a portion of merit pay. Such outcomes might well be effective in deterring repetitions of overt forms of workplace aggression, although if underlying causes persist (see below), they may serve more to drive such behavior "underground" (toward more subtle forms) than to eliminate it.

Cognitive interventions, too, may be useful in reducing the incidence and intensity of workplace aggression. Apologies have been found to be very effective in reducing anger and overt aggression, and they might produce similar effects in workplaces. However, if they are repeated frequently, their efficacy will decrease. Since overt aggression is more likely to occur when individuals' ability to think clearly is reduced (that is, in the presence of cognitive deficits), procedures that take account of this fact may also be helpful. Specifically, providing employees who are being pushed to their limit with brief respites from high-stress situations or extremely high work loads may go a long way toward reducing their tendency to lash out impulsively at others.

Finally, training in social skills may be very useful from the point of view of reducing workplace aggression. Frequently, such behavior occurs because the individuals involved are seeking to "even the score" for prior mistreatment. Thus, training managers to deliver feedback (especially negative feedback) in a more sensitive and constructive manner might well help prevent workplace aggression in many contexts. Previous research indicates that harsh, biting, or sarcastic negative feedback and negative feedback delivered in front of others can be strong precursors to anger and interpersonal conflict (Baron, 1990). Training the persons who give such feedback to do so in a more constructive manner may eliminate important causes of workplace aggression.

A Proactive Approach to Reducing Workplace Aggression

This last point suggests another approach to the issue of reducing workplace aggression—one that can be described as *proactive*. Instead of concentrating on the task of preventing repetitions of workplace aggression, such an approach focuses on removing or reducing the primary causes of such behavior from workplaces. A growing body of evidence suggests that workplace aggression often stems from perceptions of having been treated unfairly by other organizational members (Greenberg & Alge, 1998; Neuman & Baron, 1998). Thus, to the greater extent that organizations assure the presence of distributive, procedural, and interactional justice, the lower the incidence of workplace aggression is likely to be. Similarly, since direct provocation has been found to be a powerful elicitor of aggression (Anderson & Bushman, 2002), eliminating *abusive supervision*—supervisory behavior that includes sustained displays of hostile verbal and nonverbal behaviors—can go a long way toward reducing the frequency or intensity of such behavior. Finally, unpleasant environmental conditions, too, have been found to induce the negative affective states that often "set the stage" for subsequent aggression. Thus, assuring that workplaces are comfortable environmentally (that is, with respect to temperatures, noise, air quality, and so forth) may also be a useful step in preventing many forms of workplace aggression—especially, perhaps, forms that are largely emotion-driven or impulsive in nature.

In sum, basic research on aggression provides several interesting and potentially valuable leads for procedures that may be useful in preventing or reducing workplace aggression. It remains for future research to determine how effective these techniques can be and how they can best be employed for this important purpose.

Why Knowledge of the Findings of Basic Research on Human Aggression May Prove Useful

This chapter has covered a great deal of ground and has attempted to summarize a vast body of literature. In concluding, then, it seems reasonable to address the following question: Is acquaintance with the findings of basic research on aggression actually useful to investigators studying workplace aggression? In my opinion, the answer is a definite yes. Specifically, familiarity with this large body of theory and research can prove useful to the study of workplace aggression in three distinct ways.

First, as noted at the beginning, familiarity with the basic research can help prevent "reinventing the wheel." We currently know quite a lot about the nature and causes of human aggression, so why not apply these findings to the task of understanding the nature and causes of workplace aggression?

Second, working knowledge of this literature can serve as a useful source of hypotheses for researchers in the field of workplace aggression. My own graduate students have often posed the following question: Where do hypotheses for research originate? One important answer is that they are suggested by previous research. In this respect, too, the findings of basic research on aggression can prove useful. Many of the variables studied in such research are present in work settings (for example, provocations, the presence of aggressive models, norms that approve or disapprove of aggression, environmental conditions), and these factors may well play a role in determining the incidence, form, and targets of workplace aggression. These variables may well be overlooked if researchers studying workplace aggression are not conversant with past work.

Third, the findings of basic research on aggression can provide investigators studying such behavior in workplaces a rich source of theoretical and conceptual tools. In general, the more of these a field has at its disposal, the more quickly it can advance. So again, it seems to make sense to adapt as many of these as possible to efforts to understand workplace aggression. For these reasons alone, and others as well, closer conceptual ties between the two areas of investigation would appear to be well justified. The result may well be more rapid progress toward the related goals of understanding workplace aggression and managing it effectively. Regardless of any disagreements within the field, there is certainly consensus that this is what we seek, and will, ultimately, be proud to have attained.

References

Anderson, C. A. (1997). Effects of violent movies and trait hostility on hostile feelings and aggressive thoughts. *Aggressive Behavior,* 23, 161–178.

Anderson, C. A., & Bushman, B. J. (2002). Human aggression. *Annual Review of Psychology,* 53, 27–51.

Anderson, C. A., Bushman, B. J., & Groom, R. W. (1997). Hot years and serious and deadly assault: Empirical tests of the heat hypothesis. *Journal of Personality and Social Psychology,* 73, 1213–1223.

Arvey, R. D., & Jones, A. P. (1985). The use of discipline in organizational settings: A framework for future research. In L. L. Cummings & B. M. Staw (Eds.), *Research in organizational behavior* (Vol. 7, pp. 367–408). Greenwich, CT: JAI Press.

Baron, R. A. (1972). Reducing the influence of an aggressive model: The restraining effects of peer censure. *Journal of Experimental Social Psychology,* 8, 266–275.

Baron, R. A. (1977). *Human aggression.* New York: Plenum.

Baron, R. A. (1989). Personality and organizational conflict: The type A behavior pattern and self-monitoring. *Organizational Behavior and Human Decision Processes,* 44, 281–297.

Baron, R. A. (1993). Reducing aggression and conflict: The incompatible response approach, or why people who feel good usually won't be bad. In G. C. Brannigan & M. R. Merrens (Eds.), *The undaunted psychologist* (pp. 203–218). Philadelphia: Temple University Press.

Baron, R. A. (1994). The physical environment of work settings: Effects on task performance, interpersonal relations, and job satisfaction. In B. M. Staw & L. L. Cummings (Eds.), *Research in organizational behavior* (Vol. 16, pp. 1–46). Greenwich, CT: JAI Press.

Baron, R. A. (1990). Countering the effects of destructive criticism: The relative efficacy of four potential interventions. *Journal of Applied Psychology,* 75, 235–245.

Baron, R. A., & Bell, P. A. (1975). Aggression and heat: Mediating effects of prior provocation and exposure to an aggressive model. *Journal of Personality and Social Psychology,* 31, 825–832.

Baron, R. A., Neuman, J. H., & Geddes, D. (1999). Social and personal determinants of workplace aggression: Evidence for the impact of perceived injustice and the type A behavior pattern. *Aggressive Behavior,* 25, 281–297.

Baron, R. A., & Richardson, D. R. (1994). *Human aggression* (2nd ed.) New York: Plenum.

Baron, R. A., Russell, G. W., & Arms, R. L. (1985). Negative ions and behavior: Impact on mood, memory, and aggression among type A and type B persons. *Journal of Personality and Social Psychology,* 48, 746–754.

Berkowitz, L. (1989). Frustration-aggression hypothesis: Examination and reformulation. *Psychological Bulletin,* 106, 59–73.

Berkowitz, L. (1993). *Aggression: Its causes, consequences, and control.* New York: McGraw-Hill.

Berkowitz, L. (2001). *Aggression.* New York: Academic Press.

Braverman, M. (1999). *Preventing workplace violence.* London: Sage.

Bushman, B. J., & Cooper, H. M. (1990). Effects of alcohol on human aggression: An integrative research review. *Psychological Bulletin,* 107, 341–354.

Bushman, B. J., & Baumeister, R. F. (1998). Threatened egotism, narcissim, self-esteem, and direct and displaced aggression: Does self-love or self-hate lead to violence? *Journal of Personality and Social Psychology,* 75, 219–229.

Buss, A. H. (1961). *The psychology of aggression.* New York: John Wiley.

Buss, A. H. (1971). Aggression pays. In J. L. Singer (Ed.), *The control of aggression and violence* (pp. 112–130). New York: Academic Press.

Buss, D. M. (1999). *Evolutionary psychology: The new science of the mind.* Boston: Allyn & Bacon.

Caprara, G. V., Renzi, P., Amolini, P., D'Imperio, G., & Travalaglia, G. (1984). The eliciting cue value of aggressive slides reconsidered in a personological perspective: The weapons effect and irritability. *European Journal of Social Psychology,* 14, 313–322.

Carlson, M., Marcus-Newhall, A., & Miller, N. (1990). Effects of situational aggression cues: A quantitative review. *Journal of Personality and Social Psychology,* 58, 622–633.

Carver, C. S., & Glass, D. C. (1978). Coronary-prone behavior pattern and interpersonal aggression. *Journal of Personality and Social Psychology,* 36, 361–366.

Catalano, R., Novaco, R. W., & McConnell, W. (2002). Layoffs and violence revisited. *Aggressive Behavior,* 28, 233–247.

Chermack, S. T., Berman, M., & Taylor, S. P. (1997). Effects of provocation on emotions and aggression in males. *Aggressive Behavior,* 23, 1–10.

Dietz, J., Robinson, S. L., Folger, R., Baron, R. A., & Schultz, M. (2003). The impact of community violence and an organization's procedural justice climate on workplace aggression. *Academy of Management Journal,* 46, 317–326.

Dodge, K. A., & Coie, J. D. (1987). Social information-processing factors in reactive and proactive aggression in children's peers groups. *Journal of Personality and Social Psychology*, 53, 1146–1158.

Dodge, K. A., Pettit, G. S., McClaskey, C. L., & Brown, M. M. (1986). Social competence in children. *Monographs of the Society for Research in Child Development*, 51, 1–65.

Dollard, J., Doob, L., Miller, N., Mowrer, O. H., & Sears, R. R. (1939). *Frustration and aggression*. New Haven, CT: Yale University Press.

Donnerstein, E., & Donnerstein, M. (1976). Research in the control of interracial aggression. In R. G. Green & E. C. O'Neal (Eds.), *Perspectives on aggression* (pp. 133–168). New York: Academic Press.

Folger, R., & Baron, R. A. (1996). Violence and hostility at work: A model of reactions to perceived injustice. In G. R. VandenBos & E. Q. Bulato (Eds.), *Violence on the job: Identifying risks and developing solutions* (pp. 51–85). Washington, D.C.: American Psychological Association.

Fry, D. P. (1998). Anthropological perspectives on aggression: Sex differences and cultural variation. *Aggressive Behavior*, 24, 81–95.

Gantner, A. B., & Taylor, S. P. (1992). Human physical aggression as a function of alcohol and threat of harm. *Aggressive Behavior*, 18, 29–36.

Geen, R. G. (1998). Some effects of observing violence upon the behavior of the observer. In B. A. Maher (Ed.), *Progress in experimental personality research* (Vol. 8). New York: Academic Press.

Geen, R. G., & McCown, E. J. (1984). Effects of noise and attack on aggression and physiological arousal. *Motivation and Emotion*, 8, 231–241.

Greenberg, J., & Alge, B. J. (1998). Aggressive reactions to workplace injustice. In R. W. Griffin, A. O'Leary-Kelly, & J. Collins (Eds.), *Dysfunctional behavior in organizations* (Vol. 1: *Violent behavior in organizations*). Stamford, CT: JAI Press.

Glass, D. C. (1977). *Behavior patterns, stress, and coronary disease*. Hillsdale, NJ: Erlbaum.

Gustafson, R. (1990). Wine and male physical aggression. *Journal of Drug Issues*, 20, 75–86.

Hilton, N. Z., Harris, G. T., & Rice, M. E. (2000). The function of aggression by male teenagers. *Journal of Personality and Social Psychology*, 79, 988–994.

Huesmann, L. R., & Eron, L. D. (1986). *Television and the aggressive child: A cross-national comparison*. Hillsdale, NJ: Erlbaum.

Kacmar, K. M., & Baron, R. A. (1999). Organizational politics: The state of the field, links to related processes, and an agenda for future research. In G. Ferris (Ed.), *Research in personnel and human resources management* (Vol. 18). Greenwich, CT: JAI Press.

Kaukiainen, A., Salmivalli, C., Bjorkqvist, J., Osterman, K., Lahtinen, A., Kostamo, A., & Lagerspetz, K. (2001). Overt and covert aggression in work settings in relation to the subjective well-being of employees. *Aggressive Behavior,* 27, 360–371.

Lee, K., & Allen, N. J. (2002). Organizational citizenship behavior and workplace deviance: The role of affect and cognitions. *Journal of Applied Psychology,* 87, 131–142.

Lorenz, K. (1966). *On aggression.* New York: Bantam.

Marcus-Newhall, A., Pederson, W. C., Carlson, M., & Miller, N. (2000). Displaced aggression is alive and well: A meta-analytic review. *Journal of Personality and Social Psychology,* 78, 670–689.

Moeller, T. G. (2001). *Youth aggression and violence: A psychological approach.* Mahwah, NJ: Erlbaum.

Neuman, J. H., & Baron, R. A. (1998). Workplace violence and workplace aggression: Evidence concerning specific forms, potential causes, and preferred targets. *Journal of Management,* 24, 391–420.

Ohbuchi, J., & Kambara, T. (1985). Attacker's intent and awareness of outcome, impression management and retaliation. *Journal of Experimental Social Psychology,* 21, 321–330.

Ohbuchi,, J., Kameda, M., & Agarie, N. (1989). Apology as aggression control: Its role in mediating appraisal of and response to harm. *Journal of Personality and Social Psychology,* 56, 219–227.

Pederson, W. C., Gonzales, C., & Miller, N. (2000). The moderating effect of trivial triggering provocation on displaced aggression. *Journal of Personality and Social Psychology,* 78, 913–947.

Pihl, R. O., Lau, M. L., & Assad, J. M. (1997). Aggressive disposition, alcohol, and aggression. *Aggressive Behavior,* 23, 11–18.

Robinson, S. L., & Bennett, R. J. (1995). A typology of deviant workplace behaviors: A multi-dimensional scaling study. *Academy of Management Journal,* 38, 555–572.

Rosenberg, H. (1972). The cultural situation today. *Partisan Review,* Summer.

Rotton, J., Frey, J., Barry, T., Milligan, M., & Fitzpatrick, M. (1979). The air pollution experience and physical aggression. *Journal of Applied Social Psychology,* 9, 397–412.

Rotton, J., & Cohn, E. G. (2000). Violence as a curvilinear function of temperature in Dallas: A replication. *Journal of Personality and Social Psychology,* 78, 1074–1081.

Skarlicki, D. P., & Folger, R. (1997). Retaliation in the workplace: The roles of distributive, procedural, and interactional justice. *Journal of Applied Psychology,* 82, 434–443.

Strube, M. J. (1989). Evidence for the type A behavior pattern: A taxonomic analysis. *Journal of Personality and Social Psychology*, 56, 972–987.

Strube, M., Turner, C. W., Cero, D., Stevens, J., & Hinchey, F. (1984). Interpersonal aggression and the type A coronary-prone behavior pattern: A theoretical distinction and practical implications. *Journal of Personality and Social Psychology*, 47, 839–847.

Taylor, S. P., & Sears, J. D. (1988). The effects of alcohol and persuasive social pressure on human physical aggression. *Aggressive Behavior*, 14, 237–243.

Zechmeister, J. S., & Romero, C. (2002). Victim and offender accounts of interpersonal conflict: Autobiographical narratives of forgiveness and unforgiveness. *Journal of Personality and Social Psychology*, 82, 675–686.

Zeichner, A., & Pihl, R. O. (1980). Effects of alcohol and instigator intent on human aggression. *Journal of Studies on Alcohol*, 41, 265–276.

Zillmann, D. (1979). *Hostility and aggression*. Hillsdale, NJ: Erlbaum.

Zillmann, D. (1993). Mental control of angry aggression. In D. M. Wegner & J. W. Pennebaker (Eds.), *Handbook of mental control*. Englewood Cliffs, NJ: Prentice-Hall.

Zillmann, D. (1994). Cognition-excitation interdependencies in the escalation of anger and angry aggression. In N. M. Potegal & J. F Knutson (Eds.), *The dynamics of aggression*. Hillsdale, NJ: Erlbaum.

Zillmann, D., Baron, R. A., & Tamborini, R. (1981). The social costs of smoking: Effects of tobacco smoke on hostile behavior. *Journal of Applied Social Psychology*, 11, 548–561.

CHAPTER 3

Injustice, Stress, and Aggression in Organizations

Joel H. Neuman

As evidenced throughout this volume, the dark side of organizational behavior encompasses a variety of harmful actions subsumed under an assortment of labels. Although each of these behaviors could undoubtedly be studied as individual phenomena—defined in terms of their own antecedent conditions, intervening processes, and outcomes—to the extent that they involve any form of behavior directed by one or more persons in a workplace toward the goal of harming one or more others in that workplace (or the entire organization) in ways the intended targets are motivated to avoid, they represent instances of workplace aggression (Baron, this volume; Baron & Neuman, 1996; Neuman & Baron, 1997). Whereas research on workplace aggression is still in its infancy, this cannot be said for the study of aggression in other social settings—where a substantial amount of empirical and theoretical literature has accumulated. From this extant scholarship, we know quite a bit about the phenomenon, and what we know suggests that injustice and stress are among the most significant causes (and consequences) of aggression in general and workplace aggression in particular.

As I hope to demonstrate on the pages that follow, injustice, stress, and aggression (which I will refer to collectively as the *focal variables*) are ubiquitous in work settings and may have an enormous impact on the health and well-being of individuals and, ultimately, the economic prosperity and viability of organizations. To accomplish this objective, I will begin by addressing some important definitional issues associated with the focal variables and present some evidence as to their prevalence in, and potential costs to, organizations. Following this I turn my attention to conceptual issues and present a framework for understanding and exploring the relationships among the focal variables (a model consistent with contemporary theories of aggression and based on earlier research on stress) and discuss how this framework is being employed in a collaborative action research project within the United States Department of Veterans Affairs (VA) to better understand (1) the causes and consequences of workplace injustice, stress, and aggression, (2) the complex interactions among these variables, and (3) the processes and practices by which these phenomena can be effectively managed in work settings.

The Nature of Aggression, Stress, and Injustice in Organizational Settings: Definitional and Conceptual Issues

This chapter is not meant to serve as a comprehensive treatise on aggression, stress, or injustice; nor is this meant to serve as a basic primer for these subjects.[1] Nevertheless, it is important to provide some foundational information before proceeding further. To this end, in this section I will focus on some basic definitional and conceptual issues.

Workplace Aggression and Violence

As discussed in detail elsewhere (Baron, this volume; Berkowitz, 1993; Zillmann, 1979), during the 1960s and 1970s researchers struggled to find an adequate and accurate definition of aggression. The consensus that emerged holds that aggression is any form of behavior directed toward the goal of harming or injuring another living being who is motivated to avoid such treatment (Baron, 1977). This definition, along with its conceptual and empirical underpinnings, serves as the basis for the definition of workplace aggression provided earlier—any form of behavior directed by one or more persons in a workplace toward the goal of harming one or more others in that workplace (or the entire organization) in ways the intended targets are motivated to avoid. Four themes are explicit in (and central to) this definition. First, aggression involves effortful behavior; or, to put it simply, behavior that is intentional in nature. The second theme involves the nature of this intent, which is to cause harm to one or more individuals or the organization. Third, consistent with the position taken by O'Leary-Kelly, Griffin, and Glew (1996), workplace aggression involves interpersonal aggression prompted by factors within the organization—as opposed to actions motivated by factors external to the organization or initiated by organizational outsiders. Finally, the fact that individuals are motivated to avoid such treatment suggests that the behavior is neither invited nor welcomed by the target. Consistent with this definition, actions that result in unintended harm would not be considered aggressive in nature. This, of course, would exclude physical, emotional, or psychological injuries sustained as a result of accidental or unintended behavior on the part of others (for example, accidentally dropping a hammer on someone's foot or inadvertently engaging in behavior that others perceive as rude or offensive). On a related note, actions that are intended to inflict harm need not be successful for aggression to have occurred. For example, if I spread untrue and particularly vicious rumors about you in an attempt to get you fired, so that I can obtain your job, these actions would be considered aggressive even if the attempt proved unsuccessful. Even in cases of intentional harm-doing, acts are not considered aggressive if the target intentionally invites such behavior and derives pleasure from the act. Nor is it aggression if an individual engages in actions designed to be self-destructive.

Another important definitional issue regards the difference between the terms *aggression* and *violence*. O'Leary-Kelly, Griffin, and Glew ". . . propose that aggression be used to describe the potentially destructive act (the process) and violence be used to describe the consequence of the act (the outcome)" (1996, pp. 227–228). As discussed elsewhere (Baron & Neuman, 1996; Neuman & Baron, 1997, 1998), I prefer to draw a distinction based on the form and intensity of the behavior, as described next.

Forms of Aggression

Since aggression involves all forms of behavior intended to harm others, it is clear that an infinite number of behaviors could be classified as aggressive. As a result, many scholars have attempted to construct typologies for the purpose of organizing these behaviors into a more manageable number of dimensions. Of these, the most widely recognized was proposed by Buss (1961), and this has served as the basis for several studies of workplace aggression (Baron & Neuman, 1996, 1998; Baron, Neuman, & Geddes, 1999; Geddes & Baron, 1997; Neuman & Keashly, 2002). According to Buss (1961), aggression can be captured using three dimensions: (1) physical-verbal, (2) active-passive, and (3) direct-indirect. Physical aggression, as the label implies, involves physical actions on the part of the actor, whereas verbal aggression inflicts harm through words as opposed to deeds. With respect to direct forms of aggression, the actor harms the target directly, whereas in the case of indirect aggression the actor might inflict harm on something the target values or someone the target cares about, such as a protégé. Finally, active aggression requires the actor to do something to harm the target, whereas passive aggression involves withholding something that the target needs or values (refer to Table 3.1 for examples of workplace aggression falling within each of the Buss dimensions).

Regarding the distinction between aggression and violence, consistent with much theorizing in the human aggression literature, it is my position that aggression refers to all forms of intentional harm-doing behavior, whereas violence refers primarily to intense instances of harm-doing that would be characterized within the Buss (1961) typology as physical, active, and direct in nature (Baron & Richardson, 1994; Neuman & Baron, 1997).

Stressors, Stress, and Strain

Several years ago, Schuler (1980) noted that many organizational scholars had not done a very good job of distinguishing between the constructs of stressors, stress, and strain. With notable exceptions (Fox, Spector, & Miles, 2001; Jex et al., 1992; Spector, 1999; Spector et al., 2000), much confusion remains and this is probably due, in part, to the use (and overuse) of these terms in everyday language.

**Table 3.1. Sample Items from the
Workplace Aggression Research Questionnaire
(WAR-Q) Sorted into the Buss (1961) Dimensions.**

Aggressive Behavior	Active (A) Passive (P)	Direct (D) Indirect (I)
Physical		
Pushed, shoved, bumped into with unnecessary force	A	D
Assaulted with weapon or other dangerous object	A	D
Had someone interfere with your work activities	A	D
Had others storm out of a room when you entered	P	D
Been subjected to obscene or hostile gestures	A	D
Had others destroy or take resources that you needed for your job	A	I
Been excluded from work-related or social gatherings	P	D
Denied raise or promotion without being given valid reason	P	I
Verbal		
Treated in a rude or condescending manner	A	D
Negative comments made about your intelligence or competence	A	D
Been sworn at in a hostile manner	A	D
Been given the silent treatment	P	D
Had others fail to give you information that you really needed	P	I
Had someone else take credit for your work ideas	A	I
Had others fail to warn you about impending dangers	P	I
Been the target of rumors or gossip	A	I

Stress

As noted by Selye (1978), "the term stress has been used so loosely, and so many confusing definitions of it have been formulated, that I think it will be best to start by clearly stating what it is not" (p. 62). Stress is not synonymous with nervous tension, an emergency discharge of hormones, or anything that causes alarm; nor is it necessarily bad or something to be avoided. For the purpose of this chapter, stress can be viewed simply as a physiological and psychological response to demands that are perceived to be challenging or threatening (Spector, 1996), that is, stressors.

Stressors

Broadly defined, stressors are any demands, either physical or psychological in nature, encountered during the course of living. As the focus of this chapter is on organizational settings, my discussion will focus on work- or job-related stressors, conditions or situations at work that require an adaptive response on the part of the employee (Jex & Beehr, 1991). Although there are an infinite number of stimuli that might serve as stressors, organizational scholars have successfully captured many of these variables in a relatively small set of dimensions. In their review of literature on job stressors, Jex and Beehr (1991) identified issues relating to lack of control, interpersonal conflict, organizational constraints, role ambiguity, role conflict, and workload as sources of stress. In brief, to the extent that employees lack decision-making control over their jobs, experience interpersonal or role-related conflict, encounter frustration in reaching important objectives, or have to deal with high levels of ambiguity or unreasonable workloads, there is an increased likelihood that they will experience stress. Even the most casual observers of workplace behavior know that these social and situational stressors are widespread in today's leaner and meaner workplace.

Strain

Adverse reactions that develop as a result of exposure to one or more job-related stressors constitute *job-related strain*. Recent research has tended to categorize strains as involving damaging behavioral, physical, or psychological reactions (Jex & Beehr, 1991; Spector et al., 2000). Behavioral strains involve things that people may do in response to work-related stressors, such as engaging in substance abuse, increased rates of lateness and absenteeism, and other withdrawal behaviors. Psychological manifestations of strain may involve cognitive impairment (distractibility, difficulty in concentrating, ruminations) and affective or emotional disturbance (for example, job dissatisfaction, anxiety, depression). Finally, physical forms of strain may result in a wide variety of health problems (headaches, diffuse aches and pains, physical exhaustion). It is to these behavioral, physical, and psychological responses that people often refer when talking about stress, and for good reason— the only evidence we have of the presence of stress is found in these palpable reactions.

Appreciating the distinctions presented above and the underlying causal flow in the stress process (from stressors through stress to strain) is important in understanding the relationships among the focal variables and, in particular, the relationship between aggression and perceptions of injustice, to which I now turn my attention.

Organizational Justice

The term *organizational justice* was coined by Greenberg (1987) to describe theory and research related to people's perceptions of fairness (and, all too frequently, unfairness) on the job. As such, organizational justice theory is "completely descriptive in orientation—focusing on people's perceptions of what constitutes fairness, and their reactions to unfair situations" (Cropanzano & Greenberg, 1997, p. 318). Justice, according to this perspective, is in the eye of the beholder, and in work settings, where justice judgments are made on a continuing basis, there is ample opportunity for people to experience injustice—both real and imagined.

Although there are innumerable ways for people to feel mistreated, organizational justice research has tended to focus on three particular forms of justice: distributive, procedural, and interactional-interpersonal.

Distributive Justice

The modern roots of distributive justice research can be traced to Homans's (1961) "rule of distributive justice," which states that expectations among parties to a social exchange relationship are such that (1) the reward of each will be proportional to the costs of each, and (2) the net rewards, or profits, will be proportional to their investments. In short, people judge the ratio of their inputs (their investments, both in financial and nonfinancial terms) to their outcomes (what they derive from these investments) and are sensitive to any disparity in this ratio. Extending this principle to organizational settings, Adams (1965) proposed that people are motivated to avoid tension (that is, discomfort, dissonance, distress) that results from situations in which the ratio of one's own outcomes to inputs is unequal to the corresponding ratio of some comparison other.

In sum, distributive justice issues focus on individuals' perceptions of unfair treatment relating to the outcomes they receive, but research in the 1970s began to reveal that people not only focus on the "ends" (outcomes) of a social exchange but on the "means" by which those ends are (or are not) obtained.

Procedural and Interactional-Interpersonal Justice

Just as individuals are concerned with the fairness of the outcomes that they receive, they also are sensitive to the process used to determine those allocations (Thibaut & Walker, 1975) and the nature of the interactions that characterize those transactions (Bies, 1987; Greenberg, 1993).

With regard to the means, research suggests that procedures are likely to be perceived as fair to the extent that they (1) suppress bias, (2) create consistent allocations, (3) rely on accurate information, (4) are correctable, (5) represent the concerns of all recipients, and (6) are based on prevailing moral and ethical standards (Leventhal, 1976, 1980). Some practical examples of this would include procedures in which all parties have some voice in the decision-making process (Folger, 1977; Thibaut & Walker, 1975) and believe that their voice is being heard and that they have some choice in determining the outcomes. As regards interactional or interpersonal elements, a "fair" process is one in which individuals are treated with sensitivity, consideration, and politeness (Bies & Moag, 1986; Greenberg, 1993; Mikula, Petri, & Tanzer, 1990).

The Prevalence and Financial Costs of Workplace Aggression, Stress, and Injustice

Due to space constraints, my discussion of the prevalence of, and individual and organizational costs associated with, aggression, stress, and injustice will necessarily be brief. I have simply highlighted some important work and provided numerous reference citations directing the interested reader to more detailed source material. Also, it is important to note that it is difficult (if not impossible) to know, with any degree of precision, the actual prevalence of aggression, stress, and injustice in work settings or the toll they take in human or financial terms. For this reason, the data should be interpreted with caution as they are merely representative of what we believe we "know" at this time and should not be considered exhaustive or conclusive. Having said this, what we have learned to date suggests that these variables are ubiquitous in today's leaner and meaner organizations and their impact on individuals and organizations is substantial.

Workplace Violence: Fatal and Nonfatal Physical Assault

While this chapter centers on aggression and violence prompted by factors within the organization, much of the "workplace violence" literature has tended to focus on actions by organizational outsiders and, in the largest percentage of these cases, armed robbery was the motive. So rather than represent workplace aggression or violence, these acts are better captured under the heading of occupation-related aggression or violence (Mullen, 1997). Although not the central focus of this chapter, a few facts and figures are important. According to the *Census of Fatal Occupational Injuries* (CFOI), from 1992 through 1998, there were 6,714 work-related homicides. In 3,549 cases in which researchers were able to identify the perpetrators, 456 (12.8 percent) involved coworkers, 248 (7 percent) involved customers-clients, and 2,403 (67.7 percent) involved armed robbers. As best we can tell from CFOI data, the number of coworker-related incidents (the focus of this chapter) has fluctuated from a low of 10.5 percent of all work-related homicides in 1994 to a high of 15.3 percent in 1995. The most recent data available from the Bureau of Labor Statistics (BLS) show that 599 individuals were the victims of workplace homicide, and of that total 73 died at the hands of a coworker (12 percent). According to the Bureau of Justice Statistics (BJS) National Crime Victimization Survey, U.S. residents experienced more than two million violent victimizations while they were working or on duty (Bureau of Justice Statistics, 1996) costing about half a million employees 1,751,100 days of work each year, an average of 3.5 days per crime. This missed work resulted in over $55 million in lost wages annually, not including days covered by sick and annual leave (Bureau of Justice Statistics, 1994).

With respect to workplace violence research conducted by management professionals, a study of five hundred private-sector managers reporting such incidents revealed that 16 percent involved harassment, 48 percent the threat of violence, 9 percent fighting, 10 percent assault with a weapon, and 2 percent rape or sexual assault (American Management Association, 1994). Similarly, a study conducted by the Society for Human Resource Management (1996), involving 1,016 human resource professionals, found that verbal threats were the most prevalent incident (39 percent) followed by pushing and shoving (22 percent), fistfights (13 percent), assault with a weapon (1 percent), and rape or sexual assault (1 percent). Finally, in telephone interviews of six hundred full-time American workers conducted by Northwestern National Life (1993), 19 percent of the respondents reported incidents of harassment, 7 percent reported threats of physical harm, and 3 percent reported actual physical attacks. As evidenced in these reports, although workplace violence had been receiving most of the attention (each of the three reports used the term *violence* in the title), episodes of "lower-level" aggression were reported significantly more often than episodes of violence.

Workplace Aggression

Over the preceding decade, research related (in whole or in part) to workplace aggression, as defined in this chapter, has been conducted under the headings of workplace bullying (Adams & Crawford, 1992), work harassment (Björkqvist, Österman, & Hjelt-Back, 1994; Brodsky, 1976), mobbing and psychological terror (Leymann,

1990), social undermining (Duffy, Ganster, & Pagon, 2002), organizational aggression (Spector, 1975), workplace aggression (Baron & Neuman, 1996; Neuman & Baron, 1997), organization motivated aggression (O'Leary-Kelly et al., 1996), workplace violence (Kinney & Johnson, 1993; Mantell, 1994), emotional abuse (Keashly, 1998), organizational retaliatory behavior (Skarlicki & Folger, 1997), petty tyranny (Ashforth, 1994), abusive supervision (Moberg, Ritter, & Fischbein, 2002; Tepper, 2000), sexual harassment (Barling, Rogers, & Kelloway, 2001; Glomb, Munson, Hulin, Bergman, & Drasgow, 1999; Lengnick-Hall, 1995; O'Leary-Kelly, Paetzold, & Griffin, 2000; Richman et al., 1999), workplace incivility (Andersson & Pearson, 1999), counterproductive workplace behavior (Fox et al., 2001; Spector, 2001), dysfunctional, deviant, or unreliable workplace behavior (Hogan & Hogan, 1989; Robinson & Kraatz, 1998). I offer these references to demonstrate the pervasiveness of aggression-related phenomena in work settings and direct the interested reader to the above-referenced source material for more information, as well as the recent attempts to differentiate or integrate these constructs (Fox & Spector; O'Leary-Kelly, Duffy, & Griffin, 2000; Robinson & Greenberg, 1998).

Prevalence data obtained in the studies cited above suggest that persistent acts of aggression (that is, bullying and mobbing) and less frequent or isolated acts of workplace aggression are experienced by a significant segment of the working population. Based on data from fourteen Norwegian studies (involving 7,986 respondents), Einarsen and Skogstad (1996) found that as many as 8.6 percent of the respondents had been bullied at work during the previous six months. In later work involving an extensive review of empirical studies of bullying in Europe, Zapf, Einarsen, Hoel, and Vartia (2003) found that between 1 and 4 percent of employees experience serious bullying (weekly or daily episodes) and 8 to 10 percent report occasional episodes. These data also suggest "between 10 and 20 percent (or even higher) of employees may occasionally be confronted with negative social behavior at work which does not correspond to definitions of bullying but which is *stressful* [italics added] for the persons concerned nevertheless" (Zapf et al., 2003, p. 121). In one of the most comprehensive workplace bullying studies to date in the United Kingdom (Hoel & Cooper, 2000), 5,288 usable questionnaires were obtained from

12,350 respondents (overall response rate of 42.8 percent); 10.5 percent of the respondents, drawn from a diverse cross section of business sectors, had some experience with bullying. In their research on work harassment, Björkqvist, Österman, and Hjelt-Back (1994) found that as many as 30 percent of the men and 55 percent of the women had been exposed to some form of work harassment during the preceding year. In addition, 32 percent of all respondents indicated that they had witnessed others being harassed in their workplace (that is, others being subjected to "degrading and oppressive activities"). In the United States, a stratified random sample of 1,836 adults in a statewide labor survey of Michigan residents found that 27 percent reported mistreatment at work during the preceding twelve-month period and 42 percent indicated that mistreatment had occurred at some point during their working career (Keashly & Jagatic, 2000). Finally, in a recent sample of 4,801 respondents in twenty-six facilities within the U.S. Department of Veterans Affairs (VA), 1,598 of those responding (36 percent) indicated that they had experienced one or more instances of aggression on a weekly or daily basis over the preceding twelve-month period and 2,590 (58 percent) indicated that they had experienced at least one act of aggression in the previous year (Keashly & Neuman, 2002; Neuman & Keashly, 2002).

The Prevalence and Financial Costs of Stress

Unlike the more recent research on workplace aggression—especially the "low-level" forms of aggression described above—readers probably will need little convincing about the prevalence of, and costs associated with, stress in contemporary work settings. Consequently, I will spend little time "preaching to the choir," but I do feel that a few "facts" and figures are worth noting. As mentioned in the earlier discussion about aggression and violence, it is difficult to obtain precise data as to the prevalence and costs associated with stress, so these data must be considered estimates of the true scope of the problem. According to the U.S. Bureau of Labor Statistics, stress costs U.S. employers an estimated $10,000 per worker per year, and the National Institute for Occupational Safety and Health (NIOSH) estimates that 40 percent of the U.S. workforce is affected by stress, making it the number one cause of worker disability (Wojcik, 2001). Another estimate puts the cost of stress, due to absenteeism, health insurance claims, and lost productivity, at $150 billion per year, and in a survey of 700 American workers conducted by Dale Carnegie Training, 79 percent of respondents reported that work was the primary source of their stress (DeFrank & Ivancevich, 1998). Other data suggest that stress is a factor in 60 to 80 percent of all work-related injuries, a major factor in approximately 40 percent of turnovers, and a significant contributor in 75 to 90 percent of visits to primary care physicians (Atkinson, 2000; Perkins, 1994). It is important to note that aggression is an extremely salient stressor to the targets of such behavior.

Although it is difficult enough to establish a dollar value (or isolate definitive causal relationships) for stress-related illness, absence, or injury, it is of course much more difficult to establish the financial impact of more subtle and indirect consequences of stress. For example, stress may affect the organizational bottom line through its impact on interpersonal dynamics and group process. As noted by Tedeschi and Felson (1994), stress may lead to increased violations of politeness norms and thereby affect the way in which people work (or fail to work) together. In short, stress may lead to workplace incivility—instances of interpersonal injustice—to which I now turn my attention.

The Prevalence and Costs of Injustice in the Workplace

As difficult as it is to quantify the prevalence and costs associated with stress and covert forms of aggression, it is manifestly more challenging to capture these data as they relate to organizational injustice. In some instances, transgressions may be so egregious as to be obvious to all concerned; more often than not, situations are ambiguous and justice judgments are determined in a subjective (idiosyncratic) manner. To complicate matters further, even when actions are unambiguous and manifestly unjust in form or effect, there may be no formal way to capture the incident (that is, no official reporting procedure or regulatory category) or quantify its consequences. For example, how (and to whom) do you report having had your feelings hurt, and what reporting system captures the time you spend ruminating about the perceived mistreatment? Furthermore, would you believe that such an incident is serious enough to merit a formal report? Often, people choose not to report or complain about such incidents—or even more serious incidents—because they fear being seen as whiners making "mountains out of molehills." Also, targets of such injustice may believe (sometimes correctly) that formal or informal complaints to a supervisor may put them in further (and possibly greater) jeopardy. Finally, targets may choose to confront the actor directly in an attempt to restore equity or simply exact revenge (Beale, Cox, Clarke, Lawrence, & Leather, 1998).

In instances in which injustice is viewed as serious—or at least "serious enough"—people may seek redress through legal means, and the number of employment-related discrimination cases brought in U.S. federal courts clearly demonstrates the regularity with which this happens. In absolute numbers, discrimination cases doubled over a three-year period, culminating in the filing of 23,000 such actions in 1996. It has been determined that one out of every 125 federal workers (a total of 21,868 individuals) filed formal Equal Employment Opportunity Commission (EEOC) discrimination complaints in 1999.

Apart from discrimination-based claims, the evidence we have about the prevalence and cost of organizational injustice comes, almost exclusively, from survey-based research. For example, in a study of 452 employees from a diverse group of businesses, 21 percent indicated that they were dissatisfied with the degree of respect and fair treatment they received from their boss (Baron & Neuman, 1998), and in similar research, of 124,716 employees responding to justice-related questions, 47,392 (38 percent) disagreed with the statement, "People treat each other with fairness and respect" (Department of Veterans Affairs, 1997). Furthermore, 46 percent believed that disciplinary actions were applied unfairly, 52 percent thought that the distribution of work was unfair, and 40 percent believed that there was discrimination in career advancement for qualified individuals, as relates to gender, race, national origin, religion, age, cultural background, sexual orientation, or disability. In another analysis, the self-reported fairness measures cited above were aggregated at the facility level for 176 facilities in the nationwide VA system. That is, mean response ratings were established for each justice-related questionnaire item for each of the 176 facilities. These aggregated data were then correlated with actual Equal Employment Opportunity (EEO) claims filed at each facility. As can be seen in Table 3.2, the greater the perception of fair treatment for each of the justice-related behaviors listed, the fewer the number of EEO complaints that were filed at that facility. Two things seem clear: (1) perceptions of injustice are associated with actual EEO complaints, and (2) these complaints are costly to defend and even more costly to settle.

Beyond legal costs, perceptions of unfair treatment can affect productivity through their impact on employee health (Tepper, 2001), dissatisfaction and related job-withdrawal behaviors (i.e., absenteeism, lateness, "time-theft," turnover), and, more directly, through organizational retaliatory behaviors (Skarlicki & Folger,

Table 3.2. Correlations Between Aggregated Survey Data and Facility-Level EEO Discrimination Claims.

Survey Question	Correlation
Reasonable accommodations are made for persons with disabilities	–.26**
Supervisors provide fair and accurate ratings of employee performance	–.20**
Supervisors provide constructive suggestions for improving performance	–.22**
Training and career development opportunities are allocated fairly	–.22**
Supervisors support employee efforts to learn outside the job	–.24**
Career advancement occurs for qualified individuals regardless of gender, race, national origin, religion, sexual orientation, or disability	–.18*
There is trust between employees and their supervisors and team leaders	–.19*

For each survey question, respondents indicated their agreement or disagreement using the following scale: 1 = strongly disagree, 5 = strongly agree.

N = 176 facilities.

*p < .05.

**p < .01.

1997). At the risk of sounding redundant, I emphasize that in work settings—where people pay careful attention to the actions of others and are particularly sensitive to disparate treatment—opportunities for perceptions of injustice are rampant.

To fully appreciate the prevalence and organizational costs of injustice, one must understand the relationships among the focal variables, to which I now turn my attention.

The General Affective Aggression Model: A Framework for Exploring Injustice, Stress, and Aggression

Primarily used to describe the antecedent conditions and intervening processes associated with reactive (that is, affective, emotional, hostile) forms of interpersonal aggression, the General Affective Aggression Model (GAAM; Anderson, 1997; Anderson, Anderson, & Deuser, 1996; Anderson, Deuser, & DeNeve, 1995) serves as an excellent framework for understanding the interplay among the focal variables. Furthermore, this model—which is very representative of a number of modern theories of aggression (Geen, 1991)—has its roots in stress research (Lazarus & Folkman, 1984).

Referring to Figure 3.1, it can be seen that two classes of variables serve as the input for this model: social-situational and individual difference variables. Although this chapter focuses on social and situational stimuli, it should be clear to most readers that people differ (often dramatically) in their perceptions of and responses to social, situational, and environmental stimuli. For example, some individuals seem predisposed to the experience of negative affect (Watson & Clark, 1984), anxiety, and anger (Spielberger, Krasner, & Solomon, 1988) and in ambiguous situations may be inclined toward hostile attributions about the motives of others (Dodge & Newman, 1981; Dodge, Price, Bachorowski, & Newman, 1990; Kramer, 1994). In addition, people vary in their sensitivity to inequity (Huseman, Hatfield, & Miles, 1987) and their work-related responses to perceived injustice (Coyle-Shapiro & Neuman, 2004; Witt, 1991). In sum, there are many individual difference variables that relate to the experience of, and response to, stress, injustice, and aggression.

Figure 3.1. The General Affective Aggression Model.

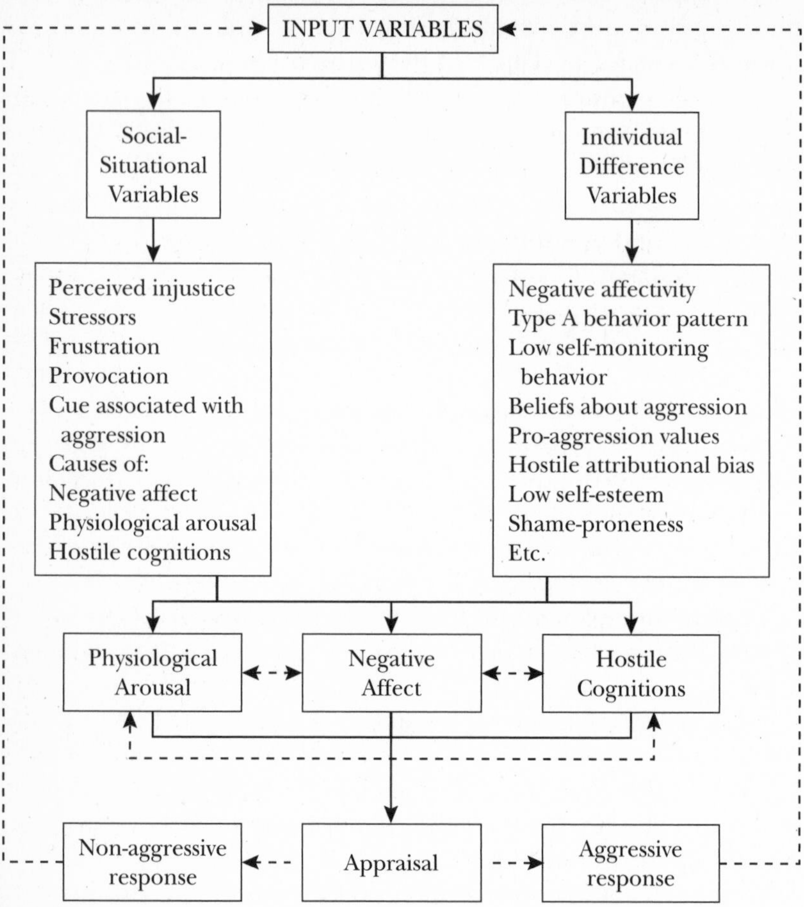

Independent of any existing trait or predisposition, stimuli may increase the likelihood of an aggressive response through their impact on three basic intervening variables (referred to collectively as *critical internal states*). According to this model, antecedents to aggression tend to (1) increase physiological arousal or excitement, (2) elicit negative affect (feelings of anger and other hostile emotions, along with outward signs of these emotions; for example, angry facial expressions), and (3) trigger hostile cognitions—induce individuals to bring hostile thoughts to mind, remember aggression-related experiences, and so on. Depending on an individual's appraisals (interpretations of the current situation and attendant thoughts, feelings, and sensations), the individual's coping ability and social skills, and the existence of possible restraining factors (for example, threat of retaliation, strict disciplinary and enforcement policies), aggression either occurs or does not occur. Of central importance to the present discussion, the GAAM also suggests that each of the three critical internal states can affect—and be affected by—the other. That is, hostile thoughts, when they occur, often may elicit negative emotions and unpleasant physiological reactions just as negative emotional reactions (such as anger) can trigger hostile thoughts and generate unpleasant physiological arousal. Finally, the process may begin with some ambiguous physiological sensation (for example, caffeine-induced jitters or physiological reactions to noise, heat, or crowding) that activates classically conditioned thoughts and emotions. Regardless of the precipitating factor, once this process begins, it may result in an escalating and intensifying cascade of hostile thoughts, negative emotions, and unpleasant physiological excitation. Depending on the intensity of the stimuli and the outcome of the subsequent appraisal process, aggression becomes a more likely—but not inevitable—result.

As suggested above, the critical internal states do not, by themselves, lead inexorably to aggression; rather, they simply set the stage for aggression. People must interpret the thoughts, feelings, and physiological sensations they are experiencing before reacting or formulating a response—identical to transactional models of stress (Cooper et al., 2001), wherein appraisal intervenes between stressors and the occurrence (or nonoccurrence) of strain. During this appraisal process, individuals ask themselves a series of questions, such as, Why am I feeling and thinking this way? Was I just treated unfairly, threatened, or actually harmed? Is there a real threat to my welfare or well-being? Was the act intentional? Are there mitigating factors? What can or should I do? What will happen if I do that? Some aspects of this process occur almost reflexively (during the initial interpretation or "primary appraisal" phase), whereas others require time and deliberation to play out (the "secondary appraisal" process). If individuals perceive the internal states as indications of threat or personal attack, they must then formulate some kind of response. This response, of course, may not involve aggression; rather, people may decide to handle the situation in a nonaggressive manner or choose to do nothing at all. This will depend, in part, on their social skills (for example, conflict management or communications skills), coping ability, or the threat of punishment, retaliation, or other adverse consequences.

Referring back to Figure 3.1, it can be seen that manifestly unfair treatment and all forms of work-related stressors (including aggression from others) may serve as input variables. Furthermore, stress, strain, and justice perceptions also play a role as intervening variables. For example, anything that elicits a stress reaction is, by definition, physiologically or psychologically arousing and, as such, may trigger one or more critical internal states. With regard to the elaboration of justice perceptions, especially in somewhat ambiguous or subtle circumstances, this is accomplished during the primary appraisal process, in which fairness interpretations are formulated. Finally, assuming that the output of this process leads to aggression against another individual, that aggression will serve as the input (stressor, perceived injustice, or act of provocation) stimulus for the targeted individual.

Empirical Connections Between Injustice, Stress, and Aggression

As demonstrated above, there is substantial conceptual support for the relationships between the focal variables, and these connections have been tested in numerous work and nonwork settings (refer to note 1 for references to some of this work). Rather than summarizing this research, I believe it more useful to focus on the Workplace Stress and Aggression Project within the United States Department of Veterans Affairs (VA), as this initiative provides a method for collecting, interpreting, and employing such empirical data to test theory and guide action in organizational settings. To that end, I present a description of the project and discuss how efforts of this kind may prove useful in (1) advancing our understanding of the causes and consequences of workplace injustice, stress, and aggression, (2) developing a better appreciation for the complex nature of the interactions between these variables, and, most important, (3) providing a mechanism for effectively managing these phenomena—and their potentially adverse consequences—in work settings.

The Genesis, Objectives, and Design of the Workplace Stress and Aggression Project

Initiated within the VA and formally begun in February 1999, the Workplace Stress and Aggression Project (herein after referred to as the VA project) is a grassroots initiative designed to better understand how stress and aggression lead to interpersonal conflict and the disruption of work-related activities and to develop workplace systems and practices to ease workplace tensions and improve employee and organizational performance. To meet these objectives, the project was implemented in three phases, only two of which have been completed to date. Consequently, the data that I report must be considered preliminary in nature. Before proceeding further, it is important to note that I am merely one member of a large project team and I gratefully acknowledge my academic and VA partners who have given so generously of their time and effort and provided me with permission to share their story in this chapter.[2]

Phase I

The initial phase of this project involved the production of an inventory of data available within the VA that could be employed for (1) use in longitudinal research, (2) testing theoretical predictions derived from the GAAM, and over time (c) exploring relationships between the focal variables and various individual- and organization-level outcomes. During this stage, one data source, in particular, attracted our attention. The "One-VA employee survey," as it is called, collected data from a nationwide sample of 125,913 individuals working in 310 VA facilities. This survey, originally developed by the Office of Personnel Management (OPM), comprises 129 items capturing many variables central to our project and this chapter (for example, distributive, procedural, and interactional justice as well as task-, role-, and environmental-stressors, and a broad array of traditional facet and global measures of job satisfaction and turnover intentions). In addition, an assortment of independent human resources-related data were obtained for each VA facility, and this included Office of Workers' Compensation Practices (OWCP) stress and violence claims, Equal Employment Opportunity (EEO) discrimination complaints, sick leave usage, disciplinary actions, and discharge data. Finally, key performance indicators (measures of important organizational outcomes, as defined by VA leadership) were obtained for use throughout all phases of the project. In the discussion that follows, I refer to these collectively as the phase I VA data.

Phase II

The second phase of the study involved the identification of facilities that would participate in the experimental (that is, intervention-based) portion of the project, the selection and training of action team members within each of the selected facilities (described below), and the administration of the Workplace Intervention Project (WIP) Survey. These efforts were guided by a core project team consisting of academic partners and VA personnel representing management, union leadership, and rank-and-file employees (please refer to note 2).

The core project team, working with VA leadership, selected eleven facilities to serve as pilot (experimental) sites and fifteen facilities to serve as comparison (control) sites. The pilot and comparison sites were matched in terms of size, demographic characteristics, and business and service lines. Within each of the eleven pilot sites, individuals were selected to form joint management-labor "action teams." These individuals were trained by the project team in the collaborative action inquiry process, which involved training in the collection, organization, and interpretation of data and its use as the basis for deep reflection, sense making, and action (Harmon, Behson, Neuman, & Keashly, 2001; Kowalski, Harmon, Yorks, Yorks, & Kowalski, 2003; Yorks, O'Neil, & Marsick, 1999; Yorks et al., 2002). These action teams worked closely with the core project team in every phase of the project. For example, they were instrumental in pilot testing the Workplace Aggression Research Questionnaire (WAR-Q, described below), the preparation of their respective facilities for the administration of the WIP survey, and the development, implementation, and evaluation of various interventions.

With respect to the WIP survey, the first part of this instrument contained selected items from the One-VA survey (ninety-one items that were found to be "key drivers" of valued organizational outcomes) that allow us to track performance over time; that is, future administrations of the One-VA survey. Part two of the WIP survey contained the Workplace Aggression Research Questionnaire (WAR-Q; Neuman & Keashly, 2002). Beyond its use as a measure of workplace aggression, the WAR-Q was employed to identify facility-specific aggression-related problems, assist in the development of situation-specific interventions designed to address those problems, and during phase III assess the effectiveness of any and all interventions. Furthermore, since the WIP survey contained both the core items from the One-VA survey, along with the new aggression questionnaire, it allowed us to correlate traditional employee justice, stress, and attitude measures with a wide range of aggressive behaviors and the causes and consequences of those behaviors.

The WAR-Q contains examples of sixty aggressive behaviors representing all dimensions of the Buss (1961) typology (the sample items shown in Table 3.1 were drawn from this survey). At this time, data have been collected from 4,801 respondents in phase II and 3,795 in phase III, for a total of 8,596 respondents. For each of the sixty items, respondents are asked to indicate the extent to which they have experienced each behavior over the preceding twelve-month period (never, once, a few times, several times, monthly, weekly, daily) and to identify the actor associated with each behavior (superior, coworker, subordinate, customer, other). Furthermore, respondents are asked to indicate what they did (if anything) in response to these behaviors, what they perceive to be the cause of these behaviors, and the extent to which they are bothered by such actions.

Throughout phase II, the project and action teams remained engaged via bi-weekly conference calls, e-mail exchanges, periodic site visits, and other face-to-face meetings. During this time, the action teams reviewed site-specific data (collected at the beginning of phase II) and compared their results to data from the larger system (that is, summary data from all eleven facilities combined). In this way, each action team was able to benchmark their data against that of the larger system and surface issues that seemed anomalous (in both positive and negative terms) by comparison. Furthermore, each action team attempted to "make sense" of their own data using their tacit knowledge of their own unique work systems and situations.

Using this process, the action teams surfaced what they believed to be "facility-specific issues" and generated assumptions as to the causes of the problems so identified. Following this, each action team attempted to test their assumptions by collecting additional data at their facility or by requesting that academics on the project team assist them in running further analyses to test their operating hypotheses. Using this collaborative action inquiry research process, the action teams proposed interventions specifically tailored to meet their needs.

Finally, and very important, the project team visited with each action team late in phase II and through structured interviews collected a good deal of qualitative data in which action team members described, in their own words, the context in which they worked. Using these verbal descriptions, the project team created "context maps" capturing the themes they heard in the interviews and graphically demonstrated the relationships among these variables. These themes represented both "negative" factors, in the form of stressors and frustrations (for example, budgetary constraints, organizational restructuring, changes in the health care or benefits systems, external political challenges, changing policies, and environmental factors), and "positive" factors (for example, working in a friendly, family-like atmosphere with dedicated and committed staff, engaging in rewarding work). Immediately after their construction, these "context maps" were shared with the interview participants to ensure that their "stories" had been accurately captured. These context maps provided important new data and also served to validate the quantitative data and provide important contextual information (to add meaning).

During phase II, the fifteen comparison sites completed the WIP survey and were provided with data analyses comparing their performance against the systemwide data for all fifteen comparison sites, similar to the process described above for the pilot facilities. The comparison sites did not, however, engage in an action team (that is, collaborative action inquiry) process and simply served as a control condition with which to judge the effectiveness of the interventions undertaken by the pilot sites.

Phase III

This phase began with the second administration of the WIP survey, which provided data for the evaluation of the interventions and, with respect to the One-VA portion of the WIP survey (that is, part I), served as the third data point in portions of our longitudinal study, exploring causal relationships between the focal variables and important organizational outcomes.

Now that you have some idea of the process employed in the Workplace Stress and Aggression Project, I present a few preliminary findings and some thoughts about the potential benefits of such an action research design. Unfortunately, as of this writing we only have preliminary data for phase III and so my comments will be necessarily brief. More detailed coverage is forthcoming in papers authored by members of the project team.

Injustice, Stress, Workplace Aggression, and Organizational Outcomes and Interventions

The relationship between injustice perceptions and workplace aggression has been well documented (Folger & Baron, 1996; Greenberg & Alge, 1998; Neuman, 2002; Torestad, 1990) and the underlying cause for this relationship is suggested in the GAAM, in which cognitive appraisal plays such an important role. One disturbing finding is the extent to which individuals perceive they are the victims of unfair treatment in organizational settings. For example, in phases II and III of the VA project, respondents identified "being treated in a rude and/or disrespectful manner" as the most frequently experienced form of workplace aggression—67 percent of those responding in phase II (2000) and 63 percent of those responding in phase III (2002). With respect to the relationship between injustice perceptions and self-reports of workplace aggression, the correlations between these two variables in phase II (2000) and phase III (2002) were $r(3844) = -.53$, $p = .000$ and $r(3087) = -.55$, $p = .000$, respectively. Furthermore, using a stepwise procedure, regressing the total aggression score from the WAR-Q on all of the original One-VA dimensions for phases II and III revealed that respect and fair treatment was the dimension most strongly associated with aggression $F(10, 5520) = 359$, $p = .000$, r-square = .30, followed by the experience of stress, which added an additional 4 percent to the variance explained (refer to Table 3.3).

In a preliminary attempt to demonstrate a relationship between "objective" measures of injustice and aggression, phase III data were collected for the mean number of EEO discrimination

Table 3.3. Total Aggression Score Regressed on All One-VA Dimensions.

Variable	Unstandardized Coefficients		Standardized Coefficients			
	B	SE	Beta	R-Square	t	Sig.
(Constant)	2.68	.048			56.251	.000
Respect	−.12	.010	−.21	.303	−11.585	.000
Stress	.08	.006	.16	.340	13.039	.000
Diversity	−.11	.009	−.17	.368	−11.842	.000
Cooperation	−.08	.011	−.13	.381	−7.926	.000
Supervisor	−.06	.009	−.11	.388	−6.635	.000
Resource	−.04	.011	−.07	.390	−4.370	.000
Planning	.03	.008	.05	.391	3.636	.000
Work family	−.03	.010	−.04	.392	−3.120	.002
Management	.04	.011	.06	.393	3.511	.000
Innovate	−.03	.010	−.05	.394	−2.835	.005

complaints filed by worker per facility along with aggregated aggression scores from the WAR-Q. In eighteen of the twenty-six facilities for which sufficient EEO data were available, there was a direct (positive) relationship between the number of EEO complaints and reports of workplace aggression, $r(18) = .44$, $p = .06$. Obviously, this is a very small sample but, as can be seen, the relationship did approach statistical significance and was in the predicted direction.

As noted earlier, stress—or more precisely, its ability to trigger strong affective responses—often creates a state of readiness or instigation to aggress, and this is true regardless the stressor (Anderson et al., 1995, 1996, 1998; Berkowitz, 1993, 1994; Zillmann, 1988). Such negative affect also has been found to be associated with reduced helping behavior (Cialdini & Kenrick, 1976; Weyant, 1978). Consequently, the connection between stress and aggression has played an important role in theoretical models of aggression (either explicitly or implicitly) since the original formulation of the frustration-aggression hypothesis (Dollard, Doob, Miller, Mowrer, & Sears, 1939). With regard to the relationship between stress and workplace aggression, individuals experiencing high levels of job stress have been found to engage in more emotional outbursts during a typical workday, are more likely to express their anger to others, and experience more work-related frustration (Boye & Jones, 1997). Similarly, Chen and Spector (1992) found a relationship between work-related stressors and interpersonal aggression, hostility, sabotage, and complaints. As one test of this relationship, during phase I of the VA project, archival data were obtained from sixty-eight VA facilities relating to OWCP claims for stress-related illness and injuries. At the same time, independent data were obtained for simple assaults from workplace violence reports within each of those sixty-eight facilities during that same reporting period. Consistent with predictions associating stress with aggression, the greater the number of OWCP stress claims filed in a particular facility, the greater the number of reports of violence within that facility, $r(68) = .39$, $p < .001$.

Organizational Outcomes

With respect to the connection between the focal variables and bottom-line organizational outcomes, some preliminary efforts have proven promising. For example, using the phase I VA data, the project team has been able to demonstrate a relationship between high-involvement work practices (HIWP) and service-related costs in the Veterans Health Administration (Harmon et al., 2003). With regard to HIWP, this includes, in part, factors related to distributive, procedural, and interactional justice (for example, employee perceptions of rewards and recognition, employee voice, interpersonal trust, and a sense of cooperation and teamwork), as well as factors that contribute to (or inhibit) work-related stress (for example, role ambiguity, empowerment, autonomy, opportunities for training and advancement). Employing structural equations modeling, HIWP was significantly related to job satisfaction and standardized cost-per-patient served in 146 VA hospitals. HIWP was associated with lower cost (had a negative total effect $\beta = -.13$). Results suggest that a one standard deviation difference in the adoption of HIWP (in this case, increasing the average response on the HIWP scale from 2.87 to 3.01 on a five-point scale) is associated with a .13 standard deviation decrease in cost—or a savings of $51.50 per patient served. For the average-sized VA health care facility serving 23,360 unique patients per year, such an improvement would represent an average annual cost savings of $1,203,040. Generalized to the national level, this would amount to an annual savings of over $175.6 million throughout the VHA health care network. Models such as these are currently being tested as relates to the impact of work climate on stress and aggression and the reciprocal and transactional linkages predicted by the GAAM and recently demonstrated by Tepper (2001).

Interventions

Space constraints do not permit a discussion of all the interventions proposed or undertaken by the pilot facilities, but I will mention that some of them involved developing systems and practices in which employees could meet regularly with leadership in their facility, the institution of formal procedures for improving communications among employees, attempts at work redesign, and the institution of programs to improve employee moral and work-related attitudes. Clearly, such initiatives are not new to organizational settings but are traditionally instituted in a top-down, one-size-fits-all manner. Most important as relates to the VA project, each of the interventions mentioned was suggested by site-specific data collected and examined by the action teams within a particular facility in concert with the project team. Consequently, there was general acceptance of, and little resistance to, the use of the interventions as they were developed by the individuals who would employ them (Coch & French, 1948; Labianca, Gray, & Brass, 2000; Lawrence, 1969). Unfortunately, at this time data are still being analyzed and the evaluation process is just beginning. However, we do have some early indication of improvement among the pilot facilities between time 1 (2000) and time 2 (2002). Comparison of the mean aggression scores (measured on five-point Likert scales, with five indicating the highest level of aggression) reveals that the pilot sites significantly lowered their aggression scores ($M^{2000} = 1.66$, $SD = .60$ and $M^{2002} = 1.60$, $SD = .58$, $F(1, 4875) = 14.19$, $p < .01$) whereas the comparison sites did not ($M^{2000} = 1.61$, $SD = .58$ and $M^{2002} = 1.56$, $SD = .59$, $F(1, 3122) = 4.28$, $p > .01$). Clearly, this represents a small numerical improvement and may reflect more statistical than practical significance; however, the action teams are reporting improvements in interpersonal interactions at their facilities, and this has led to their continued involvement with the project. After more than two years of active involvement, and in the face of increasing workloads at the VA, only one of the eleven pilot sites has withdrawn from the project and the level of engagement of the remaining ten facilities continues to be substantial. Furthermore, we are seeing early signs of fewer disciplinary actions at these sites and the action team members are using the action inquiry skills they acquired on this project to solve other work-related problems. Finally, the behaviors that we have attempted to model in our project (that is, inquiry, deep reflection, civility, and collaborative action) are being demonstrated by the teams in project meetings and on the job.

Concluding Comments

I believe that the VA Workplace Stress and Aggression Project represents a potentially important method for collecting meaningful data about complex issues over an extended period of time, using those data as the basis for data-driven workplace interventions, engaging and maintaining the commitment of "academics" and "practitioners," and implementing processes and practices that may improve the lives of those serving and being served by the organization. Central to such an endeavor is a willingness on the part of management to make sensitive information available to researchers within and beyond the organization and a readiness on the part of academic researchers to be responsive to the needs of their organizational partners. In the remaining sections, I discuss ways in which commitment and resources may be obtained and enthusiasm sustained, and I conclude with some final thoughts.

Obtaining and Sustaining Commitment and Resources

First and foremost, if an undertaking such as the VA project is to be successful, it will require a fundamental philosophical shift in thinking from a traditional "expert" or consulting model to one in which all members of the venture are truly engaged in collaboration; that is, a process of co-inquiry, participative problem solving, and joint action. Although this is not a novel idea in theory, it seems relatively rare in practice (Yorks et al., 2002). From the beginning, all members of the VA project have fully embraced this philosophy in both word and deed. For example, every aspect of the project has been developed in concert with the full participation of VA management and union leadership, rank-and-file employees, and internal and external (academic) researchers. We spent a considerable amount of time building relationships and developing and codifying memoranda of understanding and operational protocols. This "up-front" time strengthened the working relationships among all project participants and other VA partners—an important intervention in and of itself that, in turn, facilitated access to VA data for the academic researchers and provided our action team members, and other VA partners, with access to academic resources (for example, statistical analyses, literature reviews, evaluation of potential interventions, and process consultation). This process provided a means by which the needs and interests of the many participants could be met, thus seeming to elicit the motivation necessary for building and sustaining commitment.

Another important example of meeting the needs of important constituents involved the use of data to construct a "business case" that would demonstrate meaningful connections between the focal variables and important "bottom-line" outcomes (such as the one described previously linking high-involvement work practices to health care costs). This, too, served as an important mechanism for engaging management and obtaining financial and nonfinancial resources important to the continuation of the project. In short, this approach served to answer the question, What's in it for me or the organization?

Second, periodically we would reflect on critical incidents that had occurred over a given period (an exercise referred to as "harvesting the learning") so that we could learn from our successes and failures and identify patterns among seemingly discrete and disconnected incidents occurring over time. Not only did this provide valuable insight into our decision making, thereby helping improve and shape our emergent action research process, but it also revealed more data related to the focal variables—injustice, stress, and aggression. That is, through this qualitative process, we were able to identify aspects of injustice, stress, and aggression occurring within and between the various groups involved in the project (including the core project team) and, when necessary, intervene to ameliorate those tensions. Furthermore, this reflection (cognitive appraisal) process is central to the GAAM and serves as a potential intervention in moderating perceptions of injustice, stress, and aggression. In short, the project and its associated processes became an additional focus of the research and a new source of data important to understanding the dynamics among the focal variables.

Third, to facilitate our learning and provide a different and potentially more objective perspective, we periodically invited third parties to review and critique the process. This involved the use of a graduate student to conduct research on our processes and practices, as well as employing more formal venues, such as the Academy of Management and Society for Industrial and Organizational Psychology (SIOP) conferences, in which reviewers, discussants, and general audiences could react to our "stories" and statistical data and provide constructive comments (for example, Harmon et al., 2001; Yorks et al., 2002).

Fourth, although it is too early in the process to know for certain, the collaborative inquiry and action research process may have had an impact on injustice, stress, and aggression in a more direct way. As noted earlier, many of the variables that we measured, as well as many of the desirable behaviors we attempted to model, are related to high-involvement work practices. In part, the core features of these practices include involvement-empowerment and goal alignment (variables associated with increased perceptions of control and reduced stress), as well as trust and teamwork (interpersonal-interactional justice); these features, in turn, relate to lowered levels of interpersonal conflict and aggression.

As I've already said, it is too early to know with any degree of certainty whether or not stress, injustice, or workplace aggression has been reduced in the pilot facilities, but preliminary evidence is encouraging. Although we continue to "crunch the numbers," our action teams are reporting improvements at their facilities, and this improvement comes at a time of increased workloads and shrinking budgets. Although anecdotal and inconclusive in nature, this certainly is a hopeful sign.

Finally, several of the pilot facilities have collected data on their own to test various assumptions derived from our original analyses. These investigations, which were never considered a priori, are serving to further our knowledge about the focal variables and our understanding of the interpersonal dynamics and organizational contexts within which they are embedded. Since the teams now have a vested interest in the process and the outcomes, we are hopeful that these efforts will be self-sustaining, consistent with the longitudinal objectives of the project. In addition, as we disseminate this story and the underlying data throughout the VA, other sites have expressed an interest in pursuing such initiatives—thereby expanding our access and, we hope, our resources and research opportunities.

Final Thoughts

As noted in the introduction to this chapter, there are a multitude of labels being used to describe phenomena that are characterized collectively, in this volume, as dark side behaviors. This proliferation of terms and definitions may not serve to facilitate communications among researchers or help to advance theory. In addition to the difficulties posed by the lack of clarity about concepts, there has not been a standardized measure of workplace aggression and violence; consequently, researchers have used their own instruments to explore this phenomenon. Without making a pitch for the Workplace Aggression Research Questionnaire (Neuman & Keashly, 2002), it is important that we at least establish some core items and procedures for capturing the nature and prevalence of aggression and violence in work settings, provide a means of identifying the actors and targets in such incidents, capture individuals' perceptions about the causes of such behavior, measure the degree to which individuals are harmed by such encounters, and determine how individuals and organizations respond to such episodes. The WAR-Q is meant to meet those objectives, and, we hope that the WAR-Q or some other validated instrument will serve this purpose. However, questionnaires alone are not enough. As mentioned above, qualitative data serve a very important function in providing context for quantitative data and, more important, provide a means by which unsolicited, but nevertheless important, information may be obtained (that is, questions that you never thought to ask that lead to important discoveries). Also, it is important for organizations to do a better job of collecting data pertaining to stress, injustice, and aggression by creating more formal mechanisms for capturing these data.

In conclusion, regarding the prevention and management of stress, injustice, and aggression, the "remedies" will vary from situation to situation. I am convinced that whatever the solutions may be, they exist in the efforts of people working together to surface their own issues and solve their own problems. Furthermore, involving individuals in research—not as subjects but as full-fledged partners in the process—has a remarkable ability to unleash creative and constructive energy. As you will learn if you engage in such an endeavor, the process often turns out to be an important product. That is, in creating and implementing this type of partnership, centered around real problems and involving a co-inquiry process, people perceive increased control over their circumstances (lowered stress), become more sensitized to issues related to aggression, stress, and injustice, and as a result become more likely to treat each other with respect. If this weren't enough, researchers are given an opportunity to engage in meaningful research and explore important issues and their complex dynamics, culminating (ideally) with advances in theory and practice. To my way of thinking, that's not a bad day's work!

Notes

1. Space limitations prevent a thorough discussion of workplace aggression, organizational justice, and organizational stress. For comprehensive discussions related to human aggression in all its contexts, readers are directed to work by Baron and Richardson (1994), Berkowitz (1993), Geen (1991), and Tedeschi and Felson (1994). As relates to workplace aggression, refer to Baron and Neuman (1996), Neuman and Baron (1997, 1998), and O'Leary-Kelly, Griffin, and Glew (1996). The seminal work in social justice theory, and later organizational justice, includes the work of Adams (1965), Bies and Moag (1986), Blau (1964), Folger and Martin (1986), Greenberg (1987), Homans (1961), Lind and Tyler (1988), and Thibaut and Walker (1975). Other good overviews of the organizational justice literature can be found in Cropanzano and Greenberg (1997), Cropanzano and Randall (1993), and Folger and Cropanzano (1998). Finally, with

respect to the seminal research in the area of stress, refer to Lazarus and Folkman (1984), McGrath (1970), and Selye (1978). As relates to organizational stress, see Cooper, Dewe, and O'Driscoll (2001), Jex and Beehr (1991), Jex, Beehr, and Roberts (1992), Schuler (1980), Spector (1999), and Spector, Chen, and O'Connell (2000).

2. I am deeply indebted to the many people with whom I work on the VA Stress and Aggression Project. The academic partners on the core project team consist of Loraleigh Keashly, Joel Harmon, and Lyle Yorks. The VA partners include James Scaringi, Robert Petzel, Rita Kowalski, Dan Kowalski, Michelle Blakely, Oscar Williams, Anthony McRay, Odessa Johnson, Pat Russel, Ellen Kollar, Bridget Cannon, Robert Kline, Gene Mickelson, Barbara Cook, Lorena Ruley, Harley Carpenter, and Jennifer Long. Finally, I wish to thank the many action team members, facility directors, and union leaders, without whom none of this would have been possible.

References

Adams, A., & Crawford, N. (1992). *Bullying at work*. London: Virago.

Adams, J. S. (1965). Inequity in social exchange. In L. Berkowitz (Ed.), *Advances in experimental social psychology* (Vol. 2, pp. 267–299). New York: Academic Press.

American Management Association. (1994, April). Workplace violence: Policies, procedures, & incidents. *American Management Association 65th annual human resources conference & exposition onsite survey*. Washington, DC: American Management Association.

Anderson, C. A. (1997). Effects of violent movies and trait hostility on hostile feelings and aggressive thoughts. *Aggressive Behavior, 23*, 161–178.

Anderson, C. A., Anderson, K. B., & Deuser, W. E. (1996). Examining an affective aggression framework: Weapon and temperature effects on aggressive thoughts, affect, and attitudes. *Personality and Social Psychology Bulletin, 22*, 366–376.

Anderson, C. A., Deuser, W. E., & DeNeve, K. M. (1995). Hot temperatures, hostile affect, hostile cognition, and arousal: Tests of a general model of affective aggression. *Personality and Social Psychology Bulletin, 21*, 434–448.

Anderson, K. B., Anderson, C. A., Dill, K. E., & Deuser, W. E. (1998). The interactive relations between trait hostility, pain, and aggressive thoughts. *Aggressive Behavior, 24*, 161–171.

Andersson, L. M., & Pearson, C. M. (1999). Tit-for-tat? The spiraling effect of incivility in the workplace. *Academy of Management Review, 24*, 452–471.

Ashforth, B. (1994). Petty tyranny in organizations. *Human Relations,* 47, 755–777.

Atkinson, W. (2000, November/December). Managing stress. *Electrical World,* 214(6), 41–42.

Barling, J., Rogers, A. G., & Kelloway, E. K. (2001). Behind closed doors: In-home workers' experience of sexual harassment and workplace violence. *Journal of Occupational Health Psychology,* 6(3), 255–269.

Baron, R. A. (1977). *Human aggression.* New York: Plenum.

Baron, R. A., & Neuman, J. H. (1996). Workplace violence and workplace aggression: Evidence on their relative frequency and potential causes. *Aggressive Behavior,* 22, 161–173.

Baron, R. A., & Neuman, J. H. (1998). Workplace aggression—The iceberg beneath the tip of workplace violence: Evidence on its forms, frequency, and targets. *Public Administration Quarterly,* 21, 446–464.

Baron, R. A., Neuman, J. H., & Geddes, D. (1999). Social and personal determinants of workplace aggression: Evidence for the impact of perceived injustice and the Type A behavior pattern. *Aggressive Behavior,* 25, 281–296.

Baron, R. A., & Richardson, D. R. (1994). *Human aggression* (2nd ed.). New York: Plenum.

Beale, D., Cox, T., Clarke, D., Lawrence, C., & Leather, P. (1998). Temporal architecture of violent incidents. *Journal of Occupational Health Psychology,* 3, 65–82.

Berkowitz, L. (1993). *Aggression: Its causes, consequences, and control.* Philadelphia: Temple University Press.

Berkowitz, L. (1994). Is something missing? Some observations prompted by the cognitive-neoassociationist view of anger and aggressive behavior: Current perspectives. In L. R. Huesmann (Ed.), *Aggressive behavior: Current perspectives* (pp. 35–57). New York: Plenum.

Bies, R. J. (1987). The predicament of injustice: The management of moral outrage. In L. L. Cummings & B. M. Staw (Eds.), *Research in organizational behavior* (Vol. 9, pp. 289–319). Greenwich, CT: JAI Press.

Bies, R. J., & Moag, J. S. (1986). Interactional justice: Communication criteria of fairness. In R. J. Lewicki, B. H. Sheppard, & M. Bazerman (Eds.), *Research on negotiation in organizations* (Vol. 1, pp. 43–55). Greenwich, CT: JAI Press.

Björkqvist, K., Österman, K., & Hjelt-Back, M. (1994). Aggression among university employees. *Aggressive Behavior,* 20, 173–184.

Blau, P. (1964). *Exchange and power in social life.* New York: John Wiley.

Boye, M. W., & Jones, J. W. (1997). Organizational culture and employee counterproductivity. In R. Giacalone & J. Greenberg (Eds.), *Antisocial behavior in organizations* (pp. 172–184). Thousand Oaks, CA: Sage.

Brodsky, C. M. (1976). *The harassed worker.* Lexington, MA: Lexington Books.

Bureau of Justice Statistics. (1994, March). *Criminal victimization in the United States, 1992: A national crime victimization survey report* (NCJ-145125). Washington, D.C.: Bureau of Justice Statistics.

Bureau of Justice Statistics. (1996). *Workplace violence, 1992–1996* (NCJ-168634). Washington, D.C.: Bureau of Justice Statistics.

Buss, A. H. (1961). *The psychology of aggression.* New York: John Wiley.

Chen, P. Y., & Spector, P. E. (1992). Relationships of work stressors with aggression, withdrawal, theft and substance use: An exploratory study. *Journal of Occupational and Organizational Psychology, 65,* 177–184.

Cialdini, R. B., & Kenrick, D. T. (1976). Altruism as hedonism: A social development perspective on the relationship of negative mood state and helping. *Journal of Personality and Social Psychology, 34,* 907–914.

Coch, L., & French, J.R.P., Jr. (1948). Overcoming resistance to change. *Human Relations, 1,* 512–532.

Cooper, C. L., Dewe, P., & O'Driscoll, M. P. (2001). *Organizational stress: A review and critique of theory, research, and applications (foundations for organizational science).* London: Sage.

Coyle-Shapiro, J., & Neuman, J. H. (2004). The psychological contract and individual differences: The role of exchange and creditor ideologies. *Journal of Vocational Behavior, 64,* 150–164.

Cropanzano, R., & Greenberg, J. (1997). Progress in organizational justice: Tunneling through the maze. In C. L. Cooper & I. T. Robertson (Eds.), *International review of industrial and organizational psychology* (Vol. 12, pp. 317–372). New York: John Wiley.

Cropanzano, R., & Randall, M. L. (1993). Injustice and work behavior: A historical review. In R. Cropanzano (Ed.), *Justice in the workplace: Approaching fairness in human resource management* (pp. 3–20). Hillsdale, NJ: Erlbaum.

DeFrank, R. S., & Ivancevich, J. M. (1998). Stress on the job: An executive update. *Academy of Management Executive, 12,* 55–66.

Department of Veterans Affairs. (1997). [Workplace stress and aggression project]. Unpublished raw data.

Dodge, K. A., & Newman, J. P. (1981). Biased decision-making processes in aggressive boys. *Journal of Abnormal Psychology, 90,* 375–379.

Dodge, K. A., Price, J. M., Bachorowski, J. A., & Newman, J. P. (1990). Hostile attributional biases in severely aggressive adolescents. *Journal of Abnormal Psychology, 99,* 385–392.

Dollard, J., Doob, L., Miller, N., Mowrer, O. H., & Sears, R. R. (1939). *Frustration and aggression.* New Haven, CT: Yale University Press.

Duffy, M. K., Ganster, D. C., & Pagon, M. (2002). Social undermining in the workplace. *Academy of Management Journal, 45*(2), 331–351.

Einarsen, S., & Skogstad, A. (1996). Bullying at work: Epidemiological findings in public and private organizations. *European Journal of Work and Organizational Psychology,* 5(2), 185–201.

Folger, R. (1977). Distributive and procedural justice: Combined impact of "voice" and improvement on experienced equality. *Journal of Personality and Social Psychology,* 35, 108–119.

Folger, R., & Baron, R. A. (1996). Violence and hostility at work: A model of reactions to perceived injustice. In G. R. VandenBos & E. Q. Bulatao (Eds.), *Workplace violence* (pp. 51–85). Washington, D.C.: American Psychological Association.

Folger, R., & Cropanzano, R. (1998). *Organizational justice and human resource management.* Thousand Oaks, CA: Sage.

Folger, R., & Martin, C. (1986). Relative deprivation and referent cognitions: Distributive and procedural justice effects. *Journal of Experimental Social Psychology,* 22, 531–546.

Fox, S., & Spector, P. E. (Eds.). (forthcoming). *Counterproductive workplace behavior: Investigations of actors and targets.* Washington, DC: American Psychological Association.

Fox, S., Spector, P. E., & Miles, D. (2001). Counterproductive work behavior (CWB) in response to job stressors and organizational justice: Some mediator and moderator tests for autonomy and emotions. *Journal of Vocational Behavior,* 59, 1–19.

Geddes, D., & Baron, R. A. (1997). Workplace aggression as a consequence of negative performance feedback. *Management Communications Quarterly,* 10, 433–454.

Geen, R. G. (1991). *Human aggression.* Pacific Grove, CA: Brooks/Cole.

Glomb, T. M., Munson, L. J., Hulin, C. L., Bergman, M. E., & Drasgow, F. (1999). Structural equation models of sexual harassment: Longitudinal explorations and cross-sectional generalizations. *Journal of Applied Psychology,* 84, 14–28.

Greenberg, J. (1987). A taxonomy of organizational justice theories. *Academy of Management Review,* 12, 9–22.

Greenberg, J. (1993). The social side of fairness: Interpersonal and informational classes of organizational justice. In R. Cropanzano (Ed.), *Justice in the workplace: Approaching fairness in human resource management* (pp. 79–103). Hillsdale, NJ: Erlbaum.

Greenberg, J., & Alge, B. J. (1998). Aggressive reactions to workplace injustice. In R. W. Griffin, A. O'Leary-Kelly, & J. Collins (Eds.), *Dysfunctional behavior in organizations: Violent and deviant behavior* (Vol. 23, Part A, pp. 83–117). Stamford, CT: JAI Press.

Harmon, J., Scotti, D. J., Behson, S., Farias, G., Petzel, R., Neuman, J. H., & Keashly, L. (2003). Effects of high-involvement work practices on employee satisfaction and service costs in the Veterans Health Administration. *Journal of Healthcare Management.*

Harmon, J., Behson, S. J., Neuman, J. H., & Keashly, L. (2001, August 6). Quantitatively mapping the organizational causes and performance effects of workplace stress and aggression in the U.S. Department of Veterans Affairs. In J. Harmon (Chair), *Working along the practice-grounded research continuum: A collaborative academic-practitioner action-science experiment in the U.S. Department of Veterans Affairs.* Symposium conducted at the meeting of the Academy of Management, Washington, D.C.

Hoel, H., & Cooper, C. L. (2000, November). *Destructive conflict and bullying at work.* Manchester, England: University of Manchester Institute of Science and Technology.

Hogan, J., & Hogan, R. (1989). How to measure employee reliability. *Journal of Applied Psychology, 74,* 273–279.

Homans, G. C. (1961). *Social behavior: Its elementary forms.* New York: Harcourt, Brace & World.

Huseman, R. C., Hatfield, J. D., & Miles, E. W. (1987). A new perspective on equity theory: The equity sensitivity construct. *Academy of Management Review, 12,* 222–234.

Jex, S. M., & Beehr, T. A. (1991). Emerging theoretical and methodological issues in the study of work-related stress. *Research in Personnel and Human Resources Management, 9,* 311–365.

Jex, S. M., Beehr, T. A., & Roberts, C. K. (1992). The meaning of occupational stress items to survey respondents. *Journal of Applied Psychology, 77*(5), 623–628.

Keashly, L. (1998). Emotional abuse in the workplace: Conceptual and empirical issues. *Journal of Emotional Abuse, 1,* 85–117.

Keashly, L., & Jagatic, K. (2000, August 8). The nature, extent, and impact of emotional abuse in the workplace: Results of a statewide survey. In C. L. Cooper (Chair), *Exploring persistent patterns in workplace aggression.* Symposium conducted at the meeting of the Academy of Management, Toronto.

Keashly, L., & Neuman, J. H. (2002, August 12). Exploring persistent patterns of workplace aggression. In P. J. Moberg (Chair), *Workplace abuse, aggression, bullying, and incivility: Conceptual and empirical insights.* Symposium conducted at the meeting of the Academy of Management, Denver.

Kinney, J. A., & Johnson, D. L. (1993). *Breaking point: The workplace violence epidemic and what to do about it.* Chicago: National Safe Workplace Institute.

Kowalski, R., Harmon, J., Yorks, L., & Kowalski, D. (2003). Reducing workplace stress and aggression: An action research project at the U.S. Department of Veterans Affairs. *Human Resource Planning,* 26(2), 39–53.

Kramer, R. M. (1994). The sinister attribution error: Paranoid cognition and collective distrust in organizations. *Motivation and Emotion,* 18, 199–230.

Labianca, G., Gray, B., & Brass, D. J. (2000). A grounded model of organizational schema change during empowerment. *Organization Science,* 11(2), 235–257.

Lawrence, P. R. (1969). How to deal with resistance to change. *Harvard Business Review,* 47, 166–176.

Lazarus, R. S., & Folkman, S. (1984). *Stress, appraisal and coping.* New York: Springer Verlag.

Lengnick-Hall, M. L. (1995). Sexual harassment research: A methodological critique. *Personnel Psychology,* 48, 841–864.

Leventhal, G. S. (1976). The distribution of rewards and resources in groups and organizations. In L. Berkowitz & E. Walster (Eds.), *Advances in experimental social psychology* (pp. 91–131). New York: Academic Press.

Leventhal, G. S. (1980). What should be done with equity theory? In K. J. Gerneg, M. S. Greenberg, & R. H. Willis (Eds.), *Social exchanges: Advances in theory and research* (pp. 27–55). New York: Plenum.

Leymann, H. (1990). Mobbing and psychological terror at workplaces. *Violence and Victims,* 5, 119–126.

Lind, E. A., & Tyler, T. R. (1988). *The social psychology of procedural justice.* New York: Plenum.

Mantell, M. R. (1994). *Ticking bombs: Defusing violence in the workplace.* Burr Ridge, IL: Irwin Professional Publishing.

McGrath, J. E. (1970). *Social and psychological factors in stress.* New York: Holt, Rinehart, & Winston.

Mikula, G., Petri, B., & Tanzer, N. (1990). What people regard as unjust: Types and structures of everyday experiences of injustice. *European Journal of Social Psychology,* 20, 133–149.

Moberg, P. J., Ritter, B., & Fischbein, R. (2002, August 12). Predicting abusive managerial behavior: Antecedents of supervisory job performance. In P. J. Moberg (Chair), *Workplace abuse, aggression, bullying, and incivility: Conceptual and empirical insights.* Symposium conducted at the meeting of the Academy of Management, Denver.

Mullen, E. A. (1997). Workplace violence: Cause for concern or the construction of a new category of fear? *Journal of Industrial Relations,* 39, 21–32.

Neuman, J. H. (2002, April 13). The interactive effects of injustice, stress, and workplace aggression and their impact on employee satisfaction and performance. In R. W. Griffin, A. M. O'Leary-Kelly, & R. D. Pritchard (Chairs), *Frontiers series invited symposium: The dark side of organizational behavior.* Symposium conducted at the meeting of the Society for Industrial and Organizational Psychology, Toronto.

Neuman, J. H., & Baron, R. A. (1997). Aggression in the workplace. In R. Giacalone & J. Greenberg (Eds.), *Antisocial behavior in organizations* (pp. 37–67). Thousand Oaks, CA: Sage.

Neuman, J. H., & Baron, R. A. (1998). Workplace violence and workplace aggression: Evidence concerning specific forms, potential causes, and preferred targets. *Journal of Management, 24,* 391–419.

Neuman, J. H., & Keashly, L. (2002). *Development of a measure of workplace aggression and violence: The Workplace Aggression Research Questionnaire (WAR-Q).* Unpublished manuscript.

Northwestern National Life Insurance Company. (1993). *Fear and violence in the workplace: A survey documenting the experience of American workers.* Minneapolis: Author.

O'Leary-Kelly, A. M., Duffy, M. K., & Griffin, R. W. (2000). Construct confusion in the study of antisocial work behavior. In G. R. Ferris (Ed.), *Research in personnel and human resources management* (Vol. 18, pp. 275–303). Stamford, CT: JAI Press.

O'Leary-Kelly, A. M., Griffin, R. W., & Glew, D. J. (1996). Organization-motivated aggression: A research framework. *Academy of Management Review, 21,* 225–253.

O'Leary-Kelly, A. M., Paetzold, R. L., & Griffin, R. W. (2000). Sexual harassment as aggressive behavior: An actor-based perspective. *Academy of Management Review, 25,* 372–388.

Perkins, A. G. (1994). Medical costs: Saving money by reducing stress. *Harvard Business Review, 72,* 12.

Richman, J. A., Rospenda, K. M., Nawyn, S. J., Flaherty, J. A., Fendrich, M., Drum, M. L., & Johnson, T. P. (1999). Sexual harassment and generalized workplace abuse among university employees: Prevalence and mental health correlates. *American Journal of Public Health, 89*(3), 358–363.

Robinson, S. L., & Greenberg, J. (1998). Employees behaving badly: Dimensions, determinants and dilemmas in the study of workplace deviance. In C. L. Cooper & D. M. Rousseau (Eds.), *Trends in organizational behavior* (Vol. 5, pp. 1–30). Chicester, UK: John Wiley.

Robinson, S. L., & Kraatz, M. S. (1998). Constructing the reality of normative behavior: The use of neutralization strategies by organizational deviants. In R. W. Griffin, A. M. O'Leary-Kelly, & J. M. Collins (Eds.), *Dysfunctional behavior in organizations: Violent and deviant behavior* (Vol. 23, Part A, pp. 203–239). Stanford, CT: JAI Press.

Schuler, R. S. (1980). Definition and conceptualization of stress in organizations. *Organizational Behavior and Human Performance*, 25, 184–215.

Selye, H. (1978). *The stress of life* (rev. 2nd ed.). New York: McGraw-Hill.

Skarlicki, D. P., & Folger, R. (1997). Retaliation in the workplace: The roles of distributive, procedural, and interactional justice. *Journal of Applied Psychology*, 82, 434–443.

Society for Human Resource Management. (1996, April). *1996 Workplace Violence Survey*. Alexandria, VA: Society for Human Resource Management.

Spector, P. E. (1975). Relationship of organizational frustration with reported behavioral reactions of employees. *Journal of Applied Psychology*, 60, 635–637.

Spector, P. E. (1996). *Industrial and organizational psychology: Research and practice*. New York: John Wiley.

Spector, P. E. (1999). Objective versus subjective approaches to the study of job stress. *Journal of Organizational Behavior*, 20(5), 737.

Spector, P. E. (2001, May/June). Counterproductive work behavior: The secret side of organizational life. *Psychological Science Agenda*, 14(3), 8–9.

Spector, P. E., Chen, P. Y., & O'Connell, B. J. (2000). A longitudinal study of relations between job stressors and job strains while controlling for prior negative affectivity and strains. *Journal of Applied Psychology*, 85, 211–218.

Spielberger, C. D., Krasner, S. S., & Solomon, E. P. (1988). The experience, expression, and control of anger. In M. P. Janisse (Ed.), *Health psychology: Individual differences and stress*. New York: Springer Verlag.

Tedeschi, J. T., & Felson, R. B. (1994). *Violence, aggression, and coercive actions*. Washington, D. C.: American Psychological Association.

Tepper, B. J. (2000). Consequences of abusive supervision. *Academy of Management Journal*, 43, 178–190.

Tepper, B. J. (2001). Health consequences of organizational injustice: Tests of main and interactive effects. *Organizational Behavior and Human Decision Processes*, 86(2), 197–215.

Thibaut, J., & Walker, L. (1975). *Procedural justice: A psychological analysis*. Hillsdale, NJ: Erlbaum.

Torestad, B. (1990). What is anger provoking: A psychophysical study of perceived causes of anger. *Aggressive Behavior*, 16, 9–26.

Watson, D., & Clark, L. A. (1984). Negative affectivity: The disposition to experience aversive emotional states. *Psychological Bulletin,* 96, 465–490.

Weyant, J. M. (1978). Effects of mood states, costs, and benefits of helping. *Journal of Personality and Social Psychology,* 36, 1169–1176.

Witt, L. A. (1991). Exchange ideology as a moderator of job attitudes: Organizational citizenship behaviors relationship. *Journal of Applied Social Psychology,* 21, 1490–1501.

Wojcik, J. (2001). Cutting costs of stress. *Business Insurance,* 35(15), 1, 22.

Yorks, L., O'Neil, J., & Marsick, V. J. (1999). Action learning: Theoretical bases and varieties of practice. In L. Yorks, J. O'Neil, & V. J. Marsick (Eds.), *Action learning: Successful strategies for individual, team, and organizational development* (pp. 1–17). San Francisco: Berrett-Koehler.

Yorks, L., Twomey, D. F., Keashly, L., Neuman, J. H., Kowalski, D. R., Kowalski, R., Scaringi, J., Harmon, J., & Petzel, R. A. (2002, August 12). How do we know what we know? In J. Harmon (Chair), *How do we know what we think we know? Epistemic challenges of building academic-practice networks.* Symposium conducted at the meeting of the Academy of Management, Denver.

Zapf, D., Einarsen, S., Hoel, H., & Vartia, M. (2003). Empirical findings on bullying in the workplace. In S. Einarsen, H. Hoel, D. Zapf, & C. L. Cooper (Eds.), *Bullying and emotional abuse in the workplace: International perspectives in research and practice* (pp. 104–126). London: Taylor & Francis.

Zillmann, D. (1979). *Hostility and aggression.* Hillsdale, NJ: Erlbaum.

Zillmann, D. (1988). Cognition-excitation interdependencies in aggressive behavior. *Aggressive Behavior,* 14, 51–64.

CHAPTER 4

When the Dark Side of Families Enters the Workplace
The Case of Intimate Partner Violence
Carol Anne Reeves

New York—A former F.B.I. agent wielding two handguns shot and killed two colleagues yesterday at the Midtown health insurance company where they worked. . . . The police said he acted out of anger toward one of his victims after their romantic relationship cooled (Baker, 2002).

Addison, Texas—A man fatally shot and stabbed a woman inside a suburban Dallas office building Thursday. . . . Records show the suspect and the victim shared a residence in 1999 (Emily, 2002).

Goshen, Indiana—The suicidal factory worker who gunned down a co-worker and wounded six others was involved in a "love triangle" at work. . . . Co-workers said the gunman was having a problem with a male employee over a female co-worker, but neither employee was among those killed or wounded (Coyne, 2001).

Intimate partner violence (IPV) has been referred to as an epidemic in the United States (Jacobson & Gottman, 1998). The most recent nationally representative survey of IPV, conducted by the Centers for Disease Control and Prevention (CDC) and the National Institute of Justice (NIJ) (authored by Tjaden & Thoennes, 2000), indicated that over 25 percent of surveyed women and nearly 8 percent of surveyed men report having been physically assaulted, raped, or stalked by an intimate partner in their lifetime. Moreover, 1.5 million women and one million men over age eighteen report being physically assaulted, raped or stalked *annually* by an intimate partner.

Clearly, intimate partner violence is an important societal issue; but is it an organizational issue? Although the focal topics in other chapters of this book are well accepted as organizational issues, the study of intimate partner violence and the workplace is in its infancy. For example, a review of publications in the ABI (Proquest Direct) database from 1986 to the present (using search terms related to intimate partner violence and the workplace) identified only two articles that reported original research in peer-reviewed journals, and only one article appeared in a management-related journal (Barling & Rosenbaum, 1986, *Journal of Applied Psychology*). Perhaps organization scholars have been influenced by the notions held by many managers that IPV is a private family matter and not one within the purview of organizations.

To examine executives' beliefs regarding IPV, Liz Claiborne commissioned two studies by RoperASW, one in 1994 and a second in 2002, which surveyed one hundred senior executives in Fortune 1000 companies about domestic violence. They found that two-thirds of these executives believed domestic violence was a major societal problem and that their bottom line would be improved if it were addressed. Further, 91 percent of executives believed that IPV affected victims in both their private lives and their work lives. The percentage of executives who thought domestic violence was both a major societal problem and a problem for their organizations increased from 1994 to 2002, but one perception did not change—the percentage of executives who thought organizations had a major role to play in addressing it remained steady, at 12 percent (RoperASW, 2003).

This chapter has four primary purposes. First, it will serve as an introduction of IPV to organizational scholars and managers who may be unfamiliar with it. Without understanding the definition, nature, antecedents, and consequences of IPV, it is difficult for managers and scholars to understand how it can affect and be affected by organizations. Second, the chapter will make the case that intimate partner violence is an organizational issue that should be of concern to managers and researchers. Although the data available on this relationship are limited, they are compelling. Third, the chapter will integrate research on IPV with research from the organization sciences, with an emphasis on research in work-to-family and family-to-work conflict and workplace aggression. Although IPV is clearly relevant to many areas in the organization sciences, it has received very limited attention by scholars. Finally, the chapter will offer conclusions and pose questions for future research on IPV and the workplace.

Intimate Partner Violence

Studies on the prevalence and cost of intimate partner violence[1] have been conducted from the mid-1980s to the present, but the studies have revealed widely differing numbers of victims, numbers of incidents per victim, and levels of impact. The reported prevalence of IPV per 1,000 women ranges from 5.4 incidents (Bachman, 1994) to 161 incidents (Straus & Gelles, 1985, as cited in Berkowitz, 1993), and the reported costs range from $1.7 billion (Straus, 1986) to $67 billion (Miller, Cohen & Wiersema, 1995). The disparities among the statistics have been attributed to differences in definitions, sample design, survey administration, interviewing techniques, screening questions, counting rules, age populations, and sampling errors (Tjaden & Thoennes, 2000).

In an effort to minimize these discrepancies, the Centers for Disease Control and Prevention and the National Center for Injury Prevention and Control (Saltzman, Fanslow, McMahon, & Shelley, 2002) developed uniform definitions and recommended data elements for studies of IPV. They recommended that IPV include four types of violence: physical, sexual, the threat of physical or sexual violence, and psychological-emotional abuse if there has been prior physical or sexual violence, or prior threat of physical or sexual violence. Based on the uniform definitions and the work of Ganley (1995), the definition of intimate partner violence used in this chapter is *the physical or sexual violence, threat of physical or sexual violence, and psychological-emotional abuse when there has been prior violence or threats of physical or sexual violence that adults or adolescents use against their intimate partners.*

This definition of violence is consistent with the definition of workplace violence used by the Workplace Violence Research Institute, which includes physical and verbal assaults, threats, coercion, intimidation, and harassment (Duffy, O'Leary-Kelly, & Ganster, 2003).

The Nature of Intimate Partner Violence

Because many readers of this volume are unlikely to be familiar with IPV, a fairly lengthy examination of its nature, antecedents, and consequences is offered. Just as basic research on aggression can help us understand aggression in the workplace (Baron, this volume), basic research on IPV can help us understand how organizations affect and are affected by it.

Although both males and females experience violence at the hands of their intimate partners, IPV is overwhelmingly a crime committed by men against women. The NIJ-CDC study (Tjaden & Thoennes, 2000) found that 64 percent of the lifetime violence experienced by women, as opposed to 16.2 percent of the lifetime violence experienced by men, was intimate partner violence. Although Straus and Gelles (1990) reported that the frequency of violent acts is about the same in men and women, the impact of battering and its function are very different.

Women are seven to fourteen times more likely than men to experience severe IPV, such as being beaten up, choked, or threatened with a gun (Tjaden & Thoennes, 2000). And one-third of female homicides occur at the hands of their intimate partner (Rennison & Welchans, 2000). Jacobson and Gottman (1998), in their study of extremely violent couples, found *no* female batterers in their sample. Men were the only ones who used violence as a method of control, and women were the only ones who were afraid.

Although the physical and sexual violence experienced by targets of IPV may be the most obvious types of injury, psychologists have found that the most devastating outcome of IPV is psychological control. Jacobson and Gottman (1998), based on their findings from a tightly controlled study of violent couples, argued that the purpose of battering is "to control, intimidate, and subjugate another human being . . . [battering] is virtually always associated with fear and even terror on the part of the battered woman"

(p. 25). The men in their study did not batter simply to inflict physical damage; they battered because the violence allowed them to control their partner. After repeatedly battering their wives, men were able to reduce their physical violence; they could now control their partner simply through the *threat* of violence, and reduce the likelihood that they would be arrested for physical violence. Jacobson and Gottman found that the *power and control* exerted by the batterer over the victim resulted in negative consequences far greater than those that resulted from physical injury alone. [(The use of physical abuse to gain psychological control over the victim is similar to the instrumental aggression identified by Berkowitz (1993) and Baron (this volume).]

Intimate partner violence is a complex social phenomenon, one whose antecedents and consequences are difficult to identify and quantify. Certain attributes, such as alcohol and drug use, low income, and violence experienced as a child are strongly correlated with IPV (Hotaling & Sugarman, 1986; Jacobson & Gottman, 1998; Leonard & Senchak, 1996), but causality is hard to establish. For example, many drug and alcohol abusers never become batterers and, although there is a high correlation between IPV victims and substance abuse, there is a question regarding whether the substance abuse is an antecedent or a consequence of the violence. The studies discussed below identify some of the most widely accepted antecedents and consequences of intimate partner violence.

Antecedents of IPV

Social scientists have broadened their research from an examination of the "defective" personalities of batterers to examinations of the interacting influences of a number of factors. For example, Jacobson and Gottman (1998) contended that battering cannot be completely understood without taking into account the historical, political, and socioeconomic conditions in a society. Jewkes (2002) argued that, unlike diseases that have a biological basis, IPV is entirely a product of its social context and an understanding of its causes can be developed only if it is studied within many social contexts.

Although domestic violence cuts across all racial, educational, occupational, religious, age, and income groups, it is more prevalent in certain populations. Though there were no statistically significant differences between white and nonwhite victims of IPV, the NIJ-CDC study (Tjaden & Thoennes, 2000) revealed that there were differences among racial subgroups. For example, American Indian and Alaska Native women and men reported higher rates of violent victimization and rape than other racial groups, and Hispanic women were less likely than non-Hispanic women to report being raped.

Likewise, IPV is not distributed equally among income groups. Poverty and its associated stress have been identified as key contributors to the frequency and severity of IPV in countries as diverse as the United States, India, and Nicaragua (Jewkes, 2002). It is not just financial stress that contributes to increased levels of violence for lower income women. Women with lower incomes are more likely to experience abuse because they have fewer alternatives to leave the relationship (Berkowitz, 1993; Farmer & Tiefenthaler, 1997; Straus & Gelles, 1990; Tauchen, Witte, & Long, 1991). In a carefully controlled study, Farmer and Tiefenthaler (2002) found that abused women experience lower wages over the long-term. Thus, IPV has a circular economic effect on women: women who earn lower incomes are more likely to experience abuse and abused women earn lower wages, which makes them more dependent on their partner; this dependence, in turn, increases their chance of abuse. This is consistent with findings in the aggression literature (Kalmuss & Straus, 1990) that the most frequent and severe domestic violence is inflicted upon women who are economically dependent upon their partners.

Berkowitz (1993) modeled the multiplicity of factors found in domestic violence studies and grouped the factors into seven major categories. Each of these categories—family background, societal norms, personal disposition, family relationships, social status, personal stress, and situational factors—contains a number of subfactors, which can be seen in Figure 4.1. Two of these factors, social status and personal stress, are directly related to the workplace. Berkowitz argued that jobs can be a significant source of stress due to factors such as troubles with coworkers or supervisors, performance pressures, routine work, and physical exhaustion. Unemployment and other income difficulties may also lead to violence due to financial difficulties and loss of self-esteem.

Figure 4.1. Factors That Can Promote Domestic Violence.

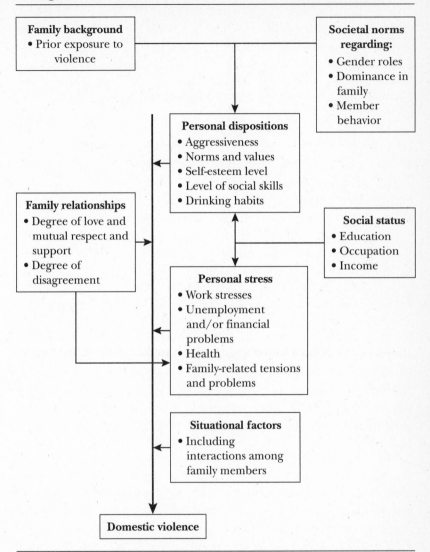

Source: Berkowitz, L. *Aggression: Its Causes, Consequences, and Control.* Philadelphia: Temple University Press, 1993, p. 244.

Consequences of IPV

Studies have found significant relationships between IPV and chronic pain, depression, substance abuse, posttraumatic stress, and other physical and mental disorders. In a meta-analysis of over fifty studies of mental health problems among battered women, Golding (1999) found that battered women were much more likely to suffer mental health problems than the general population. The weighted mean prevalence rates she found for various mental health problems were as follows:

- Depression—47.6 percent versus 10.2 – 21.3 percent in the general population
- Suicidality—17.9 percent versus 0.8 to 15.9 percent (ideation) and 0.1 to 4.3 percent (attempts) in the general population
- Posttraumatic stress disorder (PTSD)—63.8 percent versus 1.3 to 12.3 percent in the general population
- Alcohol abuse or dependence—18.5 percent versus 4.6 to 8.2 percent in the general population
- Drug abuse or dependence—8.9 percent versus 5.62 percent in the general population

Plichta and Falik (2001) also found that women who reported any type of violence were significantly more likely than women who did not experience violence to have been diagnosed with depression or anxiety or to have symptoms of depression. And intimate partner sexual violence was particularly devastating; women who experienced it reported significantly poorer physical and mental health than those who had experienced no violence or women who had experienced other forms of violence. In spite of this, their physicians did not ask or screen for violence and most women did not discuss their abuse with their physicians, even though they used health care services more frequently than nonabused women.

Overall, the annual health care costs for victims of IPV are estimated to be twice those of nonvictims, and mental health costs are up to eight times higher (Golding, 1999; Wisner, Gilmer, Saltzman & Zink, 1999). Wisner et al. (1999) found that health care expenditures for victims of IPV were $1,775 higher than that of the general population. Victims had more hospitalizations, general clinic use, mental health services use, and out-of-plan referrals. Clearly,

IPV has a significant impact on the physical and mental health of victims (Campbell, 2002).

But the costs of IPV go far beyond the costs associated with injury and death; they affect all realms of the lives of victims and their families (Hartmann, Laurence, Spalter-Roth, & Zuckerman, 1997). Costs include those associated with child well-being, housing, criminal justice, and social services. For example, costs to the criminal justice system include those associated with police protection and investigation, protective orders, prosecution, defense lawyers, court costs, incarceration, and mandatory batterer treatment programs. And the relationship between IPV and welfare costs is strong. A U.S. General Accounting Office (1998) survey of the literature on domestic violence and welfare indicated that between 55 and 65 percent of the women on welfare reported having been abused by an intimate partner. This level of victimization is much higher than the 25 percent victimization for women reported in the NIJ-CDC study. Although support provided by Temporary Assistance for Needy Families (TANF) is short-term (recipients must find work within two years and face a five-year lifetime maximum for benefits), states are permitted to grant targets of IPV a temporary exception to the work requirement while they are receiving services or gaining self-sufficiency (Raphael & Haennicke, 1999).

A long-term societal cost of IPV is borne by children who witness abuse or experience it. Costs for the well-being of children in violent homes include foster care, family services, and the "cycle of violence" that results from millions of children observing IPV every year and subsequently inflicting it on others as adults. In an examination of fifty-three studies of abusive and nonabusive couples, Hotaling & Sugarman (1986) found that 88 percent of male abusers had witnessed violence as a child and 69 percent had experienced violence. Baron (this volume) makes a similar point in his discussion of "aggressive models" who are antecedents of general aggression.

Work and home are the most important domains of adult life, but many employers continue to act as though they should or do have little relationship to each other (Morris & Curry, 1997). Rosabeth Moss Kanter (1977) coined the phrase "the myth of separate worlds" to describe managers' reluctance to address the relationship between their employees' work and home lives. Because IPV and the workplace are inseparable for most victims and batterers, the next section will integrate IPV research with studies in organization sciences.

Intimate Partner Violence as an Organizational Issue

Research from a wide variety of disciplines can be used to explore the impact of IPV on the workplace. Initial work in economics has found a strong positive relationship between IPV and absenteeism and, perhaps counterintuitively, between labor force participation and IPV (Farmer & Tiefenthaler, 2002). Role theory (Barnett & Hyde, 2001; Barnett, Marshall & Pleck, 1992) and identity theory (Burke, 1991; Burke & Reitzes, 1981, 1991) indicate that IPV should cause a great amount of distress for employees who are targets of the violence, leading to suboptimal performance in organizations.

Other "dark side" behaviors that are addressed in this book, such as alcohol and drug use, sexual harassment, incivility, workplace violence, and aggression, are all behaviors that managers and researchers consider to be legitimate organizational issues, but intimate partner violence is not traditionally regarded in the same light (Friedman, Tucker, Neville, & Imperial, 1996). Although anecdotes like those presented at the beginning of this chapter clearly indicate that intimate partner violence (IPV) is a work-related concern in at least some instances, is it a significant enough issue to warrant attention by managers and organization researchers?

Studies of intimate partner violence make a strong case that the answer to this question is unequivocally affirmative. Ruckelshaus (1996) found that 74 percent of employed battered women were harassed at work, 54 percent missed at least three days of work per month, 56 percent were late for work at least five times per month, and 75 percent used company time to call doctors, lawyers, shelters, counselors, and others because they could not do so at home. Four studies of battered women who were in shelters (Friedman & Couper, 1987; Riger et al., 1998; Shepard & Pence, 1988; and Stanley, 1992; summarized in Farmer & Tiefenthaler, 2002) reported rates of harassment ranging from 35 to 56 percent, absenteeism rates ranging from 54 to 85 percent, rates of late arrival or early departure of 62 percent, and rates of reprimand due to performance issues related to domestic violence of between 44 to 60 percent.

Intimate partner violence can affect the workplace in at least four ways: (1) when a perpetrator harasses, stalks, is physically violent toward or otherwise abuses an intimate partner in the workplace, (2) when an IPV victim's workplace performance is diminished due to abusive behavior occurring outside the workplace, (3) when a perpetrator is less productive because of past, present, or planning abusive behavior, and (4) when coworkers of perpetrators or victims are fearful for their own safety or are less productive because of the abuse being experienced or perpetrated by their coworker. In addition, IPV should be considered a workplace issue if it affects the organization. For example, if IPV causes turnover, increased health care expenditures, or litigation, the organization will experience costs above those that would have been incurred if IPV were not present. Thus, the effects of IPV go far beyond the perpetrator and the victim to all of an organization's stakeholders.

Therefore, the relevant question regarding IPV and the workplace is not whether it is a workplace behavior that should be of concern to managers and scholars. The more relevant questions are (1) what are the effects and costs of IPV for victims, perpetrators, coworkers, and organizations, and (2) how does the workplace affect IPV? Existing literature provides guidance for addressing these questions.

Intimate Partner Violence and the Workplace

Table 4.1 presents a typology that clarifies the relationship between IPV and the workplace by illustrating who is affected by IPV and the types of effects they might experience. The direct effects of IPV that are illustrated in Table 4.1 are *immediate* for victims, perpetrators, coworkers, and organizations and have a *direct* impact on the perpetrator and others. If a batterer makes harassing phone calls to a victim, the victim is directly and immediately affected. If coworkers must complete assignments that were the responsibility of absent batterers or victims, they are directly and immediately affected. If an organization failed to protect the safety of its employee(s), it becomes directly liable and will incur litigation costs should the employee(s) pursue an action against the organization.

Table 4.1. Examples of Direct and Indirect Effects of IVP.

| | Who Is Affected | | | |
	Victim	Perpetrator	Coworkers	Organization
W O R K P L A C E E E Direct (immediate)	Absences or time lost at work (for medical and legal appointments, health problems, to cover signs of IVP) Tardiness Distraction at work from IPV that occurs in the workplace (harassing phone calls, visits) Other productivity losses Injury Death Increased health care cost	Loss of job due to incarceration Absences for legal appointments Time taken from work to harass, visit, or stalk victim Other productivity losses	Injury from spill-over violence Death from spill-over violence Increased workload when either victim or perpetrator misses work Increased workload when either victim or perpetrator is less productive Increased health care premiums Less productive teams, workgroups	Bad publicity Health care costs Loss of worker productivity Litigation costs
F F E C T S Indirect (long-term)	Loss of job Loss of advancement Loss of raises Inability to fulfill potential Mental health problems (stress, depression, chronic anxiety, PTSD) Substance abuse	Substance abuse Stress	Fear that perpetrator may enter workplace Anxiety Depression Stress Substance abuse	Increased turnover Diminished organization climate

Indirect effects are more long-term and are generally the result of nonspecific, ongoing abuse. For example, although an employee might ultimately be fired as a result of frequent absences, immediate productivity losses are a more direct and immediate consequence of the abuse. Other factors, such as stress, tend to affect the victim, batterer, and coworkers (if they have been affected by the violence) over extended periods of time. These types of effects are cumulative and often subtle, such as when they lead to workplace incivility (Neuman, Pearson, this volume).[2] The indirect effects of IPV illustrated in Table 4.1 are consistent with findings related to other types of violent workplace behavior. Violent incidents can lead to feelings of guilt, depression, vulnerability, suicidal ideation, and substance abuse and range from mild anxiety to posttraumatic stress disorder (Duffy, O'Leary-Kelly, & Ganster, 2003). The work-to-family[3] and family-to-work conflict literature provides insight into how and why some of these effects occur.

Work-Family and Family-Work Conflict

Work-family conflict research (for example, Frone, 2000) explores the impact of competing role demands from work and family on employees and their employers (Greenhaus & Beutell, 1985). Over the past twenty-five years, this research has found that work and family are clearly interconnected, with each having a major influence on the other (Boles, Howard, & Donofrio, 2001; Frone, 2000; Frone, Russell & Cooper, 1992, 1997; Netemeyer, Boles, & McMurrian, 1996). Work-to-family conflict (WFC) and family-to-work conflict (FWC) studies have found that the consequences of conflict between these two primary domains are job dissatisfaction, life dissatisfaction, absenteeism, turnover, tardiness, decreased morale, stress, depression, and other mental disorders (Boles, Howard, & Donofrio, 2001; Frone, 2000; Netemeyer, Boles, & McMurrian, 1996; Rice, Frone, & McFarlin, 1992). With the exception of job dissatisfaction, which has not been tested, the same consequences have been associated with IPV.

Barling & Rosenbaum (1986) found empirical support for the relationship between work stress and domestic violence (an example of WFC). They examined whether work experiences and stressors were associated with wife abuse by comparing rates of abuse among maritally satisfied-dissatisfied and abusive-nonabusive husbands. They found that stressful work events and their negative impact were significantly related to wife abuse. Although the study was limited by a number of factors, it did provide initial evidence that negative stress from the workplace is correlated with spousal abuse by men. Jasinski, Asdigian, and Kantor (1997) reported similar results in a study of work-related stress and heavy drinking, wife assaults, and violence among Anglo and Hispanic husbands. Their research revealed that both ethnic groups experienced increased rates of husband-to-wife violence if husbands were laid off or fired in the previous year.

Intimate partner violence that enters the workplace either directly or indirectly is an obvious example of extreme family-work conflict. A target is particularly vulnerable at work because (1) it is the one place a perpetrator knows the target can be located and (2) by harassing, stalking, and threatening the target at work, perpetrators are frequently successful in their quest to get their targets fired, thus increasing the target's dependence and decreasing the probability that the relationship will be terminated (Farmer & Thiefenthaler, 1997; Gemignani, 2000; Reeves et al., 2001).

WFC studies that have examined both work-to-family and family-to-work conflict have found that WFC is more common than FWC (Frone, Russell, & Cooper, 1992). In addition to being more frequent, some scholars have found a stronger relationship between WFC and job and life satisfaction than between FWC and satisfaction. Kossek and Ozeki (1998) completed a meta-analysis of studies that examined the relationship among WFC, company policies, and job and life satisfaction. They found that, regardless of the type of measure used (WFC-FWC, WFC, or FWC), a consistent, negative relationship existed among all forms of WFC and FWC and job-life satisfaction, but that this relationship was slightly less strong with FWC. Boles, Howard, and Donofrio (2001) also found that, except for satisfaction with coworkers, WFC was a more powerful predictor of all aspects of job satisfaction (for example, pay, work itself, coworkers, supervision, and general job satisfaction) than was FWC.

It does not appear, however, that work-family conflict is a more powerful predictor than family-work conflict of more serious outcomes, such as mental health problems. Frone (2000; Frone, Russell & Cooper, 1997) found that both WFC and FWC were positively related to mood, anxiety, and substance dependence disorders, but that FWC had a consistent and stronger effect. The findings from this study are reported in Table 4.2. Although these results appear to contradict other studies of WFC, they are consistent with the results one would predict with severe FWC, such as intimate partner violence.

Because both men and women rank their roles as partners and parents higher than their roles as employees (Barnett & Hyde, 2001), their inability to manage these roles the way they wish may explain why individuals who perceive higher levels of FWC experience more negative health outcomes (Frone, 2000). Frone, Russell, and Cooper (1992) thought it possible that FWC had a greater impact than WFC on mental health outcomes because individuals might blame organizations for excessive work demands that conflict with family. In contrast, individuals who let their family life conflict with their work life might blame themselves for not being able to handle the conflict. This, in turn, might lead to "diminished perceptions of overall self-efficacy or mastery," which then lead to depression or decreased life satisfaction (1992, p. 75).

Workplace Violence and Aggression

A second stream of research that can inform our understanding of IPV and the workplace comes from studies of workplace violence and aggression. Despite its obvious relevance, there has been almost no research on family violence that enters the workplace.

Table 4.2. Frone's Findings
Regarding the Impact of WFC and FWC.

Disorder	Increase in likelihood of disorder by those reporting:	
	Work-Family Conflict	Family-Work Conflict
Mood disorder	3.13	29.66
Anxiety disorder	2.46	9.49
Substance dependence disorder	1.99	11.36

For example, Neuman (this volume) identifies sixteen areas or types of research on workplace aggression, but none of these areas includes intimate partner violence as a focus. As Neuman states, we are getting a sense of the nature and scope of workplace aggression, but a comprehensive view of workplace aggression and violence that omits IPV is incomplete.

General theories of aggression include relationships that are similar to those proposed for IPV (Martinko & Zellars, 1998). For instance, the General Affective Aggression Model (GAAM) (Anderson, 1997) suggests that aggression is triggered by a wide range of input variables. The General Workplace Affective Aggression Model (GWAAM), developed by Baron (Figure 2.2 in his chapter), extends and adapts the GAAM to include workplace-related factors and categories. A similar model of correlates of IPV was developed by Berkowitz (1993) and can be seen in Figure 4.1 in this chapter. Just as the factors in the GAAM and the GWAAM influence the nature of aggression, each of the factors in Berkowitz's model has an impact on the frequency and extent of domestic violence. Although the factors in these two models may be similar, the ongoing relationship between the batterer and the victim in intimate partner violence results in precipitating factors and outcomes that are likely to be very different, at least in some circumstances.

General aggression, workplace aggression, and IPV are related, but they are fundamentally different in important ways. For instance, the goal of aggression is to harm or injure another person (Baron, 1977). As mentioned above, the primary purpose of IPV is power and control over an intimate partner; violence is simply the means to attain this control. The types of violent behavior chosen by batterers—recurring emotional and psychological abuse, harassing phone calls, stalking—extend beyond the physical violence that characterizes both general violence and violence against an intimate partner. Many individuals who exhibit aggressive behavior toward strangers have never been violent toward their family members and vice versa. According to Hamberger, Lohr, Bonge, and Tolin (1996), two-thirds of batterers never exhibit violence toward those outside their families. And although the societal attitude toward IPV is changing in the United States and elsewhere, it is still frequently viewed as a problem that is best handled in the family, not as a crime.

Although relationships developed in the workplace are closer than those formed with acquaintances, they still do not reach the level of intimacy of partners. When violence is perpetrated by an individual with whom someone has placed their trust, the psychological impact can be particularly strong. Further, there is usually no escaping the violence. Employees who experience aggression in the workplace can usually escape from it when they leave at the end of the day. Victims of IPV are frequently tracked down in the workplace because batterers can easily find them there; they are never free from the violence. Thus, although some of the factors associated with IPV and aggression in general are similar, the consequences of violence at the hands of an intimate are likely to be far greater and longer lasting.

Other Organization Research

Although the literature regarding work-family and family-work conflict and aggression is most directly applicable to IPV and the workplace, other organization research is also informative. *Role theory* (Barnett & Hyde, 2001; Barnett, Marshall, & Pleck, 1992) and *identity theory* (Burke, 1991; Burke & Reitzes, 1981, 1991) indicate that IPV should cause a great amount of distress for employees who are targets of the violence, leading to suboptimal performance in organizations. Both work and family roles represent core components of adult identity, so impediments to identity formation and maintenance in these realms are likely to be stressful (Frone, 2000). Intimate partner violence may directly undermine a victim's ability to perform effectively at work, leading to a poor job-related self-image (Frone, Russell, & Cooper, 1997). Managers' jobs usually require them to display self-assurance, confidence, and decision-making ability. If managers are being abused by their intimate partners, it is likely that their diminished feelings of power and control in their home lives will have a negative impact on their ability to effectively manage others.

Although the management literature has long considered issues such as job security and safety from accidents, there is little research in the organizational sciences that considers employees' sense of *safety and security* from physical attack, including attacks that occur at the hands of their intimate partners. If organizations do not protect their employees from violent acts by batterers, their employees' actual and perceived safety and security will suffer. Although the findings regarding the effectiveness of restraining orders on IPV are mixed, corporate orders of protection may provide greater safety for the victim because they provide external validation that IPV is a criminal matter (Family Violence Prevention Fund, 1998).

Not only does IPV generate significant costs, but American businesses can be held *legally accountable* for IPV-related issues (Reeves et al., 2001). Employers generally have a legal duty to protect employees from injury or death if there is a safety risk in the workplace of which the employer knew or should have known but failed to take corrective action (Robertson, 1998). *Negligent security* can arise when the employer was aware that threats were being made at work (via the telephone, within the workplace itself, or through stalking outside the building), but made no effort to provide reasonable security to protect the target (and nearby others) from harm. *Negligent failure to warn* arises when an employer has specific knowledge of a threat made against the target employee but fails to warn him or her. An employer is particularly at risk if both the target and the perpetrator are employed (Perin, 1999). Thus, legal liability costs from IPV must also be considered by employers.

Conclusion

Although reliable data regarding the prevalence and cost of intimate partner violence are unavailable, all indications are that it is a major societal problem in the United States and throughout the world. More than 25 percent of women have experienced violence at the hands of their intimate partner. Nationally representative studies of IPV and the workplace have yet to be conducted, but limited studies indicate that IPV results in significant costs for employees, coworkers, batterers, and organizations. Women are far more likely than men to be battered and to experience severe forms of IPV.

Like organization aggression and stress, IPV is a complex phenomenon and has numerous antecedents and consequences. The historical, political, and socioeconomic conditions of a society must be examined in order to understand IPV. Specific antecedents of

IPV include having low income, being financially dependent, and belonging to certain racial groups. Consequences of IPV include chronic pain, depression, substance abuse, posttraumatic stress, and other physical and mental disorders. The available data on the impact of IPV on the workplace indicate that the relationship is strong and negative and affects victims, batterers, coworkers, and organizations. The workplace-related effects are both direct and long-term, and include absenteeism, turnover, lost wages, increased health care costs, stress, and decreased productivity.

Research from the literatures on work-family conflict and violence and aggression increases our understanding of IPV and the workplace. Although IPV is related to many of the variables in these literatures, its unique nature requires that it be examined independently of them. Similarly, IPV is related to role theory, identity theory, safety and security, and legal accountability. Although findings in these areas help us better understand IPV, they cannot substitute for a rigorous study of it.

So where do we go from here? We need to develop nationally representative, longitudinal studies regarding the impact of IPV on the workplace. Of particular interest are exactly how IPV affects the workplace and what are its costs. Research needs to be done regarding which workplace policies and procedures are effective in reducing IPV and mitigating its effects. Why are these policies effective? Do organizations such as CIGNA and Blue Shield of California, which are perceived as having policies that are supportive of IPV victims, experience greater commitment from victims and other employees? Are there other positive workplace outcomes, such as trust, from these policies?

Research also needs to be done on perpetrators. Too often, research on IPV focuses on the costs associated with the victim. Yet it is the perpetrator who bears ultimate responsibility for these costs. What is the work-related performance of perpetrators? Do they bring stress from the battering into the workplace? Do they have higher health care costs? Several studies (Hamberger, Lohr, Bonge, & Tolin, 1996; Jacobson & Gottman, 1998) have concluded that there are different types of batterers. Perhaps different batterer types experience different work-related outcomes from abusing others.

The blame and consequences for IPV should be placed squarely where they belong—on the perpetrators. Far too frequently it is the target who must suffer the consequences of the abuse. Indeed, more negative consequences for targets will result in more power and control for perpetrators, thus giving them incentives to increase negative outcomes, such as job loss, for the targets. A domestic violence advocate recently stated, "Just once, I would like the first question from the audience to be 'why does he batter?' rather than 'why doesn't she leave?'" (East, 2002). It is only after batterers accept responsibility for their actions that they stop the abuse, and this acceptance is rare (Jacobson & Gottman, 1998).

Finally, it is critical to address the unintended consequences that might result if employers find that IPV has a negative impact on the workplace. The first inclination of many employers might be to screen out applicants who have been or are targets of abuse. This would be the worst possible result for victims because the lack of economic resources is one of the primary reasons that victims stay with perpetrators. Fortunately, legislation has been passed in five states that prohibits the firing of IPV victims. And the Victims Economic Security and Safety Act (VESSA) that was introduced in Congress in 2001 prohibits job termination and offers workplace protections, such as unpaid time off to attend court, to targets of domestic and sexual violence. Although the costs to organizations from IPV are large, they are dwarfed by the cost of conditions such as substance abuse and heart disease, which are more frequently associated with men than women. By understanding the impact of IPV on the organization, employers can work to mitigate its effects. The ultimate objective should be to increase organizational performance by providing assistance to targets, not firing them to rid the organization of the problem.

Notes

1. Intimate partner violence is a relatively new label for violence that occurs between current or former partners. In the past, this phenomenon has been labeled domestic violence, domestic abuse, spouse abuse, battering, and wife abuse, among others. Intimate partner violence is the preferred descriptor because it encompasses violence between nonmarried couples, same-sex couples, female-male violence, and non-cohabiting couples. For this paper, intimate partner violence,

domestic violence, and battering refer to the same phenomenon, but the term used by the original authors will be used when discussing their work.

2. Of course, some severe acts, such as murder in the workplace, can have a long-lasting impact even though they are direct and immediate. However, it is unlikely that a violent event of this magnitude would not have been preceded by years of abuse.

3. Intimate partner violence is not limited to cohabiting couples, so "family" in this section is broadened to couples who share an intimate relationship with one another.

References

Anderson, C. A. (1997). Effects of violent movies and trait hostility on hostile feelings and aggressive thoughts. *Aggressive Behavior, 23,* 161–178.

Bachman, R. (1994, August). *Violence against women: A national crime victimization survey report.* Washington, D.C.: Bureau of Justice Statistics. NCJ-154348.

Baker, A. Shooting at midtown company leaves three co-workers dead. *New York Times,* Sept. 17, 2002, p. B1.

Barnett, R. C., Marshall, N. L., & Pleck, J. H. (1992). Men's multiple roles and their relationship to men's psychological distress. *Journal of Marriage and the Family, 54,* 358–367.

Barling, J., & Rosenbaum, A. (1986). Work stressors and wife abuse. *Journal of Applied Psychology, 71*(2), 346–348.

Barnett, R. C., & Hyde, J. S. (2001). Women, men, work, and family. *American Psychologist, 56*(10), 781–796.

Baron, R. A. (1977). *Human aggression.* New York: Plenum.

Berkowitz, L. (1993). *Aggression: Its causes, consequences, and control.* Philadelphia: Temple University Press.

Boles, J. S., Howard, W. G., & Donofrio, H. H. (2001). An investigation into the inter-relationships of work-family conflict, family-work conflict and work satisfaction. *Journal of Managerial Issues, 13,* 376–390.

Burke, R. J. (1991). An identity theory approach to commitment. *Social Psychology Quarterly, 54,* 280–286.

Burke, P. J., & Reitzes, D. C. (1981). The link between identity and role performance. *Social Psychology Quarterly, 44*(2), 83–92.

Burke, P. J., & Reitzes, D. C. (1991). An identity theory approach to commitment. *Social Psychology Quarterly, 54*(3), 239–251.

Campbell, J. C. (2002). Health consequences of intimate partner violence. *The Lancet, 359,* 1331–1336.

Coyne, T. Man opens fire at Indiana factory, killing one before taking his own life. *Athens Banner-Herald,* Dec. 7, 2001.

Duffy, M. K., O'Leary-Kelly, A. M., & Ganster, D. C. (2003). Antisocial work behavior and individual and organizational health. In D. A. Hofmann & L. E. Tetrick (Eds.), *Health and Safety in Organizations.* San Francisco: Jossey-Bass.

East, C. E. (2002, August). *Building networks to address intimate partner violence.* Paper presented at the Academy of Management, Denver.

Emily, J. Woman killed, suspect shot by police in Texas office shooting. *The Dallas Morning News,* Jan. 3, 2002.

Family Violence Prevention Fund. (1998). *The workplace responds to domestic violence: A resource guide.* San Francisco: FVPF.

Farmer, A., & Tiefenthaler, J. (1997). An economic analysis of domestic violence. *Review of Social Economy,* 55, 337–358.

Farmer, A., & Tiefenthaler, J. (2002). The employment effects of domestic violence. *Journal of Labor Research.*

Friedman, L. N., and Couper, S. (1987). *The cost of domestic violence: A preliminary investigation of the financial cost of domestic violence.* New York: Victim Services Agency.

Friedman, L. N., Tucker, S. B., Neville, P. R., & Imperial, M. (1996). The impact of domestic violence on the workplace. In G. R. VandenBos & E. Q. Bulatao (Eds.), *Violence on the job: Identifying risks and developing solutions.* Washington, DC: American Psychological Association.

Frone, M. R. (2000). Work-family conflict and employee psychiatric disorders: The national comorbidity survey. *Journal of Applied Psychology,* 85, 888–895.

Frone, M. R., Russell, M., & Cooper, M. L. (1992). Antecedents and outcomes of work-family conflict: Testing a model of the work-family interface. *Journal of Applied Psychology,* 77, 65–78.

Frone, M. R., Russell, M., & Cooper, M. L. (1997). Relation of work-family conflict to health outcomes: A four-year longitudinal study of employed parents. *Journal of Occupational and Organizational Psychology,* 70, 325–335.

Ganley, A. (1995). Understanding domestic violence. In C. Warshaw & A. Ganley, *Improving the healthcare response to domestic violence: A resource manual for heath care providers.* San Francisco: Family Violence Prevention Fund.

Gemignani, J. (2000). Missed opportunities in the fight against domestic violence. *Business and Health,* 18(9), 29–35.

George, J. M. (1990). Personality, affect, and behavior in groups. *Journal of Applied Psychology,* 75(2), 107–116.

Golding, J. (1999). Intimate partner violence as a risk factor for mental disorders: A meta-analysis. *Journal of Family Violence,* 14(2), 99–132.

Greenhaus, J. H., & Beutell, N. J. (1985). Sources of conflict between work and family roles. *Academy of Management Review,* 10, 76–88.

Hamberger, L. K., Lohr, J. M., Bonge, D., & Tolin, D. F. (1996). A large sample empirical typology of male spouse abusers and its relationship to dimensions of abuse. *Violence and Victims,* 11, 277–292.

Hartmann, H. I., Laurence, L., Spalter-Roth, R., & Zuckerman, D. M. (1997). *Measuring the costs of domestic violence against women and the cost-effectiveness of interventions: An initial assessment and proposals for further research.* Washington, DC: Institute for Women's Policy Research.

Hotaling, G. T., & Sugarman, D. B. (1986). An analysis of risk markers in husband to wife violence: The current state of knowledge. *Violence and Victims,* 1(2), 101–124.

Jacobson, N., & Gottman, J. (1998). *When men batter women: New insights into ending abusive relationships.* New York: Simon & Schuster.

Jasinski, J. L., Asdigian, N. L., & Kantor, G. K. (1997). Ethnic adaptations to occupational strain: Work-related stress, drinking, and wife assault among Anglo and Hispanic husbands. *Journal of Interpersonal Violence,* 12, 814–831.

Jewkes, R. Intimate partner violence: Causes and prevention. *The Lancet,* April 20, 2002, pp. 1423–1429.

Kalmuss, D. S., & Straus, M. A. (1990). Physical violence in American families: Risk factors and adaptations to violence in 8,145 families. In M. A. Straus & R. J. Gelles (Eds.), *Physical violence in American families.* New Brunswick, NJ: Transaction Publishers.

Kanter, R. M. (1977). *Work and family in the United States: A critical review and agenda for research and policy.* New York: Russell Sage Foundation.

Kossek, E. E., & Ozeki, C. (1998). Work-family conflict, policies, and the job-life satisfaction relationship: A review and directions for organizational behavior-human resources research. *Journal of Applied Psychology,* 83, 139–149.

Leonard, K. E., & Senchak, M. (1996). Prospective prediction of husband marital aggression within newlywed couples. *Journal of Abnormal Psychology,* 105, 369–380.

Martinko, M. J., & Zellars, K. L. (1998). Toward a theory of workplace violence and aggression: A cognitive appraisal perspective. In R. Griffin & A. O'Leary-Kelly (Eds.), *Dysfunctional behavior in organizations: Violent and deviant behavior.* Stamford, CT: JAI Press.

Miller, T. R., Cohen, M. A., & Wiersema, B. (1995, May). *Crime in the United States: Victim costs and consequences.* Washington, DC: National Institute of Justice.

Morris, B., & Curry, S. R. (1997). Is your family wrecking your career? (and vice versa) The dirty little secret is this: For all its politically correct talk, your company doesn't much like your kids. *Fortune*, 135(5), 70–81.

Netemeyer, R. G., Boles, J. S., & McMurrian, R. (1996). Development and validation of work-family conflict and family-work conflict scales. *Journal of Applied Psychology*, 81(4), 400–410.

Perin, S. (1999). Employers may have to pay when domestic violence goes to work. *The Review of Litigation*, 18, 365–401.

Plichta, S. B., & Falik, M. (2001). Prevalence of violence and its implications for women's health. *Women's Health Issues*, 11(3), 244–258.

Raphael, J., & Haennicke, S. (1999). *Keeping battered women safe through the welfare to work journey: How are we doing?* Chicago: Taylor Institute.

Reeves, C., O'Leary-Kelly, A., Farmer, A., Paetzold, R., & Tiefenthaler, J. (2001). *American government and business: Their individual and joint roles in addressing intimate partner violence.* Working Paper, University of Arkansas, Fayetteville.

Rennison, C. M., & Welchans, S. (2000, May). *Intimate partner violence.* Washington, DC: U.S. Department of Justice, Bureau of Justice Statistics.

Rice, R. W., Frone, M. R., & McFarlin, D. B. (1992). Work-nonwork conflict and the perceived quality of life. *Journal of Organizational Behavior*, 13, 155–168.

Riger, S., Ahrens, C., Blickenstaff, A., and Camacho, J. (1998). *Obstacles to employment of women with abusive partners.* Chicago: University of Illinois at Chicago.

Robertson, J. (1998). Addressing domestic violence in the workplace: An employer's responsibility. *Law and Inequality*, 16(2), 633–660.

RoperASW. (2003). Corporate leaders on domestic violence: Awareness of the problem, how it's affecting their business, and what they're doing to address it. New York: RoperASW. Roper Number: C205–007498.

Ruckelshaus, C. K. (1996). Unemployment compensation for victims of domestic violence: An important link to economic and employment security. *Clearinghouse Review*, Special Issue: pp. 209–221.

Saltzman, L. E., Fanslow, J. L., McMahon, P. M., & Shelley, G. A. (1999, 2002 [with revisions]). *Intimate partner violence surveillance: Uniform definitions and recommended data elements, Version 1.0.* Atlanta: National Center for Injury Prevention and Control, Centers for Disease Control and Prevention.

Shepard, M., & Pence, E. (1988). The effect of battering on the employment status of women. *Affilia*, 3(2) 55–61.

Stanley, C. (1992). *Domestic violence: An occupational impact study.* Tulsa, OK: Domestic Violence Intervention Services.

Straus, M. (1986). The cost of intrafamily assault and homicide to society. *Academic Medicine,* 102(6), 556–561.

Straus, M., & Gelles, R. (1990). *Physical violence in American families.* New Brunswick, NJ: Transaction Publishers.

Tauchen, H. V., Witte, A. D., & Long, S. K. (1991). Domestic violence: A nonrandom affair. *International Economic Review,* 32, 491–511.

Tjaden, P., & Thoennes, N. (2000, July). *Extent, nature, and consequences of intimate partner violence: Findings from the national violence against women survey.* Washington, DC: National Institute of Justice and Centers for Disease Control and Prevention.

U.S. General Accounting Office. (1998, November). *Domestic violence: Prevalence and implications for employment among welfare recipients.* Washington, DC: GAO/HEHS-99-12.

Warshaw, C., & Ganley, A. (1995). *Improving the health care response to domestic violence: A resource manual for health care providers.* San Francisco: Family Violence Prevention Fund.

Wisner, C. L., Gilmer, T. P., Saltzman, L. E., & Zink, T. M. (1999). Intimate partner violence against women: Do victims cost health plans more? *The Journal of Family Practice,* 48(6), 439–443.

PART 2

Discrimination and the Dark Side

CHAPTER 5

Subtle (and Not So Subtle) Discrimination in Organizations

Robert L. Dipboye, Stefanie K. Halverson

Not so long ago unfair discrimination in the workplace was open, tolerated, and even encouraged. Blatant discrimination against women and minorities, the disabled, and older workers only began to diminish to a substantial degree in the United States after the civil rights legislation of the 1960s. After three decades of enforcement of these laws, the workplace has become more open and tolerant. Nevertheless, a variety of groups continue to suffer from unfair treatment in the workplace despite laws, court decisions, and social pressures against discrimination. In this chapter we focus on discrimination against four groups: racial and ethnic minorities, women, older persons, and the disabled. A fifth group, gays and lesbians, is not covered here because it is the focus of another chapter in this volume. Differential treatment is not necessarily unfair but becomes unfair when it is based on "attributes irrelevant to judgment of a person's competence or worth" (Piper, 1993, p. 293) and is "selectively unjustified" (Dovidio & Gaertner, 1986, p. 3). Consistent with these views, we define unfair employment discrimination as occurring when persons in a "social category" (Jones, 1986), persons with a particular "group identity" (Cox, 1993, p. 64), or persons with certain "ascribed characteristics" (Messner, 1989, p. 71) are put at a disadvantage in the workplace relative to other groups with comparable potential or proven success (Cascio, 1998). Unfair discrimination becomes illegal when it occurs on the basis of attributes covered under the civil rights laws (for example, race and religion).

We make three primary points in this chapter. First, despite the clear progress that has been made in civil rights over the last half century, unfair discrimination in the workplace is still a problem. Second, although discrimination continues in its more blatant forms, much of today's discrimination takes a more subtle form and has slipped out of the light into the dark side of the organization. This leads to our third assertion that discrimination in the workplace is shaped not only by factors within the individuals who perpetuate the discrimination but also by factors at the group, organizational, and societal and economic levels. Moreover, these factors often conflict, and the subtlety and instability with which discrimination occurs in the workplace reflects this conflict. Those who are the perpetrators typically see themselves as unbiased, have rational justifications for their acts, and may be unaware of their own behavior and attitudes. In the maelstrom of conflicting and inconsistent pressures that can exist in an organization, active attempts to suppress biases can, with slight changes in the context, give way to unrestrained discrimination against the target.

Unfair Discrimination Is Still a Problem

It is obvious that there has been progress since the passage of civil rights legislation in the 1960s in providing greater opportunities for minority, older, female, and disabled employees. But does discrimination continue to be a significant problem? There are at least three sources of evidence showing that unfair discrimination is a continuing problem that deserves our attention.

Surveys Showing Perceived Discrimination

Opinion polls with national representative samples provide one source of evidence. Although the findings vary with the question asked, these polls tend to show that a substantial proportion of respondents perceive women, minorities, disabled, and older employees as subject to discrimination in the workplace. In a nationwide poll conducted in 2000 by NBC News, 37 percent of the total sample said that they had been discriminated against in the workplace on the basis of age, sex, disability, race, religion, or ethnicity (retrieved from Polling the Nation Survey Database, October 20, 2003; http://poll.orspub.com/poll/lpext.dll?f=templates&fn=main-h.htm). In another national poll conducted in 2002, fully 67 percent of the sample of forty-five- to seventy-six-year-old persons agreed that there is age discrimination in the workplace (American Association of Retired Persons, 2002). An NBC News–*Wall Street Journal* telephone survey in 2000 found that 44 percent of women said that they had been personally discriminated against in the workplace because of their sex and almost a third reported that they had been sexually harassed (Hunt, 2000). In another NBC News–*Wall Street Journal* poll conducted in 1995, 47 percent of those surveyed said that the disabled face unfair discrimination, 31 percent said they were treated fairly, and 11 percent said that they were given unfair preference (retrieved from Polling the Nation Survey Database, October 20, 2003; http://poll.orspub.com/poll/lpext.dll?f=templates&fn=main-h.htm). The disabled also perceive discrimination. Hallock, Hendricks, and Broadbent (1998) found that 53 percent of disabled people in their sample reported at least some discrimination and 14 percent reported discrimination as often or very often.

It is not surprising that members of groups that are targets of discrimination are more likely to see discrimination as a problem. In a random, nationwide survey of 2,203 adults in 2002, 50 percent of African Americans but only 18 percent of all adults reported that black individuals were "often" the target of workplace discrimination (Taylor, 2002). In the same survey, 27 percent of women compared to 19 percent of all adults reported that women were frequent victims of discrimination. Somewhat similar differences were reported by the Center for Workforce Development at Rutgers University (Joyner, 2002). In this survey, 28 percent of the black respondents said that they personally had suffered discrimination in the workplace and 55 percent said that they knew of a coworker who suffered discrimination. Of the Hispanics in the sample, 22 percent said that they had been the targets of discrimination and 18 percent said that they knew of a coworker who had suffered discrimination. By comparison, only 13 percent of the white persons surveyed said that they had suffered discrimination and only 6 percent said that they had observed discrimination. Feelings on the part of a group that they are the target of discrimination should be a cause of concern, even if more objective data does not support this claim. Not only are they an indicator of actual discrimination but such perceptions are also related to a variety of negative outcomes, including stress, dissatisfaction, and tension (Sanchez & Brock, 1996).

Inequalities in Labor Market Outcomes

Census and department of labor statistics provide a second source of data. Workers who are older, female, or disabled or who belong to a racial or ethnic minority are at a disadvantage in compensation, employment, and job status, compared to white, nondisabled males. The unemployment rate in 2002 for whites was 4.2 percent compared to 7.7 percent for blacks and 6.1 percent for Hispanics (U.S. Department of Labor, 2003b, tables 7 and 11). Whites who find employment are more likely to be in the management occupations than blacks and Hispanics but less likely to be handlers, equipment cleaners, helpers and laborers than blacks and Hispanics. The 2001 weekly earnings for whites was $612 compared to $487 for blacks (80 percent of whites) and $414 for Hispanics (67 percent of whites).

Of those with a work disability who were in the twenty-five to sixty-four age range in 2001, 28.7 percent were in the workforce and 8.7 percent were unemployed, whereas 78.2 percent of those without a disability in this age range were in the workforce and 3.3 percent were unemployed (U.S. Census Bureau, August 22, 2002). The average full-time earnings of disabled working persons twenty-five to sixty-four years of age was 63 percent of the earnings of persons of the same age without a disability (U.S. Census Bureau, August 22, 2002, table 3). Moreover, there is evidence that the employment status of disabled workers aged twenty-one to thirty-nine may have actually declined in the years following the passage of the Americans with Disability Act (Acemoglu & Angrist, 2001).

Of the approximately one million workers fifty-five and older who were displaced from 1997 to 1999, only 53 percent were reemployed by February 2000, compared to 80 percent of the twenty-five- to fifty-four-year-olds who were displaced during the same period. In 2002 the percentage of the civilian noninstitutional population that was not in the labor force was only 15.87 percent for those who were thirty-five to forty-four years old, compared to 17.91 percent for those who were forty-five to fifty-four years old and 38.08 percent for those who were fifty-five to sixty-four years old (U.S. Department of Labor, 2003a, table 3). Workers who are fifty-five to sixty-four are significantly less likely to be hired in firms with health care plans than in those without, and this disparity increases with the cost of the health program (Scott, Berger, & Garen, 1995).

Finally, women continue to be underrepresented in many higher paid occupations and continue to receive lower wages than men. In 2001, 78.5 percent of administrative support personnel and 77.3 percent of operators, fabricators, and laborers were men (U.S. Department of Labor, 2003b, table 11). Women rarely make it to the top positions in organizations and constitute only .4 percent of the CEOs in the Fortune 500s (Catalyst, 2000). Even when women occupy managerial positions, there is some indication that they may tend to have the title of manager without the same responsibilities (Reskin & Ross, 1992). Women working full time during 2001 had median weekly earnings that were 76 percent the earnings of men. According to a General Accounting Office study of women's pay from 1995 to 2000, the gap between the salaries of men and women widened for managers in seven of ten industries (Seglin, May 17, 2002).

Disparities in labor market outcomes alone are not sufficient proof of unfair discrimination. An alternative explanation for the disparities we have cited here is that the disadvantaged groups bring less human capital to the work situation in the form of skills, education, and experience. Although research has shown that the differences diminish once these factors are taken into account, substantial inequalities are still found (for a discussion of this research see Cohn, 2000). This research has shown that gaps in labor market outcomes as a function of race-ethnicity, gender, and age persist even after controlling for differences in human capital (Blau & Kahn, 1997; Egan & Bendick, 1994; England, 1982, 1984; Gill, 1989; Kilbourne et al., 1994; Nesbitt, 1997; Polacheck, 1981; Reskin & Ross, 1992; Valian, 2000; Wanner & McDonald, 1983; Wellington, 1994). Just how much of the disparities remain after accounting for differences in human capital is subject to continuing debate and will not be addressed in this chapter. We will simply assert that these inequalities in outcomes continue, and discrimination remains one of several viable explanations for these inequalities.

Field and Laboratory Research Showing Unfair Discrimination

As a third source of evidence, we can also point to research in the laboratory and the field demonstrating unfair discrimination. Perhaps the most direct evidence for discrimination in hiring has been provided in several field experiments in which persons from a disadvantaged group have been matched with persons from a non-disadvantaged group and have been shown to receive less favorable treatment when applying for jobs (Bendick, Brown, & Wall, 1997; Bendick, Jackson, & Reinoso, 1994; Bendick, Jackson, Reinoso, & Hodges, 1991; Bendick, Jackson, & Romero, 1996; Boggs, Sellers, & Bendick, 1993; Buchanan, 1997; Siegelman, 1999). Although the lab and field research in psychology and management has shown that unfair discrimination "can" occur and has teased out various dynamics underlying its occurrence, this research is mostly based on opportunistic samples and cannot provide the basis for estimating the extent of occurrence at a national level. The scientific surveys showing perceptions of discrimination and the research showing gaps in labor market outcomes are more convincing demonstrations, in our opinion, that there is a problem.

We believe discrimination remains a substantial problem in the work place. But what of those who disagree with our position and are convinced that unfair discrimination is infrequent and has little impact on labor market outcomes? Even if one assumes that it is a low base rate phenomenon, discrimination still occurs and can harm those who are the victims. Consequently, research is needed to understand the causes of unfair discrimination and ways to eliminate it, just as research continues on other relatively rare phenomena (for example, workplace violence, theft).

Discrimination Can Be Subtle as Well as Blatant

We would not claim on the basis of opinion polls, labor market data, or the lab and field research that inequalities in the workplace are solely the result of unfair discrimination; neither can we specify the extent to which unfair discrimination occurs. Nevertheless, we would assert on the basis of the research that unfair discrimination is neither rare nor inconsequential. Perhaps the most vivid examples of discrimination are the complaints filed with the U.S. Equal Employment Opportunity Commission (EEOC) alleging employment discrimination in the private sector. These complaints increased 4.45 percent from the previous year to 84,442 in Fiscal Year 2002 (U.S. Equal Employment Opportunity Commission, 2003). The largest single category of complaints was for race discrimination (29,910, up 3.5 percent from FY 2001), followed by sex-gender discrimination (25,536 alleged, up 1.6 percent from FY 2001). Age constitutes the third highest source of complaints in 2001 (up 14.5 percent from FY 2001). This category of complaints has shown the largest increases since 1997, and as the baby-boom generation ages is likely to increase further. The fourth highest source of complaints to the EEOC and the most ambiguous is disability (15,964, down 3 percent from FY 2001). With 43 million disabled Americans, according to the last census, this is an area where there are likely to be even greater complaints in the future. The largest increases were for national origin discrimination (9,046, up 13 percent from FY 2001) and religious discrimination (2,572, up 21 percent from FY 2001).

The cases taken to the EEOC illustrate the more blatant variety of discrimination. Consider these recent examples.

A cafeteria company agreed to pay the EEOC $175,000 fine to settle a race discrimination lawsuit. An employee who worked as a grill cook and server was told by the kitchen manager to "go back to Africa" and that "all Black people are crack heads and all they do is get drunk and live on welfare." In addition to these charges, the White general manager was accused of throwing away applications from Black applicants (Sixel, April 2, 2002).

Without admitting guilt and to avoid a major lawsuit, a large Wall Street financial firm settled for $1 million with women who had filed complaints alleging "blatant sexism" (Markon & Carroll, February 21, 2002). The women complained of being "yelled at, sworn at, and belittled by men in the company." One woman said her manager invited himself into her apartment and then refused her request for a transfer because he "would miss having (her) beautiful body around."

A Chicago-area auto dealership was ordered to pay $100,000 in damages for age discrimination (Freedman, January 7, 2002). A fifty-nine-year old applicant for a sales position was not interviewed despite twenty-four years of experience. Seven younger applicants for the same position were hired. The interviewer had noted the ages of the applicants he had interviewed. The general manager testified that he was not aware that it was illegal to discriminate on the basis of age. A jury found in favor of the plaintiff and this was upheld in a federal appeals court.

The president of a Houston manufacturer earning $225,000 was fired and his health benefits taken away after being diagnosed with a form of cancer similar to leukemia. The EEOC sued the company for violation of the Americans with Disabilities Act. The suit was settled five years after the plaintiff's death (Tedford, May 2, 2000).

As seen in these examples, blatant discrimination still exists. It is obvious, however, that this form of discrimination has become less common in the workplace. Civil rights laws have made such behavior illegal, and due in large part to the enforcement of these laws, attitudes and social norms have shifted dramatically in favor of nondiscrimination. Being seen as prejudiced is now something to be avoided. Our thesis is that unfair discrimination in today's workplace is likely to be much subtler than the behavior found in the above-mentioned examples. The following hypothetical incident illustrates the subtle variety of discrimination.

A woman working for a large corporation in a professional position feels isolated from her mostly male coworkers. An invitation is seldom extended when her coworkers go out to lunch. At meetings she often feels as though her male coworkers interrupt her and fail to give her contributions the serious consideration they deserve. She feels that when she asserts herself in meetings she is seen as overly aggressive but when she is quiet she is considered to be the "typical" passive female. The male coworkers, on the other hand, generally feel that she is qualified in several respects and would admit that she has done well in the technical aspects of her job. But they also have said in private that she lacks some of the "business savvy" and "social skills" needed for the job. They believe that like some other women and minorities she was hired because management needed to meet affirmative action goals. Recently corporate management has implemented a "rank and yank" system of 360-degree appraisal whereby the bottom performing team member each year will be fired. The feeling that she is the "weak link" has solidified and become more open since this system was announced. Still, her coworkers suspect she has an advantage and will probably survive because she is a woman.

Unlike the EEOC cases we cited, it is unlikely that formal charges of discrimination would be filed for a case such as this, and if a charge were filed, it would be unlikely to serve as a successful basis for a lawsuit. Isolation from social interactions, interruptions in meetings, or the private misgivings of coworkers provide a tenuous basis for a formal charge. Nevertheless, this example is illustrative of how discrimination can be experienced in today's workplace. In this case, aversive feelings and stereotypical beliefs are held in check out of concern with violating personal and public standards of conduct. Despite the absence of overt bias, the ambiguity and ambivalence on the part of both parties to the interaction can adversely affect the well-being and success of minority, older, female, and disabled employees. The ambiguity and ambivalence can also set the stage for what could become overt and blatant discrimination against these individuals given changes in the situation that provide a rationale or justification for the discrimination. In the remainder of this chapter we will consider how to understand discrimination of both the blatant and subtle varieties as they occur in an organizational context.

Toward a Model of Discrimination in the Organization

Greater insight into unfair discrimination in organizations is likely to come from a multilevel approach that incorporates factors at not only the individual level but also at the group, organizational, and societal and economic levels. As a step in this direction we present the model depicted in Figure 5.1. Although this model distinguishes among the different levels of causes, the outcome that is our primary concern is the act of discrimination that occurs at the level of an individual organizational participant. This act is described along four dimensions: overt-covert, intentional-unintentional, stable-unstable, and conscious-unconscious. Blatant discrimination can be characterized as unfair treatment of the target persons that is overt, conscious, intentional, and stable over time. The subtlest unfair discrimination is covert, unconscious, unintentional, and unstable over time. These four dimensions can be viewed as continua in which behavior is often at some point between the extremes.

**Figure 5.1. Acts of Unfair Discrimination
as a Function of Conflicts Among Pressures
For and Against These Acts at Various Levels.**

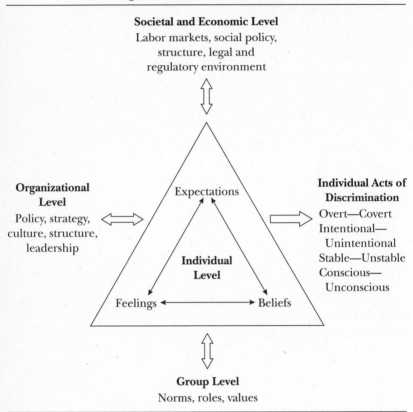

Blatant discrimination is most likely to occur when the multi-level antecedents are aligned and consistent in the pressure on the person to engage in the discriminatory act. For instance, situations exist in which organizational participants may feel strong group and organizational pressure to act in ways that unfairly discriminate against members of a group. At the same time they may have personally held feelings and beliefs that support such acts. In such an instance we would expect that the discrimination is more likely to emerge in a form that is relatively open and intentional. Moreover, we would expect the organizational participant to be aware of his or her own discriminatory behavior and to show this behavior consistently over time. Conversely, more subtle discrimination is likely when there is conflict among these various pressures. For instance, acts of discrimination are more likely to be of a subtle form when an organizational participant holds prejudicial attitudes but is restrained from acting on those attitudes as the result of organizational and group pressures against discrimination. Another situation would be where an organizational participant's attitudes and beliefs are unbiased but there are pressures at the group, organizational, and the societal and economic levels to discriminate. Still another situation might be where the pressures external to the organizational participant are aligned either in support of or opposed to discrimination. Despite the consistency among external pressures on the individual, internal conflict among the beliefs and attitudes held by the participant could still exist with regard to the target person. When there is conflict among the multilevel determinants of discrimination or conflict within the individual, one could expect that discriminatory acts that emerge are more likely to be covert, unintentional, and unconscious. Moreover, such acts in these situations are more likely to be unstable such that treatment of the target person may swing from one extreme to another given changes external to the participant. Thus, personal biases seem unlikely to appear when these acts are likely to be seen by others as biased but may emerge unrestrained when there is strong pressure from the group or organization to show "team spirit" and "fit in." In the face of such pressures, discriminatory acts can be rationalized and expressed in a form that is not aversive to the agent of the discrimination.

Individual-Level Pressures For and Against Discrimination

The typical focus in previous discussions of discrimination has been on the feelings and beliefs of the individual who commits the act of discrimination (Fiske, 1998). Although they are not the sole factor to consider, these same components are important to understanding discrimination in the organization. The primary cognitive component consists of the prototypes, schemata, and stereotypes that encourage shortcuts in the processing of information on members of groups. People hold stereotypes or schemata regarding groups and fall back on these cognitive structures in their perceptions and evaluations of individual members of these groups. In economics the term "statistical discrimination" is used to refer to the attribution of the average characteristics of the group to individual members of a group (Sattinger, 1998). The affective component consists of the emotional reactions to members of a group, which can exist in a variety of forms but is usually associated with prejudice. For instance, Stone and Colella (1996) posit several affective responses to disabled individuals, including revulsion, sympathy, discomfort, fear, resentment, frustration, anxiety-stress, and guilt. Perhaps as the result of socialization and conditioning going back to childhood, people have visceral reactions that they cannot control, that are unconscious, and may be rooted in basic psychological needs (for example, self-esteem needs). Discrimination itself is usually conceived as the behavioral component and consists of patterns of verbal and nonverbal behavior. For instance, differences in characteristic communication patterns can be responsible for problems in relationships between men and women (Haslett, Geis, & Carter, 1992) and blacks and whites (Erickson, 1979). Although discrimination can be a consequence of the cognitive and affective components, the three components can be independent or reciprocally dependent on one another. Each component may be conscious and controlled, such as when an individual intentionally discriminates against a member of a disadvantaged group. Each can also be unconscious and uncontrolled, such as when reactions to a disadvantaged person occur in an unthinking, automatic manner. Moreover, these three components can act in unison or exist in conflict with one another.

When the cognitive, affective, and behavioral factors are aligned in supporting bias against members of a targeted group, a blatant form of discrimination is the likely outcome. Discrimination against blacks can occur in the form of stereotyping of blacks, the experience of negative feelings such as disgust, fear, and dislike in the presence of blacks, and negative verbal and nonverbal behavior toward blacks. All of this may be quite conscious and intentional. However, a common theme in the social psychological research over the last two decades is that old-fashioned racism has been replaced by more subtle varieties in the form of symbolic racism (Kinder & Sears, 1981), modern racism (McConahay & Hough, 1976), racial ambivalence (Katz & Hass, 1988), and aversive racism (Dovidio & Gaertner, 2000). There are differences in these theories of racism, but there are several themes underlying these theories that characterize subtle discrimination. Although we will discuss these themes in the context of subtle racism, these same themes have been applied to discrimination against women (Glick & Fiske, 1996) and the disabled (Snyder, Kleck, Strenta, & Mentzer, 1979) and could be easily extended to older employees. The themes are as follows:

1. *Affirmation of traditional values can be a cover for prejudice.* In symbolic racism, there is old-fashioned racial hatred that is expressed in terms of the belief that blacks do not possess discipline, self-control, self-reliance, and other traditional values. Similarly, in modern racism, white individuals who are prejudiced avoid direct statements of racism but indirectly convey racism in the positions that they espouse. For instance, opposition to affirmative action may be principled and reasonable but can also be a cover-up for an underlying anti-black attitude.

2. *There is considerable ambivalence in attitudes toward members of outgroups.* Stereotypes may be predominately negative but almost always contain positive components. Katz and Hass (1988) in their theory of racial ambivalence posit that perceptions of blacks as deserving sympathy and help conflict with perceptions of blacks as deviant and not playing by the rules. One prediction of their model is that the more intense the ambivalence (that is, the more intense the negative and positive feelings), the more unstable the response. For instance, a black person may receive even greater rewards in response to good performance and more punishment in response to poor performance than would a white person (Katz & Glass, 1979).

3. *There are negative affective reactions that can be unconscious and uncontrolled.* The theory of aversive racism proposes that socialization in American culture and cognitive biases have instilled a bias among whites against blacks and other minorities. Nevertheless, there are modern norms against overt racism so that

whites cannot admit to themselves that they have these biases. There are two consequences of this. First, even well-intentioned people, who do not think of themselves as prejudiced against a group, may have rapid, automatic, racially biased associations, which would be aversive to them if they were consciously aware of them. Prejudicial attitudes may leak unconsciously into the treatment of a black person by a white person. In a demonstration of this, Vanman, Paul, Ito, and Miller (1997) had participants work with a black or white partner. More liking was reported for black partners than white partners on a self-report measure, but at the same time facial electromyography (EMG) activity indicated greater negative emotional reaction to blacks. A second consequence is automaticity in the processing of information on stereotyped groups. Payne (2001) found that subjects who were primed with photographs of black persons were more likely to identify the subsequent signal as a gun compared to subjects primed with a picture of a white person.

A second consequence of aversive racism and people's anxiety about appearing prejudiced (to themselves or to others) is that when nonegalitarian behavior can be explained in terms of something other than prejudice, people are more likely to act on their prejudice. A series of studies by Snyder and his colleagues (Snyder, Kleck, Strenta, & Mentzer, 1979) illustrates this phenomenon. Participants are asked to evaluate a movie playing on one of two monitors separated by a partition. Already sitting in front of each of the monitors is a confederate, who is either "normal" or stigmatized (for example, disabled, black). The critical manipulation is whether both monitors show the same movie or two different ones. When there are different movies showing and the individuals can attribute not sitting with the stigmatized other to personal preference for the movie, they are more likely to avoid sitting with the stigmatized person. The two-movie condition renders the motivation for the participant's avoidance of the stigmatized person ambiguous. People are more likely to avoid sitting with the minority or disabled person because their prejudice can be disguised as a legitimate preference for the other movie.

Pressures For and Against Discrimination That Are External to the Participant

In the previous discussions of the various forms of subtle discrimination, the primary emphasis in the psychological literature has been on these intraindividual events that can lead to discrimination. A common theme is that there is a conflict or tension among these factors that leads to instability and ambivalence in the treatment of the persons who are the target of discrimination. These theories also have been used to understand workplace discrimination. However, the model in Figure 5.1 is based on the assumption that other factors in addition to those at the individual level need to be incorporated to account for subtle and blatant forms of discrimination in organizations.

Group-Level Pressures

One of the strongest motives underlying human behavior in organizations is the need to belong and to be accepted by one's peers. The power of group norms and pressures to conform to these norms has been repeatedly shown in field studies and laboratory experiments. A major antecedent of unfair discrimination is conformity to the expectations of other group members (Brief, Dietz, Cohen, Pugh, & Vaslow, 2000). Group norms not only define reality for group members but also communicate how members can obtain the approval and avoid the criticisms of fellow group members. The recent allegations of harassment of women at some Wall Street firms may reflect a group culture in these companies that is dominated by young white upwardly mobile professional men (Markon & Carroll, 2002; McGeehan, 2001). Likewise, the racial graffiti that is a problem in manufacturing and production settings may reflect a group culture dominated by working class white men. Sexual harassment, racial epithets, and offensive posters are the harsher ways in which a group culture can encourage discrimination. Less obvious are other manifestations such as attending more to what some people say than others and giving more credit for accomplishments and access to information to some people over others (Ibarra, 1993).

Organizational-Level Pressures

At the organizational level, the policies, strategies, culture, structure, and top-level leadership of the organization can encourage unfair discrimination. Perry, Davis-Blake, and Kulik (1994) speculate that high levels of job title proliferation are associated with high levels of gender segregation in occupations. Also, within job ladders, if entry-level jobs are segregated by gender, the pool of individuals available for promotion will consist primarily of individuals of one gender. Another important factor is the degree of formality and standardization in human resource management procedures. When employers rely on highly subjective, unstructured, and invalidated human resource procedures without regard to the job-relatedness of these procedures, one can expect more discrimination (Finkelstein, Burke, & Raju, 1995). There is more than one underlying reason for this, including a lack of accountability that allows discrimination to go undetected and unpunished and high levels of task uncertainty that may lead decision makers to fall back on stereotypes and their feelings when making decisions about employees.

The values and behaviors of top-level management are another organizational level factor to consider. The CEO and his or her management team sets the tone for the organization. When top-level management is guilty of ageism, sexism, racism, or discrimination against the disabled, these acts of discrimination send a message to those below them in the organization. For example, one of the authors is aware of widely circulated stories within a major corporation of the CEO's womanizing and harassment of women. For some male employees in the organization this seemed to be received as a message that it was OK to be sexist as long as they espoused egalitarianism between the sexes and were not overt in their sexism. For some female employees it was a message that no matter what they did, they would still be discriminated against because they were only valued as a sex object.

Societal- and Economic-Level Pressures

At this level, there are factors such as the structure of labor markets, social policy, investments by society in human capital, and the legal and regulatory framework. Market forces are particularly important and have been largely ignored in the industrial and organizational literature. There is convincing evidence for a buffering explanation for sex segregation in occupations (see Cohn, 2000 for a discussion). In capital-intensive segments of the economy, labor costs are relatively minor and employers can afford to discriminate. In other words, these firms can afford the luxury of preferring well-paid men over women. In labor-intensive segments of the economy, cheap labor is needed to ensure a profit, and it is here that we find that a more substantial proportion of women are hired (Cohn, 2000). By contrast, in capital-intense firms personnel costs are a smaller part of the budget and the organization can afford the "luxury" of indulging their biases and discriminating against women.

Customer preference is another economic force. A recent case brought by the EEOC provides an example (U.S. Equal Opportunity Commission, March 6, 2002). In this case, the plaintiffs alleged that they had suffered racial discrimination at a drinking-water processing and delivery company. African American drivers were assigned to routes in low-income neighborhoods, which were often less profitable than routes in affluent communities. Because pay and promotion were tied to the profitability of the routes, the African American drivers received lower compensation and fewer promotions than those assigned to the affluent areas. "Black drivers understood that they would work the so-called 'ghetto routes' while Beverly Hills would be handled by White drivers" (p. 1).

It may well have been that this differential treatment was not motivated by a dislike of black drivers or an attempt to keep them down. Instead, this discrimination may well have been guided by what were seen as legitimate economic considerations. Perhaps, for instance, customers prefer drivers of the same race and are more likely to buy water if the driver is of the same race. Although we suspect that such customer preferences are often more imagined than real, and are subject to modification, in the short term they might represent realistic economic considerations. In one of the prominent court cases brought against airlines for discriminating against male flight attendants, expert witnesses argued that airline attendants should be female because passengers need and expect the nurturance of a woman (*Diaz* v. *Pan American World Airways, Inc.*). There may have been some truth to this at the time, in the sense that customers had grown accustomed to being served by women. Such arguments failed to recognize that customer tastes such as these can easily change, and after over two decades during which male flight attendants have become common, the argument seems silly in retrospect.

Discrimination in Organizations as a Role-Conflict Phenomenon

Acts of discrimination may occur as the result of any one of the factors at the individual, group, organizational, or the societal and economic level. One way to view unfair discrimination is in terms of role theory. The participant occupies a position in the organization, and expectations are communicated by those inside and outside the organization as to what behavior is desired of that person. From these expectations emerge the work role of the participant, which consists of the pattern of behavior associated with the position. Expectations for how the participant is to treat minorities, women, older, and disabled employees can be considered a type of role expectation.

One type of role conflict occurs when different people communicate conflicting expectations for whether a person should unfairly discriminate. For instance, management may communicate an expectation of nondiscrimination in the form of organizational policy, but the expectations communicated by coworkers may encourage the participant to go against policy and unfairly discriminate. Another situation might be where the expectations communicated to the participant conflict with his or her own beliefs and values. Thus, the participant may believe and feel that nondiscrimination is the right action but may perceive that he or she is expected to discriminate as the result of pressures from the work group and corporate policies. Inconsistencies among the various pressures on the individual participant depicted in Figure 5.1 could be experienced as role stress. And it is this stress that characterizes the ambivalence and instability associated with the various forms of subtle discrimination. Caught in the crossfire of inconsistent expectations, the participant may be influenced to behave in a discriminatory direction by factors that can rationalize the act.

Some Current Trends in Organizations That May Encourage Unfair Discrimination

We provide four examples of how the context might "tip" the balance in favor of discrimination in a situation characterized by conflicting pressures for and against discrimination and the role stress associated with this conflict. Paradoxically, each of these tipping points has been championed as ways that organizations can compete in an increasingly competitive global economy. We are not arguing against any of these four factors, but aim only to show how each one could have the unintended consequence of encouraging unfair discrimination in a situation in which the organizational participants are subject to conflict among the various pressures depicted in Figure 5.1.

Team Spirit Can Work Against Openness and Tolerance

One trend today is the use of team-based management whereby groups are given autonomy to select their own members, provide their own appraisals, administer their own rewards, and make important decisions about their work. Rather than having strictly defined job duties, there is flexibility in people performing each other's jobs. An unanticipated consequence of these arrangements is that groups of workers may become the primary force for socialization in the organization.

Some of the strongest resistance to diversity occurs when there is a highly autonomous group with elite status. For example, Special Forces units in the military are coming under increasing criticism for their exclusion of racial minorities and women (Kampeas, 2002). The Texas Rangers have been charged with the same criticisms (*Houston Chronicle*, 1988; Nethaway, 1995; Sixel, 1994).

Also associated with the emphasis on teams is the priority given to maintaining the cohesion and morale of the group or team. A recent charge of age discrimination against a national magazine involved a forty-year-old female college student who applied as an intern but was rejected on the basis of her age (*Washington Post*, Feb. 18, 2002). According to the editor of this magazine, "College internships, after all, thrive on a convivial, often social atmosphere where people of similar ages bond over new experiences. An older person working with a younger counterpart on routine tasks such as sending faxes or doing research would disrupt the group dynamic of the magazine's program." Another example is a major corporation that was recently charged by the EEOC with blatant harassment of women (*Washington Post,* Jan. 25, 2002). It is alleged that the company sponsored a "best breast" competition in which pictures were taken of women's chests and posted on a bulletin board so employees could vote for a winner. It was described as an attempt to "create an overall friendly productive environment."

In all of these examples, the norms of a group may have allowed members to reframe inappropriate behavior as legitimate attempts to meet the needs of the group and to develop camaraderie. Moreover, the more cohesive the group, the stronger the power of the group to gain compliance to the norms and the greater the likelihood that members will go beyond mere compliance and internalize the norms. The "we feeling" of a group can encourage a contagion effect in which normally nonbiased individuals become uninhibited in the anonymity of the group situation and engage in inappropriate behavior.

Incentive and Appraisal Systems That Encourage Competition Can Encourage Unfair Discrimination

Another trend is an attempt by organizations to increase accountability by providing regular evaluations and rewarding employees for their individual performance. As Allport (1954) noted, one of the more powerful techniques for eliminating stereotypes and reducing prejudice is to put people into situations in which they must cooperate to achieve shared goals. However, organizations may undermine attempts to achieve diversity with reward and appraisal systems that place people in competition with one another. We would argue that diversity and EEOC policies that mandate tolerance are undercut by programs such as "rank and yank" systems of performance appraisal that have the effect of pitting employee against employee. Pay for performance can have the same effect. We would go so far as to assert that the reward structures of an organization probably do more than anything else to perpetuate discrimination. Not only do systems often reward competition, but they also fail to reward and even punish the mentoring of minorities and women.

Public Assertions of Vision, Values, Objectives, and Goals Can Substitute for Action

If people are rewarded for cooperation, we might ask, What are they rewarded to accomplish? What is the common goal that they pursue? Allport (1954) suggested that contact may lead to increased tolerance when there is a common goal and people believe they must work together to achieve these goals. All major corporations today take pride in lofty expressions of what they stand for and what they hope to achieve. Leaders who are charismatic are said to be the driving force of shared goals and values. Yet charisma can be a substitute for action. Weighty pronouncements on how discrimination will not be tolerated, or how diversity is a key value, can be the prelude for inaction.

How might this occur? One possibility is that top leaders issue vision statements that are essentially lies or cover-ups. Although outright lies occur, we think that the dynamics at work here are usually more subtle. An interesting possibility is that explicit pronouncements and the championing of egalitarian values and vision can actually increase discrimination as the result of giving a moral license. Monin and Miller (2001) provide evidence of this in an experiment in which participants were given a list of statements about women under instructions to state the extent of their agreement or disagreement with each of them (for example: "Some/Most women are better off at home taking care of the children"; "Men are more emotionally suited for politics than are some/most women"). The manipulation was whether the word "some" or "most" was used in the statements. When "most" was used, the participants had the opportunity to disagree with a biased statement (for example, that "most" women need a man to protect them). In a second study that followed this induction, participants were asked to imagine that they were a manager of a small company and were given the task of deciding whether a job was better suited for a man or a woman. Those who had been given the "most" wording were more likely to state a preference for a man in the job. Similar results were found for race. The reasoning was that prior assertions that could be construed as egalitarian gave the subject "license" to subsequently discriminate. It is interesting to speculate how organizations that require employees to espouse egalitarian values might actually provide license for subsequent discrimination.

Darley (2001) has pointed out another reason that lofty, visionary statements may have an effect that is opposite of what was intended. According to Darley the mere "existence of corporate codes can cause superiors to assume that the codes are much on the minds of the subordinates, and of course this assumption may not be true. . . . The superior assumes that he or she has communicated such ethical precautions far earlier; therefore, they do not need to be a part of the present communication" (pp. 40–41). Most of the organizations found guilty of discrimination no doubt have equal opportunity and affirmative action statements that are disseminated. Moreover, many of the organizations found guilty of discrimination have as part of their vision statements endorsements of diversity. It is interesting to speculate on how the act of making such lofty pronouncements might lead to less monitoring and the assumption that there is conformity to these statements.

An Emphasis on Person-Organization (PO) Fit Can Encourage Discrimination

A major emphasis in industrial and organizational (IO) psychology and human resources (HR) that has been reinforced by court decisions and in the EEOC uniform guidelines is that the selection, appraisal, training, and compensation of employees should be based on careful, quantitative analysis of the knowledge, skills, abilities, and other attributes required in the job. As the result of a variety of factors, including increased competition and rapidly changing technologies, there has been a deemphasis of the traditional, individualistic, job-based model. Achieving a good fit to the core values of the organization has become a higher priority in many organizations than achieving a good fit to the knowledge, skills, abilities, and other characteristics required in the job (Bowen, Ledford, & Nathan, 1991; Chatman, 1991). An emphasis on "fitting in" with the values of the organization may open the door to discrimination (Brief, 1998, p. 140; Powell, 1998, p. 50).

We believe the greatest danger of a PO fit approach to HR is that these approaches are typically associated with unstructured, subjective evaluation procedures (Dipboye, 1994). When evaluation procedures are not standardized and firmly anchored in clear requirements, the individual stereotypes and prejudices of the individual evaluator are more likely to dominate. Moreover, a PO fit approach may legitimize the common rationale used in discrimination against racial minorities, women, older workers, and the disabled—that they just "don't fit in."

Conclusions

Despite progress, discrimination against racial minorities, women, older employees, and the disabled continues. There are a variety of sources of discrimination. It is not surprising that those most widely studied by psychologists are at the individual level and include cognitive and affective factors. In most organizations, however, conflict typically occurs among these individual-level antecedents and factors at the organizational, group, and societal and economic levels. The delicate balance between pressures to discriminate and pressures for tolerance and egalitarianism can easily be tipped one way or the other by this context. Thus, team management, PO fit, formal pronouncements of equal opportunity policies, and incentive systems that encourage competition may provide the release and the rationalization for acts of discrimination.

Most organizations offer neither total equality in treatment and opportunity nor blatant mistreatment of minority, women, disabled, and older employees. The more typical situation is one in which employees with good intentions are caught in the crossfire and illegal and unfair discrimination occur for what seem to be the best of reasons. But it is this subtle form of discrimination, rather than the "old-fashioned" variety, that is the more pernicious.

References

Acemoglu, D., & Angrist, J. D. (2001, October). Consequences of employment protection? The case of the Americans with disabilities act. *The Journal of Political Economy, 109,* 915–957.

Allport, G. W. (1954). *The nature of prejudice.* Cambridge, MA: Addison-Wesley.

American Association of Retired Persons. (2002, September). *Staying ahead of the curve: The AARP work and career study.* Washington, DC: AARP.

Bendick, M., Jr., Brown, L. E., & Wall, K. (1997). *No foot in the door: An experimental study of employment discrimination against older workers.* Washington, DC: Fair Employment Council of Greater Washington, Inc.

Bendick, M., Jr., Jackson, C., & Reinoso, V. (1994). Measuring employment discrimination through controlled experiments. *Review of Black Political Economy, 23,* 25–48.

Bendick, M., Jr., Jackson, C., Reinoso, V., & Hodges, L. (1991). Discrimination against Latino job applicants: A controlled experiment. *Human Resource Management, 30,* 469–484.

Bendick, M., Jr., Jackson, C., & Romero, J. H. (1996). Employment discrimination against older workers: An experimental study of hiring practices. *Journal of Aging and Social Policy, 8,* 25–46.

Blau, F. D., & Kahn, L. M. (1997). Swimming upstream: Trends in the gender wage differential in 1980s. *Journal of Labor Economics, 15,* 1–42.

Boggs, R., Sellers, J., & Bendick, M., Jr. (1993). Use of testing in civil rights enforcement. In M. Fix & R. Struyk (Eds.), *Clear and convincing evidence: Measurement of discrimination in America* (pp. 345–376). Washington, DC: Urban Institute Press.

Bowen, D. E., Ledford, G. E., Jr., & Nathan, B. R. (1991). Hiring for the organization, not the job. *Academy of Management Executive, 5,* 35–50.

Brief, A. P. (1998). *Attitudes in and around organizations.* Thousand Oaks, CA: Sage.

Brief, A. P., Dietz, J., Cohen, R. R., Pugh, S. D., & Vaslow, J. B. (2000). Just doing business: Modern racism and obedience to authority as explanations for employment discrimination. *Organizational Behavior & Human Decision Processes, 81,* 72–97.

Buchanan, J. (1997, December 14). Black citizens tell tales of bias: In wake of Dillard's verdict, other shoppers share their experiences. *Kansas City Star,* p. A1.

Cascio, W. F. (1998). *Applied psychology in human resource management.* Upper Saddle River, NJ: Prentice Hall.

Catalyst (2000). *Census of women corporate officers and top earners.* New York: Catalyst.

Chatman, J. A. (1991). Matching people and organizations: Selection and socialization in public accounting firms. *Administrative Science Quarterly, 36,* 459–484.

Cohn, S. (2000). *Race and gender discrimination at work.* Oxford, England: Westview Press.

Cox, T. (1993). *Cultural diversity in organizations. Theory, research, and practice.* San Francisco: Berrett-Koehler.

Darley, J. M. (2001). The dynamics of authority influence in organizations and the unintended action consequences. In J. M. Darley, D. M. Messick, & T. R. Tyler (Eds.), *Social influences on ethical behavior in organizations* (pp. 37–52). Mahwah, NJ: Erlbaum.

Diaz v. Pan American World Airways, Inc., 311 F. Supp. 559 (S. D. Fla. 1970).

Dipboye, R. L. (1994). Structured and unstructured interviews: Beyond the job-fit model. In G. Ferris (Ed.), *Research in personnel and human resources management, 12,* (pp. 79–123). Greenwich, CT: JAI Press.

Dovidio, J. F., & Gaertner, S. L. (1986). Prejudice, discrimination, and racism: Historical trends and contemporary approaches. In J. F. Dovidio & S. L. Gaertner (Eds.), *Prejudice, discrimination and racism* (pp. 1–34). New York: Academic Press.

Dovidio, J. F, & Gaertner, S. L. (2000). Aversive racism and selection. *Psychological Science,* 11, 315–319.

Egan, M. L., & Bendick, M., Jr. (1994). International business careers in the United States: Salaries, advancement, and male-female differences. *International Journal of Human Resource Management,* 5, 33–50.

England, P. (1982). Failure of human capital theory to explain occupational segregation. *Journal of Human Resources,* 17, 338–350.

England, P. (1984). Wage appreciation and depreciation: A test of neoclassical economic explanations of occupational sex segregation. *Social Forces,* 62, 726–749.

Erickson, F. (1979). Talking down: Some cultural sources of miscommunication in interracial interviews. In A. Wolfgang (Ed.), *Nonverbal behavior: Applications and cultural implications* (pp. 99–126). New York: Academic Press.

Finkelstein, L. M., Burke, M. J., & Raju, N. S. (1995). Age discrimination in simulated employment contexts: An integrative analysis. *Journal of Applied Psychology,* 80, 652–663.

Fiske, S. T. (1998). Stereotyping, prejudice, and discrimination. In D. T. Gilbert, S. T. Fiske, & G. Lindzey (Eds.), *The handbook of social psychology* (pp. 357–411). Boston: McGraw-Hill.

Freedman, E. (2002, January 7). Dealership owes damages in age case. *Automotive News,* 76, 16.

Gill, A. (1989). The role of discrimination in determining occupational structure. *Industrial and Labor Relations Review,* 42, 610–623.

Glick, P., & Fiske, S. T. (1996). The ambivalent sexism inventory: Differentiating hostile and benevolent sexism. *Journal of Personality and Social Psychology,* 70, 491–512.

Hallock, K. F., Hendricks, W., & Broadbent, E. (1998). Discrimination by gender and disability status: Do worker perceptions match statistical measures? *Southern Economic Journal,* 65, 245–263.

Haslett, B. J., Geis, F. L., & Carter, M. R. (1992). *The organizational woman: Power and paradox.* Norwood, NJ: Ablex.

Houston Chronicle (1988, January 14). Black troopers, NAACP allege racism within DPS, p. A12.

Hunt, A. (2000, June 22). American Opinion (A special report)—Women, politics and the marketplace—major progress, inequities cross 3 generations—grandmother, mother, daughter reveal a tempered optimism amid 'universally held views.' *The Wall Street Journal*, p. A9.

Hutchens, R. M. (1988). Do job opportunities decline with age? *Industrial & Labor Relations Review*, 42, 89–99.

Ibarra, H. (1993). Personal networks of women and minorities in management: A conceptual framework. *Academy of Management Review*, 18, 56–87.

Jones, J. M. (1986) Racism: A cultural analysis of the problem. In J. F. Dovidio & S. L. Gaertner (Eds.), *Prejudice, discrimination and racism* (pp. 279–314). New York: Academic Press.

Joyner, T. (2002, January 18). A divided workplace. *The Atlanta Journal—Constitution*, p. C1.

Kampeas, R. (2002, April 2). Elitism vs. racism? Some see efforts to diversify Special Forces as lowering of standards for sake of image. *Houston Chronicle*, p. A9.

Katz, I., & Glass, D. C. (1979). An ambivalence-amplification theory of behavior toward the stigmatized. In W. G. Austin & S. Worchel (Eds.), *The social psychology of intergroup relations* (pp. 55–70). Monterey, CA: Brooks/Cole.

Katz, I., & Hass, R. G. (1988). Racial ambivalence and American value conflict: Correlational and priming studies of dual cognitive structures. *Journal of Personality and Social Psychology*, 55, 893–905.

Kilbourne, B. S., England, P., Farkas, G., Beron, K., & Weir, D. (1994). Returns to skill, compensating differentials and gender bias: Effects of occupational characteristics on the wages of white women and men. *American Journal of Sociology*, 100, 689–720.

Kinder, D., & Sears, D. O. (1981). Prejudice and politics: Symbolic racism versus racial threats to the good life. *Journal of Personality and Social Psychology*, 40, 414–431.

Markon, J., & Carroll, J. (2002, February 21). Financial firm agrees to settle bias lawsuit. *The Wall Street Journal*, p. A3.

McConahay, J. B., & Hough, J. C. (1976). Symbolic racism. *Journal of Social Issues*, 32, 23–45.

McGeehan, P. (2001, September 9). EEOC suit targets Morgan Stanley/Bond saleswoman alleges gender bias. *The New York Times*.

Messner, S. F. (1989). Economic discrimination and societal homicide rates: Further evidence on the cost of inequality. *American Sociological Review*, 54, 597–611.

Monin, B., & Miller, D. T. (2001). Moral credentials and the expression of prejudice. *Journal of Personality and Social Psychology*, 81, 33–43.

Nesbitt, P. (1997). Clergy feminization: Controlled labor or transformative change? *Journal for the Scientific Study of Religion, 36,* 585–598.

Nethaway, R. (1995, June 21). Legendary Texas lawmen have trouble keeping peace with women. *The Atlanta Journal,* p. A11.

Payne, B. Keith (2001). Prejudice and perception: The role of automatic and controlled processes in misperceiving a weapon. *Journal of Personality and Social Psychology,* 81, 181–192.

Perry, E. L., Davis-Blake, A., & Kulik, C. T. (1994). Explaining gender-based selection decisions: A synthesis of contextual and cognitive approaches. *Academy of Management Review,* 19, 786–820.

Piper, A.M.S. (1993). Higher-order discrimination. In O. Flanagan & A. O. Rorty (Eds.), *Identity, character, and morality. Essays in moral psychology* (3rd ed.) (pp. 285–309). Cambridge: MIT Press.

Polacheck, S. (1981). Occupational self-selection: A human capital approach to sex differences in occupational structure. *Review of Economics and Statistics,* 58, 60–69.

Powell, G. N. (1998). Reinforcing and extending today's organizations: The simultaneous pursuit of person-organization fit and diversity. *Organizational Dynamics,* 26, 50–61.

Reskin, B., & Ross, C. (1992). Jobs, authority and earnings among managers: Continuing significance of sex. *Work and Occupations,* 19, 342–365.

Sanchez, J., & Brock, P. (1996). Outcomes of perceived discrimination among Hispanic employees: Is diversity management a luxury or a necessity? *Academy of Management Journal,* 39, 704–719.

Sattinger, M. (1998). Statistical discrimination with employment criteria. *International Economic Review,* 39, 205–237.

Scott, F. A., Berger, M. C., & Garen, J. E. (1995). Do health insurance and pension costs reduce the job opportunities of older workers? *Industrial and Labor Relations Review,* 48, 775–791.

Seglin, J. L. (2002, May 17). How to get a company's attention on women's pay. *The New York Times.*

Siegelman, P. (March, 1999). Racial discrimination in "everyday" commercial transactions: What do we know, what do we need to know, and how can we find out? In M. Fix & M. A. Turner (Eds.), *A national report card on discrimination: The role of testing* (Chapter 4). Washington, DC: Urban Institute.

Sixel, L. M. (1994, January 5). Texas Rangers EEOC probe calls DPS practice discriminatory. *Houston Chronicle,* p. 1.

Sixel, L. M. (2002, April 2). Prince will settle EEOC bias case/cafeteria company to pay $175,000 fine. *Houston Chronicle,* p. 2.

Snyder, M. L., Kleck, R. E., Strenta, A., & Mentzer, S. J. (1979). Avoidance of the handicapped: An attributional ambiguity analysis. *Journal of Personality & Social Psychology,* 37, 2297–2306.

Stone, D. L., & Colella, A. (1996). A model of factors affecting the treatment of disabled individuals in organizations. *The Academy of Management Review,* 21, 352–401.

Taylor, H. (2002, November 13). Workplace discrimination against, and jokes about, African Americans, gays, Jews, Muslims, and others. *The Harris Poll©,* No. 61.

Tedford, D. (2000, May 2). Houston firm settles suit in disability case. *Houston Chronicle,* p. A18.

U.S. Census Bureau (2002, August 22). Table 3, Work experience and mean earnings in 2000—work disability status of civilians 16 to 74 years old, by educational attainment and sex: 2001. Washington, DC: U.S. Census Bureau.

U.S. Department of Labor Bureau of Labor Statistics (2003a). Annual averages—Household data, employed persons by detailed occupation, sex, race, and Hispanic origin. (Retrieved October 8, 2003, from http://www.bls.gov/cps/cpsa2002.pdf)

U.S. Department of Labor Bureau of Labor Statistics (2003b). Annual averages—Household data, employment status of the civilian noninstitutional population 25 years and over by educational attainment, sex, race, and Hispanic origin. (Retrieved October 8, 2003, from http://www.bls.gov/cps/cpsa2002.pdf)

U.S. Equal Employment Opportunity Commission (2002, March 6). Court approves $1.2 million settlement between EEOC McKesson for race discrimination. (Retrieved October 8, 2003, from http://www.eeoc.gov/press/3-6-02.html)

U.S. Equal Employment Opportunity Commission (2003, February 6). Charge statistics FY 1992 through FY 2002. (Retrieved October 8, 2003, from http://www.eeoc.gov/state/charges.html)

Valian, V. (2000). *Why so slow?* London: MIT.

Vanman, E. J., Paul, B. Y., Ito, T. A., & Miller, N. (1997). The modern face of prejudice and structural features that moderate the effect of cooperation on affect. *Journal of Personality and Social Psychology,* 73, 941–959.

Wanner, R., & McDonald, L. (1983). Ageism in the labor market: Estimating earnings discrimination against older workers. *Journal of Gerontology,* 38, 738–744.

Washington Post (2002, January 25). Dial facing sexual harassment suit; Women ready to testify in key EEOC action against company.

Washington Post (2002, February 18). Massachusetts panel to study would-be intern's case against *Atlantic Monthly,* p.1.

Wellington, A. (1994). Accounting for the male/female wage gap among whites: 1976 and 1985. *American Sociological Review,* 59, 839–848.

CHAPTER 6

Sexual Harassment as Dysfunctional Behavior in Organizations

Ramona L. Paetzold

Although it came to light as a dark side of organizational behavior only about twenty years ago, sexual harassment is now an oft-studied but elusive phenomenon. Anita Hill's testimony at Clarence Thomas's confirmation hearings, the Tailhook scandal, and other high-profile allegations of inappropriate sexual behavior in organizational settings brought sexual harassment to the forefront of organizational scholarship. But workplace sexual harassment is not about sexual behavior alone, thus making its boundaries and causes difficult to establish. How should sexual harassment be characterized? Under the law, workplace sexual harassment is but one form of intentional sex discrimination. How sexual harassment is experienced by targets, and what motivates perpetrators to engage in it, may not easily be summed up by the law, however. Many organizational and social psychology researchers have considered frameworks that do not depend upon legal definitions or understandings of sexual harassment, thereby seeking to adopt more experiential perspectives on the phenomenon. Despite years of research, remaining disagreements on even the definition of the sexual harassment construct evidences the lack of accumulated knowledge within this field of study. For example, is workplace sexual harassment best viewed as a form of workplace discrimination, as the law sees it? Or is it perhaps best viewed as a form of sexual aggression or violence against women, as some organization and psychology researchers see it (Fitzgerald, 1993; O'Leary-Kelly, Paetzold, & Griffin, 2000)? Does sexual harassment require an interpretative act by the target, as the law indicates, or does it exist in the behaviors and motivations of the perpetrators themselves? Does the sexual harassment construct truly allow for women's behavior to be harassing of men, or does it by definition require that men act in inappropriate ways toward women? (See Waldo, Berdahl, & Fitzgerald, 1998.) The underlying etiology of sexual harassment—still controversial—obviously depends on the adopted definition.

Sexual harassment affects numerous employees, primarily women. Early estimates suggested that between 42 percent and 90 percent of women in organizations experienced sexual harassment (Gutek, 1985; U.S. Merit Systems Protection Board, 1981, 1988). Gutek (1985) found that over 27 percent of surveyed men indicated that they had experienced probable sexual harassment. More recent estimates of the frequency of sexual harassment suggest that the incidence rate has decreased. For example, Gruber (1990) indicated that the median percentage of women reporting sexual harassment was 44 percent, and a random telephone survey conducted by the Employment Law Alliance in 2001 found that 21 percent of women respondents and 7 percent of men respondents reported experiencing sexual harassment at work (Bureau of National Affairs, 2001). The meaning of this apparent reduction in frequency is unclear. For example, surveys create methodological problems for measuring the incidence rate of sexual harassment (Arvey & Cavanaugh, 1995). In addition, it is possible that years of clarification by the courts of patterns of behaviors that may constitute illegal sexual harassment could have reduced the reported frequency (that is, respondents may be influenced by the legal definition of sexual harassment to narrow the set of behaviors they consider to be sexually harassing). Perhaps respondents are less willing nowadays to label sex-related behaviors as offensive, because they are unwilling to place themselves in the role of victim (see Brooks & Perot, 1991; Koss, 1990; Williams, 1984). Considerations such as changing definitions of sexual harassment, the nature of the questionnaires themselves, sample selection problems, and other considerations can influence the apparent prevalence of sexual harassment at any point in time. Regardless of these interpretational problems, having even small percentages of women and men workers affected by sexual harassment signifies a serious continuing problem for both employees and organizations.

This chapter reviews the primary streams of sexual harassment research to reveal major scholarly findings about sexual harassment's etiology and effects. The review focuses on definitions for and perceptions of sexual harassment, models for explaining workplace sexual harassment, and research that investigates the responses of and effects on targets of workplace sexual harassment. It concludes with a discussion of two emerging research areas (specifically, same-sex and cross-cultural sexual harassment) as well as some existing areas that should be developed further if this dark side of organizational behavior is to be understood. Because sexual harassment is most often experienced by women targets, with men being the perpetrators, targets will be assumed to be women and perpetrators men unless otherwise noted.

What Is Workplace Sexual Harassment?

We may all agree that sexual harassment is about sex-related behavior that is in some way inappropriately connected to the workplace, but beyond that, definitions of the sexual harassment construct vary (Keyton, 1996; Legnick-Hall, 1995). The legal definition emphasizes that the behavior must be unwelcome and must be sufficient to alter the work environment, but more particularized injuries (such as economic or psychological harms) need not occur. It emphasizes the strong role that causation must play—only behaviors that evidence differential treatment because of sex can rise to the level of actionable sexual harassment. And it is insufficient for the complaining target to perceive the offensive behaviors as sexually harassing; she must convince the court that a reasonable person (or perhaps a reasonable person in her situation; Juliano & Schwab, 2001) would also find such behaviors to be sexually harassing. Thus, the legal definition of sexual harassment has an objective component (reasonableness) that goes beyond the target's own subjective experience of the behaviors. Some organizational studies have relied on the legal definition of sexual harassment (for example, Wiener & Hurt, 2000).

In contrast, a psychological definition of sexual harassment may differ considerably, focusing on the target's own actual experience of the situation. For example, Fitzgerald, Swan, and Magley (1997) define sexual harassment as "an unwanted sex-related behavior at work that is appraised by the recipient as offensive, exceeding her resources or threatening her well-being" (p. 20). More simply, Schneider, Swan, and Fitzgerald (1997), making clear their view that sexual harassment is a workplace stressor, define sexual harassment as a "workplace event that, by definition, is appraised by the recipient as stressful" (p. 403). A target's own appraisal is central to these definitions, thereby requiring that targets interpret the behaviors, make attributions about the purpose of the behaviors, and acknowledge their own experience of the behaviors in order to determine whether the behaviors constitute sexual harassment.

Obviously, targets' perceptions are essential for measuring the prevalence of sexual harassment, but they are also needed for understanding how targets experience sexual harassment, how they respond to it, and how organizational factors can be important in promoting or attenuating sexually harassing behaviors. Early attempts to identify whether targets considered their own experiences to be sexual harassment provided no guidance to subjects regarding a definition and used single-item measures (for example, Have you ever been sexually harassed?). Today, the measurement of sexual harassment experiences often relies on the self-report inventory known as the Sexual Experiences Questionnaire (SEQ) developed by Fitzgerald and colleagues (Fitzgerald, Gelfand, & Drasgow, 1995; Fitzgerald & Hesson-McInnis, 1989). This scale is a behavioral assessment instrument requiring participants to report unwanted sex-related behaviors, even if they do not consider them to be sexual harassment. The last item on the scale asks directly about sexual harassment. The scale identifies three types of harassing behaviors: gender harassment (ranging from insulting remarks to threats), unwanted sexual attention (ranging from seductive behavior to sexual assault), and sexual coercion (ranging from soliciting sex through a promise of rewards to explicit threats).

Many attempts at assessing perceptions of sexual harassment do not rely on a woman's own experiences but instead are based on laboratory studies, where written vignettes are presented (Cartar,

Hicks, & Slane, 1996; Dougherty, Turban, Olson, Dwyer, & LaPreze, 1996; Sheffey & Tindale, 1992). These vignettes ask lab participants whether they would consider the behaviors described in each vignette to be sexually harassing (or, sometimes, offensive or inappropriate in addition to being labeled as sexual harassment). Although this approach to understanding targets' perceptions of sexual harassment is common, vignettes tend to be devoid of much contextual detail, making targets' assessments somewhat difficult and ungeneralizable (Frazier, Cochran, & Olson, 1995).

The use of vignettes supports experiential findings that targets are not always willing to label behaviors they consider sexually inappropriate as sexual harassment (Barak, Fisher, & Houston, 1992; Gutek, 1985; Magley, Hulin, Fitzgerald, & DeNardo, 1999). Only the more severe, frequent, or upsetting behaviors are typically labeled as sexual harassment (Ellis, Barak, & Pinto, 1991; Hurt, Maver, & Hofman, 1999; Jones & Remland, 1992; Stockdale & Vaux, 1993; Stockdale, Vaux, & Cashin, 1995; Wilkerson, 1999). Physical behaviors are typically more likely to be perceived as sexual harassment than are verbal behaviors (Dougherty et al., 1996; Popovich, Gehlauf, Jolton, Somers, & Godinho, 1992). The relative status of the harasser (Dougherty et al., 1996; Stockdale et al., 1995), the types of jobs the target and harasser hold (Sheffey & Tindale, 1992), the amount of prior socializing between the target and the harasser (Dougherty et al., 1996), and the accounts or explanations provided for the harassment are examples of contextual factors that influence perceptions of sexual harassment. Individual-difference variables also have been found to play a role in predicting perceptions of sexual harassment. Targets with more negative attitudes toward sexual harassment may be more likely to label their own unwelcome, sex-related experiences as sexual harassment (Bergman, Langhout, Palmieri, Cortina, & Fitzgerald, 2002), as will targets holding less traditional sex-role attitudes (Foulis & McCabe, 1997; Welsh, 1999) or having more sensitivity to sexist issues (Hemmasi, Graf, & Russ, 1994).

By far, however, the greatest amount of research on factors associated with perceptions of sexual harassment has focused on the role of gender, but with equivocal results. It was generally expected that women would perceive more behaviors as sexually harassing, and such has been the case in a variety of studies

(Blakely, Blakely, & Moorman, 1995; Cartar et al., 1996; Gutek, Cohen, & Konrad, 1990; Hemmasi, Graf, & Russ, 1994; Hurt, Maver, & Hofman, 1999; Popovich et al., 1996; Tata, 2000; Wiener & Hurt, 2000). A variety of moderators has been shown to influence the relationship between gender and perceptions of sexual harassment: for example, target attractiveness (women subjects perceive more sexual harassment than do men when the hypothetical target is attractive; Cartar et al., 1996; Popovich et al., 1996), sexual humor (women subjects perceive more sexual harassment than do men when the hypothetical supervisor engages in sexual humor; Hemmasi et al., 1994), and ambiguous behavior (women subjects perceive more sexual harassment than do men when the behavior in a vignette is more ambiguous, particularly when the women were formerly targets of sexual harassment; Blakely et al., 1995). Other studies have not found gender effects (Dougherty et al., 1996), and meta-analyses have demonstrated only slight effects for gender, at best (Blumenthal, 1998; Rotundo, Nguyen, & Sackett, 2001). Thus, even the role that gender plays in identifying sexual harassment is unclear.

How Do We Explain the Occurrence of Sexual Harassment?

A variety of models have been developed to explain why sexual harassment occurs. Some receive more support than others.

Traditional Approaches

A *biological* or *sexuality-based model*, one of the earliest explanations for sexual harassment, suggests that sexual harassment is a "natural" result of sexual attraction between heterosexual men and women that is carried over into the workplace (Studd & Gattiker, 1991). Men are considered more likely to be sexual harassers ostensibly because of their greater sex drives (Kinsey, Pomeroy, & Martin, 1948). In other words, heterosexuality would be the primary predictor of sexual harassment. One version of this model is presented by the contact hypothesis, which suggests that sexual harassment is likely to occur when men and women engage in work-related contact (Gutek, Cohen, & Konrad, 1990). The role of the workplace is that of facilitating contact by arranging the amount of interaction between men and women. Gutek, Cohen, and Konrad (1990) found support for the idea that increased contact with the opposite sex at work created a more sexualized work environment and led to more reporting of sexual harassment. However, this sexuality-based model would predict that the sexually harassing behaviors should resemble courtship behaviors designed to entice women. Even early studies such as that conducted by the U.S. Merit System Protection Board (1981) have not supported this prediction (Tangri, Burt, & Johnson, 1982).

Organizational models look at organizational factors that contribute to sex-related behaviors in the workplace. Sex-role spillover theory (Gutek & Morasch, 1982) would be an example of an organizational model, whereby sex-based behavioral expectations are carried over into the workplace so that sexual harassment is linked to the nature of the job or occupation. Traditional gender roles could provide these sex-based expectations; for example, women could be expected to be dependent and nurturing or could even be viewed as sex objects. Gutek and Morasch (1982) found that women working in male-dominated jobs reported more sexual harassment than women working in female-dominated jobs, for example. Organizational climate, occupational norms, and factors such as sex ratios on the job are all examples of organizational variables that have been demonstrated to contribute to sexual harassment under this class of models (Fitzgerald, Hulin, & Drasgow, 1994; Gutek & Morasch, 1982) due to their effect on the role expectations and power distribution within the organization. This class of models has received mixed support (Gutek, 1985; Gutek & Morasch, 1982; Tangri et al., 1982).

Gender- or *power-based models* suggest that a patriarchal social system leads to sexual harassment in a way that perpetuates the economic and political dominance of men over women (Hemming, 1985; Tangri et al., 1982). These models view sexual harassment as resulting from societal or cultural power and would suggest that it could best be predicted from a nuanced consideration of gender. Gender- or power-based models have also received mixed support in the literature (Fain & Anderton, 1987; Fitzgerald, Drasgow, Hulin, Gelfand, & Magley, 1997; Gutek & Morasch, 1982; Tangri et al., 1982; Wasti et al., 2000).

These early models do not provide much focus on the harasser, thus yielding little insight into perpetrators' rationales for engaging in sexual harassment. A recent trend has been to focus on the harasser—his personality characteristics or motives that may lead him to engage in sexual harassment. Such models may be categorized as (1) those that view the harasser as acting more passively or (2) those that view the harasser as making agentic choices.

Passive Harasser Models

Misperception theory (Stockdale, 1993) suggests that men may tend to approach a woman while misperceiving her behavior, with misperception acting as a moderator variable in a stimulus-response framework. The tendency to misperceive (that is, a trait driving men to misperceive) is viewed as comprising a variety of attitudes and beliefs regarding sex-based behavior. Alternatively, misperception could be a mediator variable in the causal chain leading to sexual harassment. Stockdale (1993) argues that misperception theory can shed new light on the three models described above. For example, the biological model may account for some sexual harassment because of misperceptions of cues regarding a woman's interest. Similarly, the gender-based model may provide macro-level explanations for sexual harassment because a tendency to misperceive may result from pervasive patriarchal norms that promote beliefs about appropriate sexual behavior.

To date, the most comprehensive focus on the harasser's individual characteristics has come from the work of John Pryor and colleagues (Pryor, 1987; Pryor, La Vite, & Stoller, 1993), who focus on the propensity that perpetrators have to sexually harass. This propensity, in conjunction with organizational factors or contexts, may enhance the likelihood of sexual harassment, thereby suggesting a *person × situation* explanation for sexual harassment. The Likelihood to Sexually Harass (LSH) scale was developed by asking male participants to imagine themselves in situations where sexually coercive behaviors toward attractive women could occur without the possibility of being punished. Participants indicated their likelihood of offering job-related opportunities in exchange for sexual favors (that is, a *quid pro quo* model of sexual harassment). The LSH scale has been demonstrated to correlate moderately with other scales involving sexual aggression or hostility, such as men's Likelihood to Rape, Adversarial Sexual Beliefs, Rape Acceptance Myth, Attraction to Sexual Aggression, and Coercive Sexual Fantasy scales (Pryor, Giedd, & Williams, 1995). In addition, Pryor and others found the LSH scale to be related to gender role scales such as the Socially Undesirable Masculinity scale and that the most important situational factor to interact with LSH is organizational culture or norms (Pryor et al., 1995).

Other researchers have found LSH to be a useful predictor of sexual harassment as well (Dall'Ara & Maass, 1999; Perry, Schmidtke, & Kulik, 1998). Women have been found to have lower LSH scores than men, on average, and the distribution of men's and women's scores differ such that men have a greater variance of scores. Perry and coworkers' work suggests that LSH consists of two factors: one involving power (the first factor for women, the second factor for men) and one involving the sexual nature of the situation (the first factor for men, the second factor for women). In other words, women who sexually harass others may rely more on power motives, whereas men's motives may rely more on the sexual attractiveness or desirability of the target. However, the relevance of LSH to most workplace sexual harassment situations is not clear because LSH is based on coercive behaviors, not the type that constitute most actual occurrences of sexual harassment (Juliano & Schwab, 2001). Similar problems exist for another measure of propensity, the Sexual Harassment Proclivity Index (SHPI) (Bingham & Burleson, 1996). This measure is based on participants' placing themselves in the role of a manager wanting to date an employee and assessing their likelihood of using twenty-six date-getting strategies. Again, since the majority of sexually harassing behavior does not appear to involve a desire to date the target, the relevance of this measure to broad-based views of sexual harassment is not clear.

Another example of a relatively passive view of harasser behavior is provided by O'Donohue and his colleagues (O'Hare & O'Donohue, 1998), who have examined a multidimensional model of sexual harassment based on the existence of four preconditions required for sexual harassment to exist: motivation of the harasser, the ability to overcome internal inhibitions, the opportunity to overcome the inhibitors that exist in the external environment, and the ability to overcome resistance by the potential sexual harassment target. This model integrates aspects of all of the preceding models. For example, harasser motivation may be driven by sexual attraction or a need to dominate women. Internal inhibitions could be based on fear of punishment or a fear of being rebuked by the woman. External inhibitions could relate to organizational norms against sexist behavior. Finally, O'Donohue and colleagues argue that victim resistance plays a role in whether or not sexual harassment occurs. This factor of their model suggests that women can reduce or avoid their chances of becoming targets (for example, by exhibiting personal strength). It also implicates organizational factors that might enhance or reduce a target's resistance level, such as the percentage of women in high-status jobs. Evidence suggests that this model is a better predictor of sexual harassment than the sexuality-related, organizational, or gender models discussed earlier (O'Hare & O'Donohue, 1998).

Agentic Harasser Model

O'Leary-Kelly et al. (2000) have provided a different view of sexual harassers by drawing from the aggression literature. They first define sexual harassment as sex-based, work-related "action taken with the expectation of imposing harm on another person or forcing his/her compliance in order to achieve some valued personal goal" (p. 373). This definition shifts the focus away from target perceptions and onto the perpetrator, highlighting individual motivations for engaging in sexually harassing behavior. It is different from O'Donohue's approach, because it actually defines sexual harassment as a function of the perpetrator's expectations and motivations. For this definition, "expectation" refers to the perpetrator's beliefs that the chosen behavior may result in harm to the target. It is thus understood that certain ill-intended behaviors can constitute sexual harassment, even in the absence of the specific target's recognition of the behaviors as offensive, as long as the perpetrator expects them to cause harm. Sexual harassment can also occur, therefore, in the absence of actual negative consequences to a target, as long as the harm was expected by the perpetrator. In prior models, target harm was a requirement of both the legal (for example, altered working environment) and psychological (for example, stress-related outcomes) definitions presented earlier. For a comparison of legal, target perception-oriented, and perpetrator-motivated definitions of sexual harassment, see Table 6.1.

Table 6.1. Characteristics of
Sexual Harassment Across Definitions.

	Legal (Target Focus)	Perceptual (Target Focus)	Motivational (Perpetrator Focus)
Behavior	Unwelcome: subjective and objective	Unwelcome: subjective alone	May be unwelcome to target but need not be
Connection to sex	Causal	Related to sex	Causal
Determination of offensiveness	Subjective and objective	Subjective alone	May be offensive to target but need not be
Level of offensiveness	Sufficiently severe or pervasive	Subjective; a "stressor"	Expected to impose harm on or force compliance from target; need not be perceived as such

Why would a perpetrator engage in sexual harassment under this definition? He might have a goal of punishing the target, for example, or of presenting himself in positive ways within the organization. To achieve this goal, sexually harassing behaviors may be the behaviors of choice. They may be perceived by the perpetrator as most directly leading to the outcomes that the perpetrator desires. For example, organizational norms that normalize sexualized behavior or that minimize the effects of sexual harassment on targets may be more likely to encourage sexual harassment. In addition, individual factors such as a propensity to engage in sexually harassing behaviors (for example, as measured by either the LSH or SHPI measure discussed above) may affect the value of engaging in sexual harassment, particularly in conjunction with a variety of organizational variables (for example, minimization of sanctions).

Unlike most models of sexual harassment, this model specifically recognizes sexual harassment as a dynamic phenomenon, because it specifies that the perpetrator will perceive and interpret the target's perceptions and actions to his earlier behavior, thereby creating the possibility of continued sexual harassment through continued choices that the perpetrator makes (but see Knapp, Faley, Ekeberg, & Dubois [1997] and Glomb, Munson, Hulin, Bergman, & Drasgow [1999] for other dynamic models). The model recognizes target responses as goal-driven as well, therefore providing a theoretical mechanism for understanding target responses to sexual harassment. To date, most work on target responses has been descriptive, seeking to identify typologies of responses and link them to a variety of outcomes for the target.

Target Responses to Sexual Harassment

There are many typologies of target responses to sexual harassment, based on the variety of responses that have been observed in laboratory and field studies. Laboratory studies have employed vignettes to assess either study participants' own anticipated responses (Williams & Cyr, 1992) or their evaluations of responses within the vignettes (Remland & Jones, 1985). Field studies have asked participants to recall incidents in which they were sexually harassed and indicate how they responded (Bingham & Scherer, 1993). In general, studies have been mixed in terms of the frequencies of reported responses, their effectiveness in stopping the harassment, and their outcomes for the targets of harassment.

For example, the early U.S. Merit Systems Protection Board survey (1981) found that women tended to use informal strategies such as making a joke of the harassment (31 percent), avoiding the harasser (48 percent), ignoring the harassment (61 percent), and asking the perpetrator to stop the harassment (48 percent). Few women (13.5 percent) made formal or informal complaints to authorities, and more women sought social support from friends and coworkers than reported the harassment to their supervisor (Livingston, 1982).

More recent studies support these findings. For example, Fitzgerald, Swan, and Fischer (1995) found that more assertive coping strategies are less likely to be used by women than less confrontational ones. Other research supports the notion that many employees prefer to ignore or avoid sexual harassment, but Grauerholz (1989) found that many targets respond by talking to the perpetrator.

In an early effort to categorize the types of responses that women reported, researchers presented unidimensional taxonomies, typically based on assertiveness (Terpstra & Baker, 1989). Gruber (1989) categorized sexual harassment behaviors according to both nature and degree. Her typology involves four categories of behaviors, with nine subcategories ranging from least to most assertive. The first major category, *avoidance,* includes the subcategories of *nonrecognition* (ignoring the perpetrator), *self-removal* (removing oneself from the harassing environment by quitting or transferring), and *obstruction* (using boundaries to avoid contact with the perpetrator). The second category, *diffusion,* includes the subcategories of *masking* (pretending to play along) and *social support* (seeking support from friends, coworkers, or family). The third category, *negotiation,* includes two subcategories: *direct requests* (asking the perpetrator to stop) and *professional mediation* (seeking counseling or legal advice). The most assertive category is *confrontation,* which includes the subcategories of *personal responses* (threatening formal action or other strong behavior) and *power structure* (taking action to make the harassment known formally within the organization). This typology, although somewhat cumbersome, captures the responses that have been observed by other researchers.

More recent typologies have become multidimensional. For example, Knapp et al. (1997) have adopted a typology of coping responses based on two dimensions: focus and mode. The focus of the response may be on either the target herself or the perpetrator, and the mode can be either supported or nonsupported, depending on the amount of outside assistance sought. Wasti and Cortina (2002) summarize these response types as avoidance-denial (self—not supported), confrontation (perpetrator—not supported), social coping (self—supported), and advocacy seeking (perpetrator—supported). Although social coping is a common response strategy, the evidence provided above suggests that avoidance-denial is the most prevalent response to sexual harassment (Fitzgerald, Swan, & Fischer, 1995; Gutek & Koss, 1993). Confrontation may be the least employed coping strategy (Gutek & Koss, 1993), and advocacy seeking tends not to be used as much when the harasser is a supervisor (Bingham & Scherer, 1993).

Outcomes for Targets

It is well established that sexual harassment targets suffer a variety of negative consequences. An early study by Crull (1979) found that women who reported being sexually harassed stated that they also experienced emotional, physical, and job-related negative outcomes. These negative effects need not stem from the harassment alone, however; they may also be related to the types of responses targets employ when they experience sexual harassment. In order to understand better the types of responses in which targets engage, the resulting consequences for targets of various response types must be considered. In other words, target responses may mediate the connection between sexual harassment and ultimate outcomes that women experience. In addition, individual-level variables (for example, personality), behavioral variables (for example, severity of the harassment), and organizational-level variables (organizational support for target) may play an important role in understanding how targets respond to sexual harassment and the effects that it has on them.

Fitzgerald and colleagues have developed such an integrated model of sexual harassment (Fitzgerald, Drasgow, & Magley, 1999; Fitzgerald et al., 1995; Fitzgerald, Swan, & Magley, 1997). A recent study by Bergman, Langhout, Palmieri, Cortina, and Fitzgerald (2002) altered the original model to include formal reporting of sexual harassment as a mediator that could potentially explain stress-related harms. Formal reporting required telling an "organizational authority" about offensive sex-related behaviors (p. 231). They found that reporting did not improve and sometimes worsened health, psychological, and job outcomes. Further, they found that mediators such as organizational responses to the reporting could account for the negative effects that targets experienced. Organizational climate was found to be an important antecedent for determining whether sexual harassment will be reported, even though it did not directly influence reporting. Organizational climate affected key factors such as the frequency of sexual harassment, whether organizations had a dismissive attitude toward reporting, and the likelihood of retaliation against the reporting target, thereby indirectly influencing organizational responses.

The findings of Bergman et al. (2002) support some earlier findings that formal reporting resulted in more physical and psychological problems for women than did other forms of responses (Livingston, 1982). Earlier findings have also found that women who chose to report sexual harassment held lower organizational justice perceptions than women who chose other responses (Adams-Roy & Barling, 1998). These findings are all problematic given that the law provides greater protections for women who report sexual harassment within their organizations than for those who do not (*Burlington Industries* v. *Ellerth,* 1998; *Faragher* v. *City of Boca Raton,* 1998).

Fitzgerald and colleagues (Schneider, Swan, & Fitzgerald, 1997) have also examined the consequences of sexual harassment by considering it to fall along a stress continuum. Thus, sexual harassment may range from a "daily hassle" (that is, routine offensive comments or horseplay) to a major or traumatic life event such as sexual assault. Possible consequences of sexual harassment include organizational withdrawal attitudes and behaviors, negative psychological effects such as reduced life satisfaction and psychological well-being, and job stress. In general, working women who experienced the highest levels of harassment tended to report the worst job-related and psychological outcomes, whereas women who experienced no harassment tended to report the least negative outcomes. Even moderate levels of sexual harassment were associated with negative outcomes for women, however. The majority of women in the study did not label their experiences as sexual harassment, but they still experienced negative outcomes that could be attributed to the behaviors to which they were exposed. In fact, there were no differences in outcomes for women who labeled their experiences as sexual harassment and those who did not. Thus, failure to label behaviors as sexually harassing does not preclude women from suffering negative effects, thereby suggesting costs to organizations even when women may not indicate that they are being sexually harassed.

A study by Stockdale (1998) also examined the relationship between coping responses and job-related consequences for sexual harassment targets (both men and women). She formed two categories of coping responses, the first involving confrontational behaviors such as telling the person to stop or reporting to an authority figure. The second involved passive responses such as going along with the behavior or joking about it. Stockdale found that targets who used confrontational coping strategies experienced deteriorating perceptions of their jobs and coworkers, took more leaves of absence, and were more likely to experience a job change, and that confrontational strategies exacerbated negative consequences, particularly for men, as compared to more passive strategies. These findings are consistent with those of earlier studies (Adams-Roy & Barling, 1998; Hesson-McInnis & Fitgzerald, 1997).

Recent Developments in Sexual Harassment Research

New sexual harassment topics continue to emerge. Of these, two significant ones are same-sex sexual harassment and cross-cultural considerations of sexual harassment, each of which is discussed below. Research needs beyond these two areas are also discussed, but due to space limitations, only a select few are mentioned.

Same-Sex Sexual Harassment

Few studies have examined sexual harassment between persons of the same sex, although the law clearly recognizes such harassment as illegal as long as it is based on sex and not sexual orientation (*Oncale* v. *Sundowner Offshore Services, Inc.,* 1998). A psychological definition of same-sex sexual harassment could broadly include sexual orientation as a basis for sexual harassment, however. One of the biggest problems in studying same-sex sexual harassment is to provide an acceptable definition of such harassment (Paetzold, 1997; Stockdale, Visio, & Batra, 1999).

As has been noted, the SEQ is based exclusively on women's experiences of being harassed by men, and tends to reflect legal definitions of male-female sexual harassment (Berdahl, Magley, & Waldo, 1996). It may not even reflect men's experiences of women-initiated, sex-related behaviors at work, or at least not their attitudes toward them (Cochran, Frazier, & Olson, 1997; Gutek, 1985). Application of the SEQ to same-sex experiences is particularly problematic. Would women who receive negative remarks about women from other women tend to consider them as offensive or harassing? Similarly, would men engaging in horseplay in an organization view any resulting touching from other men as sexually harassing? If so, would it mean the same thing as when women consider touching by men to be sexually harassing? Because most same-sex sexual harassment involves male-to-male harassment (Cochran et al., 1997; Paetzold, 1997; U.S. Merit Systems Protection Board, 1981), that situation is considered most often.

For example, Waldo, Berdahl, and Fitzgerald (1998) have examined the nature of men's experiences with other men (and women) and whether those experiences are considered to be sexual harassment (using a psychological definition). They relied on the Sexual Harassment of Men (SHOM) scale to measure experiences of sexually harassing behaviors; this scale was designed by altering the SEQ to make items applicable to men. The "gender harassment" category was divided into three subscales: lewd comments, enforcement of traditional male gender roles, and negative gender-related comments about men. In general, few men experienced either sexual coercion or unwanted sexual attention, but approximately 40 percent of men experienced lewd comments, somewhat fewer experienced negative comments about men, and even fewer experienced enforcement of traditional masculine roles. Further, approximately 50 percent of the male participants indicated that their perpetrators had been male alone, as opposed to being either female or mixed (women and men both). It was unclear whether the experiences should be considered sexual harassment (from a psychological perspective), however, because the participants found most of the behaviors to be only "slightly upsetting" (p. 74).

Clearly, more work is needed to examine the behaviors, target perceptions, perpetrator motivations, and overall dynamics of the same-sex sexual harassment phenomenon. Because target perceptions can be problematic in same-sex cases, it may be particularly important to look at same-sex sexual harassment from a harasser-oriented perspective to understand motives and behavioral choices. The aggression literature, which has examined male same-sex relationships, may be useful to our understanding of this phenomenon (e.g., Regan, Bartholomew, Oram, & Landolt, 2002).

Cross-Cultural Issues in Sexual Harassment Research

Most studies of sexual harassment have focused on American women and men, subject to American laws and perspectives. Is it possible that sexual harassment is purely an American phenomenon? To date, little research has examined the cross-cultural meaning of sexual harassment (but see, for example, Chan, Tang, & Chan, 1999; Gelfand, Fitzgerald, & Drasgow, 1995; Menon & Kanekar, 1992; Pryor et al., 1997).

One recent study by Wasti and Cortina (2002) examined coping responses of targets in relation to cultural or national differences by studying Turkish, Hispanic American, and Anglo American working women. They found evidence that the typology of Knapp et al. (1997) regarding coping strategies transcended cultural boundaries. In addition, they found that Turkish and Hispanic women engaged in avoidance more than did Anglos; Hispanic women also engaged in denial more than other groups. If, in fact, the Turkish and Hispanic women can be believed to be more collectivist in nature than Anglos (this was assumed but not measured), these findings would be consistent with the notion that collectivist cultures tend to avoid conflict and maintain harmony in interpersonal relationships (Wasti & Cortina, 2002). However, there was no evidence of increased use of social coping among the "collectivist" groups, which may suggest that the outcomes are more related to considerations other than collectivism. For example, the Hispanic women were Americans and may have adopted American values through socialization. The Turkish women were professionals, most of whom had completed at least one year of college (location unknown). Their improved socioeconomic and educational statuses may have rendered them less collectivist in nature than working-class Turkish women would have been.

Cross-cultural research generally raises many difficult problems (Triandis, 1994), and these problems can be particularly important in the sexual harassment arena. Clarifying the meaning of sexual harassment, developing instruments that are content valid, recognizing differences in organizational settings and work arrangements, and interpreting behaviors in differing socio-legal contexts are just some of the difficulties cross-cultural researchers face. Nonetheless, more cross-cultural research is needed for us to understand and situate the sexual harassment construct.

Other Research Areas

In addition to the research issues described throughout the chapter, there are research questions that have remained virtually untouched. For example, little has been done to assess the longitudinal effects of sexual harassment on targets (but see Glomb et al., 1999; Munson, Hulin, & Drasgow, 2000). Cross-sectional studies do not provide much insight into the ultimate job- and health-related consequences of sexual harassment. Longitudinal research conducted in field settings would allow for interpretation of those consequences in relation to outcomes for individuals who are not sexually harassed or who experience background or ambient sexual harassment (Glomb et al., 1997). The efficacy of organizational procedures for handling sexual harassment could also be assessed longitudinally.

Dynamic empirical approaches to the study of sexual harassment are also needed. If target responses can be viewed as generating additional actions by the perpetrator, a better understanding of how sexual harassment unfolds over time—how behaviors become frequent or escalate in severity—can also be obtained. Interconnections among the models and approaches to sexual harassment may be explored via dynamic empirical approaches. For example, the biological approach may lead some men to misperceive women's behavior, particularly if the men have certain predispositions or are exposed to particular organizational factors. Organizational factors may also lead these men to act on their misperceptions. The target may perceive these actions as sexual harassment and rebuff the harasser (either directly or indirectly). At some point after being rebuffed, the harasser may engage in additional, escalating forms of sexual harassment, perhaps in accordance with the aggression model.

The aggression approach to sexual harassment also is in need of empirical study if we are to gain information about sexual harassers. For example, based on the framework of O'Leary-Kelly et al. (2000), studies are needed to provide information about goals, attributions, and behavioral hierarchies of "potential harassers." In fact, ways to measure sexual harassment must be developed if the definitions used by researchers change. In the model of O'Leary-Kelly et al., for example, sexual harassment must be measured from the perspective of the actor's likelihood of engaging in harassing behaviors to achieve specific goals. Automatic cognitions and behaviors may also be relevant to the aggression approach and should be studied empirically.

The relatively new area of same-sex sexual harassment brings with it opportunities for further study. One interesting research question could be based on the role that the gender of the harasser plays in differentiating same-sex from different-sex sexual harassment. Some sexually harassing situations could be "strong situations," such that the behaviors would be equally sexually harassing to targets regardless of whether they are exhibited by men or women. The behaviors themselves, the relationship between the target and harasser, or certain organizational or other power arrangements could lead to these strong situations. Consequences for targets may or may not be similar in these situations. For other situations, the gender of the perpetrator would be critical in determining the reaction of the target, so that same-sex and different-sex sexual harassment result from different scenarios and may have different consequences for targets.

Also, the legal view of same-sex sexual harassment has excluded male horseplay from the definition of sexual harassment (*Oncale* v. *Sundowner Offshore Services, Inc.,* 1998). Psychologically based definitions of sexual harassment need to examine what behaviors men consider to be "horseplay," when they are transformed into perceived sexual harassment, and the role that various types of touching play in that transformation. Touching may be central to perceptions of same-sex sexual harassment for men because of concerns about homosexuality (which are often raised in legal cases). In addition, the relevance of the various models for same-sex sexual harassment needs to be explored. The models were all developed within a different-sex framework, so their applicability to same-sex conditions should not be assumed.

New theorizing about sexual harassment would be welcome. Existing theories represent different research purposes, but movement toward a theoretically integrated model of sexual harassment would be useful. Sexual harassment is simultaneously a form of illegal discrimination, a workplace stressor for targets, a chosen behavioral form for perpetrators, and a problem for organizations. Continued attempts at merging these different sides of sexual harassment into a coherent theory would be useful. In addition, empirical sexual harassment research to date has focused on organizational and situational factors that lead to sexual harassment and enhance negative effects for targets. Individual difference variables have been downplayed in theoretical and empirical research, perhaps because they are believed to be outside the influence of the organization. However, they may play a bigger role than contextual variables in determining when sex-related behaviors occur and when targets will consider them to be offensive or sexually harassing. Both theoretical and empirical studies of individual differences, particularly with regard to harassers, would be of use in understanding sexual harassment.

Recent research suggests that sexual harassment may be viewed within a framework of individual and organizational ethics (Bowes-Sperry & Powell, 1999; O'Leary-Kelly & Bowes-Sperry, 2001). Not only does this approach allow for the study of harassment as a form of ethical breach, it also permits consideration of observer behavior as driven by moral considerations (O'Leary-Kelly, Tiedt, & Bowes-Sperry, in press). Further study within this framework could provide insights into the role of coworkers in helping to stop the harassment. For example, coworkers could choose to get involved in ways that directly protect the target, sanction the harasser, or make the organization aware of the unethical conduct.

Conclusion

Sexual harassment research has provided insights into a variety of aspects of the phenomenon: how it is perceived, how targets respond to it, what the consequences for targets are, and how organizations affect perceptions, responses, and consequences for targets. The research has begun to address same-sex sexual harassment and cross-cultural meanings of sexual harassment, as well as other topics not described here (such as harassment by parties "outside" of the organization, such as customers). However, greater insights into this dark side of organizational behavior require that the research addresses sexual harassment from the perspective of the harasser. Why does the harasser choose to harass? How does he or she select targets? What efforts are needed to stop the harasser? Can harassers be trained not to harass? Empirical investigation into these issues should be a focus of future research so that a more comprehensive view of sexual harassment can begin to unfold.

References

Adams-Roy, J., & Barling, J. (1998). Predicting the decision to confront or report sexual harassment. *Journal of Organizational Behavior*, 19, 329–336.

Arvey, R. D., & Cavanaugh, M. A. (1995). Using surveys to assess the prevalence of sexual harassment: Some methodological problems. *Journal of Social Issues*, 51, 39–52.

Barak, A., Fisher, W. A., & Houston, S. (1992). Individual difference correlates of the experience of sexual harassment among female university students. *Journal of Applied Social Psychology*, 22, 17–37.

Berdahl, J., Magley, V., & Waldo, C. (1996). The sexual harassment of men? Exploring the concept with theory and data. *Psychology of Women Quarterly*, 20, 524–547.

Bergman, M. E., Langhout, R. D., Palmieri, P. A., Cortina, L. M., & Fitzgerald, L. F. (2002). The (un)reasonableness of reporting: Antecedents and consequences of reporting sexual harassment. *Journal of Applied Psychology*, 87, 230–242.

Bingham, S. G., & Burleson, B. R. (1996). The development of a sexual harassment proclivity scale: Construct validation and relationship to communication competence. *Communication Quarterly*, 44, 308–325.

Bingham, S. G., & Scherer, L. L. (1993). Factors associated with responses to sexual harassment and satisfaction with outcome. *Sex Roles*, 29, 239–269.

Blakely, G. L., Blakely, E. H., & Moorman, R. H. (1995). The relationship between gender, personal experience, and perceptions of sexual harassment in the workplace. *Employee Responsibilities and Rights Journal*, 8, 263–274.

Blumenthal, J. A. (1998). The reasonable woman standard: A meta-analytic review of gender differences in perceptions of sexual harassment. *Law and Human Behavior*, 22, 33–57.

Bowes-Sperry, L., & Powell, G. N. (1999). Observers' reactions to social-sexual behavior at work: An ethical decision making perspective. *Journal of Management*, 25, 779-802.

Brooks, L., & Perot, A. R. (1991). Reporting sexual harassment: Exploring a predictive model. *Psychology of Women Quarterly*, 15, 31–57.

Bureau of National Affairs (2001, February 8). Sexual harassment: Survey finds one-fifth of women report experiencing sexual harassment at work. *Daily Labor Report*, 27 DLR A-5.

Burlington Industries v. *Ellerth*, 524 U.S. 742 (1998).

Cartar, L., Hicks, M., & Slane, S. (1996). Women's reactions to hypothetical male sexual touch as a function of initiator attractiveness and level of coercion. *Sex Roles*, 35, 737–750.

Chan, D.K.-S., Tang, C. S.-K., & Chan, W. (1999). Sexual harassment: A preliminary analysis of its effects on Hong Kong Chinese women in the workplace and academia. *Psychology of Women Quarterly*, 23, 661–672.

Cochran, C. C., Frazier, P. A., & Olson, A. M. (1997). Predictors of responses to unwanted sexual attention. *Psychology of Women Quarterly*, 21, 207–226.

Crull, P. (1979). The impact of sexual harassment on the job: A profile of the experiences of 92 women. In D. Neugarten & J. Shafritz (Eds.), *Sexuality in organizations: Romantic and coercive behaviors at work* (pp. 67–71). Oak Park, IL: Moore.

Dall'Ara, E., & Maass, A. (1999). Studying sexual harassment in the laboratory: Are egalitarian women at higher risk. *Sex Roles*, 41, 681–704.

Dougherty, T. W., Turban, D. B., Olson, D. E., Dwyer, P. D., & LaPreze, M. W. (1996). Factors affecting perceptions of workplace sexual harassment. *Journal of Organizational Behavior*, 17, 489–501.

Ellis, S., Barak, A., & Pinto, A. (1991). Moderating effects of personal cognitions on experienced and perceived sexual harassment of women at the workplace. *Journal of Applied Psychology*, 21, 1320–1337.

Fain, T. C., & Anderton, D. L. (1987). Sexual harassment: Organizational context and diffuse status. *Sex Roles*, 17, 291–311.

Faragher v. *City of Boca Raton*, 524 U.S. 775 (1998).

Fitzgerald, L. F. (1993). Sexual harassment: Violence against women in the workplace. *American Psychologist*, 48, 1070–1076.

Fitzgerald, L. F., & Hesson-McInnis, M. (1989). The dimensions of sexual harassment: A structural analysis. *Journal of Vocational Behavior*, 35, 309–326.

Fitzgerald, L. F., Drasgow, F., & Magley V. J. (1999). Sexual harassment in the armed forces: A test of an integrated model. *Military Psychology*, 11, 329–343.

Fitzgerald, L. F., Gelfand, M. J., & Drasgow, F. (1995). Measuring sexual harassment: Theoretical and psychometric advances. *Basic and Applied Social Psychology*, 17, 425–445.

Fitzgerald, L. F., Hulin, C. L., & Drasgow, F. (1994). The antecedents and consequences of sexual harassment in organizations: An integrated model. In G. Keita & J. Hurrell (Eds.), *Job stress in a changing workforce: Investigating gender, diversity, and family issues* (pp. 55–74). Washington, D.C.: American Psychological Association.

Fitzgerald, L. F., Swan, S., & Fischer, K. (1995). Why didn't she just report him? The psychological and legal implications of women's responses to sexual harassment. *Journal of Social Issues, 51,* 117–138.

Fitzgerald, L. F., Swan, S., & Magley, V. J. (1997). But was it really sexual harassment? Legal, behavioral, and psychological definitions of the workplace victimization of women. In W. O'Donohue (Ed.), *Sexual harassment: Theory, research, and treatment* (pp. 5–28). Boston: Allyn & Bacon.

Fitzgerald, L. F., Drasgow, F., Hulin, C. L., Gelfand, M. J., & Magley, V. J. (1997). The antecedents and consequences of sexual harassment in organizations: A test of an integrated model. *Journal of Applied Psychology, 82,* 578–589.

Foulis, D., & McCabe, M. P. (1997). Sexual harassment: Factors affecting attitudes and perceptions. *Sex Roles, 37,* 773–798.

Frazier, P. A., Cochran, C. C., & Olson, A. M. (1995). Social science research on lay definitions of sexual harassment. *Journal of Social Issues, 51,* 21–37.

Gelfand, M. J., Fitzgerald, L. F., & Drasgow, F. (1995). The structure of sexual harassment: A confirmatory analysis across cultures and settings. *Journal of Vocational Behavior, 47,* 164–177.

Glomb, T. M., Munson, L. J., Hulin, C. L., Bergman, M. E., & Drasgow, F. (1999). Structural equation models of sexual harassment: Longitudinal explorations and cross-sectional generalizations. *Journal of Applied Psychology, 84,* 14–28.

Glomb, T. M., Richman, W. L., Hulin, C. L., Drasgow, F., Schneider, K. T., & Fitzgerald, L. F. (1997). Ambient sexual harassment: An integrated model of antecedents and consequences. *Organizational Behavior and Human Decision Processes, 71,* 309–328.

Grauerholz, E. (1989). Sexual harassment of women professors by students: Exploring the dynamics of power, authority, and gender in a university setting. *Sex Roles, 21,* 789–801.

Gruber, J. E. (1989). How women handle sexual harassment: A literature review. *Sociology and Social Research, 74,* 3–9.

Gruber, J. E. (1990). Methodological problems and policy implications in sexual harassment research. *Population Research and Policy Review, 9,* 235–254.

Gutek, B. A. (1985). *Sex and the workplace: The impact of sexual behavior and harassment on women, men, and organizations.* San Francisco: Jossey-Bass.

Gutek, B. A., & Koss, M. P. (1993). Changed women and changed organizations: Consequences and coping with sexual harassment. *Journal of Vocational Behavior,* 42, 28–48.

Gutek, B. A., & Morasch, B. (1982). Sex-ratios, sex-role spillover, and sexual harassment of women at work. *Journal of Social Issues,* 38, 55–74.

Gutek, B. A., Cohen, A. G., & Konrad, A. M. (1990). Predicting social-sexual behavior at work: A contact hypothesis. *Academy of Management Journal,* 33, 560–577.

Hemmasi, M., Graf, L. A., & Russ, G. (1994). Gender-related jokes in the workplace: Sexual humor or sexual harassment? *Journal of Applied Social Psychology,* 24, 1114–1128.

Hemming, H. (1985). Women in a man's world: Sexual harassment. *Human Relations,* 38, 67–79.

Hesson-McInnis, M. S., & Fitzgerald, L. F. (1997). Sexual harassment: A preliminary test of an integrated model. *Journal of Applied Social Psychology,* 27, 877–901.

Hurt, J. L., Maver, J. A., & Hofman, D. (1999). Situational and individual influences on judgments of hostile environment sexual harassment. *Journal of Applied Social Psychology,* 29, 1395–1415.

Jones, T. S., & Remland, M. S. (1992). Sources of variability in perceptions of and responses to sexual harassment. *Sex Roles,* 27, 121–142.

Juliano, A., & Schwab, S. J. (2001). The sweep of sexual harassment cases. *Cornell Law Review,* 86, 548–602.

Keyton, J. (1996). Sexual harassment: A multidisciplinary synthesis and critique. In B. R. Burleson (Ed.), *Communication yearbook* (Vol. 19, pp. 92–155). Thousand Oaks, CA: Sage.

Kinsey, A. C., Pomeroy, W. B., & Martin, C. E. (1948). *Sexual behavior in the human male.* Philadelphia: Saunders.

Knapp, D. E., Faley, R. H., Ekeberg, S. E., & Dubois, C.L.Z. (1997). Determinants of target responses to sexual harassment: A conceptual framework. *Academy of Management Review,* 22, 687–729.

Koss, M. P. (1990). Changed lives: The psychological impact of sexual harassment. In M. A. Paludi (Ed.), *Ivory power: Sexual harassment on campus* (pp. 73–92). Albany: State University of New York Press.

Legnick-Hall, M. L. (1995). Sexual harassment research: A methodological critique. *Personnel Psychology,* 48, 841–864.

Livingston, J. A. (1982). Responses to sexual harassment on the job: Legal, organizational, and individual actions. *Journal of Social Issues,* 38, 5–22.

Magley, V. J., Hulin, C. L., Fitzgerald, L. F., & DeNardo, M. (1999). Outcomes of self-labeling sexual harassment. *Journal of Applied Psychology*, 84, 390–402.

Menon, S. A., & Kanekar, S. (1992). Attitudes toward sexual harassment of women in India. *Journal of Applied Social Psychology*, 22, 1940–1952.

Munson, L. J., Hulin, C., & Drasgow, F. (2000). Longitudinal analysis of dispositional influences and sexual harassment: Effects on job and psychological outcomes. *Personnel Psychology*, 53, 21–46.

O'Hare, E. A., & O'Donohue, W. (1998). Sexual harassment: Identifying risk factors. *Archives of Sexual Behavior*, 27, 561–580.

O'Leary-Kelly, A., & Bowes-Sperry, L. (2001). Sexual harassment as unethical behavior: The role of moral intensity. *Human Resource Management Review*, 11, 73–92.

O'Leary-Kelly, A., Paetzold, R. L., & Griffin, R. W. (2000). Sexual harassment as aggressive behavior: An actor-based perspective. *Academy of Management Review*, 25, 372–388.

O'Leary-Kelly, A., Tiedt, P., & Bowes-Sperry, L. (in press). Answering accountability questions in sexual harassment: Insights regarding harassers, targets, and observers. *Human Resource Management Review*.

Oncale v. *Sundowner Offshore Services, Inc.*, 118 S.Ct. 998 (1998).

Paetzold, R. L. (1997). Same-sex sexual harassment: Can it be sex-related for purposes of Title VII? *Employee Rights and Employment Policy Journal*, 1, 25–62.

Perry, E. L., Schmidtke, J. M., & Kulik, C. T. (1998). Propensity to sexually harass: An exploration of gender differences. *Sex Roles*, 38, 443–460.

Popovich, P. M., Gehlauf, D. N., Jolton, J. A., Everton, W. J., Godinho, R. M., Mastrangelo, P. M., & Somers, J. M. (1996). Physical attractiveness and sexual harassment: Does every picture tell a story or every story draw a picture? *Journal of Applied Social Psychology*, 26, 520–542.

Popovich, P. M., Gehlauf, D. N., Jolton, J. A., Somers, J. M., & Godinho, R. M. (1992). Perceptions of sexual harassment as a function of sex of rater and incident form and consequence. *Sex Roles*, 27, 609–625.

Pryor, J. B. (1987). Sexual harassment proclivities in men. *Sex Roles*, 17, 269–290.

Pryor, J. B., DeSouza, E. R., Fitness, J., Hutz, C., Kumpf, M., Lubbert, K., Pesonen, O., Erber, M. W. (1997). Gender differences in the interpretation of social-sexual behavior. *Journal of Cross-Cultural Psychology*, 28, 509–534.

Pryor, J. B., Giedd, J. L., & Williams, K. B. (1995). A social psychological model for predicting sexual harassment. *Journal of Social Issues*, 51, 69–84.

Pryor, J. B., LaVite, C. M., & Stoller, L. M. (1993). A social psychological analysis of sexual harassment: The person/situation action. *Journal of Vocational Behavior,* 42, 68–83.

Regan, K. V., Bartholomew, K., Oram, D., & Landolt, M. A. (2002). Measuring physical violence in male same-sex relationships: An item response theory analysis of the Conflicts Tactics Scales. *Journal of Interpersonal Violence,* 17, 235–252.

Remland, M. R., & Jones, T. S. (1985). Sex differences, communication consistency, and judgments of sexual harassment in a performance appraisal interview. *Southern Speech Communication Journal,* 50, 156–176.

Rotundo, M., Nguyen, D.-H., & Sackett, P.R. (2001). A meta-analytic review of gender differences in perceptions of sexual harassment. *Journal of Applied Psychology,* 86, 914–922.

Schneider, K. T., Swan, S., & Fitzgerald, L. F. (1997). Job-related and psychological effects of sexual harassment in the workplace: Empirical evidence from two organizations. *Journal of Applied Psychology,* 82, 401–415.

Sheffey, S., & Tindale, R. S. (1992). Perceptions of sexual harassment in the workplace. *Journal of Applied Social Psychology,* 22, 1502–1520.

Stockdale, M. S. (1993). The role of sexual misperceptions of women's friendliness in an emerging theory of sexual harassment. *Journal of Vocational Behavior,* 42, 84–101.

Stockdale, M. S. (1998). The direct and moderating influences of sexual harassment pervasiveness, coping strategies, and gender on work-related outcomes. *Psychology of Women Quarterly,* 22, 521–535.

Stockdale, M. S., & Vaux, A. (1993). What sexual harassment experiences lead respondents to acknowledge being sexually harassed? A secondary analysis of a university survey. *Journal of Vocational Behavior,* 43, 221–234.

Stockdale, M. S., Vaux, A., & Cashin, J. (1995). Acknowledging sexual harassment: A test of alternative models. *Basic and Applied Social Psychology,* 17, 469–496.

Stockdale, M. S., Visio, M., & Batra, L. (1999). The sexual harassment of men: Evidence for a broader theory of sexual harassment and sex discrimination. *Psychology, Public Policy, and Law,* 5, 630–664.

Studd, M. V., & Gattiker, U. E. (1991). The evolutionary psychology of sexual harassment in organizations. *Etiology and Sociobiology,* 12, 249–290.

Tangri, S. S., Burt, M. R., & Johnson, L. B. (1982). Sexual harassment at work: Three explanatory models. *Journal of Social Issues,* 38, 33–54.

Tata, J. (2000). She said, he said. The influence of remedial accounts on third-party judgments of coworker sexual harassment. *Journal of Management*, 26, 1133–1156.

Terpstra, D. E., & Baker, D. D. (1989). The identification and classification of reactions to sexual harassment. *Journal of Organizational Behavior*, 10, 1–14.

Triandis, H. C. (1994). Cross-cultural industrial and organizational psychology. In H. C. Triandis, M. Dunnette, & L. Hough (Eds.), *Handbook of industrial and organizational psychology* (Vol. 4, 2nd ed., pp. 103–172). Palo Alto, CA: Consulting Psychologists Press.

U.S. Merit Systems Protection Board (1981). *Sexual harassment in the federal workplace: Is it a problem?* Washington, D.C.: U.S. Government Printing Office.

U.S. Merit Systems Protection Board (1987). *Sexual harassment in the federal government: An update.* Washington, D.C.: U.S. Government Printing Office.

Waldo, C. R., Berdahl,, J. L., & Fitzgerald, L. F. (1998). Are men sexually harassed? If so, by whom? *Law and Human Behavior*, 22, 59–79.

Wasti, S. A., & Cortina, L. M. (2002). Coping in context: Sociocultural determinants of responses to sexual harassment. *Journal of Personality and Social Psychology*, 83, 394–405.

Wasti, S. A., Bergman, M. E., Glomb, T. M., & Drasgow, F. (2000). Test of the cross-cultural generalizability of a model of sexual harassment. *Journal of Applied Psychology*, 85, 766–778.

Welsh, S. (1999). Gender and sexual harassment. *Annual Review of Sociology*, 25, 169–190.

Wiener, R. L., & Hurt, L. E. (2000). How do people evaluate social sexual conduct at work? A psycholegal model. *Journal of Applied Psychology*, 85, 75–85.

Wilkerson, J. M. (1999). The impact of job level and prior training on sexual harassment labeling and remedy choice. *Journal of Applied Social Psychology*, 29, 1605–1623.

Williams, L. S. (1984). The classic rape: When do victims report? *Social Problems*, 31, 459–467.

Williams, K. B., & Cyr, R. R. (1992). Escalating commitment to a relationship: The sexual harassment trap. *Sex Roles*, 27, 47–72.

CHAPTER 7

Out of the Closet and Out of a Job? The Nature, Import, and Causes of Sexual Orientation Discrimination in the Workplace

Elizabeth Ann Deitch, Rebecca M. Butz, Arthur P. Brief

Abstract: Despite an increasing focus on diversity in recent decades, organizational researchers have largely ignored the experiences of lesbian, gay, and bisexual (LGB) employees. This chapter is intended to draw attention to the problem of sexual orientation discrimination in the workplace, and to encourage researchers to turn their efforts toward the study of this neglected employee population. The chapter begins with a discussion of the issues that make LGB employees a unique population for study, including the nonvisible nature of sexual orientation, the lack of federal civil rights legislation banning sexual orientation discrimination, and the general social acceptability of antipathy toward gay men and lesbians. Then, existing research regarding the incidence of sexual orientation discrimination, its antecedents, and its outcomes is reviewed. Following this review, numerous suggestions for directing future research on the issues facing lesbian, gay, and bisexual employees are advanced.

Douglas Retterer suffered constant harassment at his job, being routinely called "fag" and "queer" by his coworkers, and asked questions like, "How's your AIDS?" Two of his supervisors would frequently call him into their office over the intercom and, with coworkers watching, the supervisors would physically restrain him while prodding him with their fingers, simulating sex. After Retterer became so distraught he began having panic attacks, he filed suit against the firm, but the Ohio appeals court ruled that there is no remedy available for sexual orientation harassment under either state or federal law (Human Rights Campaign [HRC], 2001a).

When her supervisors found out she was a lesbian, "Jane" was subjected to an hour of interrogation regarding her sexual relationships. She was asked if she had fantasies about her coworkers and was accused of treating her female subordinates like a "harem." A week later, after another three-hour interrogation and two lengthy phone calls to her home, Jane was fired, despite an outstanding performance record (HRC, 2001a).

Mark Anderson's supervisor at a prestigious securities firm produced a video that was shown and distributed at the firm's biennial sales meeting. The video featured images of Anderson's car, painted by his coworkers with gay references, such as "Rump Ranger" and "1-800-Butt Boy." Although Anderson had never received any criticism regarding his work, he was fired soon after the sales meeting, being told he would "not make a good stockbroker" (HRC, 2001a).

There are approximately twenty million gay, lesbian, and bisexual persons in the United States, and a large proportion of those engage in paid work outside the home (Seck, Finch, Mor-Barak, & Poverny, 1993). Estimates of the proportion of non-heterosexual people in the American workforce put the figure at 10–14 percent (Powers, 1996). Despite an ever-increasing amount of attention to "diversity," lesbian, gay, and bisexual (LGB) workers remain virtually ignored by organizational researchers. In contrast to this lack of scientific attention, there is a growing trend by employers to attend to the issue of inclusion of LGB workers. As of the year 2001, 294 Fortune 500 companies have written nondiscrimination policies that include sexual orientation, and 145 offer domestic partner benefits to their gay and lesbian employees (HRC, 2001b). Public opinion polls also show increasing support for employment rights for gays and lesbians (Yang, 2000). This chapter is intended to encourage organizational researchers to join and facilitate this trend toward inclusiveness by expanding their definition of diversity and, correspondingly, devoting attention to the workplace experiences of LGB people.

We will begin the chapter by considering the features that make LGB employees a unique population with concerns that are somewhat different from those affecting the "diverse" groups more commonly studied (racial-ethnic minorities and women). We will include discussion of issues raised by the fact that homosexuality is not an immediately visible characteristic, that there is little legal prohibition against sexual orientation discrimination, and that prejudice against LGB people currently is more socially acceptable than overt expressions of racism or sexism. Next, we will examine the scope of the problem of sexual orientation discrimination in the workplace. After discussion of the prevalence and forms of such discrimination, we will present evidence of its impact on targets. Then, we will turn to correlates and possible antecedents of sexual orientation discrimination in the workplace, including organizational policies and climate, characteristics of coworkers and supervisors, and LGB employees' decisions to disclose their sexual orientation on the job. As we progress through this discussion of what is known regarding the antecedents, correlates, and outcomes of sexual orientation discrimination in the workplace, it will become apparent that, at this point, very little is known. Furthermore, one will see that what research does exist often provides findings that are difficult to interpret or that conflict with other findings. The void of research addressing the concerns of LGB workers will become painfully obvious. Thus, we will provide in the latter part of the chapter a coarsely articulated agenda for LGB workplace research.

LGB Employees Are a Unique Population

The majority of research on diversity and discrimination has focused upon women and racial or ethnic minorities. Some of the issues faced by these groups may be the same as those faced by LGB employees, such as confronting stereotypes and difficulties in relationships with majority-group coworkers. But the experiences of LGB employees may differ from those groups in several important ways. Below, we discuss three ways in which the LGB employee population is unique: the nonvisible nature of sexual orientation, the lack of federal civil rights protection for LGBs, and the acceptability of anti-gay prejudice. These features may alter the character of the discriminatory situations faced by LGBs, as compared to other groups, and can lead to LGBs facing issues that women and racial minorities do not encounter at all (for example, "coming out"). In light of these unique concerns, generalization of research conducted on those more well-studied groups to LGB employees may not be warranted.

Concealability of Stigma

Goffman (1963) defined a *stigma* as an attribute of a person that calls into question that person's full humanity, rendering him or her "in our minds from a whole and usual person to a tainted, discounted one" (p. 3). Homosexuality is an example of a stigma, as are minority race, disability, and gender in some contexts, in that people who possess such attributes are the object of negative stereotypes and are generally devalued in society (Crocker, Major, & Steele, 1998). However, a very important difference between LGBs and more commonly studied minorities is that homosexuality is a "concealable" stigma, in that an individual's sexual orientation is not inherently visible to others in the environment. One might think that concealable stigmas are less problematic than visible stigmas because it is possible for those who are concealably stigmatized to interact with other people without their devalued social identity being known and always filtering how everything about them is understood (Crocker et al., 1998; Frable, Platt, & Hoey, 1998). This likely leads to lower levels of some forms of discrimination being directed at individuals who do conceal their orientation. But individuals with concealable stigmas are aware that they could be devalued if their stigma were discovered, and in every new encounter with the nonstigmatized they may try to determine the attitudes of the individuals with whom they are interacting, monitor speech and behavior to avoid revealing their stigma, and worry about whether, when, and how they should reveal their stigmatizing identity (Crocker et al., 1998). Frable (1993) refers to this sort of mindfulness and worry as "social gymnastics"; those who do not possess concealable stigmas are not so burdened.

There is some evidence that LGB people do, in fact, engage in a considerable amount of these "social gymnastics" at work (Chrobot-Mason, Button, & DiClementi, 2001; Kitzinger, 1991). LGB employees report engaging in a number of identity management strategies on the job. Chrobot-Mason et al. (2001) found three common strategies in use: counterfeiting, avoidance, and integration. LGB employees who widely disclose their orientation at work attempt *integration,* that is, seeking to make a gay or lesbian identity a part of their work lives. In contrast, the other two strategies are ways to avoid disclosing one's sexual orientation. *Counterfeiting* refers to actively constructing a false heterosexual identity to present to others, such as the gay man who invented a girlfriend, "Becky," to talk about with his coworkers (Friskopp & Silverstein, 1995). *Avoidance* refers to a simple refusal to discuss one's personal life and identity and attempts to steer conversations elsewhere. Friskopp and Silverstein interviewed numerous gay and lesbian Harvard Business School alumni, and many of their interviewees spoke of "keeping their private life private." An LGB employee may use all three of the above strategies, at different times and with different people, nearly always devoting some attention to how to manage his or her stigma in each particular situation (Chrobot-Mason et al., 2001; Driscoll, Kelley, & Fassinger, 1996; Friskopp & Silverstein, 1995; Kitzinger, 1991).

Heterosexuals may underestimate the impact of nondisclosure on the daily work lives of LGB employees. Opponents of legal protection against sexual orientation discrimination commonly allege that such laws are unnecessary, because "private sexual behavior" should have no impact on the "public" workplace (Dyer, 2001; Washington for Traditional Values, 1997). However, such a separation between public and private does not exist for heterosexuals. For example, expressions of heterosexuality are apparent in displays (family photos, wedding rings), conversation, and behavior in nearly every workplace (Kitzinger, 1991). Furthermore, having an LGB identity is not merely about sex. Same-sex relationships also include nonsexual physical affection, shared goals and values, mutual support, ongoing commitment, and mundane daily activities, just as do heterosexual relationships (Herek, 1996). To be unable to even speak of one's most important relationships and activities imposes an onerous burden on closeted LGB employees. Heterosexual readers might try to imagine how difficult they would find their work lives if they could never mention a husband, wife, girlfriend, boyfriend, date, children, family outing, or any other aspect of their lives that might reveal heterosexuality. A gay man described his frustration: "Straight people say why do you have to bring being gay to work? But you know something? When straight people say 'Mary and I went to the Catskills this weekend,' or 'Our little son, Johnny, is going to MIT,' and all that stuff, they're coming out to you about their sexual orientation. They don't realize gay people aren't asking for anything special. We are just asking for equal time" (Friskopp & Silverstein, 1995, p. 87).

Furthermore, heterosexuals in the workplace often breach this supposed separation of "public" and "private" by refusing to allow LGBs to keep their lives outside of work private. For example, a gay sales manager in Illinois waved to a friend on the street; his manager observed this and, perceiving the friend to be "obviously gay," pressed the employee until he finally admitted that he had dated the friend (HRC, 2001a). A lesbian who worked for an Ohio cleaning service faced constant questioning by her supervisors about her private life and whether she had a boyfriend, and a gay male candidate for a Connecticut police department was asked directly about his sexual orientation on a polygraph (HRC, 2001a). These sorts of situations seem to be very common; LGB employees may have a hard time keeping their "private lives private," even when they want to.

Secrecy also interferes with the development of interpersonal relationships on the job. Mutual self-disclosure is vital to the formation of friendships and supportive relationships (Chelune, Sultan, & Williams, 1980; Worthy, Gary, & Kahn, 1969); thus, when LGB employees cannot engage in reciprocal disclosures, they are unlikely to form meaningful relationships on the job. This can interfere with the career development of LGBs, as they may be cut off from informal networks that can provide career guidance and information about opportunities (Boatwright, Gilbert, Forrest, & Ketzenberger, 1996). In addition, coworkers are a valuable source of social support for many people, a source that may be especially useful considering how many hours of the day one spends at work (Carlson & Perrewe, 1999; Dormann & Zapf, 1999). If closeted LGB employees fail to develop meaningful relationships with coworkers, they may suffer from the lack of that support. One lesbian Harvard alumnus explained: "Since I'm unable to be open with my coworkers about my personal life, it not only prevents me from being one of the team, but creates some stress for me. My coworkers can let off steam or indicate when they have had problems and get support from others. I don't have that kind of relationship with my colleagues" (Friskopp & Silverstein, 1995, p. 187).

Although concealing one's sexual orientation is fraught with difficulties, disclosure is not a cure-all. Even with disclosure, the need for impression management remains; its form merely changes. Individuals who are "out" on the job report being mindful of their words and actions in attempts to "correct" stereotypes about LGBs held by others. For example, a lesbian librarian explained, "There's this stereotype that all lesbians are big tough butch women in trousers and crew cuts, so I make a special effort to do my hair nicely, and wear quite feminine clothing, skirts and make-up, just to sort of say, 'look, we're not all like that'" (Kitzinger, 1991, p. 233). Another woman described attempting to dispel "butch-femme" stereotypes (which suggest that one partner has the "feminine" role, while the other plays the "male" part), saying, "Because I have short hair and a boyish figure and my lover is more conventionally feminine than I am, I feel people at work see us that way, and I hate it. So I keep dropping comments about how she fixed the car [on] the weekend while I was cooking dinner—things like that, designed to undermine their stereotypes" (Kitzinger, 1991, p. 233).

In sum, whether they disclose their sexual orientation or not, the interactions that LGB employees have with others on the job involve identity- and impression-management concerns that are unique to the invisibly stigmatized. Not only does this mean that we must be extremely cautious in generalizing results from research on visibly stigmatized groups, it also complicates research focusing specifically on LGBs. As will be noted throughout this chapter, disclosure of one's sexual orientation is likely to be related to nearly every aspect of the LGB workplace experience in complex and reciprocal ways.

Lack of Federal Civil Rights Protection

Another way in which the experience of LGBs is different from that of racial minorities and women is that in most of the United States discrimination against LGB employees is quite legal. There is currently no federal legislation prohibiting discrimination against LGBs in employment-related matters; federal courts have ruled that sexual orientation does not meet the requirements for being a "suspect class" that would be protected under current federal civil rights legislation (HRC, 2001b). Some LGB employees are protected, however, as twelve states and 122 cities and counties have enacted legislation prohibiting discrimination in employment on the basis of sexual orientation (HRC, 2001b; National Gay and Lesbian Task Force [NGLTF], 2001a).

The potential importance of such official protection from discrimination should not be underestimated in studying the work experiences of LGBs. Clearly, these laws and ordinances may directly reduce the amount of discrimination experienced by explicitly prohibiting differential treatment of gay men and lesbians in matters of hiring, firing, promotion, pay, and scope of duties (HRC, 2001b). Thus, one way in which nondiscrimination policies can prevent discrimination from occurring is by clearly specifying actions that are unacceptable. Official protection also opens an avenue for those who are discriminated against to attempt to seek redress. Without such protection, discriminatory treatment may be unlikely to be challenged for fear of retaliation (Van Den Bergh, 1994). In fact, such retaliation for complaints is not uncommon; the Human Rights Campaign (2001a) has documented numerous occasions when LGB employees were disciplined, suspended, or fired after complaining about sexual orientation discrimination. Moreover, there is some evidence that LGBs are more willing to speak out against discrimination when they enjoy employment protection. For instance, complaints to the New York City Commission of Human Rights went from 139 to 339 in just one year, after passage of a citywide ordinance prohibiting employment discrimination on the basis of sexual orientation (Poverny & Finch, 1988).

But if civil rights legislation addressing sexual orientation functions similarly to existing federal protections covering race and sex, it is unlikely to fully remedy the problem of sexual orientation discrimination. Edelman and Petterson (1999) present arguments suggesting that organizations' compliance with existing civil rights laws sometimes is only symbolic, with little substantive impact. Furthermore, they argue that the courts often are ineffectual in providing adequate redress to victims of discrimination under these laws. Nonetheless, there is evidence that numerical gains have been made in the representation of women and minorities in nontraditional and upper-level jobs (Holzer, 1996; Leonard, 1986). Collection of similar data on the representation of LGBs, however, will never be possible, due to the concealability of sexual orientation. Thus, statistical arguments of evidence of a pattern of discrimination against LGBs will not be available, and it may be difficult to evaluate the effectiveness of nondiscrimination initiatives for LGB employees. Still, the evidence that at least some organizations' responses to existing civil rights laws have achieved substantive benefits in the treatment of currently protected groups (Edelman & Petterson, 1999; Konrad & Linnehan, 1995) suggests that some improvement in the treatment of LGBs might similarly result from legal protection. Understandably, therefore, LGB activists continue to press for clear federal civil rights protection by lobbying for passage of the Employment Non-Discrimination Act (HRC, 2001b). Until such a law is passed, or the Supreme Court makes a clear statement extending current civil rights legislation to cover sexual orientation, the current "patchwork" protection remains. That fact needs to be acknowledged in research with LGB employees, as the presence or absence of workplace protection may be an important environmental influence on those employees' experiences with discrimination.

Acceptability of Heterosexism

Another important way in which the experience of LGB employees is unique is the general social acceptability of antipathy toward gay men and lesbians (Comstock, 1991; Herek, 1989). In contemporary Western society, we place people into "socioerotic categories" based upon what they do sexually (Herek, 1990). Thus, people are defined primarily as "heterosexual" or "homosexual," with occasional allowance for bisexuals or asexual individuals. Furthermore, the category "heterosexual" is clearly positively valued, whereas "homosexual" is negatively valued; and this is reflected in nearly every aspect of our culture. Indeed, due to sodomy laws, gay men and lesbians were until recently criminals in several states (NGLTF, 2001b). Heterosexual marriage is a revered institution; gay relationships cannot be officially sanctioned. Heterosexual people may hold hands in public or place pictures of their families on their desks; gay people who do the same are accused of "flaunting it" and risk rejection, denigration, and attack. Nearly all the major religions in Western society preach against homosexuality (Herek, 1990). Clearly, heterosexism pervades our culture.

A note regarding the distinction between *heterosexism* and *homophobia* may be in order at this point. We prefer the term *heterosexism* to describe prejudice against those with a homosexual orientation, entailing the belief that LGB people are inferior to heterosexual people in some way. This term is analogous to *racism* (non-white races seen as inferior) and *sexism* (women viewed as inferior). *Homophobia* implies a fearful reaction to homosexuals and is not interchangeable with the term *heterosexism,* which may or may not have a fear component (see, for example, Haaga, 1991; O'Donohue & Caselles, 1993). A distinction also needs to be made between *heterosexism,* which is an attitude, and *discrimination,* which refers to some behavior or event. In this chapter, our use of the term *discrimination* refers to negative policies, acts, or events directed toward or affecting an LGB person, or LGB people in general, that presumably result from heterosexism. Although some researchers have done so (for example, Waldo, 1999), we wish to discourage the use of the term *heterosexism* alone to refer to that discrimination, preferring instead *heterosexist discrimination* to indicate discrimination stemming from the prejudicial attitude of heterosexism.

Overt expressions of racism and sexism have become far less acceptable in recent years (Glick & Fiske, 1996; McConahay, 1986), but blatant heterosexism does not appear to have had a similar decline (Herek, 1989; Nardi & Bolton, 1991). Religious leaders and politicians frequently deliver anti-gay rhetoric in public addresses (Comstock, 1991; Herek, 1989). Senate Majority Leader Trent Lott, for instance, stated in a television interview that "he believes homosexuality is a sin," and that "you should try to show them a way to deal with that problem, just like alcohol" (Gay and Lesbian Alliance Against Defamation [GLAAD], 1998), and two Republican representatives in Oregon were asked by party leaders to leave the GOP because they had expressed support for gay rights (Mapes, 1999). Stereotypes about gay people persist in the media, regardless of their offensiveness to LGB people (Nardi & Bolton, 1991). "Dr. Laura" continues as a radio show even after the Gay and Lesbian Alliance Against Defamation began protesting Laura Schlessinger's use of terms such as "deviant," "disordered," and "biological error" to describe gays and lesbians (GLAAD, 2001). Even in children's cartoons, characters whose homosexuality is implied through their violation of gender norms typically are presented as objects of contempt and ridicule (Russo, 1989). Not only are negative media portrayals of LGB people common, positive portrayals may be protested or censored. Several local television stations refused to air an episode of the television show *Friends* featuring a lesbian commitment ceremony, and the episode of the show *Ellen* in which two women kiss was labeled with a "parental advisory" warning, normally used for explicit sex or extreme violence. Such acceptability of heterosexism also is evident in the corporate world; for example, General Motors once released a sales video that derided other auto companies for their "little faggot trucks" (Friskopp & Silverstein, 1995).

So, as prejudice against LGB people is more socially acceptable than racism or sexism, we logically may expect that discrimination against LGBs is more acceptable as well. And with such a backdrop, it is hardly surprising that many perpetrators of sexual orientation discrimination might have no qualms about publicly stating their prejudiced reasons for their actions. CPA Dan Miller's boss testified in court that he fired Miller based solely on the fact that Miller was gay (which was quite legal in that locale) (HRC, 2001a). A health care facility administrator in Iowa, who fired six employees because of their sexual orientation, told the local newspaper in an interview that when he first arrived at the company there were "at least three faggots working here and at least three dykes. That isn't the kind of atmosphere that I want to project. . . . [Gay people] are not part of society as far as I'm concerned" (HRC, 2001a).

Furthermore, due to the concealability of the stigma, many people may think they do not know any LGB people. Intergroup contact situations may pass unknown and unnoticed, thus inhibiting the formation of individualized perceptions of LGB people and allowing stereotypes to persist. Contact with gay men or lesbians has been found to be associated with more positive attitudes on the part of heterosexuals toward homosexuality and LGB people in general, but only if the heterosexual person knows of the other's orientation (Herek & Capitano, 1996; Yang, 2000). Thus, many heterosexuals still think of LGB people primarily in terms of stereotypes (Haddock, Zanna, & Esses, 1993).

Although American society still has a long way to go before LGB people enjoy full acceptance, there are certainly signs of progress. National opinion polls over the past few decades have shown steadily increasing support for equal rights for LGB people in housing, employment, and adoption, as well as less censure of same-sex relationships (Yang, 2000). A few television shows are providing more complex and individualized portrayals of LGB people (for example, *Will and Grace* and *Queer as Folk*). With each passing year, more companies adopt gay-friendly policies and more cities enact protective legislation. And we, as organizational researchers, should consider that these broader societal features and trends toward change may be stronger influences on the workplace experiences of LGB people than anything else that happens in the microcosm of a particular organization. The perpetrators of discriminatory acts are people—coworkers, supervisors, top management—not organizations or policies (although people may structure organizations and policies to discriminate or not), and these people live and function within the larger society. They bring knowledge of the prejudices and stereotypes that prevail in that society into the workplace, and, whether they consciously endorse those stereotypes or not, such ideas can still influence their actions (Chen & Bargh, 1997; Devine, 1989). Thus, a consideration of the general societal climate for LGB people, and the changes taking place in that climate, needs to be included in our research if we are to fully understand all the factors impinging upon sexual orientation discrimination in the workplace.

To recap, LGB employees differ from the groups to which much diversity research has been devoted. Perhaps the most important difference is the concealability of sexual orientation. The attendant concerns of disclosure and self-presentation affect the character of many of the interactions and experiences of LGBs in the workplace (Herek, 1989). LGB employees also differ from racial minorities and women in that federal civil rights laws do not cover sexual orientation. Thus, discrimination against LGB employees is fully legal in most parts of the United States. Finally, we have argued that overt heterosexism is more socially acceptable than blatant racism or sexism, and this relative acceptability may create a similar acceptability of discrimination against LGB employees. The forms and prevalence of such discrimination are discussed in the next section, followed by a review of the research regarding its impact on LGBs.

The Problem of Sexual Orientation Discrimination in the Workplace

Despite increasing attempts to recognize and value diversity in organizations, gay and lesbian employees are still far from enjoying full integration and acceptance in the workplace. Discrimination against workers based upon sexual orientation is unfortunately rather common. In several studies that asked gay men and lesbians whether they had experienced some form of workplace discrimination due to their sexual orientation, between 20 and 66 percent responded affirmatively (Croteau & Lark, 1995; Croteau & von Destinon, 1994; Levine & Leonard, 1984; Stoddard, 1986). The legislative counsel for the American Civil Liberties Union, speaking before the Senate Committee on Labor and Human Resources, testified that, "The ACLU receives a flood of calls from men and women who have lost or been denied jobs, or failed to receive promotions, because of discrimination based on sexual orientation" (ACLU, 1997). Badgett (1995) demonstrated that such discrimination has economic impact, in that gay men and lesbians tend to earn less than heterosexuals. And Rubenstein (2001) found that in eight of ten states that had a law prohibiting workplace discrimination against LGBs, population-adjusted complaint rates from LGBs were at least as high as those from women or ethnic minorities. One-third of a sample drawn from the membership of three national organizations of lesbian, gay, bisexual, and transgender (LGBT) individuals reported experiencing employment discrimination (Cahill, 2000). In a survey of over one thousand lawyers in Washington, D.C., 61 percent reported having witnessed or heard reports of anti-gay discrimination within their firms (van der Meide, 2000). Sexual orientation discrimination appears to be widespread, occurring in all types of industries, large firms and small businesses, major metropolitan areas, and tiny rural towns (HRC, 2001a). In this section, we intend to demonstrate that these findings and claims of discrimination are valid, and that such discrimination is damaging.

Gay, lesbian, and bisexual workers report many forms of workplace discrimination, which have been roughly classified as either formal or informal (Croteau, 1996; Levine & Leonard, 1984). *Formal discrimination* is defined as involving institutionalized procedures or official managerial decisions (Levine & Leonard, 1984). Thus, formal discriminatory actions against LGBs can include refusing to hire an applicant, terminating an employee, restricting job duties, passing an employee over for promotions, or failing to equitably reward an employee due to his or her sexual orientation. The examples of firings that opened this chapter are clear instances of formal discrimination, as are incidents such as one manager's statement that he was "not hiring any gays because there are too many problems" (HRC, 2001a, p. 20). Organizational policies that exclude same-sex partners from benefits, such as insurance and family leave, may also be classified as formal discrimination. One of Friskopp and Silverstein's (1995) gay male interviewees who was self-employed remarked, "Health insurance is really expensive as a self-insured person. If we were married, I'd be insured under [my partner's] policy" (p. 144). Any official policy or action that treats LGB people differently from heterosexual people can be viewed as formal discrimination.

Informal sexual orientation discrimination refers to negative actions directed toward LGBs because of their sexual orientation that do not directly involve organizational policies or decisions. Informal discrimination includes interpersonal animosity from coworkers or supervisors, derogatory jokes and comments regarding gays, verbal and sexual harassment, and even physical violence (Croteau, 1996; Friskopp & Silverstein, 1995; Kivel & Wells, 1998). The Human Rights Campaign's (2001a) publication documenting incidents of discrimination across the country is rife with examples of informal discrimination, such as the man who received pager messages saying, "God hates faggots and so do we," and "Death to all fags—die, queer, die," or the worker who found condoms in his locker and urine in his helmet after his coworkers learned he was gay. It appears that informal sexual orientation discrimination is not uncommon in the workplace (Croteau, 1996; Herek, 1996).

Some researchers (Waldo, 1999) have included in their conception of discrimination a construct termed "indirect heterosexism." Indirect heterosexism stems from the "heterosexual assumption" that prevails in most workplaces (and in most of American society), where all are assumed to be heterosexual unless explicitly proven otherwise (Kitzinger, 1991). Thus, closeted LGB employees may feel invisible or uncomfortable, perceiving a need to appear "sufficiently straight" in order to fit into their workplace. This discomfort is certainly real, and is likely to be an important consideration in understanding the workplace experiences of LGB employees. However, we do not believe that indirect heterosexism, which is assessed solely in terms of an employee's *perception* of a need to appear heterosexual, necessarily constitutes a form of *discrimination*. It is unclear to what extent these perceptions are a function of any feature of the workplace; such perceptions may stem from other sources, such as the attitudes of the employee's family, his or her stage of identity development and personal comfort with being gay, or perceptions of the climate for LGBs in larger society. If perceptions of indirect heterosexism are, in fact, a result of some actions or policies in the workplace, then those aspects of the workplace may certainly be considered discrimination, and it is those features that should be assessed in measures of discrimination. But we do believe that the term *discrimination* should be restricted to identifiable behaviors or procedures, and that an employee's perceptions of the need to present a heterosexual image constitute a separate construct.

Both the formal and informal discriminatory behaviors described above are specifically directed at LGB employees, or express clear antipathy toward LGB people in general. These behaviors that appear to stem from prejudice against gays and lesbians are many of the same discriminatory events faced by other stigmatized groups (for example, derogatory jokes about black people, refusing to hire a woman). However, the unique features of the LGB population may lead to these experiences having a somewhat different character. For example, due to the concealability of sexual orientation, closeted employees may hear disparaging remarks about gay people without anyone else knowing those remarks have personal relevance for the employee. Or due to the lack of legal protection in most areas, an LGB employee may experience major direct personal discrimination on the job, yet have absolutely no recourse. Thus, even when the discriminatory events are similar to those experienced by other minorities, those events might have somewhat different effects for LGB employees.

A substantial body of literature exists demonstrating that encounters with workplace discrimination are damaging to the well-being of racial and ethnic minorities (for example, Deitch et al., 2002; Jackson et al., 1996; Kessler, Mickelson, & Williams, 1999; Schneider, Hitlan, & Radhakrishnan, 2000; Williams, Yu, Jackson, & Anderson, 1997). In contrast, the literature on outcomes of sexual orientation discrimination is very sparse. The limited research that does exist suggests that such discrimination results in similar negative outcomes for LGB employees. Driscoll et al. (1996) found that gay men and lesbians who reported a "hostile work environment," characterized by heterosexism and discrimination against gays, exhibited higher stress levels than those in less hostile settings. Waldo (1999) found that experiences of heterosexist discrimination at work were associated with increased psychological distress (comprising indicators of anxiety, depression, self-esteem, and life satisfaction) and more negative health conditions on the part of LGB employees. There are accounts of discrimination leading to acute health and psychological well-being problems, such as the panic attacks suffered by Douglas Retterer, whose story opened this chapter, or the posttraumatic stress disorder that an airline employee in Denver was diagnosed with after suffering several verbal and physical attacks at work due to his sexual orientation (HRC, 2001a).

Sexual orientation discrimination also has been found to be associated with organizationally relevant attitudes and intentions. For instance, perceptions of heterosexist discrimination have been found to be related to lowered organizational commitment and job satisfaction (Button, 2001; Ragins & Cornwell, 2001a; Waldo, 1999). Moreover, discrimination has been found to be related positively to withdrawal behaviors and intentions to quit (Ragins & Cornwell, 2001a; Waldo, 1999).

In addition, a discriminatory workplace environment is likely to discourage LGB employees from disclosing their sexual orientation. Attempts to remain closeted on the job are associated with impaired well-being and negative job attitudes, associations that potentially compound the more direct negative effects of encounters with discrimination (Croteau, 1996; Herek, 1996; Kitzinger, 1991). For instance, Day and Schoenrade (1997) reported that individuals who attempted to remain closeted on the job experienced role ambiguity and conflict. Waldo (1999) found that those closeted at work exhibited lower satisfaction with life. These negative effects are not surprising, considering that concealing one's orientation on the job requires a great deal of psychological effort and perpetual vigilance (Chrobot-Mason et al., 2001). A lesbian lawyer described it as "constant monitoring" and said, "You're always on the edge when you're not being who you are. You're always being careful" (Boatwright et al., 1996, p. 219). Even outside of work, caution is required. One of Friskopp and Silverstein's (1995) interviewees related that when groups of lesbian friends stopped by her home, she always made sure the curtains were shut and the doors locked for fear her straight coworkers would pass by. Another interviewee told of a closeted friend at work who refused to go out to any gay clubs with him, saying, "How do you deal with this . . . I mean, what if somebody sees you?" (p. 161).

The alternative of disclosing one's sexual orientation on the job does appear to be associated with higher well-being, however. Studies have found that disclosure behaviors at work were associated with lower job anxiety and stress (Driscoll et al., 1996; Griffith & Hebl, 2002). In addition, a positive relationship between disclosure and global job satisfaction on the part of LGB workers has been found in some studies (Driscoll et al., 1996; Griffith & Hebl, 2002). In terms of specific facets, Ellis and Riggle (1995) found that disclosure was associated with more satisfaction with coworkers but less satisfaction with pay (possibly reflecting lower wages due to discrimination [see Badgett, 1995]), and was not significantly related to satisfaction with the job itself or with promotion opportunities. There is some indication that the responses of others in the environment to an LGB employee's disclosure matter; in the Griffith and Hebl study, the relationship between disclosure and job satisfaction was fully mediated by the tenor of coworkers' reaction to the disclosure. Such reactions are an important feature of the environment for the LGB worker who chooses to disclose, but such coworker reactions largely have been ignored in the research literature.

Personal characteristics of LGB employees also may influence the extent to which discrimination results in detriments to their well-being. Two studies have investigated associations between discrimination outcomes and the extent to which LGB employees have developed a positive personal identity as an LGB. Unlike members of many other stigmatized groups, such as racial minorities, LGBs do not usually have parental examples and guidance in developing their gay identity early in life. Thus, LGB employees may be at a variety of stages in terms of acknowledging and accepting such an identity, and even older individuals may be newly wrestling with identity concerns. Button (2001) described how, in developing a gay identity, many gay men and lesbians pass through an "immersion-emersion" phase, during which they endorse extreme positive views of their ingroup while strongly denigrating the outgroup (heterosexuals), before moving on to a stage of "internalization" where identity is more secure and more balanced and realistic views are endorsed. He found that the relationship between discrimination and satisfaction was highest for gay and lesbian employees who endorsed high immersion-emersion attitudes, thereby suggesting that individuals at that stage of identity development are more reactive to discrimination. Griffith and Hebl (2002) found that those for whom a gay identity was more central, and who were more accepting of that identity, were more likely to engage in disclosure behaviors at work and exhibited higher job satisfaction and less job anxiety. Thus, LGB employees' stage of identity development, and their comfort with a gay identity, may be important considerations in understanding their disclosure decisions, perceptions of discrimination in the workplace, and the outcomes of that discrimination.

In sum, LGB employees appear to face a substantial amount of discrimination and prejudice on the job, and their well-being, job attitudes, and workplace behaviors may be negatively affected as a result. These conclusions, however, are based on very few studies, which address a limited set of questions. As already noted, most of the research regarding workplace discrimination has focused on racial or ethnic minorities and women, and one must be cautious in attempting to generalize such research to LGB people. Research specifically directed toward exploring the experiences that LGB employees have with discrimination on the job is required to determine how such experiences are similar to those of women and racial minorities and how they differ. Specific research attention to the antecedents of sexual orientation discrimination also is sorely needed. The next section discusses a few possible antecedents that have been examined.

Potential Antecedents of Sexual Orientation Discrimination

Given that sexual orientation discrimination occurs in the workplace and has negative outcomes, what can be done about it? In order to provide suggestions and guidance for reducing such discrimination, we must understand what causes it. This section presents features of organizations, others in the workplace, and LGB employees that appear to be related to sexual orientation discrimination. However, this section refers to "potential" antecedents not only because there is very little research for firmly establishing relationships, but also because the direction of influence between these factors and discrimination is often unclear. As the existing research is primarily cross-sectional, it often is not clear whether these correlates (for example, organizational policies) are determinants or results of the prevalence of sexual orientation discrimination in the workplace. Nonetheless, the research to be presented here can provide a starting point for developing an understanding of the causes of workplace discrimination against LGBs.

Organizational Features

A few organizational features have been studied in relation to the amount and sort of sexual orientation discrimination encountered by LGB workers. These features include explicit policies and procedures, such as the provision of domestic partner benefits, as well as less overt features such as organizational climate and culture.

Even in the absence of any legal requirements, many organizations are taking steps to attempt to create a more gay-friendly workplace. They may wish to do so in order to improve recruitment and employee retention in a tight labor market, reduce productivity losses that may be associated with the stress of discrimination, or appeal to LGB consumers and investors, or they may wish to do so simply because management feels it is the right thing to do (Alpern 2002; Gardyn, 2001; Kohn, 1999; Loomis & Kass, 2002; Securities Institute of America, 1999). The most common gay-friendly policy initiative is the establishment of a specific, written company policy of nondiscrimination on the basis of sexual orientation. As of 2001, 294 of the Fortune 500 companies included sexual orientation in their official nondiscrimination policy (HRC, 2001b). Several other types of policies may be adopted by organizations who wish to be gay-friendly, including the extension of benefits (for example, insurance, family leave) to same-sex domestic partners, diversity training that includes sexual orientation concerns, support for LGB issues and activities in the larger community, and the formation of LGB employee groups (such as GALAX [Gays and Lesbians at Xerox], DuPont's BGLAD network, or the LEAGUE at AT&T).

The effect of each of these policies is difficult to determine at this point, as there is little research on their impact. A few studies have found that more gay-friendly policies are associated with less reported sexual orientation discrimination (Button, 2001; Griffith & Hebl, 2002; Ragins & Cornwell, 2001a). But Waldo (1999) found no significant relationship between organizational policies and reports of heterosexist discrimination. It may be that some policies are more effective than others—two studies have attempted to tease apart the relative value of different company policies, with conflicting results. Ragins and Cornwell (2001a) found that a written nondiscrimination policy and the provision of domestic partner benefits were negatively related to reported discrimination (experienced by oneself or observed), but the relationship of discrimination with the existence of LGB employee groups was only marginally significant, and no association was found between diversity training including LGB concerns and workplace discrimination. However, Griffith and Hebl (2002) found that reports of sexual orientation discrimination were significantly negatively related to inclusive diversity training and domestic partner benefits, as well as to written nondiscrimination policies. As did Ragins and Cornwell, the Griffith and Hebl study failed to find LGB employee groups to be associated with reported discrimination. Clearly, at this time we can draw no firm conclusions about the value of specific policies. Our stories at this point are too simple; merely correlating the existence of a policy with reports of discrimination fails to take account of features of the organization or of policy application that may affect discrimination outcomes. We need to examine additional factors that could influence when and whether policies are effective or not in reducing discrimination.

Organizational policies may be ineffective in some cases if they are only "lip service," undermined by informal organizational conditions. As noted earlier, organizational policies purportedly intended to improve the treatment of women and minorities have often been found to be only symbolic, lacking real substance (Edelman & Petterson, 1999). Furthermore, the literature on these more well-studied groups suggests that without clear accountability for actions and decisions that affect women and minorities, little progress is made (Bielby, 2000; Reskin, 2000). Although there is a lack of research assessing the extent to which gay-friendly organizational policies are enforced and the degree to which people in the organization are held accountable for their actions vis-à-vis LGB employees, anecdotal reports suggest that such enforcement and accountability may often be lacking. "Believe it or not," said one gay man, "I hear more homophobic jokes and comments from corporate counsel than from anyone else—the guy who's in charge of enforcing our nondiscrimination policy!" (Friskopp & Silverstein, 1995, p. 128). A gay man in training for the Nassau County police force reported how supervisors at the police academy snickered when discussing homosexuality during a sensitivity training workshop (HRC, 2001a). At a bank in New Mexico that had a written nondiscrimination policy, a gay man was still forced to sign an "absolute prohibition" on discussing anything about the "gay lifestyle" with any other bank employee, on or off the job, in order to hold on to a promotion (HRC, 2001a). Clearly, not all "gay-friendly" policies have substance in practice.

Indeed, there is some research evidence that assessments of informal climate may be better predictors of discrimination than official policies. Ragins and Cornwell (2001a) found that no official company policy was as strongly related to reports of sexual orientation discrimination as was respondents' perceptions of whether their same-sex partners were welcome at company events. Driscoll et al. (1996) reported a negative relationship between assessments of workplace climate (in terms of being friendly and fair to LGB workers) and reported discrimination, and Waldo (1999) found that reports of sexual orientation discrimination were related to a climate of "tolerance for heterosexism."

Another difficulty in evaluating organizational policies is that, as with much of the research this chapter covers, the direction of influence is unclear. Because the adoption of gay-friendly policies is voluntary (with the exception of a nondiscrimination policy in a locale where such is the law), those organizations that choose to enact such policies probably do so because they are more gay-friendly organizations to begin with. Therefore, these policies might be better considered as reflections of the organizational environment rather than determinants of it.

Coworkers and Supervisors

There has been some attention paid to the composition of LGB employees' immediate workplace environment and characteristics of coworkers and supervisors. One important feature of the immediate environment is the presence or absence of other LGB people. Individuals who are sole representatives of their social group tend to be viewed stereotypically and subjected to greater scrutiny than those who are not so isolated (Cohen & Swim, 1995; Kanter, 1977; Meyer, 1995; Niemann & Dovidio, 1998). Thus, the presence of more than one LGB person in a workgroup may reduce such stereotyping and scrutiny and improve the treatment of LGB employees. Three studies by Ragins and Cornwell (2000, 2001a, 2001b) have found that a higher proportion of LGB coworkers is associated with less reported sexual orientation discrimination, suggesting that departments with more openly LGB people may be less heterosexist.

As supervisors have direct influence over LGB employees and some of their coworkers, one would expect that having an LGB supervisor might reduce the amount of discrimination experienced by LGB employees. Ragins and Cornwell (2000) did find a negative relationship between having an LGB supervisor and reported discrimination. But in a later study (Ragins & Cornwell, 2001a), they found that although the simple bivariate relationship between supervisor's sexual orientation and perceived discrimination was significant, that association dropped to nonsignificance when other antecedents (coworkers' orientation, policies, and protective legislation) were included in a full path model. They point out that gay supervisors, like their employees, are vulnerable to discrimination. Thus, gay supervisors may be able to positively affect the environment for their LGB subordinates only if their own position is secure. Neither of these studies examined supervisors' experiences with discrimination. Nor does the fact that an LGB subordinate knows his or her supervisor is gay or lesbian necessarily imply that the supervisor is fully "out" on the job. If the supervisor is out only to the other LGB persons in the workplace, he or she may be unwilling to be of visible help to those subordinates. Indeed, it is possible that an LGB supervisor who is attempting to remain closeted to most others in the workplace might be even less likely to speak out against prejudice and discrimination than a sympathetic heterosexual supervisor, out of fear that a vocal stand could lead to his or her sexual orientation being discovered or suspected.

Few characteristics of those in the immediate workplace environment other than sexual orientation have been examined. One study (Ragins & Cornwell, 2000) examined the gender composition of the workgroup and found that LGB persons who were in workgroups that were mostly men reported more discrimination than those in balanced or female-dominated workgroups. There is ample evidence in the social psychology literature that men tend to hold more negative attitudes toward homosexuals (especially toward gay men) than do females (Johnson, Brems & Alford-Keating, 1997; Kite & Whitley, 1996; Whitley & Kite, 1995; Young & Whertvine, 1982). Kite and Whitley (1996) argue that cultural norms for masculinity are more rigid than those for femininity, and that males, being the ones who hold power in our patriarchal society, are the most invested in maintaining traditional gender roles and are therefore the most virulent in attacking those who are seen to threaten the social structure of gender. Therefore, males tend to be more negative toward those who deviate from traditional gender roles (which LGBs certainly do). These attitudes may translate into speech and action in the workplace, so that the more men there are in an LGB employee's workgroup, the more discrimination she or he is likely to encounter.

An LGB employee's workgroup is the most proximal environmental influence on his or her experiences. Thus, researchers need to spend more effort examining workgroup features and their relationships with sexual orientation discrimination. Considering that much sexual orientation discrimination on the job is of a direct interpersonal nature (for example, slurs and jokes, snubbing [Waldo, 1999]), more attention directed toward those with whom LGB employees have their daily interpersonal interactions seems warranted.

Targets' Disclosure Decisions

Several studies have examined associations between LGB employees' disclosure decisions and actions and the experience of sexual orientation discrimination. On the one hand, individuals who remain completely closeted on the job have been found to suffer less discrimination that is personally directed at them specifically because they are gay (Waldo, 1999). However, even when an employee attempts to conceal his or her orientation at work, such concealment may not be entirely successful, and others may still discriminate based upon suspicions or rumors (Herek, 1996). And when attempts at concealment are successful, closeted employees may experience more indirect discrimination, such as hearing more derogatory comments, jokes, and slurs about gay men and lesbians than do those who are more out, as others do not feel bound by the norms of politeness that often inhibit making such jokes or comments around a member of the targeted group (Frable, 1993).

Employees who choose to be more open on the job, on the other hand, might be expected to experience more personally directed discrimination than those who remain closeted, as, once their orientation is known, they become clearly identifiable targets for discrimination and prejudice (Frable, Wortman, & Joseph, 1997). However, workplace research has found that greater openness regarding one's sexual orientation is associated with less discrimination overall (Button, 2001; Ragins & Cornwell, 2000). The causal direction of this negative association between disclosure and discrimination is not clear, as the research to date is cross-sectional. As a possible antecedent, disclosure certainly is likely to lessen discrimination that is committed due to unthinking assumptions of heterosexuality rather than intentional antipathy on the part of others in the environment (Frable, 1993). Disclosure may also lead to a more "gay-friendly" workplace environment by helping co-workers overcome stereotypes about LGB people in favor of more individualized perceptions. One gay man described how he confronted a coworker who was joking about his sexuality, and tried to explain to the coworker how such things felt. He said, "It was interesting because he responded to that by saying, 'you know, I have to say I have never considered the idea of what it would be like if I were gay . . . but what you're saying does make some sense.'" The gay employee said that the colleague had become much more sensitive after that conversation (Friskopp & Silverstein, 1995). Thus, disclosure may serve to reduce discrimination in some instances. However, an effect in the opposite direction is also very plausible: that environments that are less heterosexist encourage disclosure. The best way to conceive of the association between disclosure and discrimination likely is as a bi-directional, iterative relationship: disclosure can reduce heterosexism in the environment, which can encourage more disclosure, which can further alter the environment, and so on. As yet, we are lacking studies that examine this process over time, studies that are definitely needed if we are to understand the ways in which personal disclosure decisions interact with the workplace environment.

Overall, research on possible antecedents of sexual orientation discrimination has focused on only a few variables, and firm conclusions are difficult to draw. Organizational policies may or may not reduce discrimination, or they may be merely a reflection of a preexisting nondiscriminatory climate. A higher proportion of female coworkers and the presence of LGB coworkers appears to be associated with less discrimination, but the value of an LGB supervisor is unclear. And the nature and direction of the relationship between disclosure and discrimination is uncertain and likely to be quite complex. Clearly, there is a need for more attention to LGB employee experiences and issues, and countless opportunities for extending our knowledge exist. Therefore, we now turn to issues and suggestions for furthering research on LGB employees and sexual orientation discrimination in the workplace.

So Where Do We Go from Here?

Organizational researchers, as we have shown, are just beginning to turn their attention to sexual orientation discrimination, so, as yet the literature is sparse. The permissible generalizable conclusions at this point appear to be limited to an acknowledgment that sexual orientation discrimination in the workplace does happen, and that it has negative outcomes for its targets in terms of job attitudes and well-being. The ways in which such discrimination and its outcomes may be related to organizational, group, or individual workplace characteristics are obviously complex, and we do not yet have enough of a body of literature to determine boundary conditions and qualifiers of the current, often conflicting, research findings (for example, those regarding the effect of various organizational policies or of having an LGB supervisor). Therefore, in the space remaining, we would like to raise some issues and make some suggestions for future research in this area.

We begin with a discussion of the difficulties and opportunities associated with studying disclosure of sexual orientation as it relates to workplace discrimination. Then we consider several features of the other people in an LGB employee's environment that may provide fruitful avenues for research. Next, we advance suggestions for examining how discrimination may affect the career development of LGBs, and then discuss the need for establishing boundary conditions and directions of influence. We consider distinctions *between* gay men, lesbians, and bisexuals, as well as how other stigmatizing conditions (for example, minority race) may interact with those identities. Finally, we raise some methodological issues, including concerns with measurement and sampling. We hope that these numerous suggestions will emphasize the opportunities available for meaningfully advancing the knowledge regarding sexual orientation discrimination in the workplace, and inspire researchers to turn their efforts toward a consideration of LGB employees.

The Issue of Disclosure

As noted earlier, the fact that homosexuality is not a visible characteristic is one major factor that makes LGB employees different from more researched minority groups; it is also a factor that makes LGB research complicated. First of all, disclosure is a complicated concept to define and measure. Disclosure is not a one-time event, and one should not view LGB employees as simply "out" or "not out" on the job. Rather, the *degree* to which an employee is out at work should be considered. Such considerations may include addressing the number of others in the workplace to whom an LGB employee has disclosed, the relationships of those individuals to the employee, and the nature of the disclosure (for example, direct verbal disclosure versus some sort of "display" through clothing or jewelry). Furthermore, the reactions of those to whom an LGB employee discloses are likely to be important determinants of the employee's subsequent experiences on the job and future disclosure decisions (Griffith & Hebl, 2002). Merely asking whether one's coworkers know of one's sexual orientation does not assess how comfortable those coworkers are about it. The situation may be one in which, as one gay man put it, "it was okay to be gay as long as I never talked about it" (Kitzinger, 1991, p. 232). As Hodges and Hutter (1974) pointed out, "To share the knowledge of one's homosexuality with non-gay people, but never to speak of it, is to tacitly agree that, like bad breath, homosexuality is something embarrassing, best left unmentioned." This situation seems to be fairly common; several of Friskopp and Silverstein's (1995) interviewees described a similar environment in which, "I know they know, and they know I know they know, but we never acknowledge they know in words." Thus, we might expand our understanding of disclosure issues by asking not just whether coworkers know of one's sexual orientation, but whether speaking of it is permissible or discouraged.

Furthermore, organizational research tends to examine outness at only one point in time. Coming out at work is a process, and the way that process unfolds is likely to be an extremely important determinant (and result) of the workplace experiences of an LGB employee. Consider a gay employee who decides to disclose his sexual orientation to a coworker. If that coworker reacts positively, the employee may feel less stress on the job now that he has an "ally," and he may then decide to disclose to some others. But if that coworker reacts negatively, the employee may well refrain from engaging in any further disclosure. Perhaps the issue then "goes away." But perhaps the coworker, who now knows but is not accepting, begins to engage in discriminatory behaviors toward the gay employee. Perhaps that coworker tells others in the workplace, and the environment becomes more unfriendly—or more supportive, depending on the reactions of those others. Our failure to examine this process of coming out and its results may account for conflicting findings regarding the relationship of disclosure to experienced discrimination, with supportive reactions possibly leading to less discrimination and hostile reactions leading to more discrimination and more negative outcomes. Clearly reactions are important; recall that the one study that did ask about coworker reactions found that such reactions completely mediated the relationship between disclosure and job satisfaction (Griffith & Hebl, 2002)—and that study only asked about "my coworkers" as a whole, not reactions to each step in the disclosure process. Examining that entire process, and reactions along the way, could be very helpful in clarifying how disclosure is related to sexual orientation discrimination and its outcomes.

The reactions to and results of one LGB employee's disclosure also are likely to have a strong influence on any other closeted LGBs in the workplace. LGB workers commonly use others' observed experiences to gauge probable outcomes if they themselves were to disclose, as is exemplified by one lesbian's comment that, "I would never come out to my supervisor because there was a woman who did and she went through hell! My supervisor mocked her and abused her and eventually fired her. I know I would be too" (Kitzinger, 1991, p. 226). Thus, when closeted LGB employees view more open LGBs being treated poorly, their own fear of disclosure and discrimination is likely to increase. Indeed, the fear of disclosure may be an important variable for study in the examination of LGBs' workplace experiences. Ragins and Cornwell (2001) assessed such fear, in addition to actual disclosure, and found that the fear of disclosure (but not actual disclosure!) was significantly related to psychological strain, work and career attitudes, and career outcomes.

Not only is "fear of disclosure" a construct worthy of study on its own, the fact that such fear can exist highlights another important issue: not all workplace disclosure of sexual orientation is voluntary. Certainly, being "outed" against one's will is likely to have different results than self-determined disclosure that is the result of a thoughtful personal decision. "Outing" may be more likely to happen in organizations that are less gay-friendly, as there may be a higher proportion of LGBs who are closeted (and thus able to be outed), and outing in hostile organizations may be used as a sort of "weapon" against an LGB employee. As one (closeted) lesbian was told by her boss: "I love to get a bunch of people together and go down to one of those gay piano bars after doing a big deal. . . . You never know who you're going to see from your competition. All you gotta do is see 'em there and you've got 'em beat for the next job. You never know who might be a hidden faggot. It's so easy to start a whispering campaign" (Friskopp & Silverstein, 1995, p. 189).

Even if the outing is not malicious, the reactions of others to learning about an employees' orientation secondhand may be less positive than with direct personal disclosure. Herek and Capitano (1996) found that, of heterosexual people who had a gay or lesbian friend, those who had been personally told by their friend held more positive attitudes toward LGBs in general than did those who found out indirectly. Current measures that merely ask whether coworkers and supervisors "know" do not capture whether an LGB employee discloses personally and willingly, or is outed involuntarily. How others came by that knowledge may be very important in determining the results of the disclosure for the LGB employee.

Concealment of one's sexual orientation at work also may result in "spillover" into other life domains. Certainly, the anxiety and strain associated with remaining closeted is likely to have a negative impact on the LGB person away from work. Remaining closeted on the job can also create strains within an LGB employee's romantic relationships. Partners may feel they are a source of shame, or may exert pressure for the employee to come out. One gay man said, "It's like wearing armor at work, and it's difficult to shed that armor when I get home—not to feel tense, alert for danger, defensive, when I want to be open and trusting with Mike" (Kitzinger, 1991, p. 228). A lesbian explained how her partner "resents it that I have to keep her existence a secret; she feels as though I must be ashamed of her," and another woman stated that she felt her partner was "pressuring me to be more public . . . in a sense, she's taken away my right to make my own decision" (Kitzinger, pp. 229, 233). Another gay man stated that his relationship was suffering, with him feeling he was implicitly saying to his partner, "Okay, prove to me you're worth all this hassle I'm going through at work" (Kitzinger, p. 232). Research examining the specific ways in which workplace concealment of sexual orientation may affect relationships outside of work could be useful in understanding associations between LGB workplace experiences and general well-being.

Finally, as noted throughout the earlier parts of this chapter, disclosure appears to be related to everything—to discrimination (Waldo, 1999), organizational policies and climate (Button, 2001), well-being (Driscoll et al., 1996), and job attitudes (Ragins & Cornwell, 2001a). And these relationships are likely bi-directional and interrelated, thereby making attempts to tease apart cause-and-effect relationships impossible, based only upon logic and cross-sectional research. Again, we must begin to examine the disclosure process, its antecedents, and its outcomes over time if we are to meaningfully further our knowledge in this area. The complications to research posed by considerations of disclosure will be likely to appear daunting to those considering studying LGB employees. Nonetheless, it seems that disclosure must be dealt with if attempts to understand LGB workplace experiences are to be fruitful.

Characteristics of Other People in the Workplace

As noted earlier, few features of the people in the LGB employee's immediate environment have been studied. The previous section mentioned issues of coworkers' reactions to disclosure; characteristics that might influence those reactions, as well as the propensity to discriminate, are worthy of study. In terms of demographic features, little beyond gender has been examined. Several other possible coworker traits that could be explored are suggested by the social psychology literature regarding attitudes toward homosexuality and LGB people, even though that research does not specifically address sexual orientation *discrimination* or workplace issues.

One feature that has been found to relate to heterosexist attitudes is belief in and endorsement of traditional norms regarding acceptable gender roles. Ideas of "appropriate" traits, appearance, and behavior for men and women are socially shared and prescribed (Lindsey, 1997). Children are socialized early about "normal" gender roles and learn to ostracize those who do not conform (Lindsey,

1997; Pharr, 1997). Thus, some of the antipathy toward LGB people may stem from their violation of "acceptable" gender roles. Considerable research does attest to the fact that those who most strongly believe in traditional gender roles hold the most negative attitudes toward homosexuals (Krulewitz & Nash, 1980; Kurdek, 1988; Newman, 1989; Whitley, 1987). Sexual orientation discrimination often includes allegations of being "gender-inappropriate," such as the male headwaiter who was fired for being "too feminine" and "too flamboyant," or the staffing services supervisor who was criticized because her voice was too "heavy and masculine" (HRC, 2001a). Therefore, the coworkers who most strongly endorse traditional gender roles also may be those who are most likely to engage in sexual orientation discrimination.

Religiosity also has been found to relate to attitudes about homosexuality; those who score higher on measures of religiosity generally hold more heterosexist attitudes (Johnson et al., 1997; Vanderstoep & Green, 1988). Gentry (1986) found that those who participated in religious functions more frequently reported more discomfort around homosexual people, and Maret (1984) reported that those who held fundamentalist religious beliefs held more heterosexist attitudes. Thus, features of individuals' religious beliefs and activities may influence their propensity to discriminate against their LGB coworkers.

Some personality traits have been found to relate to heterosexist attitudes; empathy is negatively related to heterosexism (Johnson et al., 1997) and authoritarianism is positively related to negative attitudes toward homosexuality (Haddock et al., 1993; Herek, 1984). More negative attitudes are expressed by Republicans than by Democrats (Bierly, 1985). Age is also correlated with attitudes; older individuals tend to be more heterosexist (Kurdek, 1988). Beliefs about the nature of homosexuality may also be determinants of people's attitudes toward LGB people. Several studies have found that those who believe homosexuality is "chosen" or "learned" endorse more heterosexist attitudes than do those who believe a homosexual orientation is genetically or physiologically determined (Aguero, Block, & Byrne, 1984; Ernulf, Innala, & Whitam, 1989; Whitley, 1990). Thus, many coworker characteristics might be investigated as possible causes or correlates of discrimination against LGBs on the job.

Supervisors certainly deserve more attention. Because they have power over LGB employees, whether a supervisor is supportive, indifferent, or hostile can be very important. Many LGBs have reported supervisors who did nothing in response to interpersonal discrimination, such as a supervisor of a gay Detroit postal worker, who did nothing to intervene when the employee complained of coworkers leaving AIDS brochures and lewd graffiti at his workstation and calling him a "fag" who "sucks dick" (HRC, 2001a). There are numerous instances of LGB employees who were told by their supervisors that they themselves were the problem, such as the manufacturing plant worker in Maine who complained of constant harassment by coworkers and was told by his supervisor that he was failing to work effectively as a team member (HRC, 2001a). Sometimes supervisors are the worst source of antipathy and abuse, as in the case of Douglas Retterer that opened this chapter. However, supportive managers may be very valuable, as was the case for one of Friskopp and Silverstein's (1995) interviewees who described how much he was helped in being honest with his clients by support from above: "What helped me . . . was speaking to my boss and saying, 'Look, we all know that personal conversations are a part of doing business and all these situations come up. My preference is to act honestly and nondeceptively. Is the company willing to abide by its standards and support me in doing that?' He had to stop and think and [said] yes. . . . if they're willing to lose business rather than sacrifice their principles, that really empowers me" (Friskopp & Silverstein, 1995, p. 127).

Supervisors' perceptions of the general social climate for LGBs also may influence the extent to which they discriminate against LGB employees. Perpetrators of discrimination sometimes deny personal prejudice, instead citing the prejudice of others as a reason for their own actions. For example, a police officer in Los Angeles was told to conceal her sexual orientation because the department was "not yet ready to accept gays," and the CFO of an aircraft parts manufacturer was terminated because the board felt that customers would be reluctant to do business with the company if they knew he was gay (HRC, 2001a). The general social acceptance of heterosexism described earlier can make it seem "appropriate" for businesses to accommodate the prejudices of their employees and clients. However, supervisors are likely to differ in how widespread they believe blatant heterosexism to be, and the extent to which they feel that accommodating such heterosexism is acceptable; these variables may be relevant in determining a supervisor's likelihood to discriminate.

Finally, there has been no attention devoted to subordinates of LGBs. Hostile subordinates can threaten an LGB supervisor's effectiveness and provide a rationale for discrimination from those further up the ladder. For example, stockbroker Michael Armentrout was denied a promotion after the regional vice president was told by a broker that the people in the branch Armentrout was to manage would not work for a gay man (HRC, 2001a). Clients or customers, as well, can cause difficulties, by being openly hostile, withdrawing business, or complaining to superiors. For example, a customer of a funeral home in Idaho, upon finding out that the manager of the home was gay, called his superiors in the main office and threatened to withdraw her future-services contract, as she would never use a funeral home that employed a gay person. The manager was subsequently fired (HRC, 2001a). Thus, all those with whom LGBs interact on a daily basis at work—coworkers, supervisors, subordinates, and clients—are likely to be important influences on the LGB employee's encounters with discrimination and the results of those experiences.

Career Development

Heterosexism and discrimination are likely to affect the career paths of many LGBs. Certainly, direct, formal discrimination, such as being fired or passed over for promotion, is detrimental to career development. But LGBs also may curtail their own career options and choices based on experienced or expected heterosexism and discrimination. A gay consultant related how he "was on the partnership track for many years, but it's harder to be closeted the longer you are there and the older you get. It seemed my career prospects would be better if I left, which is what I did" (Friskopp & Silverstein, 1995, p. 104). They may reject the possibility of employment in organizations that seem hostile, or may be clearly "out" in the hiring process to allow such companies to "self-select" out of the LGB person's consideration. As one lesbian who is out on her résumé succinctly stated, "If they don't want to hire me because I'm gay, I don't want to work there anyway" (Friskopp & Silverstein, p. 223). (One can "come out" on a résumé by listing things like involvement in gay rights organizations.) Finally, some LGB people may completely change the industry in which they work in an attempt to achieve a more amenable environment. For example, one gay man described how he left his job as a builder, where it was necessary to constantly "prove you're a he-man" and where the men he worked with seemed "to be driven by a pathological need to prove they're not gay." He became a hairdresser instead, saying, "I wanted to work somewhere where I could be free to be who I am" (Kitzinger, 1991, p. 230). It appears that heterosexism and discrimination may have a profound effect on the career paths of LGB people.

Boundary Conditions

There has been little research on sexual orientation discrimination that has examined anything as a potential moderator of relationships of interest. For example, disclosure may have interactive effects with other variables under study. As such, an examination of disclosure as a possible moderator of relationships being studied may help establish boundary conditions for those effects. Nearly all the studies to date are either simple correlational research, or tests of multivariable path models that assess mediation but not moderation. We must look for moderation if we are ever to make sense of conflicting findings. For example, we earlier alluded to the possibility that the relationship between having an LGB supervisor and having experienced discrimination may be moderated by the extent to which that supervisor is out in the workplace, in that supervisors who are themselves closeted may be of little help to their LGB subordinates. Many other such possibilities exist: perhaps the relationships between organizational policies (for example, inclusive diversity training) and discrimination vary depending on coworker attitudes or gender, or whether the policies are backed up by actions or are just "lip service." Maybe the strength of associations between discrimination and well-being indicators depend upon the supportiveness of one's supervisor, or the type of industry, or the source of the sample, or features external to the workplace such as having a supportive family. The point is that antecedent-discrimination-outcome relationships are highly unlikely to be precisely the same for all LGB employees in all workplaces; we must look for qualifiers and boundary conditions.

Antecedents, Outcomes, or Both?

Difficulties with determining the direction of influence in relationships of variables with sexual orientation discrimination have been alluded to throughout this chapter. For example, we are unable to determine the extent to which policies influence discrimination versus a discriminatory environment's influence on the likelihood of the adoption of gay-friendly policies. Or it is unclear whether workgroups with more LGB people create a more gay-friendly environment, or whether gay-friendly environments simply attract more LGB workers. Once again, to assess these complex relationships, researchers will have to conduct longitudinal research. Long-term studies are admittedly difficult, but the question of effect direction is of vital importance if organizational researchers are to provide any guidance for facilitating change in organizations.

Lesbians and Gay Men
Versus Bisexuals (and Transgenders)

We have used the acronym "LGB" throughout, combining bisexuals with lesbians and gay men. Some studies regarding sexual orientation discrimination have explicitly included bisexuals (Waldo, 1999) whereas others appear to have included only those who self-identified as gay or lesbian (Button, 2001; Ellis & Riggle, 1995). But there has yet to be any examination of the ways in which bisexuals may be different from those who are exclusively homosexual. Bisexuals may have unique concerns with developing an identity, feeling well-identified with neither heterosexual nor homosexual people (or with both). Furthermore, some antipathy toward bisexuals may be found in the gay and lesbian community, with bisexuals referred to as "fence-sitters," viewed as questionable allies unwilling to fully relinquish "heterosexual privilege" (Duberman, 1999). In addition, the treatment of bisexuals by others in their workplace is likely to vary greatly depending upon whether they are in a relationship with a same- or opposite-gender person at a given time. Thus, combining bisexuals and homosexuals in research may not be warranted. Certainly, researchers should look for differences between bisexual and homosexual respondents, and research specifically devoted to examining the experiences of bisexuals is needed.

Occasionally, one will see the acronym LGBT, referring to lesbian, gay, bisexual, and *transgender* individuals. Transgenders do share some of the same concerns as LGB people, as prejudice and discrimination against transgenders likely have similar roots in rigid stereotypical ideas about gender roles as does heterosexism (Pharr, 1997). But gender-identification and sexual orientation are two very different constructs—most gay men are gender-identified as male, and most lesbians are gender-identified as female (Earnshaw, 1991). Transgender individuals, however, have a gender identity inconsistent with their physiology at birth. They may choose to surgically alter their physical gender or not, and their sexual orientation vis-à-vis their "chosen" gender may be heterosexual, homosexual, or bisexual. Even where LGBs are covered by a nondiscrimination law, transgender people usually are not. Only one of the eleven states with a nondiscrimination law, Minnesota, includes gender identity as an impermissible basis for discrimination (HRC, 2001b). There is no research of which we are aware that specifically examines the workplace experiences of transgenders; such research could be a fascinating undertaking. But we do wish to emphasize the distinction between gender identity and sexual orientation, a distinction that can be lost when everyone who does not conform to their traditional assigned gender role is lumped together as "LGBT."

Lesbians Versus Gay Men

Even when research examines only those with an exclusively homosexual orientation, there is a tendency to combine gay men and lesbians. Few studies have looked to see whether gay male participants differed from lesbians in any way. In two studies that did, neither Ragins and Cornwell (2000) nor Griffith and Hebl (2002) found any differences in the reported incidence of discrimination, although Griffith and Hebl did report that the lesbians in their study were more accepting of their identity than were the gay men.

Chrobot-Mason et al. (2001) found that lesbians used identity management strategies in a somewhat different way than did gay men. Conceptually, there is reason to expect that the experiences of gay men may differ from those of lesbians. The social psychology literature provides ample evidence that people tend to hold considerably more negative attitudes toward gay men than toward lesbians (Whitley & Kite, 1995). However, in the workplace, lesbians may face a "double stigma" of being both female and homosexual. Some have argued that homosexuality is not the same stigma for males as for females (Kite & Whitley, 1996). Furthermore, some concerns are not shared by gay men and lesbians, such as concern for the "gender gap" in wages and job opportunities, which hits lesbian couples doubly hard but may actually be a benefit to gay male couples. Friskopp and Silverstein (1995) found that as gay men moved up the corporate ladder and gained seniority and power, they usually felt less vulnerable to sexual orientation discrimination. Lesbians, however, were very aware of their rarity, simply as *women,* at top organizational levels, and felt their positions more precarious as they rose in the hierarchy. Researchers need to consider the experiences of gay men and lesbians separately to determine points of commonality and difference.

Additional Stigmatizing Conditions

Just as lesbian women might be additionally stigmatized by their female gender in some employment contexts, other stigmatizing characteristics may complicate the work experiences of LGBs. The combination of minority race and minority sexual orientation may be especially difficult. Crow, Fok, and Hartman (1995) conducted a laboratory study that indicated that black homosexuals were more likely than white gay men and lesbians to be discriminated against in hiring (although heterosexuals of any race or gender were preferred over all homosexual applicants, even the white, male ones). However, Ragins and Cornwell (2000) found that LGBs of color were no less likely to come out at work than white LGBs and were more likely to come out when their supervisor was of the same race, suggesting that minority race may provide a common ground even for those who do not share a similar sexual orientation. But their sample was derived from national gay organizations, whose membership may be more likely to be out at work than are LGBs who do not join such groups. In contrast, Friskopp and Silverstein (1995) reported that their interviewees were less likely to disclose their sexual orientation if they possessed another stigmatizing condition: "They said they were already unusual enough at their companies and didn't want to spend any more difference capital on the gay issue" (p. 167). More study is required to understand how other stigmas, not just race but also disability, obesity, advancing age, or minority religion, for example, may interact with homosexuality in determining the workplace experiences of LGBs.

Measurement Issues

The facts that there is no legal protection against sexual orientation discrimination in most states and that many LGB people are not "out" to all others in their workplaces mean that researchers must be especially careful to protect confidentiality. In order to not inadvertently "out" someone, researchers usually do not want to reveal that someone is taking part in a study at all. These concerns have led to research based almost entirely on self-report measures. Self-report data on discrimination can be problematic, as actual discriminatory incidents cannot be dissociated from people's attributions for those incidents (Gomez & Trierweiler, 2001). There is also the potential for method bias when all measures are self-reports (Schmitt, 1994; Spector, 1987). Researchers should attempt to be creative in obtaining other data, for example, by asking everyone in a workplace (heterosexuals and homosexuals) for information regarding climate and attitudes, perhaps vis-à-vis "diversity" in general (including race, gender, disability, age, and so forth) to avoid an obvious focus on sexual orientation. In addition, some data on specific organizations are publicly available; for example, the Human Rights Campaign publishes a report called the *State of the Workplace for Lesbian, Gay, Bisexual and Transgendered Americans* every year, which tracks gay-relevant policies of all Fortune 500 companies. Researchers should try to make use of such resources to supplement self-report data.

Another concern is the lack of measures specifically developed upon, or validated with, LGB samples. We must continue to devote efforts to developing appropriate measures for the study of sexual orientation discrimination. Furthermore, we must be cautious in using measures developed for other populations. In a study by one of the authors of this chapter, an established measure of social support functions (Davis, Morris, & Kraus [1998], Social Provisions Checklist) exhibited a factor structure in the LGB sample different from what has been reported for other types of samples, in that the supposedly separate support functions of emotional and informational support were not differentiated in the LGB sample (Deitch, 2002). These sorts of differences should be attended to, not just because they suggest existing measures may be inadequate, but also because they may indicate true, unique features of the operation of constructs and processes in LGB populations.

Sampling

Finally, a major difficulty with studying members of a concealably stigmatized group is obtaining a sample, as such individuals need to explicitly identify themselves to be included in research. Every sampling strategy is likely to produce a sample that is skewed in some direction. Several studies have obtained samples from the mailing lists of activist organizations (Day & Schoenrade, 1997); these samples probably include more gay-identified and politically aware individuals than the larger LGB population. Also, because membership in those organizations typically requires the payment of dues, such samples are likely to exclude LGB persons of lower socioeconomic status. Unless one specifically targets minority LGB organizations (such as Ragins & Cornwell, 2000, who recruited from an African American LGB group and a Latina-Latino group), samples gleaned from activist organizations are also likely to be disproportionately white. Other studies have recruited at community events such as gay pride rallies (Waldo, 1999), which will be likely to draw primarily those who are "out" and self-accepting of their gay identity.

Certainly, gaining access to closeted individuals for study is extremely difficult. A snowball sampling technique (as employed by Button [2001] and Driscoll et al. [1996], for example), whereby respondents are asked to recruit other LGB people they know, may gain some closeted individuals. As the Internet appears to be a resource of growing importance for individuals who are not yet out to explore aspects of gay life and gay identity (McKenna & Bargh, 1998), in the aforementioned study by one of the authors of this chapter, a strategy of recruiting on the Internet for a Web survey was employed, including a snowball sampling component (Deitch, 2002). This strategy did gain some closeted individuals, but also resulted in a sample that was far too educated to possibly be representative in that respect (40 percent of the respondents held postgraduate degrees).

Furthermore, once a sample has been obtained there is no way even to accurately identify the population to be sampled so that representativeness can be assessed. For example, is a sample that is 15 percent closeted representative? How could we ever know? We just must accept that no single study, whether based on an Internet sample, a sample from activist organizations, or a sample gleaned at community events, will ever achieve a truly representative sample of gay men and lesbians. The best way to deal with this problem is for many similar studies to be conducted on different subsets of the gay and lesbian population acquired via different sampling strategies so that the consistency of results in varied subpopulations can be evaluated. Findings that hold across different types of samples then may be generalized with more confidence to the larger population of gay men and lesbians, and findings that do not generalize may help establish boundary conditions.

This rough agenda for research is just a beginning. We have attempted to highlight some of the substantive issues requiring attention, including possible antecedents of sexual orientation discrimination in the workplace, outcomes of that discrimination, and the role of disclosure of sexual orientation. We also have raised some difficulties with pursuing research on sexual orientation, such as measurement concerns and challenges in obtaining samples. Even acknowledging these difficulties, we have attempted to demonstrate the tremendous potential for interesting and meaningful research regarding LGB employees. We hope that organizational researchers will tap this potential by pursuing some of the research issues we have raised here, as well as developing further directions for studying workplace discrimination based on sexual orientation.

Conclusions

Lesbian, gay, and bisexual people are a sizable minority in America, and most LGB people, like everyone else, work for a living. There is evidence that these employees experience substantial discrimination in the workplace. Many LGB individuals are fired or denied promotions and rewards for reasons that have no relation to their job performance. LGB employees may be subjected to harassment and verbal abuse or even physically assaulted on the job due to their minority sexual orientation. This discrimination clearly has a negative impact on those who are its targets, causing stress and anxiety and damaging physical health and psychological well-being. Such discrimination may be organizationally costly as well, leading to negative job attitudes, the potential loss of talented workers, and the possible alienation of LGBs as customers and consumers.

But despite the growing focus on "diversity" in recent years, the concerns of LGB employees have been virtually ignored by organizational researchers. There has been very little study of the workplace experiences of LGB employees and their encounters with discrimination on the job. The causes of such discrimination and the processes by which it affects employees are poorly understood. Without an understanding of the factors that underlie sexual orientation discrimination, useful suggestions for ways to counter it cannot be developed, and thus LGB employees continue to suffer mistreatment on the job.

We hope that by pointing out just a few of the potentially interesting research questions in this area, we have encouraged researchers to help rectify this lack of knowledge. Studies show slow but consistent trends toward greater integration and acceptance of LGBs in society (Yang, 1999) and many organizations would welcome clear guidance regarding how to reduce sexual orientation discrimination and become more gay-friendly companies (HRC, 2001b). Providing such guidance is our responsibility as organizational researchers, and we hope this chapter spurs researchers' interest and increases the attention devoted to lesbian, gay, and bisexual employees.

References

Aguero, J. E., Bloch, L., & Byrne, D. (1984). The relationships among sexual beliefs, attitudes, experience, and homophobia. *Journal of Homosexuality, 10,* 95–107.

Alpern, S. (2002). Gay & lesbian workplace rights: An issue for investors. Available: http://www.planetout.com/pno/money/article.html?sernum=49.

American Civil Liberties Union (1997). Testimony on the Employment Non-Discrimination Act: Hearings before the Senate Committee on Labor and Human Resources, 105th Congress, S. 869.

Badgett, M.V.L. (1995). The wage effects of sexual orientation discrimination. *Industrial and Labor Relations Review*, 48, 726–739.

Bielby, W. T. (2000). Minimizing workplace gender and racial bias. *Contemporary Sociology*, 29, 120–129.

Bierly, M. M. (1985). Prejudice toward contemporary outgroups as a generalized attitude. *Journal of Applied Social Psychology*, 15, 189–199.

Boatwright, K., Gilbert, M., Forrest, L., & Ketzenberger, K. (1996). Impact of identity development upon career trajectory: Listening to the voices of lesbian women. *Journal of Vocational Behavior*, 48, 210–228.

Button, S. B. (2001). Organizational efforts to affirm sexual diversity: A cross-level examination. *Journal of Applied Psychology*, 86, 17–28.

Cahill, S. (2000). *What's at stake for the gay, lesbian, bisexual, and transgender community in the 2000 presidential elections*. New York: NGLTF Policy Institute.

Carlson, D. S., & Perrewe, P. L. (1999). The role of social support in the stressor-strain relationship: An examination of work-family conflict. *Journal of Management*, 25, 513–540.

Chelune, G. J., Sultan, F. E., & Williams, C. L. (1980). Loneliness, self-disclosure, and interpersonal effectiveness. *Journal of Counseling Psychology*, 27, 462–468.

Chen, M., & Bargh, J. A. (1997). Nonconscious behavioral confirmation processes: The self-fulfilling consequences of automatic stereotype activation. *Journal of Experimental Social Psychology*, 33, 541–560.

Chrobot-Mason, D., Button, S. B., & DiClementi, J. D. (2001). Sexual identity management strategies: An exploration of antecedents and consequences. *Sex Roles*, 45, 321–336.

Cohen, L. L., & Swim, J. K. (1995). The differential impact of gender ratios on women and men: Tokenism, self-confidence, and expectations. *Personality and Social Psychology Bulletin*, 21, 876–884.

Comstock, G. D. (1991). *Violence against lesbians and gay men*. New York: Columbia University Press.

Crocker, J., Major, B., & Steele, C. (1998). Social stigma. In D. T. Gilbert, S. T. Fiske, & G. Lindzey (Eds.), *The handbook of social psychology* (Vol. 2, 4th ed., pp. 504–553). New York: McGraw-Hill.

Croteau, J. M. (1996). Research on the work experiences of lesbian, gay, and bisexual people: An integrative review of methodology and findings. *Journal of Vocational Behavior*, 48, 195–209.

Croteau, J. M., & Lark, J. S. (1995). On being lesbian, gay, or bisexual in student affairs: A national survey of experiences on the job. *NAPSA Journal*, 32, 189–197.

Croteau, J. M., & von Destinon, M. (1994). A national survey of job search experiences of lesbian, gay, or bisexual student affairs professionals. *Journal of College Student Development, 35,* 40–45.

Crow, S. M., Fok, L. Y., & Hartman, S. J. (1995). Priorities of hiring discrimination: Who is at greatest risk—women, blacks, or homosexuals? *Academy of Management Best Paper Proceedings,* 443–448.

Davis, M. H., Morris, M. M., & Kraus, L. A. (1998). Relationship-specific and global perceptions of social support: Associations with well-being and attachment. *Journal of Personality and Social Psychology, 74,* 468–481.

Day, N. E., & Schoenrade, P. (1997). Staying in the closet versus coming out: Relationships between communication about sexual orientation and work attitudes. *Personnel Psychology, 50,* 147–163.

Deitch, E. A. (2002). Concealable stigma and well-being: The role of social identity as a buffer against sexual orientation discrimination in the workplace. Unpublished doctoral dissertation, Tulane University, New Orleans.

Deitch, E. A., Barsky, A., Butz, R. M., Brief, A. P., Chan, S.S.Y., & Bradley, J. C. (2002). Subtle yet significant: The existence and impact of everyday racial discrimination in the workplace. *Human Relations.* Under review.

Devine, P. G. (1989). Stereotypes and prejudice: Their automatic and controlled components. *Journal of Personality and Social Psychology, 56,* 5–18.

Dormann, C., & Zapf, D. (1999). Social support, social stressors at work, and depressive symptoms: Testing for main and moderating effects with structural equations in a three-wave longitudinal study. *Journal of Applied Psychology, 84,* 874–884.

Driscoll, J. M., Kelley, F. A., & Fassinger, R. E. (1996). Lesbian identity and disclosure in the workplace: Relation to occupational stress and satisfaction. *Journal of Vocational Behavior, 48,* 229–242.

Duberman, M. B. (1999). *Left out: The politics of exclusion.* New York: Basic Books.

Dyer, R. (2001). Who cares how they get their jollies? Available: http://journal.maine.com/op-ed/rdyer/homosexuals.

Earnshaw, J. (1991). Homosexuals and transsexuals at work: Legal issues. In M. J. Davidson & J. Earnshaw (Eds.), *Vulnerable workers: Psychosocial and legal issues* (pp. 241–257). London: John Wiley.

Edelman, L. B., & Petterson, S. M. (1999). Symbols and substance in organizational response to civil rights law. *Research in Social Stratification and Mobility, 17,* 107–135.

Ellis, A. L., & Riggle, E.D.B. (1995). The relation of job satisfaction and degree of openness about one's sexual orientation for lesbians and gay men. *Journal of Homosexuality, 30,* 75–85.

Ernulf, K. E., Innala, S. M., & Whitam, F. L. (1989). Biological explanation, psychological explanation, and tolerance of homosexuals: A cross-national analysis of beliefs and attitudes. *Psychological Reports,* 65, 1003–1010.

Frable, D.E.S. (1993). Being and feeling unique: Statistical deviance and psychological marginality. *Journal of Personality,* 61, 85–110.

Frable, D.E.S., Platt, L., & Hoey, S. (1998). Concealable stigmas and positive self-perceptions: Feeling better around similar others. *Journal of Personality and Social Psychology,* 74, 909–922.

Frable, D.E.S., Wortman, C., & Joseph, J. (1997). Predicting self-esteem, well-being, and distress in a cohort of gay men: The importance of cultural stigma, personal visibility, community networks, and positive identity. *Journal of Personality,* 65, 599–624.

Friskopp, A., & Silverstein, S. (1995). *Straight jobs, gay lives: Gay and lesbian professionals, the Harvard Business School, and the American workplace.* New York: Scribner.

Gardyn, R. (2001). A market kept in the closet. *American Demographics,* 23, 36–43.

Gay and Lesbian Alliance Against Defamation (1998). GLAAD links journalists and Internet community with progressive organizations responding to Trent Lott's disparaging and homophobic remarks. Available: http://www.glaad.org/org/press/?record=1191.

Gay and Lesbian Alliance Against Defamation (2001). GLAAD's Laura Resource Center. Available: http://www.glaad.org/org/topics/index.html?topic=108.

Gentry, C. S. (1986). Social distance regarding male and female homosexuals. *Journal of Social Psychology,* 127, 199–208.

Glick, P., & Fiske, S. T. (1996). The ambivalent sexism inventory: Differentiating hostile and benevolent sexism. *Journal of Personality and Social Psychology,* 70, 491–512.

Goffman, E. (1963). *Stigma: Notes on the management of spoiled identity.* Englewood Cliffs, NJ: Prentice-Hall.

Gomez, J. P., & Trierweiler, S. J. (2001). Does discrimination terminology create response bias in questionnaire studies of discrimination? *Personality and Social Psychology Bulletin,* 27, 630–638.

Griffith, K. H., & Hebl, M. R. (2002). The disclosure dilemma for gay men and lesbians: "Coming out" at work. *Journal of Applied Psychology,* 87, 1191–1199.

Haaga, D.A.F. (1991). "Homophobia"? *Journal of Social Behavior and Personality,* 6, 171–174.

Haddock, G., Zanna, M. P., & Esses, V. M. (1993). Assessing the structure of prejudicial attitudes: The case of attitudes toward homosexuals. *Journal of Personality and Social Psychology,* 65, 1105–1118.

Herek, G. M. (1984). Beyond "homophobia": A social psychological perspective on attitudes toward lesbians and gay men. *Journal of Homosexuality, 10,* 1–21.

Herek, G. M. (1989). Hate crimes against lesbians and gay men: Issues for research and policy. *American Psychologist, 44,* 948–955.

Herek, G. M. (1990). The context of anti-gay violence. *Journal of Interpersonal Violence, 5,* 316–333.

Herek, G. M. (1996). Why tell if you're not asked? Self-disclosure, intergroup contact, and heterosexuals' attitudes toward lesbians and gay men. In G. M. Herek, J. B. Jobe, & R. M. Carney (Eds.), *Out in force: Sexual orientation and the military* (pp. 197–225). Chicago: University of Chicago.

Herek, G. M., & Capitano, J. P. (1996). "Some of my best friends": Intergroup contact, concealable stigma, and heterosexuals' attitudes toward gay men and lesbians. *Personality and Social Psychology Bulletin, 22,* 412–424.

Hodges, A., & Hutter, D. (1974). *With downcast gays: Aspects of homosexual self-oppression.* Toronto: Pink Triangle Press.

Holzer, H. (1996). *What employers want: Job prospects for the less-educated.* New York: Russell Sage Foundation.

Human Rights Campaign (2001a). *Documenting discrimination.* Washington, DC: HRC.

Human Rights Campaign (2001b). *State of the workplace for lesbian, gay, bisexual and transgender Americans 2001.* Washington, DC: HRC.

Jackson, J. S., Brown, T. N., Williams, D. R., Torres, M., Sellers, S., & Brown, K. (1996). Racism and physical and mental health status of African Americans: A thirteen year national panel study. *Ethnicity and Disease, 6,* 132–147.

Johnson, M. E., Brems, C., & Alford-Keating, P. (1997). Personality correlates of homophobia. *Journal of Homosexuality, 34,* 57–69.

Kanter, R. M. (1977). *Men and women of the corporation.* New York: Basic Books.

Kessler, R. C., Mickelson, K. D., & Williams, D. R. (1999). The prevalence, distribution, and mental health correlates of perceived discrimination in the United States. *Journal of Health and Social Behavior, 40,* 208–230.

Kite, M. E., & Whitley, B. E. (1996). Sex differences in attitudes toward homosexual persons, behaviors, and civil rights: A meta-analysis. *Personality and Social Psychology Bulletin, 22,* 336–353.

Kitzinger, C. (1991). Lesbians and gay men in the workplace: Psychosocial issues. In M. J. Davidson & J. Earnshaw (Eds.), *Vulnerable workers: Psychosocial and legal issues* (pp. 223–257). London: John Wiley.

Kivel, B. D., & Wells, J. W. (1998). Working it out: What managers should know about gay men, lesbians, and bisexual people and their employment issues. In A. Day (Ed.), *Workplace diversity: Issues and perspectives* (pp. 103–115). Washington, DC: NASW.

Kohn, S. (1999). *The domestic partnership organizing manual.* New York: NGLTF Policy Institute.

Konrad, A. M., & Linnehan, F. (1995). Formalized HRM structures: Coordinating equal opportunity or concealing organizational practices? *Academy of Management Journal, 38,* 787–820.

Krulewitz, J. E., & Nash, J. E. (1980). Effects of sex-role attitudes and similarity on men's rejection of male homosexuals. *Journal of Personality and Social Psychology, 38,* 67–74.

Kurdek, L. A. (1988). Correlates of negative attitudes toward homosexuals in heterosexual college students. *Sex Roles, 18,* 727–738.

Leonard, J. S. (1986). The effectiveness of equal employment law and affirmative action regulation. *Research in Labor Economics, 8,* 319–350.

Levine, M. P., & Leonard, R. (1984). Discrimination against lesbians in the work force. *Signs, 9,* 700–710.

Lindsey, L. L. (1997). *Gender roles: A sociological perspective.* Upper Saddle River, NJ: Prentice Hall.

Loomis, J., & Kass, R. (2002, March 22). Boycott boosts diversity awareness. *The Journal News* [electronic version]. Available: http://www.thejournalnews.com/diversitydollars/articles/24divboycotts.html.

Mapes, J. (1999, June 6). Hill takes no-nonsense approach to role in House. *The Oregonian,* p. A4.

Maret, S. M. (1984). Attitudes of fundamentalists toward homosexuality. *Psychological Reports, 55,* 205–206.

McConahay, J. B. (1986). Modern racism, ambivalence, and the Modern Racism Scale. In J. F. Dovidio & S. L. Gaertner (Eds.), *Prejudice, discrimination, and racism* (pp. 91–125). San Diego: Academic Press.

McKenna, K.Y.A., & Bargh, J. A. (1998). Coming out in the age of the Internet: Identity "demarginalization" through virtual group participation. *Journal of Personality and Social Psychology, 75,* 681–694.

Meyer, I. (1995). Minority stress and mental health in gay men, *Journal of Health Sciences and Social Behavior, 36,* 38–56.

Nardi, P. M., & Bolton, R. (1991). Gay-bashing: Violence and aggression against gay men and lesbians. In R. Baenninger (Ed.), *Targets of violence and aggression* (pp. 349–400). Amsterdam: Elsevier Science.

National Gay and Lesbian Task Force (2001a). NGLTF civil rights map. Available: http://www.ngltf.org/downloads/civilmap00801.gif.

National Gay and Lesbian Task Force (2001b). NGLTF sodomy law map. Available: http://www.ngltf.org/downloads/sodomymap.gif.

Newman, B. S. (1989). The relative importance of gender role attitudes to male and female attitudes toward lesbians. *Sex Roles, 21,* 451–465.

Niemann, Y. F., & Dovidio, J. F. (1998). Relationship of solo status, academic rank, and perceived distinctiveness to job satisfaction of racial/ethnic minorities. *Journal of Applied Psychology,* 83, 55–71.

O'Donohue, W., & Caselles, C. E. (1993). Homophobia: Conceptual, definitional and value issues. *Journal of Psychopathology and Behavioral Assessment,* 15, 117–195.

Pharr, S. (1997). *Homophobia: A weapon of sexism.* Berkeley, CA: Chardon Press.

Poverny, L. M., & Finch, W. A., Jr. (1988). Integrating work-related issues on gay and lesbian employees into occupational social work practice. *Employee Assistance Quarterly,* 4(2), 15–29.

Powers, B. (1996). The impact of gay, lesbian, and bisexual workplace issues on productivity. *Journal of Gay and Lesbian Social Services,* 4, 79–90.

Ragins, B. R., & Cornwell, J. M. (2000). *Heterosexism in the workplace: Does race and gender matter?* Paper presented at the conference: Psychological and Organizational Perspectives on Discrimination in the Workplace: Research, Theory and Practice, Houston.

Ragins, B. R., & Cornwell, J. M. (2001a). Pink triangles: Antecedents and consequences of perceived workplace discrimination against gay and lesbian employees. *Journal of Applied Psychology,* 86, 1244–1261.

Ragins, B. R., & Cornwell, J. M. (2001b). *Walking the line: Fear and disclosure of sexual orientation in the workplace.* Paper presented at the Annual Meeting of the Academy of Management, Washington, D.C.

Reskin, B. F. (2000). The proximate causes of employment discrimination. *Contemporary Sociology,* 29, 319–328.

Rubenstein, W. B. (2001). Do gay rights laws matter? An empirical assessment. *Southern California Law Review,* 75, 65–119.

Russo, V. (1989). *Nelly toons: A look at animated sissies.* Presentation at the 13th Lesbian and Gay Film Festival, San Francisco.

Schmitt, N. (1994). Method bias: The importance of theory and measurement. *Journal of Organizational Behavior,* 15, 393–398.

Schneider, K. T., Hitlan, R. T., & Radhakrishnan, P. (2000). An examination of the nature and correlates of ethnic harassment: Experiences in multiple contexts. *Journal of Applied Psychology,* 85, 3–12.

Seck, E. T., Finch, W. A., Mor-Barak, M. E., & Poverny, L. M. (1993). Managing a diverse workforce. *Administration in Social Work,* 17, 67–79.

Securities Institute of America (1999). Diversity guide on gays and lesbians. Available: http://www.sia.com/diversity/pdf/GAY_LESBIAN.PDF.

Spector, P. E. (1987). Method variance as an artifact in self-report affect and perceptions at work: Myth or significant problem? *Journal of Applied Psychology,* 72, 438–443.

Stoddard, T. (1986, February 14). It isn't a "gay rights" bill. *The New York Times,* p. 15.

Van Den Bergh, N. (1994). From invisibility to voice: Providing EAP assistance to lesbians at the workplace. *Employee Assistance Quarterly*, 9, 161–177.

Van der Meide, W. (2000). *Legislating equality: A review of laws affecting gay, lesbian, bisexual and transgender people in the United States.* New York: NGLTF Policy Institute.

Vanderstoep, S. W., & Green, C. W. (1988). Religiosity and homonegativism: A path-analytic study. *Basic and Applied Social Psychology*, 9, 135–147.

Waldo, C. R. (1999). Working in a majority context: A structural model of heterosexism as minority stress in the workplace. *Journal of Counseling Psychology*, 46, 218–232.

Washington for Traditional Values (1997). Civil rights or another agenda? The probable motivations and practical consequences of Initiative 677. Available: http://www.e-z.net/wtv/I-677_Full_General_Brief.htm.

Whitley, B. E. (1987). The relationship of sex-role orientation to heterosexuals' attitudes toward homosexuals. *Sex Roles*, 17, 103–113.

Whitley, B. E. (1990). The relationship of heterosexuals' attributions for the causes of homosexuality to attitudes toward lesbians and gay men. *Personality and Social Psychology Bulletin*, 16, 369–377.

Whitley, B. E., & Kite, M. E. (1995). Sex-differences in attitudes toward homosexuality: A comment on Oliver and Hyde (1993). *Psychological Bulletin*, 117, 146–154.

Williams, D. R., Yu, Y., Jackson, J. S., & Anderson, N. B. (1997). Racial differences in physical and mental health. *Journal of Health Psychology*, 2, 335–351.

Worthy, M., Gary, A. L., & Kahn, G. M. (1969). Self-disclosure as an exchange process. *Journal of Personality and Social Psychology*, 13, 59–63.

Yang, A. (2000). *From wrongs to rights, 1973–1999: Public opinion on gay and lesbian Americans moves toward equality.* New York: NGLTF Policy Institute.

Young, M., & Whertvine, J. (1982). Attitudes of heterosexual students toward homosexual behavior. *Psychological Reports*, 51, 673–674.

PART 3

The Dark Side of Interpersonal Influence

CHAPTER 8

The Dark Side of Politics in Organizations

Angela T. Hall, Wayne A. Hochwarter,
Gerald R. Ferris, Michael G. Bowen

Abstract: Organizational scientists have tended to investigate work-place politics as a negative phenomenon. Here, we examine this per-spective, exploring the underlying reasons that have led scholars to assume that political behavior results in negative experiences for individuals and organizations. In this effort, we contend that work-place politics may be perceived negatively because political behav-ior impedes or obstructs rational decision making and blurs the relationship between effort and subsequent reward. Moreover, highly politicized environments also make psychological investment risky in that individuals are not as likely to commit emotional resources if it is perceived that the organization will not value their contributions. We also point out that most operational definitions of work politics fail to consider the neutral, or even beneficial, out-comes of political behavior, instead focusing almost exclusively on destructive manifestations of politics. Finally, we propose avenues for future research and suggest that exploring the positive, nega-tive, and the neutral aspects of politics is a necessary step toward understanding the broader aspects and contributions of political behavior to organizational life.

It's not what you know; it's who you know!
—POPULAR ADAGE

> Before I served as a consultant to Kennedy, I had believed, like most academics, that the process of decision-making was largely intellectual and all one had to do was walk into the President's office and convince him of the correctness of one's view. This perspective I soon realized is as dangerously immature as it is widely held (Kissinger, 1979, p. 39).

Hear the word "politics," and chances are something negative comes to mind. This negative perception, what we will refer to as the "dark side" perspective of political behavior, is the subject of this chapter. Here, we critically examine the nature of organizational politics as a "dark side" phenomenon, assess why it has come to be viewed as such by organizational scientists, investigate key issues that need to be adequately addressed in order to more representatively reflect the full scope and domain of the politics construct, and provide some directions for future research in this important area. Some of the issues we consider deal with definitional questions, whereas others suggest that there are measurement issues that might require systematic attention. The purpose of this chapter is thus to address issues surrounding the dark side perspective in a manner that will help refine subsequent theory and research in this growing area of study. In the process, we hope to present the negative characterization of organizational politics as but one possible perspective, and to call for a change in research focus to one that more broadly considers the realities of human interaction in work organizations.

The Dark Side Perspective

The dark side perspective of politics was not formed in a vacuum. Rather, there are rational reasons for this dark side perspective that are based in history and in the traditional scholarly view of this construct.

Some "Rational" Reasons for a Dark Side Perspective

Throughout human history, one fundamental problem that has faced our species is "interrelatedness." Like it or not, we have to share space, organize, live, and work together in some fashion. Because of this, the nature of interaction and how people organize and govern those interactions (that is, political behavior) have been the subjects of much thought and discussion over the course of human existence.

Over the centuries, political philosophers have debated—and taken sides over—the role of politics in human interaction. In ancient times, for example, Aristotle (Barnes, 1995) wrote that man is *by nature* a political animal and that politics is the most important human activity because it is the process by which societies work toward the universal good: a *rationally* and fully developed civilization. Since then, many, including Cicero (Everitt, 2002), St. Augustine (1994), and St. Thomas Aquinas (McInerny, 1993), have generally agreed with Aristotle's arguments, writing from what is called the *Aristotelian tradition*. Others, however, have disagreed, arguing, among other things, that the ends of political behavior are anything but universal and "good." Machiavelli (1984), Hobbes (1994), and Mill (1982), for example, agreed that behavior must be *rational* in order to preserve the human species, but that the idea of a clear-cut universal conception of the "good" in political discourse would lead to ideological and actual warfare.

In more recent times, nineteenth-century German sociologist and political economist Max Weber believed that political behavior was the root cause of inefficiency in societal institutions. Because of this, Weber (1947) argued that an ideal bureaucratic form of organizations could provide a solution to the problem of politics run amok. His solution, a formal theory of bureaucracy, was that organizations should be characterized by the "rational" and impersonal regulation of inferior-superior relationships, rather than by political machinations and influence. According to Weber, the most important and pervasive characteristic of bureaucracy (that is, one that explains all the others to some extent) is a system of control based on *rational* rules: rules meant to design and regulate the whole organization on the basis of technical knowledge, rather than political influence. Only if organized this way, Weber argued, could organizations achieve maximum efficiency.

It is relevant to note that today, in sharp contrast to Weber's beliefs about ideal bureaucracies, the word *bureaucratic* is oftentimes used to imply inefficiency and dysfunctionality in organizations. The reason frequently given for this is that modern bureaucracies typically are characterized by the overpoliticization of decision processes, resulting in many organizations that are slow, ineffective, and unresponsive to current business conditions (Deming, 1986).

A fundamental reason for the dark side perspective of political behavior might be, then, that political behavior is seen as obstructing or impeding what should otherwise be *rational* decision processes. This explanation is possible, given the common term—*rationality*—that has often been used in historical discussions of politics to describe how interaction *should* occur. Because violations of the *ideal* rational decision-making model are generally thought to be bad (that is, a deviation from norms of rationality; Dawes, 1988; Thompson, 1967), and this assumption is so ingrained in our culture that it underlies much of the research conducted today in the social sciences (compare with Kissinger, 1979; see also Bowen, 1987), one might expect some negativity toward, and a reluctant acceptance of, political processes and behaviors. Indeed, as citizens of the United States, we are taught to understand and respect the trade-offs between the inefficiencies of the democratic political process in government, on one hand, and concerns about effectively maintaining citizens' involvement in democratic processes, on the other. We have all, with exceptions of course, perhaps learned to concede the *bad* with the *good* of our democracy.

The results of a study of workplace politics by Gandz and Murray (1980) also illustrate these points. That research showed that 90 percent of survey respondents thought politics was common in organizations, 89 percent indicated that successful executives must be good politicians, and 76 percent responded that political behavior increases as one rises higher in an organization. Despite these attitudes, however, 55 percent of respondents felt that politics is detrimental to efficiency, and 48.6 percent thought that top management should attempt to rid organizations of political behavior.

Research on Organizational Politics and the Dark Side

Scholars have begun taking a systematic look into the nature of political behavior in organizations since the mid-1950s, when French (1956) suggested that it represented a meaningful area of scientific inquiry (see also Burns, 1961; March, 1962). Much of the scholarly research on the topic since then, proceeding under the assumption that politics is a "dark side" phenomenon, has indeed confirmed the notion that political behavior carries with it undesirable consequences for individuals, groups, and organizations (Cropanzano, Howes, Grandey, & Toth, 1997; Eisenhardt & Bourgeois, 1988).

So, too, research has shown perceptions of politics to be associated with lower levels of job satisfaction, job involvement, and work group cohesion (Ferris & Kacmar, 1992; George & Jones, 1996); that those acting politically do so to manipulate resources that might not come their way under more authorized means (Burns, 1961; Pettigrew, 1973); and that organizational politics has been positively associated with increased intent to turnover (Anderson, 1994) and higher job anxiety (Ferris, Frink, Bhawuk, Zhou, & Gilmore, 1996). Moreover, it is thought that political behavior seems to represent tactics that are neither sanctioned nor endorsed by the organization (Mayes & Allen, 1977; Mintzberg, 1983), and that individuals act politically to either obtain or protect what is perceived as desirable (Allen, Madison, Porter, Renwick, & Mayes, 1979; Cropanzano, Kacmar, & Bozeman, 1995; Ferris, Russ, & Fandt, 1989; Pfeffer, 1981).

From this research, one might conclude that the cornerstone of political activity at work might be the maintenance of one's self-interest, and that self-interest can work to either the advantage or the disadvantage of the organization as a whole. As a result, it is most unlikely that one would find the rules and procedures for successful politicking in any employee handbook, or management textbook, for that matter (compare with Pfeffer & Salancik, 1978, p. 213).

Today, there are various definitions of organizational politics in the literature (see Ferris, Adams, Kolodinsky, Hochwarter, & Ammeter, 2002; Kacmar & Baron, 1999, for reviews). At the core of virtually all of these is the exercise of social influence (Ferris et al., 1989; Mayes & Allen, 1977; Porter, Allen, & Angle, 1981).

In this vein, consider the definition of organizational politics offered by Pfeffer (1992). Arguing that the concepts of power and organizational politics are closely related, Pfeffer defined organizational politics as "the exercise or use of power, with power being defined as potential force" (1992, p. 14). Because of this, Pfeffer suggested that the development and use of power in organizations is regarded negatively because (1) people generally do not like to consider the *means* that are often necessary to get things done; (2) people have learned in school that success in life is a matter of *individual* effort, ability, and achievement and is not accomplished in cooperation with others; and (3) people believe that intellectual analysis, leading to *right* and *wrong* answers, can be used to solve, and judge solutions to, problems in a world where things are seldom clear-cut, obvious, and knowable with any real certainty. About these reasons, Pfeffer (1992) wrote with some apparent frustration: "It is as if we know that power and politics exist, and we grudgingly admit that they are necessary to individual success, but we nevertheless don't like them" (p. 15).

Political Behavior at Work

Recognizing this apparent love-hate conflict in our thinking, a distinction is now being made in the literature between *perceptions* of politics or political behavior and political behavior *itself*. Unlike previous scholarly work, this research suggests that perceptions of politics and political behavior are distinct constructs (Harrell-Cook, Ferris, & Dulebohn, 1999; Hochwarter, in press). In general, this research has asked whether political behavior can serve to mitigate many of the harmful effects of perceptions of politics on work outcomes. As a result, the study by Harrell-Cook et al. (1999) found that self-promotion behaviors (that is, a specific form of political behavior) moderated the relationship between perceptions of politics and two work outcomes: satisfaction with supervision and intent to leave.

Extending this research stream, Hochwarter (in press) hypothesized that political activity not only would serve to ameliorate the harmful effects of perceptions of politics, but also would be seen by some as beneficial. Results from this study provided three important findings. First, perceptions of politics and political activity were unrelated ($r = .01$, *ns*), providing additional evidence of construct uniqueness (Harrell-Cook et al., 1999). Second, those failing to participate in political activities reported lower levels of job satisfaction and affective commitment, thus suggesting that a failure to "play politics" led to potentially harmful results. Finally, the bivariate relationship between perceptions of politics and job satisfaction was *positive* ($r = .44$, $p < .10$) for those actively participating in the political arena. This finding calls into question the generally agreed-upon view that heightened levels of politics always lead to lower levels of job satisfaction. Studies such as these clarify the importance of examining whether employing political behavior or influence tactics might, at a minimum, negate many of the destructive consequences of perceptions of politics.

An earlier indirect attempt to address this question was undertaken by Dulebohn and colleagues (Dulebohn, 1997; also Dulebohn & Ferris, 1999). These studies found that the use of political behavior or influence tactics can represent an informal mechanism of voice with fairness-enhancing effects similar to those found for more formal voice mechanisms. Voice effects of political behavior might be expected to give individuals greater perceptions of control over their environment. These perceptions, in turn, might be associated with lower perceptions of politics, or perhaps the lesser degree to which politics is perceived as a threat.

Forms of Social Influence and Political Behavior

Several studies have examined the effects of upward influence, as a surrogate measure of political behavior. For example, Harrell-Cook et al. (1999) used the self-promotion and ingratiation subscales by Wayne and Ferris (1990) as measures of upward influence to represent political behavior. Further, Valle and Perrewé (2000) used proactive (Kipnis, Schmidt, & Wilkinson, 1980; Schriesheim & Hinkin, 1990) and reactive (Ashforth & Lee, 1990) upward influence strategies to tap political behavior. Finally, Hochwarter (in press) simply asked respondents to indicate their level of political activity (for example, "I am actively involved in politics at work") to assess involvement in political behavior.

Yet, although an upward influence framework might be useful for the examination of political behaviors in the workplace, it might explain only part of the story. Individuals engage in upward influence tactics for numerous reasons, many of which are unrelated to managing a political environment (Kipnis et al., 1980; Rao, Schmidt, & Murray, 1995; Thacker & Wayne, 1995). Moreover, research by Kacmar and Carlson (1998) provides strong evidence that impression management tactics represent only a small subset of behaviors that are generally deemed to be political.

In addition, when researchers measure only upward influence tactics, they ignore other hierarchical levels that might be important targets of politicking. Past research has established both the use and the utility of downward and lateral influence tactics (Yukl, Guinan, & Sottolano, 1995; Yukl & Tracey, 1992). For example, managers often use downward influence tactics to motivate their employees (Falbe & Yukl, 1992).

Finally, upward influence tactics (for example, ingratiation) are normally considered to be harmless attempts at impression management. Consequently, these behaviors are typically not viewed in a negative light. However, political behaviors are typically deemed to be injurious and rooted in self-interest, such as sabotaging the work of a coworker who does not support one's position (Hochwarter, Witt, & Kacmar, 2000). Thus, by concentrating on upward influence tactics alone, researchers will discount the dark side of organizational politics.

Why Do Perceptions of Politics Cause Adverse Reactions?

Let us now again consider why political environments might be viewed with such disdain. One answer is offered by Cropanzano et al. (1997), who maintained that environments burdened with politics are inherently risky. When environments are political, individuals attain desired outcomes by accruing power and influence. Because not everyone will be successful via these means, some will be relegated to outsider status. If resources and rewards are viewed as unattainable, dissatisfaction and tension should ensue. Accordingly, the immediate environment becomes more unpredictable because the unwritten rules for success change as the power of those playing the political game varies. This uncertainty blurs the relationship between performance and desired outcomes, thus causing employees to question whether it is in their best interest to try to contribute to the objectives of the organization.

Further, it is unlikely that political activity would prosper in environments where infinite resources exist. Because this environment does not exist in contemporary organizations, in resource-scarce political environments there are destined to be winners and losers. Winners are likely to be those who play the political game effectively, whereas losers are those who fail to play or play poorly (Hochwarter, in press). Cropanzano et al. (1997) further suggested that individuals not only are unlikely to achieve desired outcomes (for example, pay, recognition, promotion, work-related resources), but they also run the risk of losing what they already have. When the environment is free of politics (or at least reduced levels are present), the relationship between one's contribution and subsequent rewards is more direct. In such cases, employees are more likely to perceive their investment in the firm as less risky.

Moreover, politics often leads to a desecration of the psychological contract (Robinson & Morrison, 1995). Critical to the maintenance of this implied contract is a continuing, mutually beneficial relationship between employer and employee. As such, environments perceived to be political in nature are not likely to support a bilateral commitment to the psychological contract. For example, conceptualizations of organizational politicking often discuss behaviors that are designed to promote or protect the self-interests of the actor (Allen et al., 1979; Ferris & Judge, 1991). Examples of self-serving political behaviors include taking credit for the accomplishments of others and furthering one's own agenda at the expense of organizational goals (Mintzberg, 1983). If it is perceived that individuals are endangering the interests of the firm to fulfill personal objectives, it is unlikely that key organizational players will feel obligated to offer support through the maintenance of employee psychological well-being.

In sum, these arguments suggest that politics affect the reward expectations that individuals hold. When environments are perceived to be political, the rules of the game change as policies, protocol, and conscientious behavior are replaced with gamesmanship, unwritten norms, and rewards based on influence. Because rewards are allocated on non-merit-based factors instead of performance (Rusbult, Campbell, & Price, 1990), it is not surprising that adverse reactions result, and that the dark side label persists.

Unresolved Research Issues

Although there is a developed stream of research on organizational politics, there still exist critical areas on this topic that warrant further examination by organizational scholars. We now address these unresolved research issues.

Behavioral Versus Outcome Origins of the Dark Side Perspective

An important, yet unresolved, issue in this area relates to whether the dark side perspective of politics is driven by actual behaviors in which people engage, or based on the outcomes that organizational politics produces. We argue that this dark side label is driven by *both* behaviors and outcomes. With respect to outcomes, extant research strongly suggests a significant positive relationship between organizational politics and such adverse outcomes as job anxiety and intent to turnover(Anderson, 1994).

Moreover, increased organizational politics has been associated with lower job satisfaction and lower organizational commitment (Ferris & Kacmar, 1992; Hochwarter, in press). It is important to note, however, that these findings might be an artifact of the measurement tools that have been used to operationalize organizational politics as an *insidious* phenomenon. For example, the Perceptions of Organizational Politics scale (POPS; Kacmar & Carlson, 1997) contains items that only capture "bad politics" (for example, "People in this organization build themselves up by tearing others down"). As such, this scale only taps the absence or presence of destructive politics. Disagreeing with items in this scale does not connote "good" politics or "neutral" politics but simply an absence of "bad" politics.

Furthermore, research on political behavior also has generally emphasized an actor's role in the manipulation process (Schriesheim & Hinkin, 1990); the outcomes associated with such behavior are usually found to be negative. It should be noted, however, that political activity is often attributed to individuals in the organization who hold high positions and who have high legitimate power (Madison, Allen, Porter, Renwick, & Mayes, 1980). These key individuals can be critical in shaping the perceived political climate; that is, the shared perception of "the way things are done around here" (Reichers & Schneider, 1990, p. 22).

Consequently, in addition to the potential negative outcomes of organizational politics, another fundamental force driving the dark side perspective might be the perceived political behaviors of just a few key people. It is thus possible that the dark side label is, in part, the result of a disproportionately weighted process driven by the dysfunctional behavior of a small, yet influential, group, such as key top managers or certain departments or units of the organization that are generally considered to be critical.

The actions of a select few are capable of shaping the perceived political climate of an organization through the process of social contagion; that is, the idea that thoughts and feelings about an issue "can be communicated from one individual to another and ultimately spread and be maintained across entire networks or groups" (Degoey, 2000, p. 54). The concept of social contagion has roots in social psychology and suggests that reality is constructed, and that the attitudes of an individual can be influenced by the expressed attitudes and behaviors of others (Salancik & Pfeffer, 1978; Weick, 1969).

A key implication of applying social contagion theory, or related theories such as social information processing theory (Salancik & Pfeffer, 1978), to organizational politics is the inference that actual, accurate, and valid perceptions of politics are not as relevant as a construed reality when individuals interpret and label political behavior. Indeed, people operate on and react to their perceptions of reality, not objective reality per se (Lewin, 1936). With respect to perceptions of political behavior, the tenets of social contagion theory suggest that even if an organization is largely apolitical, the perceptions of politics and behaviors of critical individuals, units, or departments can cause employees to view the entire organization as highly political. This "pockets of politics" argument is an interesting one, but one that has not received much empirical attention to date (Ferris, Adams, Kolodinsky, Hochwarter, & Ammeter, 2002).

Interpretation and Labeling of Politics: Cognitive and Affective Processes

Another aspect of the politics interpretation process that has been addressed in the literature concerns attributions of intentionality. Specifically, Ferris, Bhawuk, Fedor, and Judge (1995) argued that whereas organizational politics and organizational citizenship behavior appear, at first, to be polar constructs, they can reflect identical behaviors (for example, offering to stay after work hours to help out your supervisor could be viewed as either citizenship or political). Thus, the fundamental difference between citizenship behavior and political behavior is the perceiver's *attribution* of the actor's intentions. To this point, Ferris et al. (1995) have offered a model of the process by which individuals assess whether behavior is to be labeled as political (that is, with selfish motives), or as altruistic citizenship. This process includes an assessment of whether the perceiver personally benefits or suffers from the behavior at issue.

Moreover, the label "political" might be simply an attribution made by individuals when things have gone wrong; that is, when desired or preferable outcomes have not occurred. Specifically, Kakabadse and Parker (1984) argued that each individual has a set of "purposive" or cognitive maps that drive behavior. When individuals view behavior that is not aligned with or threatens their own cognitive maps, they are inclined to label that behavior as political. In light of this, questions about individuals' enactments (Weick, 1969) of observed political behaviors become important. Because of the nature of enactment processes, two avenues of research that might assist in the development of an understanding of the enactment processes underlying the labeling of politics are (1) political skill and (2) emotions.

Political Skill

Political skill has been defined as "an interpersonal style construct that combines social astuteness with the ability to relate well, and otherwise demonstrate situationally appropriate behavior in disarmingly charming and engaging manner that inspires confidence, trust, sincerity, and genuineness" (Ferris, Perrewé, Anthony, & Gilmore, 2000, p. 30). Political skill is thus believed to affect the successful execution of influence behaviors.

It has been argued that political skill should moderate the relationship between political behavior and perceptions of politics (Ferris, Harrell-Cook, & Dulebohn, 2000). The essential argument here is that the tactics of those who are highly politically skilled appear to others as legitimate, whereas the tactics of those who have low political skill are labeled as "political"; that is, negative or harmful.

A related, yet still untested, theoretical view is that of *political skill deficiency* (Ferris, Frink, & Galang, 1993), in which it is argued that important organizational information is transmitted to only select groups. Under this view, some individuals are not provided opportunities to establish meaningful social relationships with individuals in the organization who could assist them in developing their political skills. Because these individuals are not privy to such political information (for instance, "the ropes" of the organization; whom to get in with, whom not to cross), they are unable to develop the skills necessary for them to be as successful in the organization.

The political skill deficiency view tentatively argues that the selective transmission of information creates two groups: privileged insiders who are "in the know," and outsiders who are unaware. These "outsiders" might, in turn, be more likely to interpret behaviors in their work environment as political, particularly because they are not as likely to be the beneficiaries of favorable outcomes and work-related rewards.

Emotions

Another area that might assist researchers in understanding the processes behind the labeling and interpretation of political behavior is that of emotions in the workplace (Arvey, Renz, & Watson, 1998). Emotions are typically defined as "intense, generally short-lived, feelings that are focused on a specific object or target (the stimulus) and typically interrupt thought processes" (Arvey et al., 1998, p. 106). Research suggests that emotions can have both affective and behavioral outcomes (Staw & Barsade, 1993) and that an important distinction can be made between "felt" and "displayed" emotions (Rafaeli & Sutton, 1989). This latter distinction refers to the difference between emotions that are experienced as opposed to those that are expressed. This distinction is thought to be important because individuals might feel one way but may express a converse emotion as part of the *emotional labor* associated with a given job (Hochschild, 1979, 1983).

Building from this, the concept of emotional labor provides an important link between emotions and organizational politics (Ferris, Hochwarter, Douglas, Blass, Kolodinsky, & Treadway, 2002). Specifically, individuals might use "strategic" expressions of emotions as influence tactics (Ferris et al., 1995). However, not every individual will be equally successful in that endeavor, as it might be that those who are highly politically skilled would appear to others as expressing legitimate emotions. Conversely, individuals who observe the use of emotions by those who are less politically skilled would be more likely to interpret those influence attempts as illegitimate or manipulative. Thus, in order to better understand the interpretation and labeling of political behavior, researchers should examine the use of emotions as an influence tactic. Moreover, further research on this topic might reveal that it is the use of emotional expression as an influence tactic by those who are low in political skill that might help explain why organizational politics has garnered its dark side label.

Mitigating and Harmful Effects Within the Dark Side Perspective

Research has indicated that the dysfunctional consequences of perceptions of politics can be mitigated through an awareness that one is in control and has an understanding of how things work, as well as the extent to which one is involved or has a voice in the work environment (Ferris, Brand, Brand, Rowland, Gilmore, King, Kacmar, & Burton, 1993; Ferris et al., 1996; Gilmore, Ferris, Dulebohn, & Harrell-Cook, 1996). Other recent studies have shown that organizational commitment (Hochwarter et al., 1999) and supervisor-subordinate goal congruence (Witt, 1998) act as moderators of the politics-outcomes relationships as well.

Continuing in this line of inquiry, Hochwarter and Treadway (2002) examined the moderating potential of affective disposition (that is, negative and positive affect). Results indicated that those with both high negative (NA) and positive affect (PA) reported lower levels of job satisfaction in political environments. That study suggests that high NAs will report lower levels of job satisfaction because they tend to view their immediate environment with disdain (Hochwarter, Kiewitz, Castro, Perrewé, & Ferris, 2003; Watson, Clark, & Tellegen, 1988). The study also suggests that high PAs will report dissatisfaction because the rewards coveted by the employee are not likely to be obtained by traditional work-related outcomes. In another study, Hochwarter et al. (2003) examined the influence of collective efficacy and positive affect on the politics-job satisfaction relationship. Results demonstrated that groups having high positive affect coupled with high collective efficacy and low positive affect coupled with low collective efficacy reported the lowest levels of job satisfaction. This study was the first to examine the relationship between dispositional and situational moderators of the perceptions of politics and work outcomes simultaneously

Finally, in asking what factors might augment the harmful effects of perceptions of politics, Bozeman, Perrewé, Hochwarter, and Brymer (2001) found that self-efficacy exacerbated the relationship between perceived politics and certain organizational outcomes (that is, commitment and job satisfaction). That study concluded that highly efficacious individuals would view political environments with more contempt because political gamesmanship, not performance, would predict rewards.

Directions for Future Work

In light of the present review, we believe that what is lacking in the literature is research that helps clarify what actions or tactics might be considered political behavior, and whether those actions can be functional or dysfunctional for the organization. There too is clearly a need for in-depth examinations of the situational and dispositional factors that predict the occurrence of political behavior.

Toward a More Integrative Theory of Political Behavior in Organizations

Future research also is needed to develop a theory of political behavior that integrates the two largely independent streams of work on perceptions of politics and political actions. This theory would require researchers to (1) consider political behavior as a multidimensional phenomenon, (2) articulate the conditions under which we might predict dark side political behavior, and (3) investigate the condition under which politics might take on a more neutral or even positive tone. In this regard, it might be useful to investigate potential mediating variables. For example, Hochwarter, Kacmar, Perrewé, and Johnson (2002) found that perceived organizational support mediated the relationship between perceptions of politics and work outcomes.

The research results reviewed here suggest that politics is viewed negatively when it leads to a lack of psychosocial support. Building on this work, it could be that perceived politics leads to adverse outcomes when it cultivates cynical attitudes toward the organization (Andersson, 1996; Andersson & Bateman, 1997). Described as a "dislike for and distrust of others" (Cook & Medley, 1954, p. 418), cynicism might represent an important intermediate linkage between perceptions of politics and work outcomes, as has been suggested recently by Ferris, Adams et al. (2002) in their revised model of perceptions of politics.

Alternatively, politics could lead to constructive outcomes. For example, organization members might view politics positively if it is perceived that a failure to participate in politics would lead to adverse organization outcomes (for example, failure to secure federal funding, performance that leads to layoffs). In addition, politics might be viewed favorably if the individuals are well-versed at playing the political game. Research reported earlier (Hochwarter, in press) has indicated that some political environments are viewed favorably by job incumbents. It is plausible that one could report that politics is bad for others who are not competent in playing the game, but "good for me because I either enjoy or see participation in politics as a way to maximize my returns." However, before scholars are able to answer these questions more definitively, the measures used to empirically assess political activities need to be critically examined and, in many cases, fine-tuned.

Measurement of Organizational Politics

With a new theory and definition of politics that captures the full construct domain more inclusively and representatively, we will need psychometrically sound measurement instruments that reflect an appropriate balance of the tone or perspective. As we have suggested, research has generally characterized political activity as a disreputable fact of organizational life. Measures used to capture this phenomenon have embraced this view, as many of the frequently used scales capture only the negative attributes of political behavior (Kacmar & Carlson, 1997; Kacmar et al., 1999). Research will be enhanced if value-neutral measures are employed to capture the full range of potential scores for perceptions of politics. Qualitative studies that explore individuals' perceptions of positive, negative, and neutral aspects of politics should also further this end.

Similarly, new measures need to consider level-of-analysis issues. Contained within the POPS measure are political activities that occur at the levels of the individual (for example, "Telling others what they want to think is sometimes better than telling the truth"), group ("There has always been an influential group in this department that no one ever crosses"), and organization ("Promotions around here are not valued much because how they are determined is so political"). Despite previous research indicating that respondents are able to differentiate between the levels on which organizational politics occurs (that is, on the individual, group, or organizational level) (Hochwarter et al., 2003; Maslyn & Fedor, 1998), most studies have used the scale in its entirety, as opposed to using a subscale designed to measure politics at a specific level.

To address this concern, Hochwarter, Kacmar et al. (2002) developed a measure of perceptions of politics that included three unique organization levels (that is, at one's current level, at one level above one's current level, and at the highest levels in the organization). The original model proposed by Ferris et al. (1989) and the revised model (Ferris, Adams et al., 2002) both reflect that individual, job-work, and organization factors influence perceptions of politics. For organizational politics research to significantly advance, however, researchers must examine antecedents to perceptions of politics that occur at multiple levels of analysis, not just those that exist at the individual level.

Finally, Pfeffer's (1992) propositions and our suggestion that political behavior might be, at base, viewed as a dark side phenomenon because it obstructs or impedes rational decision making strike us as worthy of systematic examination. This is particularly true if Pfeffer and others are correct that gaining and utilizing political power is an essential skill, a skill not generally taught, and indeed mostly avoided, in management education. Taking this argument further, some scholars view politics as an important and often necessary element of organizational functioning. This view can be found, for example, in research suggesting that organizational politics is critical to a theoretical understanding of change and the change process (Burns, 1966; Mangham, 1979) and in research suggesting that active politicking is an essential element of successful organizational development (Dunphy & Stace, 1988). Perhaps, on the one hand, as Frost and Egri (1991) suggested, political behavior is not only inevitable but also necessary to the development of creativity and thoughtful deliberation. On the other hand, perhaps political skill can also be a survival mechanism for those whose performance would otherwise be rated as incompetent.

Beyond these points, a look at other literatures provides insights on this issue. For example, some writers in business ethics, such as Badarraco (1997), have argued that to get things done, ethical leaders must learn to successfully play politics while remaining true to ethical principles. Also, writers on leadership and change management (Kotter, 1996; O'Toole, 1995; Quinn, 1996) essentially have argued that leaders bring about successful change efforts only through the effective use of power and influence. In short, it seems clear that political behavior in organizations is multidimensional and multifaceted, and that research in the area would greatly benefit from scholars breaking down paradigmatic and disciplinary boundaries to be better able to generate new questions, and broader insights, about the phenomenon.

Conclusion

In this chapter we have explored some reasons for the "dark side" perspective of organizational politics, reviewed research from the two streams in the scholarly literature on political behavior and perceptions of political behaviors, and suggested some areas that researchers might pursue productively. We also discussed how research has overwhelmingly linked organizational politics to adverse outcomes for a variety of theoretical reasons, and raised the possibility that a significant cause of the profusion of negative findings might be linked to paradigmatic and measurement issues. By operationalizing organizational politics as a negative phenomenon, researchers are unable to identify the potential neutral or positive effects of political activities. Politics can, indeed, reflect a negative and destructive "dark side," and we need to develop a more informed scholarly understanding of that side of the phenomenon. However, this appears to capture only part of the full construct of politics.

As we develop a more informed understanding of the full range of perspectives on political behavior, we should be better able to see how, where, and why politics can be bad or good and how to control it; that is, when politics is functional or useful and when it is destructive. Exploring the positive, negative, and the neutral aspects of politics is a constructive avenue for future research and a necessary step toward understanding the broader aspects and contributions of political behavior to organizational life.

References

Allen, R. W., Madison, D. L., Porter, L. W., Renwick, P. A., & Mayes, B. T. (1979). Organizational politics: Tactics and characteristics of its actors. *California Management Review,* 22, 77–83.

Anderson, T. P. (1994). Creating measures of dysfunctional office and organizational politics: The DOOP and short for DOOP scales. *Psychology,* 31, 24–34.

Andersson, L. (1996). Employee cynicism: An examination using a contract violation framework. *Human Relations,* 49, 1395–1418.

Andersson, L., & Bateman, T. (1997). Cynicism in the workplace: Some causes and effects. *Journal of Organizational Behavior,* 18, 449–469.

Arvey, R. D., Renz, G. L., & Watson, T. W. (1998). Emotionality and job performance: Implications for personnel selection. In G. R. Ferris (Ed.), *Research in personnel and human resources management* (Vol. 16, pp. 103–147). Stamford, CT: JAI Press.

Ashforth, R., & Lee, R. (1990). Defensive behavior in organizations: A preliminary model. *Human Relations,* 43, 621–648.

Badarraco, J. L. (1997). *Defining moments: When managers must choose between right and wrong.* Boston: Harvard Business School Press.

Barnes, J. (1995). *The complete works of Aristotle,* Vol. 1. Princeton, NJ: Princeton University Press.

Bowen, M. G. (1987). The escalation phenomenon reconsidered: Decision dilemmas or decision errors? *Academy of Management Review,* 12, 52–66.

Bozeman, D. P., Perrewé, P. L., Hochwarter, W. A., & Brymer, R. A. (2001). Organizational politics, perceived control, and work outcomes: Boundary conditions on the effects of politics. *Journal of Applied Social Psychology,* 31, 486–503.

Burns, T. (1961). Micropolitics: Mechanisms of institutional change. *Administrative Science Quarterly,* 6, 257–281.

Burns, T. (1966). On the plurality of social systems. In J. Lawrence (Ed.), *Operational research and the social sciences* (pp. 321–356). London: Tavistock.

Cook, W., & Medley, D. (1954). Proposed hostility and pharisaic-virtue scales of the MMPI. *Journal of Applied Psychology,* 38, 414–418.

Cropanzano, R., Howes, J. C., Grandey, A. A., & Toth, P. (1997). The relationship of organizational politics and support to work behaviors, attitudes, and stress. *Journal of Organizational Behavior,* 18, 159–180.

Cropanzano, R. S., Kacmar, K. M., & Bozeman, D. P. (1995). Organizational politics, justice, and support: Their differences and similarities. In R. S. Cropanzano & K. M. Kacmar (Eds.), *Organizational politics, justice, and support: Managing the social climate of the workplace* (pp. 2–18). Westport, CT: Quorum Books.

Dawes, R. M. (1988). *Rational choice in an uncertain world.* San Diego: Harcourt Brace Jovanovich.

Degoey, P. (2000). Contagious justice: Exploring the social construction of justice in organizations. In B. M. Staw & R. I. Sutton (Eds.), *Research in organizational behavior* (Vol. 22, pp. 51–102). Oxford, UK: JAI/ Elsevier Science.

Deming, W. E. (1986). *Out of the crisis.* Cambridge: The Massachusetts Institute of Technology Center for Advanced Engineering Study.

Dulebohn, J. H. (1997). Social influence in justice evaluations of human resources systems. In G. R. Ferris (Ed.), *Research in personnel and human resources management* (Vol. 15, pp. 241–291). Greenwich, CT: JAI Press.

Dulebohn, J. H., & Ferris, G. R. (1999). The role of influence tactics in perceptions of performance evaluations' fairness. *Academy of Management Journal, 42,* 288–303.

Dunphy, D., & Stace, D. (1988). Transformational and coercive strategies for planned organizational change: Beyond the OD model. *Organization Studies, 3,* 317–334.

Eisenhardt, K. M., & Bourgeois, L. J. (1988). Politics of strategic decision making in high velocity environments: Toward a midrange theory. *Academy of Management Journal, 31,* 737–770.

Everitt, A. (2002). *Cicero: The life and times of Rome's greatest politician.* New York: Random House.

Falbe, C. M., & Yukl, G. (1992). Consequences for managers of using single influence tactics and combinations of tactics. *Academy of Management Journal, 35,* 638–653.

Ferris, G., Adams, G., Kolodinsky, R., Hochwarter, W., & Ammeter, A. (2002). Perceptions of organizational politics: Theory and research directions. In F. J. Yammarino & F. Dansereau (Eds.), *Research in multi-level issues,* Volume 1: *The many faces of multi-level issues* (pp. 179–254). Oxford, UK: JAI Press/Elsevier Science.

Ferris, G. R., Bhawuk, D.P.S., Fedor, D. B., & Judge, T. A. (1995). Organizational politics and citizenship: Attributions of intentionality and construct definition. In M. J. Martinko (Ed.), *Advances in attribution theory: An organizational perspective* (pp. 231–252). Delray Beach, FL: St. Lucie Press.

Ferris, G. R., Brand, J. F., Brand, S., Rowland, K. M., Gilmore, D. C., King, T. R., Kacmar, K. M., & Burton, C. A. (1993). Politics and control in organizations. In E. J. Lawler, B. Markovsky, J. O'Brien, & K. Heimer (Eds.), *Advances in group processes* (Vol. 10, pp. 83–111). Greenwich, CT: JAI Press.

Ferris, G. R., Frink, D. D., Bhawuk, D.P.S., Zhou, J., & Gilmore, D. C. (1996). Reactions of diverse groups to politics in the workplace. *Journal of Management, 22,* 23–44.

Ferris, G. R., Frink, D. D., & Galang, M. C. (1993). Diversity in the workplace: The human resources management challenges. *Human Resource Planning,* 16, 41–51.

Ferris, G. R., Harrell-Cook, G., & Dulebohn, J. H. (2000). Organizational politics: The nature of the relationship between politics perceptions and political behavior. In S. B. Bacharach & E. J. Lawler (Eds.), *Research in the sociology of organizations* (Vol. 17, pp. 89–130). Stamford, CT: JAI Press.

Ferris, G. R., Hochwarter, W. A., Douglas, C., Blass, F. R., Kolodinsky, R. W., & Treadway, D. C. (2002). Social influence processes in organizations and human resources systems. In G. R. Ferris & J. J. Martocchio (Eds.), *Research in personnel and human resources management* (Vol. 21, pp. 65–127). Oxford, UK: JAI Press/Elsevier Science.

Ferris, G. R., & Judge, T. A. (1991). Personnel/human resources management: A political influence perspective. *Journal of Management,* 17, 447–488.

Ferris, G. R., & Kacmar, K. M. (1992). Perceptions of organizational politics. *Journal of Management,* 18, 93–116.

Ferris, G. R., Perrewé, P. L., Anthony, W. P., & Gilmore, D. C. (2000). Political skill at work. *Organizational Dynamics,* 28, 25–37.

Ferris, G. R., Russ, G. S., & Fandt, P. M. (1989). Politics in organizations. In R. A. Giacalone & P. Rosenfeld (Eds.), *Impression management in the organization* (pp. 143–170). Hillsdale, NJ: Erlbaum.

French, J. (1956). A formal theory of social power. *Psychological Review,* 63, 181–194.

Frost, P., & Egri, C. (1991). The political process of innovation. In L. L. Cummings & B. M. Staw (Eds.), *Research in organizational behavior* (Vol. 13, pp. 229–295). Greenwich, CT: JAI Press.

Gandz, J., and Murray, V. (1980). The experience of workplace politics. *Academy of Management Journal,* 23, 237–251.

George, J. M., & Jones, G. R. (1996). The experience of work and turnover intentions: Interactive effects of value attainment, job satisfaction, and positive mood. *Journal of Applied Psychology,* 81, 318–325.

Gilmore, D. C., Ferris, G. R., Dulebohn, J. H., & Harrell-Cook, G. (1996). Organizational politics and employee attendance. *Group and Organization Management,* 21, 481–494.

Harrell-Cook, G., Ferris, G. R., & Dulebohn, J. H. (1999). Political behaviors as moderators of the perceptions of organizational politics—work outcomes relationships. *Journal of Organizational Behavior, 20,* 1093–1106.

Hobbes, T. (1994). *Leviathon: With selected variants from the Latin edition of 1668.* E. Curley (Ed.). Indianapolis: Hackett.

Hochschild, A. (1979). Emotional work, feeling rules, and social structure. *American Journal of Sociology, 85,* 551–575.

Hochschild, A. R. (1983). *The managed heart: Commercialization of human feeling.* Berkeley: University of California Press.

Hochwarter, W. (in press). The interactive effects of pro-political behavior and politics perceptions on job satisfaction and affective commitment. *Journal of Applied Social Psychology.*

Hochwarter, W., Kacmar, C., Perrewé, P., & Johnson, D. (2002). *Perceived organizational support as a mediator of the relationship between politics perceptions and work outcomes: A multi-level analysis.* Paper presented at the Academy of Management, 62nd Annual National Meeting, Denver.

Hochwarter, W., Kiewitz, C., Castro, S., Perrewé, P., & Ferris, G. (2003). Positive affectivity and collective efficacy as moderators of the relationship between perceived politics and job satisfaction. *Journal of Applied Social Psychology, 33,* 1009–1035.

Hochwarter, W., & Treadway, D. (2002). The interactive effects of negative and positive affect on the politics perceptions–job satisfaction relationship. Working paper.

Hochwarter, W. A., Perrewé, P. L., Ferris, G. R., & Guercio, R. (1999). Commitment as an antidote to the tension and turnover consequences of organizational politics. *Journal of Vocational Behavior, 55,* 277–297.

Hochwarter, W. A., Witt, L. A., & Kacmar, K. M. (2000). The moderating effects of perceptions of organizational politics on the conscientiousness-sales performance relationship. *Journal of Applied Psychology, 85,* 472–478.

Kacmar, K. M., & Baron, R. A. (1999). Organizational politics: The state of the field, links to related processes, and an agenda for future research. In G. R. Ferris (Ed.), *Research in personnel and human resources management* (Vol. 17, pp. 1–39). Stamford, CT: JAI Press.

Kacmar, K. M., & Carlson, D. S. (1997). Further validation of the Perceptions of Politics scale (POPS): A multi-sample approach. *Journal of Management, 23,* 627–658.

Kacmar, K. M., & Carlson, D. S. (1998). The dysfunctional aspect of political behavior in organizations. In R. W. Griffin, A. M. O'Leary-Kelly,

& J. Collins (Eds.), *Dysfunctional behavior in organizations* (Vol. 23, pp. 195–218). Greenwich, CT: JAI Press.

Kacmar, K. M., Bozeman, D. P., Carlson, D. S., & Anthony, W. P. (1999). A partial test of the perceptions of organizational politics model. *Human Relations,* 52, 383–416.

Kakabadse, A., & Parker, C. (1984). Towards a theory of political behaviour in organizations. In A. Kakabadse & C. Parker (Eds.), *Power, politics, and organizations: A behavioural science view* (pp. 87–108). London: John Wiley.

Kipnis, D., Schmidt, S., & Wilkinson, I. (1980). Intraorganizational influence tactics: Exploration in getting one's way. *Journal of Applied Psychology,* 65, 440–452.

Kissinger, H. (1979). *The White House years.* Boston: Little, Brown.

Kotter, J. (1996). *Leading change.* Boston: Harvard Business School Press.

Lewin, K. (1936). *Principles of topological psychology.* New York: McGraw-Hill.

Machiavelli, N. (1984). *The prince.* New York: Bantam Classics. (Originally published 1532.)

Madison, D., Allen, R., Porter, L. W., Renwick, P., & Mayes, B. (1980). Organizational politics: An exploration of managers' perceptions. *Human Relations,* 33, 79–100.

Mangham, I. (1979). *The politics of organizational change.* Westport, CT: Greenwood Press.

March, J. (1962). The business firm as a political coalition. *Journal of Politics,* 24, 262–278.

Maslyn, J., & Fedor, D. B. (1998). Perceptions of politics: Does measuring different foci matter? *Journal of Applied Psychology,* 84, 645–653.

Mayes, B., & Allen, R. (1977). Toward a definition of organizational politics. *Academy of Management Review,* 4, 672–677.

McInerny, R. M. (1993). *Commentary on Aristotle's Nicomachean Ethics (Thomas Aquinas's Aristotelian Commentaries Series).* Chicago: Dumb Ox Books.

Mill, J. S. (1982). *On liberty.* New York: Viking Press. (Originally published 1859.)

Mintzberg, H. (1983). *Power in and around organizations.* Englewood Cliffs, NJ: Prentice-Hall.

O'Toole, J. (1995). *Leading change: Overcoming the ideology of comfort and the tyranny of custom.* San Francisco: Jossey-Bass.

Pettigrew, A. (1973). *The politics of organizational decision making.* London: Tavistock.

Pfeffer, J. (1981). Management as symbolic action: The creation and maintenance of organizational paradigms. In L. L. Cummings &

B. M. Staw (Eds.), *Research in organizational behavior* (Vol. 3, pp. 1–52). Greenwich, CT: JAI Press.

Pfeffer, J. (1992). *Managing with power: Politics and influence in organizations.* Boston: Harvard Business School Press.

Pfeffer, J., & Salancik, G. R. (1978). *The external control of organizations: A resource dependence perspective.* New York: Harper & Row.

Porter, L. W., Allen, R. W., & Angle, H. L. (1981). The politics of upward influence in organizations. In L. L. Cummings & B. M. Staw (Eds.), *Research in organizational behavior* (Vol. 3, pp. 109–149). Greenwich, CT: JAI Press.

Quinn, R. (1996). *Deep change: Discovering the leader within.* San Francisco: Jossey-Bass.

Rafaeli, A., & Sutton, R. I. (1989). The expression of emotion in organizational life. In L. L. Cummings & B. M. Staw (Eds.), *Research in organizational behavior* (Vol. 11, pp. 1–42). Greenwich, CT: JAI Press.

Rao, A., Schmidt, S., & Murray, L. (1995). Upward impression management: Goals, influence strategies, and consequences. *Human Relations, 48,* 147–167.

Reichers, A., & Schneider, B. (1990). Climate and culture: An evolution of constructs. In B. Schneider (Ed.), *Organizational climate and culture* (pp. 5–39). San Francisco: Jossey-Bass.

Robinson, S., & Morrison, E. (1995). Psychological contracts in OCB: The effect of unfulfilled obligations on civic virtue behavior. *Journal of Organizational Behavior, 16,* 289–298.

Rusbult, C., Campbell, M., & Price, M. (1990). Rational selective exploitation and distress: Employee reactions to performance-based and mobility-based reward allocations. *Journal of Personality and Social Psychology, 59,* 487–500.

Salancik, G. R., & Pfeffer, J. (1978). A social information processing approach to job attitudes and task design. *Administrative Science Quarterly, 23,* 224–253.

Schriesheim, C., & Hinkin, T. (1990). Influence tactics used by subordinates: A theoretical and empirical analysis and refinement of the Kipnis, Schmidt, and Wilkinson subscales. *Journal of Applied Psychology, 75,* 246–257.

St. Augustine. (1994). *City of God* (Reprint edition). New York: Modern Library. (Originally published 426.)

Staw, B., & Barsade, S. (1993). Affect and managerial performance: A test of the sadder-but-wiser vs. happier-and-smarter hypothesis. *Administrative Science Quarterly, 38,* 304–331.

Thacker, R., & Wayne, S. (1995). An examination of the relationship between upward influence tactics and assessments of promotability. *Journal of Management, 21,* 739–756.

Thompson, J. D. (1967). *Organizations in action.* New York: McGraw-Hill.

Valle, M., & Perrewé, P. L. (2000). Do politics perceptions relate to political behaviors? *Human Relations, 53,* 359–386.

Watson, D., Clark, L., & Tellegen, A. (1988). Development and validation of brief measures of positive and negative affect: The PANAS scale. *Journal of Personality and Social Psychology, 54,* 1063–1070.

Wayne, S., & Ferris, G. (1990). Influence tactics, affect, and exchange in supervisor-subordinate interactions: A laboratory experiment and field study. *Journal of Applied Psychology, 75,* 487–499.

Weber, M. (1947). *Max Weber: The theory of social and economic organization,* A. M. Henderson & Talcott Parsons (Trans.). New York: The Free Press. (Originally published 1920.)

Weick, K. E. (1969). *The social psychology of organizing.* Reading, MA: Addison-Wesley.

Witt, L. A. (1998). Enhancing organizational goal congruence: A solution to organizational politics. *Journal of Applied Psychology, 83,* 666–674.

Yukl, G., Guinan, P., & Sottolano, D. (1995). Influence tactics used for different objectives with subordinates, peers, and superiors. *Group and Organization Management, 20,* 272–297.

Yukl, G., & Tracey, J. (1992). Consequences of influence tactics used with subordinates, peers, and the boss. *Journal of Applied Psychology, 77,* 525–535.

CHAPTER 9

Under-the-Table Deals
Preferential, Unauthorized, or Idiosyncratic?
Denise M. Rousseau

Individual workers can seek special treatment or working conditions differing from what their coworkers receive. In spite of the advantages workers or their employers might receive from such arrangements, these deals skirt the dark side of organizational life. Special treatment can leave a trail of injustice and resentment, all the while eroding the organization's legitimacy—particularly from the perspective of third parties, the coworkers of that individual with the special deal. Unless third parties learn of such deals, the worker and managers involved may not even acknowledge them publicly. This under-the-table quality of many person-specific employment arrangements makes their dynamics, and often their very existence, difficult to discern.

This chapter attempts to *put on the table* the variety of forms such arrangements take, addressing the organizational complications arising from special treatment for individual workers (as well as its potential advantages). It first introduces three distinct types of person-specific arrangements, focusing particularly on one type, the idiosyncratic employment arrangement, which has the potential to fuel innovation in human resource practice and expand the choices available to workers and employers in crafting their relationship. But the potential benefits of idiosyncratic arrangements can be severely limited by their "look alike" counterparts from the dark side of the employment relationship: preferential treatment (for example, politics and favoritism) and unauthorized appropriations (misrepresentation and theft). Moreover, poorly managed idiosyncratic arrangements can themselves create adverse consequences for all parties involved. The chapter addresses the slippery slope of poorly managed idiosyncratic arrangements, where these are construed by third parties to represent preferential favoritism or unauthorized appropriation. In particular, how well idiosyncratic arrangements are managed plays a role in the dynamics surrounding many well-established constructs in organizational behavior, from leader-member exchange to the many dimensions of justice. Finally, this chapter addresses how idiosyncratic employment arrangements can be implemented in ways that are functional for all parties involved.

Many of the things contemporary knowledge workers look to their employers for are seemingly contradictory. On the one hand, workers value flexibility in their relationship with an employer to better meet their personal needs. The schedule that lets one employee coach kids' soccer after school differs from that permitting another to run a trading business on an extended lunch break. Enabling workers to conduct a satisfying nonwork life requires a certain willingness to customize on the part of the employer. Yet consistency in treatment and comparability in outcomes are the building blocks of fairness. Fair treatment typically entails comparable arrangements across workers. We prize membership in organizations where all people are treated fairly but where our own special needs and individuality also are embraced. Workers seek treatment that affirms their individual value and self worth ("I am special") as well as their employer's overall fairness and positive identity ("Everybody thinks this is a great place to work"). As one of my colleagues put it: "I want to be part of an organization that treats everybody well and me just a little bit better."

An upside of the flexibility versus fairness dilemma can be found in the idiosyncratic employment arrangements (Rousseau, 2001; in press) whereby workers with valued skills negotiate with employers so that the needs of both are met. Such voluntary and sometimes public agreements offer the parties involved an opportunity to creatively meet personal as well as organizational needs in ways that promote the comfort level of coworkers who might otherwise look askance on any arrangement differing from their own. But one dilemma in creating individualized arrangements is the fine line between a win-win solution of mutual benefit and those deals that hint or even smack of favoritism. To explicate the difference we next examine the several forms person-specific employment arrangements can take.

Person-Specific Employment Arrangements

What is my nature? It is characterized by diversity, by life of many forms, utterly immeasurable.
St. Augustine, *Confessions*

Person-specific employment arrangements refer to employment conditions whereby an individual obtains valued resources that differ from his or her coworkers. Although substantial benefits can come to workers and firms from customizing their terms of employment, human beings are acutely sensitive to differences in treatment. These differences are particularly salient when the individuals involved belong to the same work group or are otherwise interdependent day-to-day. Organizational accommodations to individuals have been studied as part of the normal give-and-take in work relationships (Abrahamson, 1966) and in response to the special needs of the disabled (Colella, 2001). How socially acceptable such accommodations are continues to be a concern. Employers often take great pains to downplay differential treatment while continuing to provide it under the table. The prevalence of secrecy despite public downplaying of difference is evidence of the inept and disingenuous ways employers handle otherwise justifiable differential treatment. This lack of appropriate handling of idiosyncratic arrangements exacerbates the dark side of person-specific arrangements.

There are three types of person-specific employment arrangements (Table 9.1):

1. *Preferential*—Favored treatment offered to a worker by an agent of the firm, usually the immediate manager or supervisor, to

strengthen their personal relationship, as in the case of lowered performance standards for a worker who is a friend of the boss.

2. *Unauthorized*—Confiscation of employer resources by a worker without authorization, as in the case of theft or misrepresentation.

3. *Idiosyncratic*—Negotiation between a worker and an employer for different arrangements based upon that worker's needs and his or her value to the firm, as in the case of a highly skilled designer who is allowed to take a one-of-a-kind sabbatical for a year to travel abroad. Idiosyncratic arrangements are often initiated by the worker, but employers themselves can initiate them for workers with distinct capabilities or those willing to undertake special duties (Rousseau, in press).

The first two arrangements are dysfunctional, creating adverse consequences for the firm's legitimacy, by eroding trust between workers and management and undermining cooperation among coworkers. The third arrangement, idiosyncratic, can be highly functional but only if its distinction from the other two is conveyed and maintained.

Preferential Treatment

An exemplar: A small tool-and-die shop authorizes one-hour lunch breaks for all its employees. The owner's cousin who works in the shop often takes off at lunch for an hour and a half or more. The facility manager scolds all other workers if they don't return in an hour. Trying to curry favor with this influential cousin, the manager says nothing when the cousin shows up two hours late.

Table 9.1. Facets of Person-Specific Arrangements.

	Preferential	Unauthorized	Idiosyncratic
Process	Favoritism, politics	Usurped	Negotiation
Basis	Relationship	Rule-breaking	Value to firm
Beneficiary	Worker and boss	Worker	Worker and employing firm

Preferential arrangements take the form of favoritism and crony-ism whereby managers (or other agents of the firm) favor certain workers over others based on personal relations or political ties. The primary basis for preferential treatment is a personal relationship between the individuals involved. Such arrangements often serve to strengthen the bond between the parties, permitting them to meet each other's needs at the expense of coworkers, colleagues, or the larger firm. The classic example of preferential treatment is the "non-obvious promotion" John DeLorean (1979) described in his book *On a Clear Day You Can See General Motors*. The ticket to pro-motion in the GM of the 1960s according to DeLorean was for a junior manager to cultivate a relationship with a senior executive. Executives in turn were on the look out for bright young people many rungs down the hierarchy. Giving a position up in the cor-porate ladder to a very junior manager created a bond whereby junior managers were beholden to senior executives for their cur-rent career success and continued opportunities. The loyalty derived from such self-interest served the political interests of the executives, though it did nothing to enhance the overall compe-tence of GM's management.

Political in nature, these preferential arrangements undermine the legitimacy of the formal organization while advancing the per-sonal interests of its agents (Pearce, 2001; Pearce, Bigley, & Branyiczki, 1998). It could be argued that playing favorites might benefit the firm by gaining a lackey willing to do an employer's bidding. Nonetheless, such arrangements are predicated upon personal connections and not on the individual capabilities that add value to the firm.

The dysfunctional consequences of preferential treatment are amplified when a workforce is demographically or culturally di-verse (Cox, 1993; Rousseau, 1995). Information selectively trans-mitted to certain groups permits their members to develop the political acumen to use the firm's formal and informal systems to their advantage (Ferris et al. 1993; 1996). Limited experience with the *organization-specific* political skills required to navigate a firm's hierarchy is one factor that shapes the inferior opportunities and sense of injustice women and minorities often experience (Dreher & Cox, 1998). Moreover, demographic similarity is a factor that shapes the quality of the relationship between supervisor and subordinate (Tsui, Porter, & Egan, 2002). Relationship quality—in particular, high leader-member exchange—is associated with greater career success (Brass, 2001). By virtue of demographic characteristics and cultural background, some workers have better access to valued resources than others, thus increasing the likelihood that some workers access special arrangements based upon the inside information their demographic advantages bring them. To the extent that workers get resources by negotiating with managers who trust them, what would seem to be justified flexibility for one worker and his or her manager may seem like an unfair advantage from the perspective of coworkers from different backgrounds.

The dynamics of preferential treatment are seldom studied simultaneously from the perspectives of beneficiaries and disadvantaged third parties. For instance, organizational scholars tend to view strong leader-member exchange (LMX) relationships as a net positive to the organization and to the employment relationship (Graen & Cashman, 1975; Graen & Scandura, 1987). We note that at least in the early work on dyadic exchanges involving leaders and subordinates, the existence of both in-groups and out-groups was recognized (Dansereau, Graen, & Haga, 1976). However, the consequences of the presence of one high LMX relationship upon other members of the work group have been largely ignored. This look at the dark side of special employment arrangements suggests that it is important to ask, What is the impact of that particular high-quality relationship on the other subordinates that the manager supervises? Relative standing within their work group is a salient issue for workers (Firebaugh, 1980; Frank, 1985). Any special treatment a worker receives from his or her high LMX supervisor can generate dysfunctional consequences for his or her peers, and for the work group generally.

Organizational politicking is closely tied to how responsive to their needs workers believe their employer is. But of course that relationship is negative. The correlation between Perceived Organizational Support (POS), measured using the 1986 POS scale of Eisenberg et al., and the widely used Perceptions of Organizational Politics scale (POPS; Kacmar & Ferris, 1991) is a whopping –.80 despite evidence that these are separate constructs (Cropanzano, Howes, Grandey, & Toth, 1997). Not merely the support itself but how organizations provide that support, broadly as policy or discriminately via managerial discretion, may determine whether workers construe it as fair and justified.

When reward allocations are determined primarily by personal relationships, as was the case in communist countries, a sense of injustice is pervasive within firms and often in the society as a whole (Pearce, 2001; Pearce, Branyiczki, & Bigley, 2000). Pearce quotes Haraszti's (1977) story of distrust among factory workers in communist Hungary: "Supplementary wages are our most frequent topic of conversation with the foremen. They have at their disposal a relatively large wage sum for the adjustment of individual wages. No one knows exactly how much, nor whether all or part of it is used up. . . . One thing is certain: the foremen resist paying supplementary wages. Each worker therefore concludes that if there are too many demands, less will be left for him . . . so each worker treats what he gets as a supplemental wage as a secret" (Pearce, 2001, p. 87).

Even in the context of human resource systems that attempt to base reward decisions upon worker contributions and market value, personal factors still can enter in. A worker's *true* contribution to the firm is unknowable in all but a few organizational settings. Things aren't always what they appear to be. Assessments are often subjective (objective indicators of contribution or value can be difficult to come by) and coworkers often have only incomplete information regarding the bases for managerial decisions. Recently, an administrator in my university, a man I view as very concerned about his staff and the organization, expressed surprise when some employees charged him with favoritism. He had recently promoted X into the position her former boss had held: "X was the only person who had done some of the work [her boss] had performed. When [the boss] left, we didn't even post the job, but just promoted X. Then people started complaining about a fix being in. There was no reason for them to think this."

What was a logical choice to the administrator, who possessed certain information about X's competence, can be favoritism to others who lack that information (or perhaps possess different information). Failure to follow a consistent and public promotion process in this case led to a perception of favoritism, even when the decision was effectively based on legitimate, job-related criteria. Coworkers also had difficulty discerning whether X, who had performed aspects of her boss's job, was conscientious and competent or manipulative and ingratiating. Although the administrator may not care what X's motives were, her coworkers were less sanguine and held a variety of disparate opinions that the process did nothing to resolve.

Unauthorized Taking

An exemplar: A department store salesperson sets aside an expensive swimsuit, waiting until the price is marked down after the season before buying it herself.

Unauthorized arrangements arise where a worker violates organizational rules, taking employer resources for personal use without permission. These illicit practices benefit the worker and include explicit activities such as employee theft (for example, embezzlement, misappropriation of equipment and supplies; Hollinger & Clark, 1983) and subtle behavior such as misrepresenting one's relationship to the firm for personal gain (for example, making false claims regarding one's title or position). When supervisors look the other way, such as when a convenience store manager lets the night-shift worker take groceries without paying to make working that shift more attractive, an arrangement that benefits both worker and manager is still unauthorized by the firm itself (Greenberg and Scott, 1996).

Although criminality and antisocial motivations pertain to aspects of unauthorized appropriation, some illicit behavior can be better understood from the perspective of social exchange (Greenberg & Scott, 1996). Social exchange research helps address the dynamics of illicit acts in settings in which situational factors to some extent condone or even legitimate the behavior. Illicit acts commonly include committing controlled larceny (whereby workers are permitted to take certain merchandise or set it aside until its price is reduced; Zeitlin, 1971), taking bribes (Henry, 1981), or stealing time to do personal business on the job (Bradford, 1976).

These accommodations can form part of a technically illegal, but nonetheless normative, invisible wage structure (Ditton, 1977; Greenberg & Scott, 1996). Inequitable treatment by the employer is one basis of employee theft (Greenberg, 1993), whether that inequity is objectively evident or only subjectively experienced. Fueled by both social acceptance and personal rationalization, illicit accommodations can create a psychological contract promoting deviance (Rousseau & Parks, 1993).

The consequences of illicit accommodations are multifaceted. They reduce the legitimacy of the formal organization when rule breaking becomes institutionalized. Initial motivations for deviance can be to restore equity under conditions of low pay or other unfair work conditions. The rationalization that deviance is payback for poor employer treatment complicates attempts to create a more open and trust-based employment system. These effects can spill over to coworkers by giving rise to group norms promoting illicit acts. Attempts to realign the interests of workers and employer can meet with wide resistance in settings where formal systems are viewed with suspicion and under-the-table practices are commonplace (Leatherwood & Spector, 1991).

Idiosyncratic Arrangements

An exemplar: As its business has grown, a consulting firm is having difficulty staffing its auditing engagements. Auditors traditionally stay in this functional area, sit for their certification examination, then get promoted as an audit partner, or else they leave to join a client firm. An auditor whose career goal is to become a tax consultant agrees to accept another auditing assignment under the condition that he will then be reassigned to another partner—whose specialty is tax.

Idiosyncratic arrangements are employment terms that are negotiated between an individual worker and an employer. Either the firm or the individual worker can initiate the negotiation. What makes these individual arrangements different from other person-specific employment is that both worker and firm benefit and some features of the arrangement differ from those that coworkers experience. (Note that for purposes of this chapter we are ignoring the distinct arrangements groups of workers such as core employees receive; Rousseau & Wade-Benzoni, 1995.) Such individual arrangements differ both from standardized ones that employees access as a group (for example, benefits allocated to full-time employees) and those based upon the particular positions workers hold (for example, more flexible work hours and vacations that a firm's professionals enjoy in contrast to its nonprofessional staff). Idiosyncrasy can be as explicit and clear-cut as different pay for the same work. Also, it can be as subtle as having greater autonomy and latitude on the job than one's peers enjoy.

A common motivator for workers to seek idiosyncratic arrangements is pursuit of individual flexibility to meet personal needs, such as enriching or de-stressing life outside of work. Arlie Russell Hochschild's book *Time Bind* (1997) is replete with examples of local arrangements made to the subject firm's valued workers in order to attract or retain them (from flexible work hours to one-year sabbaticals to make underwater photographs of coral reefs!). Klein, Berman, and Dickson's (2000) study of lawyers observed similar responsiveness to worker demands for flexibility but, in that sample, only in cases consistent with institutionally legitimated reasons (mothers caring for their children, but not fathers; demands from family but not personal hobbies).

Employers are motivated to offer idiosyncratic arrangements for numerous reasons, among these are to attract hard-to-find talent, retain valued employees, motivate workers when extra contributions are needed, and convey responsiveness to special worker needs. Idiosyncratic arrangements make a job more valuable to a worker and may be difficult for another employer to match.

The timing of idiosyncratic arrangements makes a difference. Workers who participate in them interpret such arrangements differently depending upon whether they arise due to pre-employment negotiation *(ex ante)* or once the worker is on the job in the context of an employment relationship *(ex post)*. Workers who negotiate idiosyncratic arrangements once they are on the job are more likely to view these as signals of organizational support than are those who negotiated accommodations at the time of hire (Rousseau, 2002; Rousseau & Kim, 2003). Some *ex post* idiosyncratic arrangements are offered in order to reinforce what Coyle-Shapiro and Kessler (2002) refer to as "proactive reciprocity" to motivate a worker to provide special, greater, or more flexible contributions in the future, in effect to build worker loyalty to the employer (Rousseau, in press). Moreover, *ex post* arrangements are more likely to entail career-enhancing opportunities (for example, preferred assignments, visibility) that require a degree of familiarity between the worker and firm in order for these to be negotiated (Rousseau, 2002). It can be more difficult to ask for certain conditions *ex ante* because recruits are likely to have relatively limited knowledge of the firm's work, customers, and internal operations. In contrast, *ex post* deals reflect negotiations in the context of a relationship with greater trust and shared information on the part of the parties involved.

The challenge of creating idiosyncratic deals that serve the interest of both worker and firm lie in creating arrangements that third parties view as fair; in particular, immediate coworkers. Idiosyncratic arrangements that otherwise fulfill the needs of worker and employer can erode the quality of the principals' relationships with third parties who perceive these arrangements as unjust. Fairness is nonetheless easier to achieve in idiosyncratic arrangements than in the other two because the former are created to enhance achievement of organizational goals and often entail workers who make a special or distinctive contribution to the firm. A major barrier to creating "just" idiosyncratic arrangements is the blurry boundary between idiosyncratic arrangements and those that are preferential or illicit.

Gray Areas

The boundaries among these forms of person-specific arrangement patterns can be ambiguous (Figure 9.1). Both illicit and idiosyncratic arrangements can come about under conditions in which the worker has a special relationship with his or her immediate manager. It is not uncommon for people with close ties to senior management to have unique employment roles. "Special assistants," "advisors," and long-standing "consultants" who serve at the discretion of a powerful manager very often have personal ties as well as their own distinctive competencies to thank for the particular roles they hold. Similarly, preferential treatment sometimes borders on the illicit. Consider the driver for a highly successful entrepreneur on the South Side of Chicago. The driver, who had been a boyhood friend of his boss, took "walking around money" out of the cash box to show off to his friends. Seldom spending it, he usually put the wad of cash back at the end of the day. The entrepreneur knew about his friend's behavior and looked the

**Figure 9.1. Blurry Boundaries
Among Person-Specific Employment Practices.**

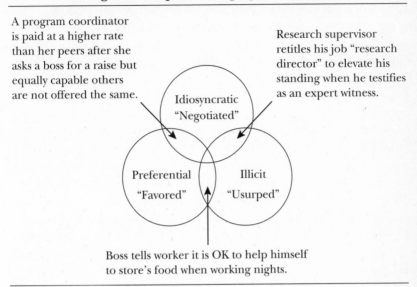

A program coordinator
is paid at a higher rate
than her peers after she
asks a boss for a raise but
equally capable others
are not offered the same.

Research supervisor
retitles his job "research
director" to elevate his
standing when he testifies
as an expert witness.

Idiosyncratic
"Negotiated"

Preferential
"Favored"

Illicit
"Usurped"

Boss tells worker it is OK to help himself
to store's food when working nights.

other way. Whether this situation is illicit or preferential depends
on the perspective taken, and points to the tension between the
objective and perceptual nature of person-specific arrangements.
In the case of the South Side entrepreneur's friend, the arrangement exists at the border between the illicit and preferential.

Idiosyncratic arrangements flirt with the dark side more often
where they border on the preferential: "From my first year working with the restaurant my employer provided 'special perks' to
keep me satisfied. I was paid more than my peers. I interpreted this
to mean they found me valuable and wanted me to stay. . . . It's sad
to say but this restaurant was very political. . . . I never realized how
much more I was on the 'inside' than some others. I guess I took
much for granted. It was in talking to people who were frustrated
by the politics that I realized how strong an element it was with this
company" (thirty-four-year-old former restaurant manager).

In businesses where there is little formal performance appraisal
or systematic employee development, it can be tough to keep idiosyncratic arrangements distinct from preferential ones. Such is the

case when one worker receives more latitude in choosing assignments because he or she is highly trusted. When that worker's skills develop more rapidly than his colleagues, it is not surprising that he is chosen for promotion over less favored peers. Nonetheless, without clear standards for evaluating performance, this worker's promotion is unlikely to be understood as legitimate (that is, performance-based).

The illicit also can become the idiosyncratic. An organizational psychologist believed that her formal job title, personnel research supervisor, was low in status compared to her professional peers. She printed up business cards giving herself the title of personnel research *director* to make it easier to obtain expert witness opportunities. Eventually, her manager learned about this embellishment. Worrying that the false title might surface when this psychologist was about to testify before the state legislature on the company's behalf, the manager quickly changed the psychologist's title to personnel research director. This circumstance is a form of acquiescence (Rousseau, 1995) whereby parties to the employment arrangement accept the terms that one or the other has usurped.

The Slippery Slope to the Dark Side

The slippery slope to the dark side of person-specific employment arrangements is the confusion of idiosyncratic arrangements with their dysfunctional counterparts. Although treating individuals with respect according to their needs and individual interests is valuable for the person and the firm, how this differential treatment is handled spells the difference between being seen in the eyes of third parties as acting in good faith or unjustly.

I argue that to date the field of organizational behavior has been relatively ineffective in guiding either scholars or managers to deal with the difficulties arising when individuals seek to be treated fairly, equally, *and* differently. Equal treatment need not mean the *same* treatment. We have failed to address simultaneously the *three* parties affected by the typical employment relationship: the employer, the worker, and his or her coworkers. The fundamental limitation has been the scant attention that organizational behavior (OB) scholars have given to the dynamics associated with relative standing among members of a work group. We first address the dilemma of relative standing and then examine its implications for justice issues and leader-member exchange in employment relations.

The Dilemma of Relative Standing

Idiosyncratic arrangements can throw the internal equities within the organization out of kilter. Such arrangements are behind the broad array of resources employers offer high performers relative to their lower-performing counterparts (Gerhart & Milkovich, 1992). Nonetheless, idiosyncratic arrangements can give rise to the "appearance of preferential treatment" even when the basis is a legitimate organizational goal such as worker retention or reward for high performance.

The relative standing individuals have in relation to peers plays a substantial role in the dark side of organizational life. Social standing is largely a within-group process. Or as Robert Frank (1985, p. 8) suggests: "Our 'needs' depend very strongly on those with whom we *choose* to associate closely." A utility function for individual status needs could be operationalized as "feel bad whenever you are less well provided for than your peers." Consider millionaire baseball players feeling cheated and taken advantage of because of even higher salaries offered to peers: "To be 50 or 60 on the pay scale doesn't sit well in my stomach. . . . I signed a contract, but no, I'm not happy with it anymore because baseball is business just like any other job. There are A players, B players and C players. I have been an A player for a long time" (Frank Thomas as quoted in Berkow, 2001, p. D2).

Status in local hierarchies may be a thing of considerable value. Although negative consequences arise from being at the bottom, being higher in the hierarchy accesses valued resources that are often in fixed supply (training, money, opportunities, choice). Frank (1985) argues that paying people their marginal product (the economist's ideal) seldom occurs in reality, as people at the top of the hierarchy access special gains from their position aside from pay and others at the bottom incur special costs. The presence of nonmonetary payouts to high-status members puts pressure on employers to reduce variation in pay. (Indeed paying people their marginal product would be perceived as an unfair wage structure if high performers also were accorded more respect and recognition than lower-performing peers.) In effect a "fair" wage should compensate people for where they stand in their respective earning hierarchies.

The dynamics of idiosyncratic arrangements point out why in understanding differential treatment it is important to address simultaneously the vantage points of employer, focal employee, and coworkers. Though many core concepts in organizational research involve these three parties, theory and research seldom take into account *all three perspectives* at the same time. I suggest, however, that core organizational behavior concepts, including leader-member exchange and all three forms of justice (procedural, distributive, and interactive) can better inform scholars and practitioners regarding how idiosyncratic arrangements can be made functional through simultaneous consideration of the vantage point of all three parties. Moreover, the conditions under which legitimated idiosyncratic arrangements arise have powerful implications for research on leader-member exchange and justice in the workplace.

Procedural Justice

Procedural justice pertains to beliefs regarding the fairness of procedures governing decisions. Originally conceptualized in terms of formal procedures (Masterson, Lewis, Goldman & Taylor, 2001; Thibaut & Walker, 1975), procedural justice extends to informal procedures used by those with power to make decisions. It leads to greater overall satisfaction with decision-making experiences. One key feature of procedural justice is voice, the opportunity to express one's point of view and influence the proceedings (Greenberg, 1996; Tyler, 1988). Procedural justice is more highly related to certain attitudinal outcomes, such as satisfaction, than is distributive justice (Alexander & Ruderman, 1987). It completely mediates the relationship between participation and satisfaction, highlighting the link between voice and fairness (Roberson, Moye, & Locke, 1999). Those idiosyncratic arrangements negotiated by workers can be construed as a form of voice that individuals exercise over their conditions of employment.

Though voice is a central feature of procedural justice, workers in the same firm do not necessarily have or avail themselves of the same opportunities for input into the decisions affecting them. Freeman and Rogers (1999) in a national survey of American workers found that workers who were of higher occupational status were more likely to exercise the opportunity to avail themselves of an employer's open-door policy. Believing one's self to have standing in one's employing firm may be a necessary condition for exercising voice. If voice is not equally accessed, or importantly exercised, it increases the likelihood that procedural justice is confounded with status issues in firms.

Voice is only one facet of procedural justice. Other features of procedural justice may be more difficult to execute in the context of idiosyncratic arrangements, particularly when these arise due to novel circumstances with which the firm has limited experience. Aside from voice, conditions of procedural justice include accuracy, representativeness, bias suppression, and consistency (Leventhal, 1980), and these can be difficult to achieve in the new or nonroutine situations often characteristic of idiosyncratic arrangements.

Employers often find it difficult to use personnel processes characterized by procedural justice when issues arise that are outside their prior experience. Procedural justice typically involves some degree of standardized practice in implementing personnel actions (for example, terminations, layoffs, and introduction of no-smoking policies; Greenberg, 1996). A base of experience is required to create procedures and implement them consistently and effectively (Pearce, Branyiczki, & Bigley, 2000). In consequence, standardizing idiosyncratic arrangements is difficult since they often are a response to special demands or needs. (As one respondent commented in Lee, MacDermid, and Buck, 2000: "Don't get rigid about flexibility," p. 1221.) For example, when law and accounting firms began affirmative action programs to promote women, they had little experience and fewer policies regarding pregnant professionals or nursing mothers. In early phases of adapting to such a change in human resource practice, inconsistency is inevitable. Diversity of interests in the labor force makes complete standardization of practices difficult, though cafeteria-type benefit arrangements are an exemplar of the standardization of flexibility (Barringer & Milkovich, 1997). Nonetheless, despite pressures for standardization, some degree of inconsistency is necessary for experimentation and to recruit new workers from non-traditional backgrounds. Procedural justice research provides little guidance on how to experiment fairly.

Distributive Justice

Distributive justice refers to the fairness with which individuals evaluate the outcomes they and others receive. Individuals can have a variety of standards of comparison for evaluating distributive justice (for example, market, contribution, or comparison to others). The choice of comparison depends on the distribution rule used (for instance, equal pay for equal work, preexisting agreement, need). Distributive fairness is to a great extent a function of social comparison (Goodman, 1974). Remember the millionaire baseball player described above who feels cheated by the even higher salaries offered to peers.

Because idiosyncratic arrangements create special treatment for one worker, they challenge the conventions of distributive fairness (for example, salary surveys, benchmarks, and preestablished criteria). For this reason, idiosyncratic arrangements often are associated with obfuscation, that is to say, practices that limit the ability of coworkers to make comparisons. Pay secrecy policies are the exemplar of comparison-reducing practices, since they attempt to suppress communication between coworkers regarding compensation (Rosen, 1981). Informal practices also discourage comparison by suppressing information ("don't tell anyone") or making arrangements difficult to verify ("don't put it in writing"). Unfortunately, this failure to make transparent the conditions giving rise to idiosyncratic arrangements means that potentially legitimate person-specific arrangements often wind up having the same dysfunctional consequences of their less legitimate counterparts.

Complicating the picture, workers can seek out idiosyncratic arrangements to compensate for what they believe to be otherwise unfair or inequitable treatment. When workers seek redress from employers whom they perceive to have violated their psychological contract, the remedial action taken sometimes takes the form of an idiosyncratic arrangement such as a special assignment that substitutes for a promotion that failed to materialize (Rousseau, Robinson, & Kraatz, 1992). These remedies arise following employee complaints and often are directly negotiated by workers with their own manager or his or her superior (Rousseau, 1995). In an intriguing parallel, employee theft can occur when managers turn a blind eye toward workers appropriating company supplies and equipment for their personal use, as a means to informally compensate the worker for low wages or otherwise inadequate employment arrangements (for example, having to work undesirable shifts; Greenberg & Scott, 1996). Supervisory collusion in worker pilfering is an extra-legal adjunct to the firm's reward system, what Ditton (1977) called the "invisible wage structure." To date, research on distributive justice has largely ignored the less monetizable, intrinsic, and social rewards that workers derive from employment. It also has ignored the offsets workers seek to make organizational practices more distributively fair, if only for themselves as individuals. Idiosyncratic arrangements commonly involve negotiations over employment terms other than money (Rousseau, Ho, & Kim, 2003), thus suggesting that distributive justice research needs to be better informed regarding the broader array of exchanges arising in employment.

Interactional Justice

Interactional justice refers to the quality of interpersonal treatment received during the execution of an organizational decision or process (Bies & Moag, 1986). Bies and Moag maintain that employee attributions for the source of interactional justice generalize to the person carrying out the procedure (for example, one's manager or a human resource staff member) whereas procedural justice is attributable to the entity whose procedures are involved (for example, the firm). Interactional justice predicts supervisor-related outcomes whereas procedural justice accounts for organization-related ones (Masterson, Lewis, Goldman, & Taylor, 2001; Masterson & Taylor, 1996). In contrast to the typical focus of interactional justice—that is, whether a recipient feels treated respectfully—at issue more often in idiosyncratic arrangements is the treatment of third parties. The worker with the idiosyncratic agreement is an active participant, negotiating his or her own terms at least to some extent. Participants are likely to believe themselves to be treated more fairly in terms of interactional justice than do their peers.

Social accounts shape perceptions regarding interactional justice. As explanations made in an attempt to influence how parties interpret a decision, accounts can alter beliefs regarding the decision's legitimacy, the responsibility that decision makers have for the decision or its outcome, their motives for an action, or perceptions of the action's unfavorability (Sitkin & Bies, 1993). Idiosyncratic accommodations are by definition influenced by both the worker and the employer, reflecting both their interests and making each responsible for its terms. Under conditions of idiosyncratic arrangements, the principals to the negotiation are in a position to negotiate based on their own personal beliefs regarding what is legitimate and acceptable. However, third-party perceptions regarding the deal's legitimacy and unfavorability can vary. Anticipating reactions of peers and coworkers is important to implementation of idiosyncratic arrangements.

When idiosyncratic arrangements are made to accommodate circumstances not covered by existing procedures, they are likely to engender one of two responses: disclosure coupled with an explanation for the arrangement (that is, a social account) or secrecy. Social accounts that explain the basis for idiosyncratic arrangements can enhance their legitimacy, but doing so requires that the arrangement (its existence if not all its terms) is made public. Secrecy exists when the idiosyncratic arrangement is not publicized, and thus no account is likely to be offered. Although secrecy can be a means of protecting recipients from an embarrassing disclosure (for example, a medical condition precipitating some accommodation), more often it is employed to keep coworkers from feeling inequitably treated or making a similar request. Such conditions erode both transparency of the personnel action and equality of outcomes workers experience. Since open and honest communication gives rise to interactional justice (Bies & Moag, 1986), secrecy is expected to be negatively related to interactional justice. In contrast, a social account focusing on the legitimacy of the accommodation can enhance both interactional justice and signal the organization's respect for individuals.

Leader-Member Exchange

LMX refers to a high-quality relationship between a manager and his or her subordinate based upon strong ties of loyalty trust, mutual respect, and emotional attachment. High-LMX relationships are related to the satisfaction, performance, and retention of the workers party to the relationship (Graen & Uhl-Bien, 1995). Moreover, managers are more likely to give broad latitude to their high-LMX subordinates in shaping their own roles, crafting tasks in ways that those workers find personally gratifying, and otherwise permitting high-LMX workers to shape their work experience along lines that reflect their own interests and needs (Graen &

Scandura, 1987). Not an unmitigated good, such strong ties require time and energy to maintain, are difficult to break, and can close off other opportunities (Brass, 2001). We know little of how high-managerial investment in certain subordinates affects their relationships with *other* subordinates. How promotion, development, support, and recognition are allocated within the workgroup is likely to be influenced by the nature of a manager's relations with individual group members. It is likely that workers who are party to a high-LMX relationship are advantaged in their ability to garner valued resources from their manager. Thus, the consequence of a high-LMX relationship upon coworkers not party to it can be adverse, yet researchers have largely ignored the impact of high-LMX relationships on low-LMX coworkers not party to them. In one of the few studies examining the contextual effects in relation to LMX, Conglisier and Schriesheim (2000) find evidence of numerous contextual factors shaping subordinate LMX perceptions (for example, leader power and reward climate). However, the impact of within-group variance in the quality of the supervisor-to-subordinate relationship has not yet been investigated. I would anticipate, however, that a major concern to low-LMX coworkers would be the extent to which the manager and the broader firm were viewed as just.

Implications

Idiosyncratic arrangements differ from the narrow array of resources typically examined in justice research in that they span the broad array of resources exchanged in employment. Distributive justice research largely addresses monetizable resources (pay, promotion, development opportunities; Adams, 1965), ignoring less monetizable resources such as interpersonal support. Procedural justice research addresses the process whereby firms allocate resources to workers with a focus on consistency in treatment, but it is relatively silent on flexibility (Tyler, 1988). Interactional justice research focuses specifically on relational issues of respect (Bies & Moag, 1986) but fails to address the potentially distributive quality of respect shown to one worker but not others. Moreover, the constituencies of idiosyncratic arrangements are arrayed differently than in traditional justice research. Although workers are recipients of employer-initiated conditions in the three "justices" described above, both workers and employers are principals playing an active role in shaping the terms of a worker-initiated idiosyncratic arrangement. In the latter context, pertinent fairness judgments rest in the minds of third parties, typically coworkers who would compare their own work arrangements to those of the focal worker. The vantage point of third parties is particularly critical to understanding the implications of idiosyncratic arrangements, since the potential array of resources exchanged varies in both salience and visibility, two conditions not addressed in traditional justice studies.

Idiosyncratic arrangements benefit both the worker and employer who negotiated them. Since their basis lies in the needs of individual worker and firm, in contrast to preferential and illicit arrangements, both principals are inclined to see this arrangement as fair. Third parties, in particular, coworkers, are likely to have more complex and varied reactions to idiosyncratic arrangements. Anticipation of third-party reactions is one factor influencing what worker and employer are willing to negotiate and the processes involved in creating idiosyncratic arrangements (Rousseau, in press). Another research domain, LMX has been largely silent on how coworkers react to their manager's having a particularly high-quality relationship with one of their peers. The notion that the LMX is an unmitigated good merits greater scrutiny, particularly in terms of coworker reactions and whether the resources exchanged between supervisors and their valued subordinates aversely affect the opportunities available for other subordinates.

In Support of Idiosyncratic Arrangements

Despite the obviously slippery slope between idiosyncratic arrangements and their dark side counterparts, I advocate for the continued need to develop and enhance use of idiosyncratic arrangements and for more systematic research on them.

Why do person-specific arrangements arise in the first place? Individual differences, and their increasing salience, are one answer. In contemporary firms individuals often work in micro-environments of their own design (sales staff operating out of their house and car, book editors who use Starbuck's for an office, financial traders for New York firms working from Tel Aviv and Tel-luride). Prevalence of such practices creates both opportunities for and expectations of employment arrangements compatible with individual preferences and needs (Rousseau, 1997; Weick, 1996). Over one hundred years of scientific psychological research indicates the inherent differences between people (Galton, 1879). Early industrial psychologists recognized that the organizational environment often had restrictive effects on the maximum use of individual capacity (Viteles, 1932; p. 109). The shift from the highly structured organization of the past to the more flexible organizing of contemporary work means that as traditional structures loosen, individuals have a greater hand in shaping their own working conditions. In this context, organizational control increasingly focuses more on job performance and business outcomes and less on how workers behave and the means they choose to achieve the firm's objectives.

This shift co-occurs with the need to find appropriate ways of motivating workers for whom the promise of job security is no longer credible (Rousseau & Shperling, 2003). Employers need new ways to motivate and retain valuable workers. Where traditional incentives such as seniority and retirement benefits have lost their credibility, and too long a stay in a firm can hamper one's employability, employers are challenged to create an employment relationship with a valued worker with which a firm's competitors would have a difficult time competing. In response, employers have expanded the resources they provide as inducements. This expansion of resources is what Bloom and Milkovich (1996, p. 26) call the "bundle of valued returns." Shifting how we think about compensation away from cash-based pay to the relationship among all valued returns, Bloom and Milkovich argue that how workers react to almost any compensation decision is influenced by other valued returns included in the bundle. Incentive pay's impact on behavior can depend upon the presence of other elements in the bundle, such as job security or autonomy, as well as the overall quality of the employment relationship. Having a quality relationship and an opportunity to work on preferred projects can add value to one's compensation package and amplify the performance that incentive pay is intended to promote. Moreover, adding more intangibles to the bundle makes it less likely that the worker can be lured away by another firm, since intangibles can be difficult to negotiate *ex ante*. Competitors would have a difficult time matching a mixed bag of cash, intrinsic job features, and relational advantages.

Finally, idiosyncratic arrangements that mix various resources also promote third-party perceptions of fairness by reducing comparison and making assessments of injustice more difficult. Broader bundles allow a mix of inducements based on resources that particular individuals value differently. High performers are often underpaid compared to their marginal product but receive a broader array of resources (from status and flexibility to other perks and higher pay) than average performers (Gerhart & Milkovich, 1992). This mix permits exchanges that are valued by the high performer but whose components are less likely to trigger a sense of inequity on the part of colleagues. Colleagues who might otherwise object to extraordinarily higher pay for a peer often can accept that star's getting a little more respect, since that respect may be legitimate in the eyes of the peer or not even particularly salient. One consequence of this differential reward pattern for high performers is that star performers in investment banks have been found to have lower turnover than nonstars despite their greater marketability. Special perks made available to stars by an employer can also make stars more resistant to outside offers, thus allowing them to remain in the firm to develop firm-specific capabilities that reinforce their star status and making it likely that they can be more productive by staying where they are. The connection between special treatment and development of firm-specific capabilities is likely to be mutually reinforcing and can account for the finding that individuals who have been high performers for some time are much less likely than new stars to switch employers (Groysberg & Nanda, 2002).

Organizational Practice

It's in the implementation where one can separate the flexibility of idiosyncratic arrangements from the favoritism and exploitation characteristic of preferential treatment and unauthorized arrangements. The hallmark of legitimate and functional differences in treatment between individual workers is the existence of three conditions:

- *Transparency.* It is public knowledge within the firm that an individual's employment conditions differ from his or her peers and the process whereby that negotiation has occurred is communicated to organization members.
- *Equality.* Other individuals could have negotiated similar conditions if they had met the standards that such a negotiation requires (for example, contribution or value to the firm) or valued those conditions in the first place (for example, preferring to work reduced or greater hours than the norm).
- *Differentiation.* Respect for individual differences is inherent in the social setting's values. Firms that focus on results rather than behavioral conformity may be in a better position to negotiate with workers in crafting customized employment relations because they are tolerant of different ways of getting the job done.

These three principles respect the dignity and value of all parties to the employment negotiation: worker, employer, and third parties such as coworkers whose social standing is affected by the treatment their fellows receive. Careful implementation based on these principles keeps clear the boundary between idiosyncratic arrangements and their dysfunctional counterparts (Rousseau, in press).

Conclusion

This chapter has taken a close look at circumstances wherein a worker has an employment arrangement that differs from his or her peers. It has examined the process whereby differential treatment arises and is socially interpreted, particularly where workers are active in creating work conditions that meet their personal needs. One central theme is that there are at minimum three parties to the typical employment relationship: the employer, a worker, and his or her coworkers. Viewing an individual's distinctive employment arrangement from the perspective of third parties as well as its principals raises important issues regarding the dynamics of several traditional concepts in organizational research ranging from LMX to forms of justice. Features distinguishing idiosyncratic employment arrangements from their dark side counterparts, preferential treatment and unauthorized taking, provide a basis for flexible treatment for individual workers that is fair to all. By shining a light on the dark side of person-specific employment arrangements, we can better discern how to create beneficial idiosyncratic arrangements, thus avoiding the pitfalls of their destructive counterparts.

Acknowledgments

Work on this chapter was supported by a H. J. Heinz II Professorship. Special thanks are due to Anne O'Leary-Kelly and a reviewer for insightful feedback and to Carole McCoy for constructing the graphics.

References

Abrahamson, M. (1966). *Interpersonal accommodation.* Princeton, NJ: Van Nostrand.

Adams, J. S. (1965). Inequity in social exchange. In L. Berkowitz (Ed.), *Advances in experimental social psychology.* New York: Academic Press.

Alexander, S., & Ruderman, M. (1987). The role of procedural and distributive justice in organizational behavior. *Social Justice Research, 1,* 177–198.

Barringer, M. W., & Milkovich, G. T. (1997). A theoretical exploration of the adoption and design of flexible benefit plans: A case of human resource innovation. *Academy of Management Review, 23,* 305–324.

Berkow, I. (2001). 'The big hurt' Feeling pained by his contract. *The New York Times,* February 26, 2001, D2.

Bies, R. J., & Moag, J. S. (1986). Interactional justice: Communication criteria of fairness. In M. H. Bazerman, R. Lewicki, & B. Sheppard (Eds.), *Research on negotiations in organizations* (Vol. 1, pp. 43–55). Greenwich, CT: JAI Press.

Bloom, M. C., & Milkovich, G. T. (1996). Issues in managerial compensation. In C. L. Cooper & D. M. Rousseau (Eds.), *Trends in organizational behavior, 3,* 23–49.

Bradford, J. A. (1976). A general perspective on job satisfaction: The relationship between job satisfaction and sociological, psychological, and cultural variables. Unpublished doctoral dissertation, Department of Sociology, University of California, San Diego (quoted in Greenberg and Scott, 1996).

Brass, D. J. (2001). Social capital and organizational leadership. In S. J. Zaccaro & R. J. Klimoski (Eds.), *The nature of organizational leadership: Understanding the performance imperatives confronting today's leaders.* San Francisco: Jossey-Bass.

Collela, A. (2001). Coworker distributive fairness judgments of the workplace accommodation of employees with disabilities. *Academy of Management Review*, 26, 100–116.

Conglisier, C. C., & Schriesheim, C. A. (2000). Exploring work unit context and leader-member exchange: A multilevel perspective. *Journal of Organizational Behavior*, 21, 487–513.

Cox, T. (1993). *Cultural diversity in organizations: Theory, research, and practice.* San Francisco: Berrett-Koehler.

Coyle-Shapiro, J.A-M., & Kessler, I. (2002). Reciprocity through the lens of the psychological contract: Employee and employer perspectives. *European Journal of Work and Organizational Psychology*, 11, 1–18.

Cropanzano, R., Howes, J. C., Grandey, A. A., & Toth, P. (1997). The relationship of organizational politics and support to work behaviors, attitudes and stress. *Journal of Organizational Behavior*, 18, 159–180.

Dansereau, F., Graen, G., & Haga, W. J. (1975). A vertical dyad linkage approach to leadership within formal organizations: A longitudinal investigation of the role-making process. *Organizational Behavior and Human Performance*, 13, 46–78.

DeLorean, J. Z. (1979). *On a clear day you can see General Motors.* Grosse Pointe, MI: Wright Enterprises.

Ditton, J. (1997). Perks, pilferage, and the fiddle: The historical structure of invisible wages. *Theory and Society*, 4, 39–71.

Dreher, G. F., & Cox, T. H. (2000). Labor market mobility and cash compensation: The moderating effects of race and gender. *Academy of Management Journal*, 43, 890–900.

Ferris, G. R., Frink, D. D., Bhawuk, D., Zhou, J., & Gilmore, D. C. (1996). Reactions of diverse groups to politics in the workplace. *Journal of Management*, 22, 23–44.

Ferris, G. R., Frink, D. D., & Galang, M. C. (1993). Diversity in the workplace: The human resources management challenges. *Human Resources Planning*, 16, 41–51.

Firebaugh, G. (1980). Groups as contexts and frog ponds. In K. H. Roberts & L. Burstein (Eds.), *Issues in aggregation. New Directions for Methodology of Social and Behavioral Science* (Vol. 6). San Francisco: Jossey-Bass.

Frank, R. (1985). *Choosing the right pond: Human behavior and the quest for status.* New York: Oxford.

Freeman, R. B., & Rogers, J. (1999). *What workers want.* Ithaca, NY: Cornell University Press.

Galton, F. (1879). Psychometric experiments. *Brain*, 2, 472–474.

Gerhart, B., & Milkovich, G. T. (1992). Employee compensation: Research and practice. In M. D. Dunnette & L. M. Hough (Eds.), *Handbook in industrial and organizational psychology* (pp. 481–569). Palo Alto, CA: Consulting Psychologists Press.

Goodman, P. S. (1974). An examination of referents used in the evaluation of pay. *Organizational Behavior and Human Performance*, 12, 170–195.

Graen, G., & Cashman, J. F. (1975). A role-making model of leadership in formal organizations: A developmental approach. In J. G. Hunt & L. L. Larson (Eds.), *Leadership frontiers.* Carbondale: Southern Illinois University.

Graen, G. B., & Scandura, T. A. (1987). Toward a psychology of dynamic organizing. *Research in Organizational Behavior*, 9, 175–208.

Graen, G. B., & Uhl-Bien, M. (1995). Relationship-based approach to leadership: Development of leader-member exchange (LMX) theory over 25 years: Applying a multi-level, multi-domain perspective. *Leadership Quarterly*, 6, 219–247.

Greenberg, J. (1993). Stealing in the name of justice: Informational and interpersonal moderators of theft reactions to underpayment inequity. *Organizational Behavior and Human Decision Processes*, 54, 81–103.

Greenberg, J. (1996). *The quest for justice on the job.* Thousand Oaks, CA: Sage.

Greenberg, J., & Scott, K. S. (1996). Why workers bite the hand that feeds them? Employee theft as a social exchange process. *Research in Organizational Behavior*, 18, 111–156.

Groysberg, B., & Nanda, A. (2002, June). *Does stardom affect job mobility? Evidence from analyst turnover in investment banks.* Paper presented at Career Evolutions conference sponsored by Harvard Business School, London.

Henry, S. (1981). *Can I have it in cash? A study of informal institutions and unorthodox ways of doing things.* London: Astragal Books.

Hochschild, A. R. (1997). *Time bind: When work becomes home and home becomes work.* New York: Metropolitan.

Hollinger, R. D., & Clark, J. P. (1983). *Theft by employees.* Lexington, MA: Lexington Books.

Kacmar, M., & Ferris, G. R. (1991). "Perceptions of organizational politics scale" (POPS): Development and construct validation. *Educational and Psychological Measurement*, 51, 193–205.

Klein, K. J., Berman, L. M., & Dickson, M. W. (2000). May I work part-time? An exploration of predicted employer responses to employee requests for part-time work. *Journal of Vocational Behavior*, 57, 85–101.

Leatherwood, M. L., & Spector, L. C. (1991). Enforcements, inducements, expected utility and employee misconduct. *Journal of Management*, 17, 533–550.

Lee, M. D., MacDermid, S. M., & Buck, M. L. (2000). Organizational paradigms of reduced-load work: Accommodation, elaboration, and transformation. *Academy of Management Journal*, 43, 1211–1226.

Leventhal, G. S. (1980). What should be done with equity theory? In K. J. Gergen, M. S. Greenberg, & R. H. Willis (Eds.), *Social exchange: Advances in experimental social psychology.* (pp. 27–55) New York: Plenum.

Masterson, S. S., Lewis, K., Goldman, B. M., & Taylor, M. S. (2001). Integrating justice and social exchange: The differing effects of fair procedures and treatment on work relationships. *Academy of Management Journal*, 43, 738–746.

Masterson, S. S., & Taylor, M. S. (1996). *The broadening of procedural justice: Should interactional and procedural components be separate theories?* Paper presented at the annual meeting of the Academy of Management, Cincinnati.

Pearce, J. L. (2001). *Organization and management in the embrace of government.* Mahwah, NJ: Elrbaum.

Pearce, J. L., Bigley, G. A., & Branyiczki, I. (1998). Procedural justice as modernism: Placing industrial/organizational psychology in context. *Applied Psychology: An International Review*, 47, 371–396.

Pearce, J. L., Branyiczki, I., & Bigley, G. A. (2000). Insufficient bureaucracy: Trust and commitment in particularistic organizations. *Organization Science*, 11, 148–162.

Roberson, Q. M., Moye, N. A., & Locke, E. A. (1999). Identifying a missing link between participation and satisfaction: The mediating role of procedural justice perceptions. *Journal of Applied Psychology*, 84, 585–593.

Robinson, S. L. (1995). Violation of psychological contracts: Impact on employee attitudes. In L. E. Tetrick & J. Barling (Eds.), *Changing employment relations: Behavior and social perspectives.* Washington, D.C.: American Psychological Association.

Rosen, S. (1981). The economics of superstars. *American Economic Review*, 71, 845–858.

Rousseau, D. M. (1995). *Psychological contracts in organizations: Understanding written and unwritten agreements.* Newbury Park, CA: Sage.

Rousseau, D. M. (1997). Organizational behavior in the new organizational era. *Annual Review of Psychology*, 48, 515–546.

Rousseau, D. M. (2001). The idiosyncratic deal: Flexibility versus fairness? *Organizational Dynamics*, 29, 260–273.

Rousseau, D. M. (2002, August). *When workers bargain for themselves (and career advantage).* Paper presented at Academy of Management meetings, Denver.

Rousseau, D. M., Ho, V. T., & Kim, T. G. (2003). *How I-deals shape psychological contracts.* Unpublished manuscript. Carnegie Mellon University, Pittsburgh.

Rousseau, D. M., & Kim, T. G. (2003). *Idiosyncratic deals: When workers bargain for themselves.* Unpublished manuscript. Carnegie Mellon University, Pittsburgh.

Rousseau, D. M., & Parks, J. M. (1993). The contracts of individuals and organizations. *Research in Organizational Behavior,* 15, 1–43.

Rousseau, D. M., Robinson, S. L., & Kraatz, M. S. (1992, May). *Renegotiating the psychological contract.* Paper presented at the Society for Industrial and Organizational Psychology meetings, Montreal.

Rousseau, D. M., & Shperling, Z. (2003). Pieces of the action: Ownership, power and the psychological contract. *Academy of Management Review*

Rousseau, D. M., & Wade-Benzoni, K. A. (1995). Changing models of attachment. In A. Howard (Ed.), *The changing nature of work. Foundation of Industrial/Organizational Psychology* (Vol. 5, pp. 290–322). San Francisco: Jossey-Bass.

Rousseau, D. M. (in press). *I-deals: When individual workers bargain for themselves.* New York: M. E. Sharpe.

Sitken, S. B., & Bies, R. J. (1993). Social accounts in conflict situations: Using explanations to manage conflict. *Human Relations,* 46, 349–370.

St. Augustine (1991). *Confessions.* Translated by H. Chadwick. Oxford: Oxford University Press.

Thibaut, J., & Walker, L. (1975). *Procedural justice: A psychological analysis.* Hillsdale, NJ: Erlbaum.

Tsui, A. S., Porter, L. W., & Egan, T. (2002). When both similarities and dissimilarities matter: Extending the concept of relational demography. *Human Relations,* 55, 899–929.

Tyler, T. R. (1988). What is procedural justice? Criteria used by citizens to assess the fairness of legal procedures. *Law and Society Review,* 22, 103–135.

Viteles, M. S. (1932). *Industrial psychology.* New York: Norton.

Weick, K. H. (1996). Enactment in the boundaryless career: Organizing as we work. In M. B. Arthur and D. M. Rousseau (Eds.), *The boundaryless career: A new employment principle for a new organizational era* (pp. 40–57). New York: Oxford University Press.

Zeitlin, L. R. (1971, June). A little larceny can do a lot for employee morale. *Psychology Today,* pp. 22, 24, 26, 64.

CHAPTER 10

Extreme Careerism
The Dark Side of Impression Management
Virginia K. Bratton, K. Michele Kacmar

In an age of economic downturn and cutbacks, career management is an important activity for many members of the workforce. In an effort to proactively manage their careers, many individuals seek promotional opportunities as well as methods through which to advance themselves and their careers. Although careerism has been a topic of interest for quite some time, there have been relatively few examinations of this construct (Feldman, 1985, 1996; Feldman & Weitz, 1991). Here we examine *extreme careerism,* which is the propensity to pursue career advancement, power, or prestige through any positive or negative nonperformance-based activity that is deemed necessary.

As our definition suggests, careerist individuals often engage in nonperformance-based activities to achieve their personal and career goals (Feldman, 1985). One way this can be accomplished is through the use of impression management (IM) (Ferris, Judge, Rowland, & Fitzgibbons, 1994; Wayne, Liden, Graf, & Ferris, 1997). IM has been defined as the process through which individuals manipulate information about themselves so that others perceive them as they desire to be viewed (Schlenker, 1980). The actual manipulation of information is accomplished by enacting IM tactics.

As frequently occurs with human behaviors, IM tactics can be positive (such as modesty), or negative (for example, when one blames others for undesirable behavioral outcomes). Although extreme careerists may rely on positive influence behaviors, in keeping with the theme of this book we focus here on the use of negative IM. We define negative IM as either aggressive or defensive actions taken usually at another's expense in order to protect or enhance one's own image. It is important to increase our understanding of extreme careerism and negative IM for many reasons. An increased organizational awareness of these constructs and the behaviors associated with them can lead to better management and policies in the workplace. These improvements, in turn, can help decrease the use of negative IM techniques and, more important, reverse the trend of increasing negativism in the workplace in the form of aggression, violence, and organizational cynicism.

The goal of this chapter is to contribute to the accumulation of knowledge on extreme careerism and negative IM. By drawing upon the extant literature, we propose a general model of extreme careerism, which is depicted in Figure 10.1. Included in this model are what we view as the major contextual, individual, and behavioral components of extreme careerism. The model also illustrates the potential outcomes of extreme careerists' use of negative IM. Although we endeavored to include what we view as the key components of extreme careerism, we recognize that not all of the relevant variables have been integrated into our model. Thus, our depiction of extreme careerism should be viewed as a general rather than comprehensive model.

Contextual and individual antecedent variables directly affect an actor's use of negative IM tactics. As is suggested in Figure 10.1, extreme careerism embodies the front end of the model. Although context certainly shapes this concept—as do individual trait and dispositional variables—the most defining characteristic here is behavioral. The behaviors employed within extreme careerism are negative IM tactics. The use of negative IM tactics will lead to outcomes at multiple levels in the organization, and the outcomes loop back into context at the front end of the model. In the sections that follow we will examine each component of the model in more detail, starting with the components of extreme careerism.

Figure 10.1. Model of Extreme Careerism.

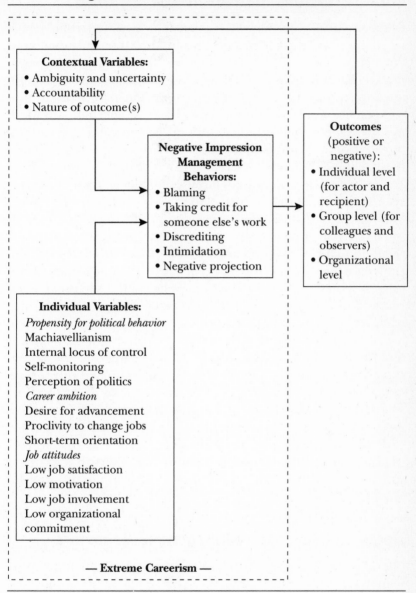

What Is "Extreme Careerism"?

Feldman (1985) introduced the concept of "new careerism," which he defined as "the propensity to pursue career advancement through nonperformance-based means" (Feldman & Weitz, 1991, p. 237). Several themes underlie beliefs about new careerism and are applicable to the current discussion. The first theme is that competence alone is insufficient for career advancement. In order to fully achieve their advancement goals, new careerists can use interpersonal relationships they have formed. Another theme is that the use of IM tactics to create the image of being successful is as effective in attaining career advancement as actually being successful. One final theme relates to careerist orientations toward time. Careerist individuals believe that in the long run their personal goals do not align with organizational goals; therefore, they will tend to focus attention and effort on short-term tactics. These tactics are aimed at personal advancement rather than long-term organizational success (Feldman & Weitz, 1991). There has been support for this conceptualization of careerism and the existence of careerist individuals in the workplace (Kacmar & Carlson, 1998).

Although Feldman's (1985) work can serve as a basis for our discussion, we wish to differentiate "extreme careerism" from "new careerism" based on the types of behaviors exhibited by the individual toward achieving his or her career goals. The behaviors referred to here are IM tactics. Although new careerism acknowledges the role of IM in creating more promotable images for careerist individuals, it is relatively silent on the types of IM techniques that careerists tend to employ. We assert that extreme careerism draws primarily, but not exclusively, upon negative IM techniques.

Negative Impression Management Behaviors

One of the first researchers to discuss IM was sociologist Erving Goffman in 1959. He suggested that people are like actors who behave as though they are fulfilling a role and by doing so build their social identities. These role-induced behaviors are consciously exhibited in order to influence how people are perceived and consequently treated by others. A steady stream of research that began in the

1970s and extends to the present day has established IM in the workplace as an important area of inquiry (Becker & Martin, 1995; Rosenfeld, Giacalone, & Riordan, 1995; Wayne & Liden, 1995).

Most researchers conceptualize IM in a broad sense, as a fundamental and common part of all interactions between people (Rosenfeld et al., 1995). Such a perspective on IM does not necessarily restrict the concept to negative, selfish acts. Rather, this perspective depicts IM as a broad group of behaviors that may be aimed at multiple audiences, evolve from a broad range of motives that are not limited to those of a selfish and ulterior nature, and result in both positive and negative outcomes for the actor, his or her coworkers, and the overall organization.

A few researchers, however, have taken a more restrictive view of IM by conceptualizing it as a "form of interpersonal manipulation occurring in very confined settings . . . as something basically bad, involving actions performed primarily to attain the upper hand over others, or to deceive them" (Rosenfeld et al., 1995, p. 6). Although IM was not initially conceived in this "dark" light, it was developed in research to characterize an extreme form of behavior. It is this restrictive view of IM that more accurately represents the concept of negative IM.

Negative IM is associated with negative behaviors and outcomes, and is strongly linked to Machiavellianism, which is the self-interested exploitation of another for one's personal gain. It also can be related to "instrumental aggression," which is aggressive behaviors that are performed for reasons apart from causing harm (Berkowitz, 1992). Instrumental aggression can be regarded as a means to an alternative end (Geen, 1990). This can be extended to negative IM in that at some level within the organization, these behaviors are typically harmful when they are not intended to cause harm but rather to provide instrumental gain for the actor.

A variety of negative IM tactics have been described in the literature. Figure 10.1 provides a list of a few of the more established tactics. More details about these tactics are provided in the following paragraphs. The common undercurrent of these tactics is the instrumentality of the negative social behaviors (Mohamed, Gardner, & Paolillo, 1999). In the case of extreme careerism, it is the goal of gaining promotion, power, prestige, and other rewards within an organization.

Blaming

Blaming typically occurs after a predicament, which is defined by Schlenker (1980) as an event that causes others to doubt the background, personality, behavior, ability, or intentions of the actor. When someone blames others, the actor is admitting that a given act was wrong but does not accept responsibility for the act. Rather, the actor assigns blame or responsibility to someone else. This tactic is a type of excuse in that the actor tries to alter the way others think about a bad event rather than trying to alter the event itself. For example, an extreme careerist who lost a major account might blame a coworker for this negative event. This IM tactic serves two purposes. First, it protects the actor's reputation as an effective account manager and it also harms the reputation of the coworker on whom the event was blamed, perhaps eliminating this coworker as a competitor for organizational rewards and promotions.

Taking Credit for Someone Else's Work

Another way an actor can compromise competitors is by taking credit for their work. One way this can occur is by implementing an entitlement tactic, which has sometimes been described in the literature as a form of acclaiming (Schlenker, 1980; Tedeschi & Melburg, 1984). Entitlements occur following some positive outcome or event. Using this tactic, the actor tries to increase his perceived responsibility for the positive outcome or event even when he is not directly responsible. For example, an extreme careerist would claim that he was responsible for a particularly high-profile sale in order to bolster his impression as a competent and talented salesperson. In so doing, the careerist also would prevent his coworkers from building their sales reputations and from receiving organizational rewards or attention from their superiors that they have earned.

Discrediting

Discrediting involves attempts to lessen the favorable qualities of another. These attempts are made with the objective of enhancing the actor's personal reputation by downplaying positive qualities of a competitor. Cialdini (1989) reasoned that there might be a propensity for such behavior in managers who consider certain subordinates to be potential rivals. Such managers will conceivably decrease their evaluations of the performance of these subordinates, thereby limiting or even derailing their career progress.

Intimidation

Intimidators seek to be feared in contrast to ingratiators who seek to be liked. Whereas ingratiators dangle a carrot, intimidators brandish a big stick (Rosenfeld et al., 1995). When using this aggressive self-presentation tactic, individuals strive to achieve the image of being dangerous, such as a person whose threats and warnings must be heeded in order to avoid negative consequences (Arkin & Sheppard, 1989). Jones and Pittman (1982) described intimidators as those who send the message that they have the power to generate a level of discomfort and even produce "psychic pain" (p. 238). Intimidators typically exert pressure in a downward direction; however, it is possible for such tactics to entail upward influence. For instance, an employee can threaten her superior with a discriminatory lawsuit if she does not get promoted. Jones and Pittman (1982) describe such upward influence as "counterpower intimidation." Extreme careerists are most likely to employ intimidation tactics when they are acting in a contracted relationship such as the employer-employee relationship, they have the leverage to impose discomfort upon a target, the target lacks the aptitude or desire to strike back, and when they are prepared to surrender any possibility of being held in positive esteem by the target (Jones & Pittman, 1982). Intimidating tactics may be used to obtain agreement from others, protect or defend one's reputation, garnish social rewards (such behavior might be the norm in a particular organization), and fulfill interpersonal objectives when one believes behaviors supporting a positive social image will not succeed in this regard (Leary & Miller, 1986).

Negative Projection

Negative projection involves an exaggeration of the degree that an actor is impeded in his ability to perform so as to avoid the unpleasant consequences of his performance or a related event. This is a form of self-handicapping (Becker & Martin, 1995) that has been described in the literature as strategically "shooting yourself in the foot." For example, extreme careerists may exaggerate their inability to speak in public settings in order to avoid having to participate in an ill-fated presentation. Here, by self-handicapping their presentational abilities, careerists avoid the more negative consequences of being associated with a disastrous presentation.

Contextual Variables: When Do People Use Negative Impression Management?

It is generally agreed upon in the literature that certain contexts give rise to political behavior. Here we examine three commonly investigated contextual variables that we anticipate will give rise to the use of negative IM by extreme careerists. Drawing on previous research, we develop propositions for the following contextual antecedent variables: ambiguity and uncertainty (Ferris, Fedor, & King, 1994; Ferris, Russ, & Fandt, 1989), accountability (Fandt & Ferris, 1990; Ferris, Fedor, & King, 1994; Tetlock, 1985), and the nature of outcomes (Ferris, Fedor, & King, 1994).

Ambiguity and Uncertainty

A workplace can be characterized as ambiguous and uncertain when a lack of clarity exists regarding several aspects within it. For example, unclear performance expectations lead to unclear evaluation criteria in performance appraisal. When evaluation criteria are unclear, greater reliance on personal characteristics, which are generally not related to work behaviors, may be the result. Such ambiguity provides for the opportunity for individuals to employ IM so as to influence the outcomes of such processes (Ferris et al., 1989). With this increased opportunity to perform IM overall comes the increased opportunity to use negative IM techniques as well. For example, in a work situation where an employee is unclear as to the criteria upon which her performance is to be evaluated, this employee may be more likely to resort to a negative IM technique such as discrediting in order to enhance her personal reputation and job promotability while disqualifying the competition.

PROPOSITION 1: *Higher levels of organizational ambiguity and uncertainty will be related to increased use of negative IM behaviors.*

Accountability

Accountability has been depicted as a key influence on the expression of political behavior. It can be defined as the extent to which a person is held responsible for a given outcome (Fandt & Ferris, 1990). Many researchers in accountability have examined the motivation for symbolic or tangible gains (Baumeister, 1982; Fandt & Ferris, 1990; Schlenker, 1980). Individuals are motivated to seek symbolic gains, such as approval and respect, and tangible gains, such as promotions and salary increases, from those to whom they are accountable (Tetlock, 1985). Tetlock and others (Tetlock, 1992; Tetlock, Skitka, & Boettger, 1989) have shown that individuals, in an effort to deal with increased accountability, are more inclined to anticipate responses and modify their decisions and behaviors in order to obtain positive responses. Thus, individuals who are held accountable for their work behaviors may be more likely to engage in defensive and protective IM tactics (Ferris, Fedor, & King, 1994; Tedeschi & Melburg, 1984). For example, an accountable employee might resort to intimidation in a downward direction in order to attain the desired performance toward achieving the given outcome for which he is accountable. As mentioned previously, when an individual feels that behaviors supporting a positive social image will not contribute toward accomplishing a given objective, he will be more likely to resort to a negative IM technique such as intimidation.

PROPOSITION 2: *Individual accountability will be related to increased use of negative IM behaviors.*

The Nature of Outcomes

The nature of outcomes refers to whether the anticipated outcomes of a given situation are expected to be negative or positive (Ferris, Fedor, & King, 1994). As mentioned earlier, IM techniques will differ depending upon whether the actor is held accountable for that outcome. Yet regardless of the actor's level of accountability, she will be inclined to distance herself from a negative outcome through the use of negative IM. For example, blaming others is an example of a negative IM technique that would be employed when anticipating a negative outcome for which the actor did not wish to be responsible, as the actor here seeks to distance herself as much as possible from the negative result (Ferris, Fedor, & King, 1994). For positive outcomes, savvy extreme careerists want to be associated with such results and therefore increase the perception of their accountability for these results. In such situations, actors would be more likely to use entitlements or simply take credit for another's work (Gardner & Martinko, 1998).

PROPOSITION 3: *Extreme careerists will use negative IM in order to distance themselves from negative events and associate themselves with positive events.*

Individual Variables: Why Do People Use Negative Impression Management?

Our examination of individual variables is based on a synthesis of the work done by Ferris and others (Ferris et al., 1989; Ferris, Fedor, & King, 1994; Ferris & Kacmar, 1992) in the area of political behavior with the research by Feldman and Weitz (1991) in the area of careerism. In the following paragraphs, we consider three key constructs that give rise to the application of negative IM by individual actors: propensity to behave politically (Ferris, Fedor, & King, 1994), desire for mobility or career ambition (Feldman & Weitz, 1991; Judge, Cable, Boudreau, & Bretz, 1995), and job attitudes (Feldman & Weitz, 1991).

Propensity to Behave Politically

Research suggests that some individuals are predisposed to exhibit political behaviors in general (Ferris, Fedor, & King, 1994; Ferris et al., 1989). Political behaviors are defined as "the management of shared meaning," focusing on the "subjective evaluations and interpretations of meaning" (Ferris, Fedor, & King, 1994, p. 4). Defining a behavior in a given situation as political is a function of the traits of the actor, the perceiver, the situation, and the ensuing cognitive assessments conceived by the perceiver. Here we focus on the actor. Modeling the work of Ferris and others, we expect that the following individual variables will influence whether a person will exhibit political behavior: Machiavellianism, locus of control, self-monitoring, and perception of politics.

Machiavellianism

Individuals who are Machiavellians (Machs) will do virtually anything in order to promote their personal interests (Christie & Geis, 1970). Negative conceptions of IM have been related to this personality trait in the literature (Rosenfeld et al., 1995). High Machs are predisposed to engage in manipulative and opportunistic behaviors. In the appropriate setting, such individuals can be anticipated to zealously enhance their self-interests. Research supports the connection between Machiavellianism and careerism by demonstrating a link between high Machs and higher levels of work-related prestige as well as earnings (Turner & Martinez, 1977). There is also research indicating the propensity of high Machs to manage the impressions of others (Ferris, Fedor, & King, 1994; Pandey, 1981). It is thus expected that high Machs will be more likely to employ negative IM techniques than low Machs.

PROPOSITION 4A: *Individuals who are high Machiavellians will be more likely to use negative IM behaviors than those who are low Machiavellians.*

Locus of Control

Individuals with an internal locus of control believe that they can change their environment (Bandura, 1977). They feel that they have a high degree of control over the process and outcomes of their given situations and can take steps to elicit more favorable outcomes (Ferris et al., 1989). Given their mindset, it follows that these individuals will be more likely to engage in negative IM as a means of creating their own destiny.

PROPOSITION 4B: *Individuals who have an internal locus of control will be more likely to use negative IM behaviors than individuals who have an external locus of control.*

Self-Monitoring

Those who are high self-monitors have the ability to evaluate and regulate their behaviors (Snyder, 1987). Such individuals search their environments for social cues and shape their behavior in accordance with these cues. In other words, high self-monitors interpret their environments and modify their actions accordingly. Past research has demonstrated the importance of this construct in career management, finding that high self-monitors are more likely than low self-monitors to achieve job promotions. This may be because high self-monitors are better able to adapt their behavior to their work environments (Kilduff & Day, 1994). With their ability to perceive opportunities in the environment and behave opportunistically in accordance with that environment, high self-monitors will have a greater propensity to successfully engage in negative IM than their low-self-monitoring counterparts. For example, an employee who denies his connection to a notoriously poor performing coworker must first recognize that others in the organization negatively perceive this coworker. A high self-monitor will be more effective in such an endeavor.

PROPOSITION 4C: *Individuals who are high self-monitors will be more likely to use negative IM behaviors than will low self-monitors.*

Perceptions of Politics

One last individual variable is the perceived political climate of the organization. It stands to reason that the greater the level of perceived politics, the more likely it is that careerist individuals will exhibit political behaviors. Because the actual political climate depicting a given context may or may not be accurately perceived by the actor, we propose that it is in fact the actor's perceptions of politics (Ferris et al., 1989; Ferris, Fedor, & King, 1994; Ferris & Kacmar, 1992) that influences her employment of negative IM. As suggested by Ferris et al. (1989), one possible reaction to perceived politics is that it may prompt opportunistic activity by changing the nature of the work situation and in so doing encourage others to "play the game or at least [provide] others with the opportunity to do so" (p. 161). With this in mind, the following proposition is offered.

PROPOSITION 4D: *Increased perceptions of politics will be related to increased use of negative IM behaviors.*

Career Ambition

The individual-level construct of career ambition is described by Judge et al. (1995) simply as the desire to get ahead. Feldman and Weitz (1991) further develop this construct by finding support for the link between a careerist orientation and the desire and disposition to change jobs. Echoing Feldman and Weitz's (1991) description of careerists, we also assert that career ambition in the proposed model will include short-term orientations in job behaviors. Such short-term orientations will better allow for negative IM, for individuals are more likely to "rock the boat" if they foresee that they will soon be disembarking. Thus, we conceptualize career ambition as a synthesis of these three factors (the desire to get ahead, the proclivity to change jobs, and short-term orientations in job behaviors) and expect that high levels of career ambition will lead to the use of negative IM behaviors.

PROPOSITION 5: *Individuals with high levels of career ambition will be more likely to use negative IM behaviors.*

Job Attitudes

Feldman and Weitz (1991) noted that careerists have low levels of job satisfaction, motivation, job involvement, and organizational commitment. One explanation for these negative job attitudes may be the incongruity that often exists between the personal goals of an extreme careerist and the goals of the overall organization. That is, extreme careerists may be less hesitant to exhibit negative IM in situations perceived to be instrumental. The absence of thought about the repercussions on coworkers and the overall organization of using these tactics virtually requires that the person engaging in such tactics possess low levels of job attitudes such as job satisfaction or organizational commitment.

PROPOSITION 6: *Individuals with lower levels of (1) job satisfaction, (2) motivation, (3) job involvement, and (4) organizational commitment will be more likely to use negative IM behaviors.*

Outcomes: What Is the Impact of Negative Impression Management?

The model depicted in Figure 10.1 indicates that negative IM behaviors may lead to both functional and dysfunctional outcomes at multiple levels within the organization. It is beyond the scope of the current discussion to go into detail in this area; however, it is important to acknowledge that, like IM behaviors in general, negative IM behaviors may lead to positive outcomes. For example, at the individual level, employment of such tactics may lead to desired promotions. At the group and organization levels, negative IM behaviors may coincide with behavioral norms. In other words, individuals exerting such tactics may be merely fulfilling organization- or group-level behavioral expectations.

However, eventually the negative IM behaviors employed by extreme careerists will lead to negative outcomes at some level in the organization. For example, at the individual level the overuse of a negative IM tactic such as blaming may result in a negative impression, such as of one who shirks work responsibilities (Rosenfeld et al., 1995). At the same time, individuals who are blamed for negative organizational outcomes can be expected to suffer psychologically as well as in terms of reduced organizational rewards and recognition.

Furthermore, excessive career advancement achieved through the vehicle of negative IM may place unqualified individuals or low performers in key positions within a group or organization, a result that may cause lower levels of organizational performance. For example, an extreme careerist who often discredits her coworkers may distort performance evaluations within the organization to the point that accurate assessments can no longer be used to gauge the overall performance or improvement of an organization or workgroup (Gardner & Martinko, 1998).

Indeed, it seems that the potential long-term negative outcomes outweigh any short-term benefit that can be derived from the negative IM behaviors employed by extreme careerists. Based on this discussion, the following exploratory proposition is offered.

PROPOSITION 7: *The use of negative IM may lead to negative outcomes at multiple levels within an organization (individual level, group level, and organizational level).*

One last note regarding the outcomes of negative IM. As depicted in Figure 10.1, a feedback loop exists between outcomes and contextual variables. Here we infer that it is only logical that the outcomes of negative IM will feed into and influence contextual variables for future actions. If the tactics are successful in achieving the actor's desired outcomes, then the feedback will be of a reinforcing nature, contributing to greater levels of ambiguity and uncertainty. If the outcomes of the actor's behavior are negative, however, the nature of feedback here will lessen the configuration of context variables such that the future use of negative IM behaviors will be less likely.

PROPOSITION 8: *The multiple level outcomes of negative IM will feedback to influence the contextual variables that function as antecedents in the model.*

Conclusion

In this present age of organizational cutbacks and recession, extreme careerism is a construct increasing in its visibility in the workplace. With extreme careerism comes the increased employment of negative IM techniques. Although such "dark behaviors" do not necessarily result in dysfunctional organizational outcomes, in most cases they are likely to result in harmful individual, group, and organization-level outcomes.

The challenge for practitioners is to shape the organizational context to control the use of negative IM. This may be accomplished through increased effort to eliminate the uncertainty and ambiguity within an organization's environment. For example, practitioners can take appropriate action by devising and enforcing human resources procedures and policies, basing rewards on performance, conducting objective performance evaluations, and encouraging open communication as to how things get done within the organization.

The challenges for future researchers are to refine and clarify the concept of extreme careerism by empirically exploring antecedents leading to the use of negative IM behaviors, develop a measure for such behaviors, and better analyze the multiple level outcomes associated with extreme careerism. With additional study in this area, we can increase our understanding of extreme careerism and negative IM. Ideally we can learn to discourage such behaviors so as to improve organizational performance and the overall attitudes held by employees about their jobs and their organizations—in spite of cutbacks and economic recession.

References

Arkin, R. M., & Sheppard, J. A. (1989). Self-presentation styles in organizations. In R. A. Giacalone & P. Rosenfeld (Eds.), *Impression management in the organization* (pp. 125–139). Hillsdale, NJ: Erlbaum.

Bandura, A. (1977). *Social learning theory.* Englewood Cliffs, NJ: Prentice-Hall.

Baumeister, R. (1982). A self-presentational view of social phenomena. *Psychological Bulletin, 19,* 2–36.

Becker, T. E., & Martin, S. L. (1995). Trying to look bad at work: Methods and motives for managing poor impressions in organizations. *Academy of Management Journal, 38,* 174–200.

Berkowitz, L. (1992). *Aggression: Its causes, consequences, and control.* Philadelphia: Temple University Press.

Christie, R., & Geis, F. L. (1970). *Studies in Machiavellianism.* New York: Academic Press.

Cialdini, R. B. (1989). Indirect tactics of image management: Beyond basking. In R. A. Giacalone & P. Rosenfeld (Eds.), *Impression management in the organization* (pp. 45–56). Hillsdale, NJ: Erlbaum.

Fandt, P. M., & Ferris, G. R. (1990). The management of information and impressions: When employees behave opportunistically. *Organizational Behavior and Human Decision Processes, 45,* 140–158.

Feldman, D. C. (1985). The new careerism: Origins, tenets, and consequences. *The Industrial Psychologist, 22,* 39–44.

Feldman, D. C. (1988). *Managing careers in organizations.* Glenview, IL: Scott Foresman.

Feldman, D. C. (1996). Managing careers in downsizing firms. *Human Resource Management, 35*(2), 145–161.

Feldman, D. C., & Weitz, B. A. (1991). From the invisible hand to the gladhand: Understanding a careerist orientation to work. *Human Resource Management, 30,* 237–257.

Ferris, G. R., Fedor, D. B., & King, T. R. (1994). A political conceptualization of managerial behavior. *Human Resource Management Review, 4,* 1–34.

Ferris, G. R., Judge, T. A., Rowland, K. M., & Fitzgibbons, D. E. (1994). Subordinate influence and the performance valuation process: Test of a model. *Organizational Behavior and Human Decision Processes, 58,* 101–135.

Ferris, G. R., & Kacmar, K. M. (1992). Perceptions of organizational politics. *Journal of Management, 18,* 93–116.

Ferris, G. R., Russ, G. S., & Fandt, P. M. (1989). Politics in organizations. In R. A. Giacalone, & P. Rosenfeld (Eds.), *Impression management in the organization.* Hillsdale, NJ: Erlbaum.

Gardner, W. L., & Martinko, M. J. (1998). An organizational perspective of the effects of dysfunctional impression management. In R. W. Griffin, A. O'Leary-Kelly, & J. M. Collins (Eds.), *Dysfunctional behavior in organizations: Non-violent dysfunctional behavior* (pp. 69–125). Stamford, CT: JAI Press.

Geen, R. G. (1990). *Human aggression.* Pacific Grove, CA: Brooks/Cole.

Goffman, E. (1959). *The presentation of self in everyday life.* Garden City, NY: Doubleday.

Jones, E. E., & Pittman, T. S. (1982). Toward a general theory of strategic self-presentation. In J. Suls (Ed.), *Psychological perspectives on the self.* Hillsdale, NJ: Erlbaum.

Judge, T. A., Cable, D. M., Boudreau, J. W., & Bretz, R. D. (1995). An empirical investigation of the predictors of executive career success. *Personnel Psychology, 48,* 485–519.

Kacmar, K. M., & Carlson, D. S. (1998). A qualitative analysis of the dysfunctional aspects of political behavior in organizations. In R. W. Griffin, A. O'Leary-Kelly, & J. M. Collins (Eds.), *Dysfunctional behavior in organizations: Non-violent dysfunctional behavior* (pp. 195–217). Stamford, CT: JAI Press.

Kilduff, M., & Day, D. V. (1994). Do chameleons get ahead? The effects of self-monitoring on managerial careers. *Academy of Management Journal, 37*(4), 1047–1060.

Leary, M. R., & Miller, R. S. (1986). *Social psychology and dysfunctional behavior.* New York: Springer-Verlag.

Mohamed, A. A., & Gardner, W. L. (1996). *An exploratory study of defamation: An organizational impression management perspective.* Paper presented at the 1996 Academy of Management meetings, Cincinnati, Ohio.

Mohamed, A. A., Gardner, W. L., & Paolillo, J.G.P. (1999). A taxonomy of organizational impression management tactics. *Advances in Competitiveness Research,* 108–130.

Pandey, J. (1981). A note about social power through ingratiation among workers. *Journal of Occupational Psychology,* 54, 65–67.

Rosenfeld, P., Giacalone, R. A., & Riordan, C. A. (1995). *Impression management in organizations: Theory, measurement, practice.* New York: Routledge.

Schlenker, B. R. (1980). *Impression management: The self-concept, social identity and interpersonal relations.* Monterey, CA: Brooks/Cole.

Snyder, M. (1987). *Public appearance, private realities: The psychology of self-monitoring.* New York: Freeman.

Tedeschi, J. T., & Melburg, V. (1984). Impression management and influence in the organization. In S. B. Bacharach & E. J. Lawler (Eds.), *Research in the sociology of organizations* (Vol. 3, pp. 31–58). Greenwich, CT: JAI Press.

Tetlock, P. E. (1985). Accountability: The neglected social context of judgment and choice. In L. L. Cummings & B. M. Staw (Eds.), *Research in organizational behavior* (Vol. 7, pp. 297–332). Greenwich, CT: JAI Press.

Tetlock, P. E. (1992). The impact of accountability on judgment and choice: Toward a social contingency model. In M. P. Zanna (Ed.), *Advances in experimental social psychology* (Vol. 25, pp. 331–377). New York: Academic Press.

Tetlock, P. E., Skitka, L., & Boettger, R. (1989). Social and cognitive strategies for coping with accountability: Conformity, complexity, and bolstering. *Journal of Personality and Social Psychology,* 57, 632–640.

Turner, C. F., & Martinez, D. (1977). Socioeconomic achievement and the Machiavellian personality. *Social Psychology Quarterly,* 40, 325–336.

Ungar, S. (1984). Self-mockery: An alternative form of self-presentation. *Symbolic Interaction,* 7, 121–133.

Wayne, S. J., & Liden, R. C. (1995). A longitudinal study on the effects of impression management on performance ratings. *Academy of Management Journal,* 38, 232–260.

Wayne, S. J., Liden, R. C., Graf, I. K., & Ferris, G. R. (1997). The role of upward influence tactics in human resource decisions. *Personnel Psychology,* 50(4), 979–1006.

CHAPTER 11

Psychological Contract Breach and Violation in Organizations

Sandra L. Robinson, Graham Brown

An important and prevalent "dark side" of organizational behavior is that of psychological contract breach and violation. Psychological contract breach reflects one's perception that another has failed to fulfill his or her obligations to one; psychological contract violation refers to the emotional reaction to that interpretation of a breach experience. Psychological contract breach is not only a specific type of dysfunctional behavior, it may also both influence and lead to other dysfunctional behaviors and share with those behaviors some common antecedents and consequences. Research shows that contract breach and violation is both a prevalent and costly problem in current organizations (Robinson, 1996; Rousseau, 1995). For example, it has been found that from 50 to 81 percent of employees reported the breach of specific obligations by their employer (Conway & Briner, 2002; Robinson & Rousseau, 1994; Turnley & Feldman, 1999b). As the nature of employment relationships continue to evolve and trends toward downsizing, restructuring, and organizational change continue, the occurrence and importance of psychological contracts and their violation will increase.

In this chapter we introduce and review the literature on this dysfunctional and deviant behavior in organizations. We examine where prior research on psychological contract breach and violation has taken us and what we have learned along the way, as well as explore interesting directions in this domain. Although this area of study is relatively new, numerous studies have been published in recent years, and we believe it is a good time to pull them together, take stock, and encourage additional research on this significant phenomenon.

The chapter is structured as follows. First, we address the conceptual and definitional issues surrounding psychological contracts, in general, and breach and violation, in particular. Next, we discuss the antecedents and consequences of contract breach and violation. We follow this with a discussion of the practical implications for managers and organizations of the empirical research done to date on this phenomenon. Finally, we explore methodological challenges to studying psychological contract breach and violation, as well as some general guidelines for future research on this topic.

Conceptual and Definitional Issues

The concept of psychological contracts was originally identified over thirty years ago by Argyris (1960), Levinson, Price, Munden, and Solley (1962), Schein (1965), and Kotter (1973) as mutual expectations in employment relationships. More recently, Rousseau (1989) reintroduced the concept, defining it more precisely as individuals' perceptions of what they owe one party and what that party owes them in return. From this reconceptualization a new wave of empirical and theoretical research on this phenomenon has emerged.

The almost exclusive focus of these studies has been on the psychological contracts held by employees regarding their relationship with their employer. Moreover, the majority of these studies have been focused on the employees' experience that their employer has breached or violated their psychological contract. In this sense, it is one of the few research domains addressing the dark side of organizational behavior that is focused on dysfunctional *managerial* behavior rather than dysfunctional *employee* behavior.

Although the terms *breach* and *violation* have been used interchangeably in the literature, more recent theoretical precision has led to a distinction between these two terms. According to Morrison and Robinson (1997), *breach* refers to the cognitive awareness that something promised has not been received, whereas *violation* entails the emotional experience emanating from the interpretation of that breach in a given context. Thus one may observe a breach but not necessarily experience a violation. Despite this conceptual distinction, however, most empirical studies have tended to use the terms interchangeably and use the term *violation* when in fact only breach is measured. For the purposes of this chapter, we will use these different definitions for *breach* and *violation*.

Psychological contract breach and violation can be readily conceptualized as specific forms of deviant, aggressive, and antisocial behavior. Consistent with definitions of deviance (Robinson & Bennett, 1995), incidents of psychological contract breach and violation are perceived to violate significant and commonly accepted organizational norms, such as those involving justice, good faith, and fair dealing. Psychological contract breach and violation is akin to other forms of antisocial behavior because they have the potential to bring significant harm to the organization and its members (Robinson & Greenberg, 1999). In some cases, contract breach and violation may resemble workplace aggression if such acts by the employer are intended to inflict harm on the employee (O'Leary-Kelly, Griffin, & Glew, 1996).

Key Characteristics

There are several important characteristics of the psychological contract that distinguishes it from related concepts. It is important to understand these characteristics in order to appreciate the frequency and impact of psychological contract breach and violation. The first noteworthy characteristic of the psychological contract is that it is inherently subjective and perceptual (Rousseau, 1989). There is no "objective reality" per se as the psychological contract, and its fulfillment or breach resides in the eye of the person who possesses it. As such, two parties in the same relationship, who share the same formal contract, will have somewhat unique psychological contracts (Morrison & Robinson, 1997). One party may perceive or experience a contract breach or violation where another has no such perception.

Although the terms of the psychological contract are perceptual, they are nonetheless extremely influential. Indeed, it is ultimately only the perception of one's obligations, not any formal contract, that guide and direct behavior. Moreover, the experience of psychological contract breach and violation is every bit as real and painful to the individual as a readily observable breach or the violation of a legally binding condition. This definitional characteristic of psychological contract breach and violation is consistent with definitions of victimization that recognize the critical role that victim's perceptions play in defining its existence (Quinney, 1974). That is, only the victim of the aggressive or harmful act can rightly define the act as such.

Another important characteristic of the psychological contract is that it entails a sense of obligation (Robinson, 1996; Rousseau, 1989). These obligations emanate not only from explicit promises, but also from a variety of other sources such as behavior, communications from various agents of the organization, administrative documents, organizational practices, socialization, and colleagues, to name a few (Rousseau, 1995). Thus, the psychological contract involves not what a given party might expect to give or receive or would desire to give or receive, but rather what that party believes *should* be given or received because one of the other parties is *obligated* to provide it to another. Thus, all obligations create expectations but not all expectations involve obligation. For example, you may expect, based on past experience, to have a big office with blue walls, but that does not mean that you believe your employer is obligated to provide such an office. Indeed, the negative impact of contract breach, because it involves unfulfilled obligations, goes well beyond the impact of mere unmet expectations (Robinson, 1996; Robinson & Rousseau, 1994).

Finally, the psychological contract and its violation, unlike expectations, centers around an ongoing exchange in the context of a relationship (Robinson & Rousseau, 1994; Rousseau, 1989). Although the contract itself resides in the cognition of the individual, it is about the person's perception and belief that obligations are exchanged in a relationship; that is, one provides a set of goods or services to another in return for one's entitlements. Within this relational context is the notion of trust whereby one believes he can provide his side of the bargain because he trusts that the other will follow suit (Robinson, 1996). It is because breach and violation inherently take place in the context of a trusting relationship that its occurrence can be so damaging. When a violation occurs, it not only means that one is *not* getting something one desired or expected but, moreover, that a trusted other betrayed a trust and failed to live up to norms of reciprocity and goodwill that one expects in an ongoing relationship.

Antecedents

As we will later demonstrate, psychological contract breach is prevalent and, as with most forms of dysfunctional behavior in organizations, its consequences are often severe. As such, understanding factors causing or increasing the likelihood of breach and violation is paramount. The findings from research on the antecedents of contract breach and violation may help reduce the occurrence of breach or mend the wounds that surface when it does occur. Despite the importance of this research focus, however, we still know relatively little about what causes breach and violation.

There is some agreement that psychological contract breach emanates from one of two sources. The first source is reneging, whereby purposeful breach occurs because the breaching party is aware of his or her obligations but is either unwilling or unable to fulfill some terms of the contract (Morrison & Robinson, 1997). Reneging is what most of us usually think of as a breach, especially in relation to the dark side of organizational behavior. One reason for reneging is that the organization may be unwilling to fulfill the contract because it perceives that the employee's performance has fallen short and thus the organization is no longer obligated to follow through on its side of the bargain (Morrison & Robinson, 1997). In this sense, reneging may reflect a form of revenge (Bies & Tripp, 1998) or, at a minimum, restoration of equity (Adams, 1963). For example, Robinson and Morrison (2000) found that an employee's lowered performance was correlated with the subsequent experience of breach by the employer, possibly because the organization failed to fulfill its obligations, since the employee did not live up to his or hers.

In other cases, reneging may come about as a result of disruption (Rousseau, 1995), whereby the organization is unable to fulfill its obligations, such as during financial downturns or organizational change (Appelbaum & Donia, 2000). Some evidence for this relationship was reported by Robinson and Morrison (2000), who found that reports of organizational change were positively related to experiences of breach eighteen months later.

The second source of contract breach is incongruence. Incongruence reflects inadvertent breach that occurs when parties in a relationship have different perceptions of what they owe one another (Morrison & Robinson, 1997). Incongruence can result from ambiguous contracts, weak or poor communication between the parties, or different cognitive schemata of the two parties resulting in differing perceptions of what and how much is owed. Factors such as the lack of a pre-hire contact and lack of a formal socialization experience, which increase incongruence, have been found to be related to greater breach (Robinson & Morrison, 2000).

Another noteworthy factor influencing contract breach is that of vigilance, or the extent to which someone is monitoring the contract and becomes aware of a discrepancy between what she is owed and what she receives (Morrison & Robinson, 1997). The greater the vigilance, the more likely someone is to see a breach and experience a violation. Morrison and Robinson (1997) identified several factors that may affect vigilance and thus the likelihood of breach. Uncertainty, such as when there is organizational change or when the employee is new, is one factor that may increase vigilance about a contract. The nature of the relationship will also play a role. For example, if trust is low or if the relationship is one that is highly transactional or quid pro quo in nature, parties are more likely to monitor one another. Perceived costs and benefits of detecting a breach may also have an impact on vigilance. For example, when an employee's employment alternatives are many, the costs of detecting a breach are low and the benefits high, thus one will be motivated to be vigilant. Robinson and Morrison (2000) found that breach was more likely when organizational change was high, the employee had a history of breach with former employers, and employment alternatives were high, thus suggesting that these factors increase breach by heightening vigilance.

Future research is needed to empirically examine additional predictors of contract breach and violation. One interesting avenue is to explore attributes of the victims themselves. Most research on the "dark side" of organizational behavior has tended to focus on the motives, attitudes, and attributes of the perpetrators (Greenberg & Scott, 1996; O'Leary-Kelly et al., 1996; Robinson & Bennett, 1995). However, the study of deviance in general, and psychological contract breach and violation in particular, could benefit greatly from borrowing from the tradition of victimology (Felson & Steadman, 1983; Sparks, Genn & Dodd, 1977) by exploring the attributes of victims in predicting abuse, aggression, and tyranny. Some research has found that those with prior breach experience with one employer are more likely to experience a breach with their current employer (Robinson & Morrison, 2000). Possibly those who have experienced prior violation are more likely to vigilantly monitor their current employer's actions to avoid repeat experiences of abuse, but because of their vigilance, they are also more likely to see and report it again. Some employees may be inherently distrusting (Rotter, 1967) or be "perpetual victims" who see and interpret a breach wherever they go, regardless of the actions of the other party. A more intriguing explanation is that some individuals may repeatedly seek out "abusive" employers and end up in relationships with them either because their options for employment are limited or because of some psychological tendency on their part.

Other predictors of psychological contract breach and violation that are worth exploring include some of the known antecedents of other types of antisocial, deviant, and aggressive behavior in organizations. As just one example, we know that stress from financial pressure, poor work environment, intrusion, workload, and other stressors can exacerbate the occurrence of violence and harm-doing in the organization by its members (Baron & Neuman, 1996; Chen & Spector, 1992; Crino & Leap, 1989; Giacalone & Greenberg, 1997; Hollinger & Clark, 1982). Quite possibly, parallel provocations experienced by the organization itself, such as during economic downturns, drastic change, or uncertain times, will increase the likelihood that the organization will hurt its employees through breach and violation.

Consequences

Although few studies have explored the causes of contract breach, a comparatively large number of studies have examined its consequences. This is not surprising given that what seems to pull together researchers fascinated with the dark side of organizational behavior is their shared interest in the dysfunctional consequences of such behavior. As Robinson and Greenberg (1999) point out, despite the many constructs and definitions of antisocial and deviant behavior, researchers universally address the potential of those behaviors to cause harm. Psychological contract breach is no exception in this regard; as the research clearly shows, contract breach considerably and negatively affects both employee attitudes and behaviors. We will now discuss some of these negative outcomes in detail.

Attitudinal Consequences

In terms of attitudes, numerous empirical studies have shown a negative relationship among (1) contract breach and commitment (Bunderson, 2001; Coyle-Shapiro & Kessler, 1998; Hopkins, Hopkins, & Mallette, 2001; Kickul, 2001b; Lester, Turnley, Bloodgood, & Bolino, 2002; Robinson, 1996; Robinson & Rousseau, 1994), (2) satisfaction (Bunderson, 2001; Lester & Kickul, 2001; Martin & Peterson, 1987; Porter, Pearce, Tripoli, & Lewis, 1998; Robinson & Rousseau, 1994), and (3) a positive relationship between psychological contract breach, violation, and intentions to quit (Robinson, 1996; Robinson & Rousseau, 1994). Raja, Johns, and Ntalianis (2003) found both psychological contract breach and violation to be negatively related to commitment and satisfaction and positively related to turnover intentions. In addition, breach has been associated with lowered trust (Robinson, 1996), lowered perceived organizational support (Coyle-Shapiro & Kessler, 1998), and possibly perceptions of injustice (Cropanzano & Prehar, 2001; Liao-Troth, 1999). Andersson (1996) suggests that breach may also be a primary determinant of employee cynicism. Although not empirically demonstrated, the link between breach and cynicism is intriguing because we believe that cynicism is not only an outcome of breach but may also cause perceptions of breach and subsequent feelings of violation.

It is apparent that psychological contract breach leads to a host of negative attitudes in the workplace: about one's job, the organization itself, and one's relationship to the organization. It is important to note that this pattern is similar to that found with other deviant behaviors in organizations, in that behaviors such as workplace aggression, harassment, and sabotage also decrease employee morale, increase stress, and alter attitudes regarding one's satisfaction and willingness to remain in the organization (Giacalone & Greenberg, 1997; Robinson & Greenberg, 1999).

Behavioral Consequences

Empirical studies have also demonstrated the impact of breach on actual employee behavior. Employees who have experienced a contract breach with their employer, in comparison to those who have not, are more likely to quit the organization (Guzzo, Noonan, & Elron, 1994; Robinson, 1996; Turnley & Feldman, 1999a). In addition, psychological contract breach has been found to be negatively related to both self-rated performance (Robinson, 1996) and supervisor-rated performance (Lester et al., 2002). Some good exemplars of this relationship between breach and performance have been noted: Llewellyn (2001) found breach to be related to service delivery problems, and Farmer and Fedor (1999), in a study of volunteers in a nonprofit organization, showed that contract breach decreased the volunteers' involvement in the organization. Breach also appears to negatively impact extra-role performance and citizenship behavior (Coyle-Shapiro & Kessler, 1998; Morrison & Robinson, 1997; Robinson, 1996).

Unfortunately, this decline in both performance and organizational citizenship behavior (OCB) may become, ironically, justification for the organization to further breach the employees' psychological contract. Morrison and Robinson (1997) argued that organizations might be more likely to breach a contract to the extent that they believe that the employee is not valuable or that the employee has cut back on his or her obligations. Thus an employee who withdraws OCB or reduces their performance may be more likely to experience additional contract breaches down the road. In such a situation, both employee and employer will hold the other responsible for starting this downward spiral of unfulfilled obligations (Bies, Tripp, & Kramer, 1997).

Of particular interest is the suggestion that psychological contract breach by the employer actually causes subsequent deviant behavior in the employee (Kickul, 2001b; Turnley & Feldman, 1999b). Thus not only is psychological contract breach a type of dysfunctional and antisocial behavior but also it may breed more such behavior. Both the sense of injustice and the threat to self emanating from psychological contract breach can create frustration, aggression (Felson, 1982; Morrill, 1992), and revengeful behavior (Bies & Tripp, 1998; Skarlicki & Folger, 1997). Consistent with these arguments, Kickul (2001b) reported that the greater the perceived injustice in the breach experience, the stronger the relationship between breach and subsequent deviant behavior. As Andersson and Pearson (1999) articulate, employees and organizations can begin to engage in tit for tat, with hurtful behavior from one party spurring similar behavior from another, thus creating a cycle of abuse within the relationship.

The pattern we derive from the above studies on consequences of psychological contract breach is self-evident. Clearly, breach has significant negative ramifications for both the attitudes and behaviors of employees. Moreover, some research has shown that these negative ramifications can be seen more than eighteen months after their occurrence. In a study by Robinson (1996), contract breach could predict turnover, in-role performance and citizenship behavior eighteen months later, after controlling for factors such as pay, number of pay increases, and number of promotions. Likewise, Bunderson (2001) found that breach had an impact on turnover several years later. But the question posed by Kickul (2001b) remains; that is, when does the impact of contract breach abate? How far out may we go in time to measure consequences of prior breach and still see its lasting effects?

What is missing from the above set of studies is research examining the relationship between psychological contract breach and negative affect. We can think of only a few exceptions. Kickul (2001a, b) and Conway and Briner (2002) show that breach is related to negative affect and a sense of violation. Likewise, Robinson and Morrison (2000) found that breach is significantly, but only moderately, correlated to the emotional experience of violation. Perhaps this dearth is merely reflective of the past avoidance of emotions in the study of organizational behavior more generally and workplace deviance and dysfunction more specifically. Given the obvious emotions generated from behaviors such as breach, theft, harassment, aggression, and the like, it is actually surprising that more attention has not been given to emotions in this domain. We hope that future research addressing this lapse will enrich our understanding of this phenomenon.

Although the outcomes of psychological contract breach seem clear, we know proportionally less about *why* this relationship exists. Much theory abounds, yet very few studies have actually examined the underlying psychology involved by empirically assessing the mediators of this relationship. Our current belief is that psychological contract breach creates negative attitudes and behaviors for several interrelated reasons. The most obvious is that breach results in the loss of desired or expected returns. Such loss, much like distributive injustice or unmet expectations (Adams, 1963), is bound to produce negative attitudes. But more important, psychological contract breach involves a sense of violated trust or betrayal by a trusted other (Robinson and Rousseau, 1994; Rousseau 1989). The individual believes that he lived up to his side of the bargain yet the trusted other took advantage of his trust and did not reciprocate. Such actions undermine trust, norms of reciprocity and fair dealing, and the goodwill one needs to continue in an ongoing relationship. It is this socio-emotional aspect of contract breach, similar to feelings of procedural injustice (Folger & Greenberg, 1985; Lind & Tyler, 1988) in the context of a trusting relationship, that has the most impact on subsequent attitudes and behavior.

In exploring this issue empirically, Robinson (1996) demonstrated that the relationship between trust and outcome variables was mediated by trust above and beyond that which could be accounted for by unmet expectations. However, much more empirical research is clearly needed in order for us to fully understand why psychological contract breach and violation have the severe consequences that we observe.

Moderators of the Breach-Outcome Relationships

Along with main effects of breach, research is also beginning to explore moderators of the breach-outcome relationship. That is, under what conditions is breach more likely to have an impact and when is it less likely? When does breach lead to violation and when does it not? Which employees will be most hurt by transgressions and which employees will overlook them? It is apparent that similar transgressions can lead to very different outcomes, depending upon the individuals involved and the context in which the transgression occurs. From a practical standpoint, it may be important to address this issue because, although organizations may not be able to always prevent mismanaging and breaching employees' psychological contracts, they may be able to manage how, when, and why it is done in such a way to offset its negative consequences. In our review of the literature that has examined moderators of the breach-outcome relationship, we have organized the moderators from micro to macro in nature, ranging from characteristics of the individual to specifics of the contract itself to the larger context in which the breach experience occurs.

Individual Characteristics

It is apparent that employees will not view the same transgressions the same way. Indeed, before an injury such as a breach can be addressed, it first has to be identified as such, labeled as injurious, and attributed to someone (Felstiner, Abel, & Sarat, 1980). At each step of this process, individual differences, perceptions, and interpretations come into play. Just as victims may differ in their experience of treatment by aggressors (Quinney, 1974) or employees in the same work environment may vary in their perceptions of justice (Ployhart & Ryan, 1997; Schminke, Ambrose, & Noel, 1997), so too can employees possess different perceptions of the breach experience.

Turnley and Feldman (1999b) have suggested that individuals with a negative affect trait will be less likely to interpret ambiguous information in a positive fashion and thus will be more likely to make negative attributions and experience a greater sense of violation. Similarly, Andersson (1996) conjectured that those rating high on Machiavellianism would be most inclined to perceive and interpret breaches in a negative light. In an empirical study, Raja, Johns, and Ntalianis (2003) found that the personality traits of equity sensitivity and external locus of control actually enhanced the relationship between perceptions of breach and feelings of violation. Given the subjective and idiosyncratic nature of psychological contracts, this is an open avenue for future research.

In addition to personality, the relationship between breach and outcomes may also depend, in part, on the type of employee involved. McLean-Parks, Kidder, and Gallagher (1998) suggested that the experience of contract breach might be different for contingent workers than regular employees. Similarly, employees with few job alternatives or many investments, compared to those with many alternatives and few investments, may be more sensitive to contract breach (Kersi & Frazier, 2001; Turnley & Feldman, 1999b). One potential explanation for this effect is that constraints, such as non-transferable investments and few job alternatives, make the relationship more valuable and thus make the treatment one receives in that relationship much more critical. However, as we have argued, such constraining conditions may also make the recognition and acknowledgment of a breach that much more painful, and thus one may instead be motivated to avoid or deny its occurrence.

Employees also enter the organization with different allegiances and expectations that may moderate the influence of breach. Larwood, Wright, Desrochers, and Dahir (1998) examined differences between employees with different latent roles—cosmopolitan and local—in terms of their contracts and their experience of contract breach by their employers. Cosmopolitans, in comparison to locals, were more likely to enter with an existing psychological contract whereas locals tended to develop one from on-the-job socialization. Thus cosmopolitans perceived a poorer fit between the job and their psychological contract. This would suggest that they are more likely to experience breach and violation, and when they do, they are more likely to consider leaving and less likely to engage in political activity to change the situation.

Situational Factors

The specific characteristics of the situation, event, or process involved in the breach experience will also alter how it's interpreted and the impact it has. One such characteristic is the nature of the obligations that are unfulfilled. Employees will vary in terms of what they view as a breach and also the importance they place on particular obligations (Martin & Peterson, 1987; Porter et al., 1998). Bunderson (2001), studying doctors in a health care setting, found that professional breaches, those focused more on the core values of being a member of the profession, produced more significant responses than administrative breaches. Along similar lines, Farmer and Fedor (1999) suggested that breach of relational obligations, those that address socio-emotional concerns such as support and job security, may produce more severe reactions than breach of transactional obligations, which are more economic in nature, such as pay and benefits. Likewise, Turnley et al. (2003) found that contract fulfillment of relational aspects of the contract were more influential on employees' behavior than transactional aspects such as pay. Perhaps these findings collectively suggest that the more important the obligations are that are breached, the more significant the negative outcomes. Indeed, Conway and Briner (2002) found just that; to the extent that the breached obligations were important, they were more likely to lead to a sense of violation.

Another important aspect of the particular situation in which breach occurs is the degree to which procedural justice and distributive justice are perceived to be present or absent. Morrison and Robinson (1997) argued that to the extent that the procedure was relatively fair, in terms of demonstrating respect and offering social accounts and such, breach would not necessarily lead to violation and the subsequent negative repercussions. Similarly, Sparrow (1996) argued that breach may have few to no consequences if both procedural justice and distributive justice are met (if such a scenario is possible). As already noted, Kickul (2001b) found that when breach was high and procedural and interaction justice were low, breach had a stronger impact on workplace deviance. Similarly, Robinson and Morrison (2000) found a three-way interaction among degree of breach, perceived fairness, and degree of negative attribution on feelings of violation. That is, the experience of violation was more severe when breach was high, perceived fairness was low, and negative rather than positive attributions were made.

Clearly, the type of attributions that the individual makes for the breach will play a key role in the interpretation of that breach and the subsequent sense of violation. Given the subjective, perceptual nature of the psychological contract and its fulfillment, contract transgressions can be viewed quite differently, depending upon the perceived cause. As Lester et al. (2002) pointed out, a perceived cause of incongruence may be more palatable than an attribution of reneging. However, the results thus far are inconclusive on this issue. Turnley, Bolino, Lester, and Bloodgood (2003) found that employee perceptions regarding the reasons for breach did not matter, arguing that a breach may be sufficient enough to create an experience of violation. Charness and Levine (2000), however, found that breach in the form of layoffs were more acceptable when they were attributed to reduced product demand rather than employee suggestions. Morrison and Robinson (1997) mentioned that social accounts, which influence the attribution process, may reduce the likelihood that breach will be interpreted as a violation and thus lessen the consequences. In support of this argument, Turnley and Feldman (1999a) found that the provision of adequate justification lessened the impact that breach had on turnover intentions (though, curiously, it did not weaken the relationship between breach and voice, loyalty, or neglect). Perhaps the reason for these differential findings is that intentions of turnover are hidden and thus unpunishable outcomes and therefore are not constrained like behavioral responses such as voice, loyalty, or neglect.

The role of prior trust that the employee has in the employer has been explored as another potential situational moderator. In a series of experiments, Koehler and Gershoff (2003) found that more trusted parties in comparison to less trusted parties were punished more for committing betrayals. They suggested that the more trusted parties are punished more severely because their actions are considered more consequential as they more greatly violate social order. Thus, for example, we should be more outraged when the organization that violates its employees' contract is one that is trusted and respected than when it is one for whom our expectations about ethical conduct are already low. These results suggest that high prior trust should actually make the likelihood of violation greater. However, Robinson (1996) found that high prior trust actually reduced the impact of breach on in-role performance, extra-role performance, and turnover intentions—the reason being that, consistent with research on cognitive biases, prior positive attitudes such as trust lead one to be less vigilant and likely to notice a breach, as well as more likely to make a positive attribution for the incident. Robinson et al. (2003) further explored these possible alternative influences of prior trust in a scenario-based study. They found that although high prior trust weakens the relationship between breach and negative attributions, high prior trust will actually make the response to breach even more negative when the attribution is seen as negative. Thus, up to a point, prior trust may inoculate employees against experiencing a breach; however, if the evidence is so strong that one cannot help but interpret the breach as a violation, the sense of violation will be stronger when prior trust is high rather than low.

Contextual Factors

Finally, as Guest and colleagues (Guest & Conway, 1997; Guest, Conway, Briner, & Dickmann, 1996) have rightly noted, it is essential that we consider the importance of the context and organizational climate in influencing both the contract and how it is maintained. Just as the context is important to the labeling and experience of workplace deviance (Bennett & Robinson, 1997; Robinson & Bennett, 1995) so too does it matter to the psychological contract breach experience. Morrison and Robinson (1997) spoke of the importance of how breach will be interpreted in light of the larger social contract, including the norms of exchange and the legal and social environment. For example, a breach in a context where trust is highly important may be interpreted quite differently than in one where everyone anticipates self-interested behavior.

Context also includes national cultural differences, such as the degree of hierarchy and centrality of work values, which guide interpretation and attention to contextual influences (Kiesler & Sproull, 1982).These cultural differences may result in unique interpretations and reactions to breach and violation. This is a very important set of variables for us to consider as we seek to be able to generalize our results to workers in a variety of cultural contexts.

Clearly we have very little research on the role of context, and much more is needed. Future research ideally will examine the experience of breach across different legal contexts, national cultures, and organizational and industrial climates. We may learn just how generalizable our results are thus far, and we may also understand how variable the relationships are when considered in different contextual arenas.

In summary, we have learned that psychological contract breach and violation is prevalent, that its consequences are dire, and that the effects can be seen up to three years after an incident occurs.

The negative effects of violation emanate from material losses coupled with a sense of betrayal by someone previously trusted in the context of an ongoing relationship. These negative effects are stronger than the motivating effects of pay and promotion, as well as the impact of unmet expectations. As Baumeister, Bratslavsky, Finkenauer, and Vohs (2001) have demonstrated, "bad" events have a stronger impact in general than "good events." We have also identified a number of moderators of the breach-outcome relationship, including individual factors such as the personality, job, and role of the victim; situational factors such as degree of justice, the nature of the obligations involved, and the types of attributions that are made; as well as the larger social and cultural context. Much work remains to be done on the consequences of contract breach. In particular, we need more empirical evidence regarding the factors that moderate the relationship between breach and violation and between violation and consequences. Indeed, we know that not all employees will interpret and experience the same breach in the same way. We could also benefit from research that addresses the underlying psychology involved in the breach experience. For example, studies looking at mediators of the above relationships would be of great use.

Practical Implications

The study of psychological contract breach and violation has inherent practical value. Given the prevalence of psychological contract breach and violation in today's workplace, organizations and their managers benefit from knowing what happens when breach and violation occur, and what actions they can take to either mitigate its negative effects or prevent breach and violation altogether.

To date, the collective efforts of researchers have reached some clear conclusions that have important implications for practicing managers. First, there is evidence that breach and violation are very common. Even with good intentions or efforts on the part of organizations and their managers, some degree of breach may still occur. The reasons are twofold. First, organizational change may prevent some contract terms from being fulfilled as originally intended. Second, incongruence resulting from unique individual perceptions of what each party owes the other may lead to breach.

Thus, even employers with the best intentions may sometimes inadvertently fail to live up to perceived obligations on the part of the employee.

In addition, the impact of contract breach and violation by the employer has significant implications for employees and their organizations. We know breach can and does negatively affect employees' attitudes and behaviors and that those effects can be seen far into the future. Organizations that are unable to reduce the occurrence or impact of contract breach are more likely to have higher turnover, reduced citizenship behavior, and a decline in work performance. The implications of lost trust as a result of breach are even more significant, as we know the loss of trust can be significantly detrimental to the organization's well-being (Dirks & Ferrin, 2002). Although the actual cost to the bottom line resulting from contract breach has not be calculated, we can assume it is extremely high.

Third, not all employees will have the same experiences or reactions to breach. Even if breach is inevitable, managers and organizations may be able to manage the experience to reduce the likelihood of violation and hence the negative reactions that follow. That is, there are actions that organizations can take to reduce the likelihood that a breach will be perceived as a violation, and also how its employees will react to the breach if it is perceived as such. Although we currently have limited empirical evidence on what these actions should be, some theory suggests the following. Organizations should only promise what they can deliver—not just now but also at some future time. This can be a challenge because organizations are increasingly under constant change and it is difficult to predict what they can provide to their employers in the future. In addition, recruiters, who are usually a primary influence on employees' psychological contracts, are often overzealous in their pursuit to get employees on board and thus they may overcommit to things that they cannot necessarily ensure will be forthcoming by others at a later time.

Also, organizational agents, those responsible for making promises and those responsible for executing obligations, need to maintain coordination. Poor coordination and miscommunication will be likely to result in incongruence and breaches when none were intended. Unfortunately, given the many actors involved in creating and maintaining the psychological contract of the employee and the constant changes that most organizations face today, achieving this level of coordination and agreement is difficult.

More important, explicit communication about expectations and obligations between organizational agents and employees is critical. This communication has to begin at the outset and continue throughout the relationship. It is only through regular and repeat dialogue that differences in perceptions (incongruence) can be uncovered and resolved. It is better for the organization to identify and change employees' contracts in ways that match what the organization is willing and able to deliver on than to surprise the employee later with a contract breach resulting from incongruence.

To reduce the repercussions of contract breach, it is very important for the organization to build trust with its employees. As Robinson (1996) showed, prior trust in the employer may serve as a sort of inoculation against breach. Prior trust reduces the likelihood that a potential transgression will be interpreted as a breach, and if a breach is witnessed it is more likely to be interpreted in a positive light. When prior trust is low, however, breaches are more likely to be noticed and employees are much more likely to make a negative attribution about it. Of course, building trust does not serve as a panacea and with it comes risk as well. As Robinson et al. (2003) found, if prior trust is high and the employee ends up feeling violated, she or he will actually be more harmed and distraught than if his or her prior trust had not been so high. In such a case, as Shakespeare stated, "hell hath no fury like a lover scorned."

Finally, if a breach does occur, research suggests that attempts to offer justifications may be worthwhile (Cobb & Wooton, 1998). However, to the extent that the individual is harmed by the breach, she or he is less likely to accept the organization's justification (Jones & Davis, 1965; Lester et al., 2002). In addition, if a breach is inevitable, attempts by the organization to maintain distributive and procedural justice remain very important for reducing the harmful effects of breach.

These are but some recommendations that are suggested by the literature on how to offset and manage psychological contract breach and violation. The bottom line is that organizations and their managers need to learn about psychological contracts and continually manage and maintain them if they want to avoid breach or lessen the repercussion of contract violation when it does occur.

Methodological Challenges

From its inception, the empirical study of psychological contract breach and violation has been fraught with empirical difficulties and barriers. Some of these challenges have been surmounted and some remain to be resolved by future researchers. We hope that as we move ahead, the rigor we employ continues to improve along with our content knowledge.

One of the biggest problems facing those studying in this area is that psychological contracts and the experience of contract breach are *psychological* phenomenon. Therefore, they have to be dependent on self-report, whether in interviews or surveys. In addition, individuals are not necessarily cognizant of the terms of their contract until that contract is broken. Moreover, they are *psychologically idiosyncratic*; that is, each individual has a unique psychological contract. This makes standardized surveys, the most typical measurement method we use, only rough approximations of respondents' actual contracts. Also, the terms of the contract are in constant flux. Thus a contract assessed at one time may be different from the contract that is assessed six months later. Finally, individuals have a multitude of contracts with different organizational parties—the organization itself, one's supervisor, one's peers or team group members, and so forth. Confusion about which terms are part of which contract may be difficult to report, assess, and observe. For all these reasons, it is especially difficult to capture the actual psychological contract of the individual, a necessary condition to studying contract breach and violation.

When it comes to measuring contract breach, the challenges are even greater. The most ideal measure would be one that can capture contract breach and experiences of violation as they take place. If possible, we would assess the "actual" contract terms just moments before a breach takes place (because the contract is constantly changing, to measure it much before an actual breach may not be capturing the contract as it was when it was broken). Such an ideal measure would also assess the breach as soon as it took place and then capture the unfolding experience of breach and violation over time from that point onward.

As we hope you can see at this point, it is difficult to study psychological contracts with our current methods. What we suggest for future studies is the following. First, we should continue with standardized surveys, recognizing, of course, that only a subset of contract terms that can be assumed to be shared by the sample are included in the measure. To determine the appropriate subset, significant pilot testing is needed to develop a survey instrument that is most useful to the particular sample for a given study. The same set of contract terms must be used for both the pre- and postbreach measures of the contract. Second, both pre- and postbreach measures of the psychological contract need to be measured. Depending upon the nature of the design and the context in which breach is studied, the timing for those measures will vary. On the one hand, you need a close enough time frame to capture a relatively accurate prebreach measure of the contract. On the other hand, you need a long enough time frame to ensure that you get enough variance on psychological contract breach. Finally, given the inherent problem with difference scores, you need to employ some methods that rely on alternatives to difference scores (see, for example, Edwards & Parry, 1993). Another challenge of measuring contract breach is to determine what exactly to measure.

Do you ask about fulfillment of the contract or nonfulfillment? These are not necessarily the same thing. Technically speaking, the breach should involve not only the discrepancy between what you were promised and what was received but should also take into account the individuals' perception of how well they have fulfilled their side of the bargain. This is something most prior studies have not yet done.

In addition, do you assess specific nonfulfillment of terms of the contract or a more global measure about how well the contract has been fulfilled? We lean toward using a more global measure, as it offsets the problem of having a standardized survey of contract terms that are not necessarily applicable to everyone and that inevitably leave out significant contract terms. But it is very important to note that the type of measure one uses will probably produce very different results. As Turnley and Feldman (1999b) noted, the extent of breach and the magnitude of the problem depends on how the breach is reported and measured. Turnley (1996; c.f. Turnley & Feldman, 1999b), for example, found that 81 percent of respondents reported receiving less on at least one job factor but only 24 percent said that the organization failed to keep promises overall. How long do people remember breach and the magnitude of breach? Are all breaches the same? These are also important questions.

These are but some of the challenges we are facing as we study psychological contract breach and violation. Those working in the area are probably familiar with these problems and others, but our aim here is merely to highlight some of the issues that are important and some potential solutions to these issues.

Additional Directions for Future Research

We previously addressed some future directions around filling specific gaps in the literature. We now briefly turn our attention to some very general suggestions regarding all future research on psychological contract breach and violation. First, future research on contract breach and violation could be enriched by taking a decidedly more process-oriented perspective, looking at how the interpretation and reaction to contract breach and violation evolves and unfolds over time. Most of the empirical research has been conducted at one point in time. Even studies that have employed a longitudinal design (Coyle-Shapiro & Kessler, 1998, 2000; Porter et al., 1998; Robinson, 1996) do not necessarily capture dynamics per se, just snapshots of some variables at different points in time. One good exception to the above is a study by Conway and Briner (2002) that examined contract breach and violation over a ten-day period. Using a diary method, they were able to track employees' immediate perceptions of contract breach and their evolving psychological states over time with regard to those experiences. Future studies may use this study as a potential model for examining the actual process of contract breach and violation as it occurs.

Second, future research on breach and violation may expand to include more parties and contexts. In other words, we need to consider more types of employees other than the traditional manager. Some studies have examined physicians (Bunderson, 2001), franchisors (Kersi & Frazier, 2001), internal customers and suppliers (Llewellyn, 2001), and volunteers (Farmer & Fedor, 1999), but much more diversity is needed if we seek to fully understand how employees in general react to this prevalent form of dysfunctional behavior in organizations. We also need research that examines perpetrators other than employers, such as employees or team members, as well as victims other than employees, such as organizations.

Third, more attention has to be given to the employers' perspective, which has thus far been largely omitted from the equation.

Although there have been some notable exceptions (Coyle-Shapiro & Kessler, 2000; Lester et al., 2002; Porter et al., 1998; Shore & Barksdale, 1998), most studies have only considered the employees' perspective. Neglecting the employer's side misrepresents a core aspect of the psychological contract that is embedded within an exchange relationship (Guest, 1998). Moreover, as Coyle-Shapiro and Kessler (2000) suggest, adding in the employer means identifying a source of contract breach, namely, incongruence between the employees' and the employers' perspectives.

Finally, future explorations of psychological contract breach and violation need to bridge more effectively with the larger literature on workplace deviance, dysfunction, and antisocial behavior. Thus far, these literatures have remained apart yet they have much in common. As we have demonstrated, they are conceptually similar, with shared antecedents and consequences. Moreover, contract breach and other forms of "dark" behavior may casually affect one another. Finally, the theories developed to explain other forms of dysfunctional workplace behaviors, such as injustice, frustration-aggression, and learning theory, may be valuable for helping us better understand the phenomenon of psychological contract breach and violation.

These are just some potential research directions that we hope to see in the future. We believe that this is a rich area to conduct research, and the possibilities at this point are many.

Conclusion

Our goal in this chapter has been to review the literature thus far on psychological contract breach and violation as a form of dark, dysfunctional, and harmful workplace behavior. We hope that the chapter serves as a good starting point for those beginning to immerse themselves in the topic, as well as a ready resource for those working in or planning to work in this area. This is a new and growing area of study and we hope that interesting insights into the experience of psychological contract breach will be uncovered in the years ahead.

References

Adams, J. S. (1963). Toward an understanding of inequity. *Journal of Abnormal and Social Psychology, 67,* 422–436.

Andersson, L. M. (1996). Employee cynicism: An examination using a contract violation framework. *Human Relations,* 49, 1395–1418.

Andersson, L. M., & Pearson, C. (1999). Tit for tat? The spiraling effect of incivility in the workplace. *Academy of Management Review,* 24, 452–471.

Appelbaum, S. H., & Donia, M. (2000). The realistic downsizing preview: A management intervention in the prevention of survivor syndrome (part 1). *Career Development International,* 5, 333–358.

Argyris, C. (1960). *Understanding organizational behavior.* Homewood, IL: Dorsey.

Baron, R. A., & Neuman, J. H. (1996). Workplace violence and workplace aggression: Evidence on their relative frequency and potential causes. *Aggressive Behavior,* 22, 161–173.

Baumeister, R. F., Bratslavsky, E., Finkenauer, C., & Vohs, K. D. (2001). Bad is stronger than good. *Review of General Psychology,* 5, 323–370.

Bennett, R. J., & Robinson, S. L. (1997). Workplace deviance: Its definition, its nature and its causes. In R. J. Lewicki, B. H. Sheppard, & R. J. Bies (Eds.), *Research on negotiation in organizations* (Vol. 7). Greenwich, CT: JAI Press.

Bies, R. J., & Tripp, T. M. (1998). The many faces of revenge: The good, the bad, and the ugly. In R. W. Griffin, A. O'Leary-Kelly, & J. Collins (Eds.), *Dysfunctional behavior in organizations,* Vol. 1: *Violent behaviors in organizations,* pp. 23, 49–68. Greenwich, CT: JAI Press.

Bies, R. J., Tripp, T. M., & Kramer, R. M. (1997). At the breaking point: A social cognitive perspective on vengeance and violence in organizations. In J. Greenberg & R. Giacalone (Eds.), *Antisocial behavior in organizations,* pp. 18–36. Newbury Park, CA: Sage.

Bunderson, J. S. (2001). How work ideologies shape the psychological contracts of professional employees: Examining doctors' responses to perceived breach. *Journal of Organizational Behavior,* 22, 1–25.

Charness, G., & Levine, D. I. (2000). When are layoffs acceptable? Evidence from a quasi-experiment. *Industrial and Labor Relations Review,* 53, 381–400.

Chen, P. Y., & Spector, P. E. (1992). Relationships of work stressors with aggression, withdrawal, theft and substance abuse: An explanatory study. *Journal of Occupational and Organizational Psychology,* 65, 177–184.

Cobb, A. T., & Wooton, K. (1998). The role social accounts can play in a 'justice intervention.' In W. Pasmore & R. Woodman (Eds.), *Research in organizational change and development* (73–115). Greenwich, CT: JAI Press.

Conway, N., & Briner, R. B. (2002). A daily diary study of affective responses to psychological contract breach and exceeded promises. *Journal of Organizational Behavior*, 23, 287–302.

Coyle-Shapiro, J., & Kessler, I. (1998). The psychological contract in the UK public sector: Employer and employee obligations and contract fulfillment. In S. J. Havlovic (Ed.), *Academy of management best paper proceedings*, San Diego.

Coyle-Shapiro, J., & Kessler, I. (2000). Consequence of psychological contact for the employment relationship: A large scale survey. *Journal of Management Studies*, 37, 903–930.

Crino, M. D., & Leap, T. L. (1989). What HR managers must know about employee sabotage. *Personnel*, 66, 31–32, 34–36, 38.

Cropanzano, R., & Prehar, C. A. (2001). Emerging justice concerns in an era of changing psychological contracts. In R. Cropanzano (Ed.), *Justice in the workplace* (Vol. 2, pp. 245–269). Mahwah, NJ: Erlbaum.

Dirks, K. T., & Ferrin, D. L. (2002). Trust in leadership: Meta-analytic findings and implications for research and practice. *Journal of Applied Psychology*, 87, 611–628.

Edwards, J. R., & Parry, M. E. (1993). On the use of polynomial regression equations as an alternative to difference scores in organizational research. *Academy of Management Journal*, 36, 1577–1613.

Farmer, S. M., & Fedor, D. B. (1999). Volunteer participation and withdrawal: A psychological contract perspective on the role of expectation and organizational support. *Nonprofit Management and Leadership*, 9, 349–367.

Felson, R. B. (1982). Impression management and the escalation of aggression and violence. *Social Psychology Quarterly*, 45, 245–254.

Felson, R. B., & Steadman, H. J. (1983). Situational factors in disputes leading to criminal violence. *Criminology*, 21, 59–74.

Felstiner W. L., Abel, R. L., & Sarat, A. (1980). The emergence and transformation of disputes: Naming, blaming, claiming. *Law & Society Review*, 15, 631–654.

Folger, R., & Greenberg, J. (1985). Procedural justice: An interpretative analysis of personnel systems. In K. Rowland & G. Ferris (Eds.), *Research in personnel and human resource management* (Vol. 3, pp. 141–183). Greenwich, CT: JAI Press.

Giacalone, R. A., & Greenberg, J. (Eds.). (1997). *Antisocial behavior in organizations.* Thousand Oaks, CA: Sage.

Greenberg, J., & Scott, K. S. (1996). Why do workers bite the hands that feed them: Employee theft as a social exchange process. In B. M. Staw & L. L. Cummings (Eds.), *Research in organizational behavior* (Vol. 18, pp. 111–156). Greenwich, CT: JAI Press.

Guest, D., & Conway, N. (1997). *Employee motivation and the psychological contract.* London: CIPD.

Guest, D. E. (1998). Is the psychological contract worth taking seriously?" *Journal of Organizational Behavior,* 19, 649–664.

Guest, D. E., Conway, R., Briner, R., & Dickmann, M. (1996). The state of the psychological contract in employment. *Issues in People Management,* 16. London: CIPD.

Guzzo, R. A., Noonan, K. A., & Elron, E. (1994). Expatriate managers and the psychological contract. *Journal of Applied Psychology,* 79, 617–626.

Hollinger, R. C., & Clark, J. P. (1982). Formal and informal social controls of employee deviance. *Sociological Quarterly,* 23, 333–343.

Hopkins, W. E., Hopkins, A. A., & Mallette, P. (2001). Diversity and managerial value commitment: A test of some proposed relationships. *Journal of Managerial Issues,* 13, 288–306.

Jones, E. E., & Davis, K. E. (1965). From acts to dispositions: The attribution process in person perception. In L. Berkowitz (Ed.), *Advances in experimental social psychology* (Vol. 2). Orlando, FL: Academic Press.

Kersi, D. A., & Frazier, G. L. (2001). The severity of contract enforcement in interfirm channel relationships. *Journal of Marketing,* 65, 67–81.

Kickul, J. R. (2001a). Promises made, promises broken: An exploration of employee attraction and retention practises in small business. *Journal of Small Business Management,* 39, 320–335.

Kickul, J. R. (2001b). When organizations break their promises: Employee reactions to unfair processes and treatment. *Journal of Business Ethics,* 29, 287–307.

Kiesler, S., & Sproull, L. (1982). Managerial response to changing environments: Perspectives on problem sensing from social cognition. *Administrative Science Quarterly,* 27, 548–570.

Koehler, J. J., & Gershoff, A. D. (2003). Betrayal aversion: When agents of protection become agents of harm. *Organizational Behavior and Human Decision Processes,* 90, 244–261.

Kotter, J. P. (1973). The psychological contract: Managing the joining-up process. *California Management Review,* 15, 91–99.

Larwood, L., Wright, T. A., Desrochers, S., & Dahir, V. (1998). Extending latent role and psychological contract theories to predict intent to turnover and politics in business organizations. *Group and Organization Management,* 23, 100–123.

Lester, S. W., & Kickul, J. (2001). Psychological contracts in the 21st century: What employees value most and how well organizations are responding to these expectations. *Human Resource Planning,* 24, 10–21.

Lester, S. W., Turnley, W. H., Bloodgood, J. M., & Bolino, M. C. (2002). Not seeing eye to eye: Differences in supervisor and subordinate perceptions of and attributions for psychological contract breach. *Journal of Organizational Behavior,* 23, 39–56.

Levinson, H., Price, C. R., Munden, K. J., & Solley, C. M. (1962). Men, management, and mental health. Cambridge, MA: Harvard University Press.

Liao-Troth, M. (1999). The effects of psychological contract strength and violation on organizational commitment and organizational justice. Paper presented at the annual meeting of the Academy of Management, Chicago.

Lind, E. A., & Tyler, T. (1988). *The social psychology of procedural justice.* New York: Plenum.

Llewellyn, N. (2001). The role of psychological contracts within internal service networks. *The Service Industries Journal,* 21, 211–226.

Martin, J. E., & Peterson, M. M. (1987). Two-tier wage structures: Implications for equity theory. *Academy of Management Journal,* 30, 297–315.

McLean Parks, J., Kidder, D. L., & Gallagher, D. G. (1998). Fitting square pegs into round holes: Mapping the domain of contingent work arrangements onto the psychological contract. *Journal of Organizational Behavior,* 19, 697–730.

Morrill, C. (1992). Vengeance among executives. *Virginia Review of Sociology,* 1, 51–76.

Morrison, E. W., & Robinson, S. L. (1997). When employees feel betrayed: A model of how psychological contract violation develops. *Academy of Management Review,* 22, 226–256.

O'Leary-Kelly, A. M., Griffin, R. W., & Glew, D. J. (1996). Organization-motivated aggression: A research framework. *Academy of Management Review,* 21, 225–253.

Ployhart, R. E., & Ryan, A. M. (1997). Toward an explanation of applicant reactions: An examination of organizational justice and attribution frameworks. *Organizational Behavior and Human Decision Processes,* 72, 308–335.

Porter, L. W., Pearce, J. L., Tripoli, A. M., & Lewis, K. M. (1998). Differential perceptions of employers' inducements: Implications for psychological contracts. *Journal of Organizational Behavior,* 19, 769–782.

Quinney, R. (1974). The social reality of crime. In A. S. Blumberg (Ed.), *Current perspectives on criminal behavior: Original essays in criminology* (pp. 35–47). New York: Alfred A. Knopf.

Raja, U., Johns, G., & Ntalianis, F. (2003). The impact of personality on psychological contract dynamics. Working paper, Concordia University, Montreal, Quebec, Canada.

Robinson, S. L. (1996). Trust and breach of the psychological contract. *Administrative Science Quarterly,* 41, 574.

Robinson, S. L., & Bennett, R. J. (1995). A typology of deviant workplace behaviors: A multi-dimensional scaling study. *Academy of Management Journal,* 38, 555–572.

Robinson, S. L., Dirks, K., & Ozcelik, H. (2003). Untangling the knot of trust and betrayal: The relationship between prior trust and the experience of psychological contract violation. Working paper, University of British Columbia, Vancouver.

Robinson, S. L., & Greenberg, J. (1999). Employees behaving badly: Dimensions, determinants and dilemmas in the study of workplace deviance. In D. M. Rousseau & C. Cooper (Eds.), *Trends in organizational behavior* (Vol. 5, pp. 1–23). New York: John Wiley.

Robinson, S. L., & Morrison, E. W. (2000). The development of psychological contract breach and violation: A longitudinal study. *Journal of Organizational Behavior,* 21, 525–546.

Robinson, S. L., & Rousseau, D. M. (1994). Violating the psychological contract: Not the exception but the norm. *Journal of Organizational Behavior,* 15, 245–259.

Rousseau, D. M. (1989). Psychological and implied contracts in organizations. *Employee Responsibilities and Rights Journal,* 2, 121–139.

Rousseau, D. M. (1995). *Psychological contracts in organizations.* Thousand Oaks, CA: Sage.

Rotter, J. B. (1967). A new scale for the measurement of interpersonal trust. *Journal of Personality,* 35, 657–665.

Schein, E. (1965). *Organizational psychology.* Englewood Cliffs, NJ: Prentice-Hall.

Schminke, M., Ambrose, M. L., & Noel, T. W. (1997). The effect of ethical frameworks on perceptions of organizational justice. *Academy of Management Journal,* 40, 1190–1207.

Shore, L. M., & Barksdale, K. (1998). Examining the degree of balance and level of obligation in the employment relationship: A social exchange approach. *Journal of Organizational Behavior,* 19, 731–744.

Skarlicki, D. P., & Folger, R. (1997). Retaliation for perceived unfair treatment: Examining the roles of procedural and interactional justice. *Journal of Applied Psychology,* 82, 434–443.

Sparks, R. F., Genn, H. G., & Dodd, J. (1977). *Surveying victims: A study of the measurement of criminal victimization, perceptions of crime, and attitudes to criminal justice.* New York: John Wiley.

Sparrow, P. R. (1996). Transitions in the psychological contract: Some evidence from the banking sector. *Human Resources Management Journal,* 6(4), 75–92.

Turnley, W. H. (1996). *Reconceptualizing the nature and consequences of psychological contract violations.* Doctoral dissertation, University of South Carolina, Columbia.

Turnley, W. H., Bolino, M. C., Lester, S. W., & Bloodgood, J. M. (2003). The impact of psychological contract fulfillment on the performance of in-role and organizational citizenship behaviors. *Journal of Management, 29,* 187–206.

Turnley, W. H., & Feldman, D. C. (1999a). The impact of psychological contract violations on exit, voice, loyalty, and neglect. *Human Relations, 52,* 895–922.

Turnley, W. H., & Feldman, D. C. (1999b). A discrepancy model of psychological contract violations. *Human Resource Management Review, 9,* 1–20.

PART 4

The Dark Side in Other Places

CHAPTER 12

Alcohol and Drug Use in the Workplace

Michael M. Harris

U.S. employers generally regard substance use as an important workplace problem. It is hardly surprising, then, that a 2001 American Management Association survey indicated that 67 percent of major U.S. firms used some form of drug testing. Although this number reflected a small decline from previous years (for example, 81 percent in 1996), the report noted that changes in questionnaire format may have explained these apparent differences and 67 percent still reflects a large number of organizations conducting drug testing.

In this chapter, I will discuss key issues concerning the use of alcohol and drugs as they relate to the workplace. The scope of this chapter is limited in at least two important ways. First, there are certain other substances that might be classified as drugs, such as tobacco products and caffeine, which will not be addressed in this chapter. These substances are not reviewed here because they are quite different in nature from alcohol and drug use and have been far less frequently studied by industrial and organizational (I-O) psychologists.

Second, I do not cover Employee Assistance Programs (EAPs) in this chapter. EAPs are workplace programs designed to ameliorate a variety of organizational problems, including substance use. Although they were reviewed in some detail in Harris and Heft (1992), there was very limited new research in this area, and the bulk of this literature appears to be outside the relevant I-O psychological framework.[1]

The remainder of this chapter is divided into four major sections. First, I review the construct of substance use in the workplace, including measurement issues. The next two sections focus on substantive issues, which are summarized in Figure 12.1. Specifically, I review research addressing the outcomes of substance use in the workplace, followed by a discussion of workplace determinants of substance use. In the fourth major section of the paper, I discuss some methodological issues in the study of substance use in the workplace.

The Construct of Substance Use

In this section, I will discuss the definition, measurement, and nomological network of substance use in the workplace.

Figure 12.1. Overview of Model of Antecedents and Consequences of Substance Use in the Workplace.

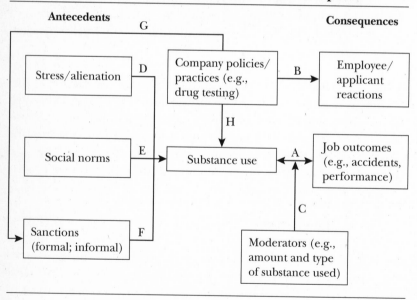

Definition

At first glance, one might think that it would be simple to define substance use in the workplace. More careful consideration suggests a number of reasons that this is a more difficult undertaking. First, what is meant by the term *substance?* Typically, what is meant is alcohol as well as illegal narcotics, such as marijuana and cocaine. But what about legal substances, such as Valium, that might be taken in inappropriate doses or without a prescription? I would suggest that such variables be included in any measure of substance use. Second, the phrase *in the workplace* is quite unclear. Does it refer only to substances used in the workplace facility? In today's world, even the distinction between a workplace facility and a non-workplace facility is often blurred. For the purposes of this chapter, I will not differentiate between substance use that physically occurs in a workplace facility from substance use that is outside of a workplace facility. Thus, the phrase *in the workplace* is somewhat of a misnomer, in that the literature does not always differentiate between substance use at work and substance use away from work. Nevertheless, as will be mentioned later in this paper, where one drinks alcohol or uses illegal substances may be an important determinant of subsequent behavior.

Measurement Issues

Substance use may be measured in different ways. The present discussion will focus on the measurement implications for research, rather than practical, purposes. It is appropriate to begin by dividing measures that are based on self-reports from those that use biological indicators (for example, urine samples). Indeed, many of the studies reviewed in this chapter have used self-report measures.

Self-Report Measures

Because substance use is potentially a sensitive topic (indeed, it may reflect a serious workplace infraction, if not illegal behavior) and respondents may be tempted to conceal the truth, concerns have been raised as to how much underreporting occurs. This is not a simple question to answer and, as it turns out, there are various factors that can affect the amount of underreporting that occurs.

One major determinant of underreporting that has been considered is the mode of administration. If conducted in an interview setting, for example, the perceived similarity (for instance, in terms of values and background) between the interviewer and the respondent has been found to affect the degree of underreporting (Johnson, Fendrich, Shaligram, Garcy, & Gillespie, 2000). Another factor affecting underreporting may be whether respondents are told their answers will be anonymous versus confidential. Although one study found that manipulating a promise of anonymity versus a promise of confidentiality did not affect the amount of underreporting, Richter and Johnson (2001) noted that the manipulation may simply not have worked. A third factor that may affect the amount of underreporting is the use of different media, such as mail questionnaires versus touch-tone telephone formats; some studies have found significant differences between these media (Richter & Johnson, 2001). Finally, it should be noted that most of this research has been conducted in settings other than the workplace, including law enforcement settings and government-funded household surveys. To what degree underreporting occurs in workplace research has rarely been examined; whether tactics such as controlling for social desirability effects would help reduce underreporting is unknown (Harris & Heft, 1992).

Aside from administration mode, self-report measures of substance use in the workplace have employed at least three measurement models. First, substance use has been subsumed as one indicator of workplace counterproductivity. Bennett and Robinson (2000), for example, developed a two-dimensional scale of workplace counterproductivity. One dimension, which they termed "interpersonal deviance," focused on counterproductive behavior targeting another individual (for example, cursing someone at work). The second dimension, which they termed "organizational deviance," included such behaviors as littering and using an illegal drug or alcohol on the job. Bolin and Heatherley (2001) created a measure of counterproductive behavior. Based on a factor analysis, they grouped the items into several dimensions, such as absenteeism, privilege abuse (for example, eating food at work without paying for it), and substance abuse, which included separate items for alcohol and drug use. Not surprisingly, each of the dimensions was predicted by a different set of variables. It is interesting that whereas only about 4 percent of the variance was explained in substance abuse, a much higher amount of variance was explained in the other dimensions (about 10 to 16 percent of the variance). The assumption that substance use is part of the repertoire of inappropriate workplace behaviors needs to be more carefully considered. We need to be cautious in lumping substance use together with other forms of workplace counterproductivity because this behavior may differ in significant ways from other forms of inappropriate workplace conduct. First and foremost, substance use may not be under the volitional control of the individual. It may be a kind of addiction. Indeed, under the Americans with Disabilities Act, alcoholism is a disability. Second, substance use is viewed as a coping technique in the stress literature (Latack, 1986). This is quite different from viewing substance use as a counterproductive or "deviant" behavior. Third, as reviewed later, substance use may, *under certain circumstances,* have some beneficial effects. This is a radical departure from the inherent assumption in studying other forms of counterproductive behavior in the workplace.

A second approach assumes that substance use should be studied in isolation from other behaviors. Scholars using this approach have measured substance use in terms of frequency and quantity to assess the total amount consumed within a given time frame. Stein et al. (1993), for example, examined adult use of alcohol, marijuana, hard drugs (for example, LSD), and cocaine.

A third approach focuses on substance use problems rather than amount of consumption. Galaif, Newcomb, and Carmona (2001), for example, measured a latent construct they called "polydrug problems," which used three manifest variables: alcohol problems, marijuana problems, and cocaine problems. Typical items included how often the respondent "had a hangover" and "gotten nauseated and vomited" from each of these sources. Whether such measures are more (or perhaps less) affected by underreporting than consumption is unknown. Individual differences in the effects of substance use (some substance users may be more susceptible to such problems by virtue of their physiological makeup) may also account for considerable variance here. Finally, substance use problems may be more relevant to assess alcohol effects rather than illegal substance effects.

Biological Measures

There are a variety of biological measures of substance use, including tests of urine, blood, saliva, and hair. Although biological measures might be assumed to be more accurate than self-report measures, Richter and Johnson (2001) pointed out a number of limitations in using biological measures for research purposes, including that they tend to assess relatively recent substance use (for example, most traces of substance use leave urine within a few days), they do not indicate amount of substance used, and mistakes can occur (for example, laboratory mix-ups). Thus, biological measures are not necessarily ideal measures of substance use.

To assess convergent validity, a number of studies have compared self-report measures to biological measures of substance use. Although studies conducted in the 1980s showed relatively good agreement between the two methods, more recent research has shown that self-report measures appear to underestimate the amount of drug use. Indeed, a recent report argued that the use of self-reports should be seriously questioned in terms of their accuracy (Richter & Johnson, 2001). It is not surprising, however, that a number of complexities emerge. Wish, Hoffman, and Nemes (1997), for example, suggested that underreporting may vary by type of drug (for example, heroin may be underreported) and the amount used (heavy users may be more likely to report accurately than light users). Finally, Cook, Bernstein, and Andrews (1997) conducted a workplace study comparing self-reported drug use, urinalysis, and hair tests for drugs. Depending on which self-report technique was employed, the amount of underreporting varied. Overall, though, thirty-nine subjects testing positively to a urinalysis test did not report use of any drugs, and fifty-four subjects who reported using drugs tested negatively with the urinalysis test. Thus, the method of measuring substance use remains problematic and requires further study. At the very least, multiple measurement methods appear advisable.

Nomological Network

Two different explanations have been offered for the linkage between substance use and job outcomes. One explanation is that substance use directly affects cognitive functioning (for example, alters one's eye-hand coordination), and in turn may increase the chance of an accident or a decrease in performance. Unfortunately, there has been little specific discussion in the workplace context as to whether this is a long-term or short-term effect. As discussed later in this chapter, current methodologies make it difficult, if not impossible, to determine whether the effect is long-term or short-term.

A second explanation is that the relationship between substance use and job outcomes is due to a third variable; that is, people who use substances such as marijuana are also less responsible or conscientious and therefore suffer from other problems, such as poorer work performance. According to this explanation, there is no causal relationship between substance use and job outcomes. To date, there has been very little research examining these two explanations either directly or indirectly (Harris & Trusty, 1997). If the latter explanation is correct, for example, one might predict that any relationship between substance use and job outcomes would be accounted for by conscientiousness.

I believe that most hypothesizing in this area has been quite simplistic. Research by Kandel and Chen (2000) suggests, for example, that there are different types of drug users. Specifically, they identified four groups of marijuana users, who differed in a variety of respects, including presence of psychopathology, affiliation with other marijuana users, and involvement in typical adult social roles (for example, marriage). Their findings suggest that styles of drug use may lead to different outcomes. Conceivably, then, some drug users may suffer from symptoms that cause work-related impairments, whereas for others the relationship between substance use and negative job outcomes is due to a spurious relationship. Still others may actually benefit from alcohol use in some way, much as moderate amounts of alcohol consumption have been shown to have some health benefits. I return to this point again later in the chapter.

What Is the Effect of Substance Use on Job Outcomes?

In this section, I examine links A and C in Figure 12.1 and, to a lesser degree, link B. Whether substance use affects job outcomes is a very practical, as well as theoretically interesting, question. From a naïve point of view, the answer seems almost obvious—of course substance use will affect job outcomes. But more careful thought suggests that the question is not quite so obvious. First, substance use in what context? An office worker drinking a glass of wine at a winter holiday party is quite different from a pilot having the same glass of wine just before he or she is scheduled to fly an airplane. Second, the kind of substance used (for example, a beer versus cocaine) may have a dramatic effect on the results. Although there have been a number of studies regarding the effect of substance use on workplace behavior, the conclusions are somewhat mixed.

Traditional Validity Studies

Harris and Heft (1993) thoroughly reviewed traditional validity studies that examined illegal substance use. It is noteworthy that there has been practically no new research on this topic since the early 1990s. Most of these studies have used urinalysis. Harris and Heft (1993) located six validation studies. Two of them used a concurrent validity design. Both of these studies, however, suffered from possible design problems; for example, both of them included subjects who were tested "for cause," indicating that they were included for particular problems that they exhibited, such as poor performance. Thus, these studies may have produced inflated estimates of drug test validity. In addition, there were some unexpected results (for example, drug-positive employees had on average more promotions than the comparison group).

Four studies used a predictive design. Of those four studies, one of them (Blank and Fenton, 1989) used a Navy sample. Although there was a significant difference in the turnover rate of applicants who tested positive for marijuana versus those who did not, the fact that marijuana-positive applicants were assigned to a special program may have led to the higher turnover rate. A second study (Parish, 1989) failed to find any significant differences between the twenty-two applicants who tested positive and the 158 who did not test positive.

Two well-designed, large-sample predictive validity studies were done for the U.S. Postal Service. Based on a sample of over four thousand hired applicants, Normand et al. (1990) reported a statistically significant relationship with absenteeism and involuntary turnover. Relationships with accidents and injuries were not statistically significant. Although Normand et al. did not report an effect size, Harris and Heft (1993) estimated a correlation of .09 between drug test results and absenteeism and asserted that the effect size was likely to be even lower for involuntary turnover. Thus, Harris and Heft argued that the relationship, albeit statistically significant, was very small. Finally, a similar study reported by Zwerling et al. (1990) based on about 2,500 hired applicants reported statistically significant relationships with all criteria, except for voluntary turnover. However, no effect sizes could be calculated for their study.

Other Studies

Although many other studies have been reviewed elsewhere (Harris and Trusty, 1997), one recent study conducted by Hoffmann and Larison (1999) is worth examining here. Using self-report surveys, Hoffmann and Larison tested the relationship between a variety of illegal drugs, days drunk, and symptoms of dependence with workplace accidents and termination. Their sample was the 1994 National Household Survey of Drug Abuse, which contains over nine thousand workers from a large cross-section of occupations. Contrary to the expectation that greater substance use would be related to workplace accidents, Hoffmann and Larison found that there was practically no relationship. The only exception was for those who used cocaine between one to three years ago, in which case they had a lower chance of being in an accident compared to those who had never used cocaine. No other substance use variables (for example, symptoms of dependence) were related to accident rate.

Unlike accident rate, however, the likelihood of being fired from one's job did increase for those who used substances. For example, weekly users of marijuana and cocaine were far more likely to be fired than those who never used these substances. Similarly, respondents who reported symptoms of dependence were far more likely to be fired.

Contrary to the evidence regarding the negative effects associated with substance use in the workplace, Harris and Greising (1998) reviewed several studies indicating that higher drug and alcohol use was associated with higher wages. Using econometric techniques to take into account the possibility of a reverse causal relationship (that is, higher wages allow the individual to purchase more drugs and alcohol), Gill and Michaels (1992) and Register and Williams (1992) both reported a positive relationship between substance use and wages and suggested that substance use may relieve tension, thereby enabling employees to work more effectively. Although these findings would conflict with the notion that substance use decreases productivity in the workplace, Harris and Greising (1998) offered some possible explanations; chief among them is that different patterns of substance use appear to have different effects. Register and Williams (1992) found, for example, that on-the-job marijuana use was negatively related to wages earned.

It is important to note that all of these studies suffer from the same limitation that the self-report or urinalysis test does—not ascertaining when the respondent was using the substance. None of these studies indicate whether the person was under the influence on the job at the time of an accident or had hangovers at work. Thus, it may be that people who use alcohol and illicit drugs at work are more prone to accidents at the time of use. I think the implication of these papers is that mere substance use alone does not necessarily explain or cause accidents. This does not preclude the notion that on-the-job substance use causes accidents. Hence, the pattern of usage may perhaps be the most important determinant of the effects of substance use.

The research reviewed above raises a number of questions. First, is substance use really a workplace problem? Second, is drug testing fair? Third, is drug testing an effective tool compared to the alternatives? Finally, might not the relationship between drug use and job outcomes be moderated by the amount of substance used or by the specific substance used? Each of these questions is considered next.

Is Substance Use a Workplace Problem?

Perhaps one of the more interesting debates is whether substance use is truly a workplace problem. First, conclusions about the extent to which substance use is a problem may depend on the nature of the job one is considering (some related evidence regarding substance use in different occupations is presented below). Second, one might question how to define the term "problem." Does a problem mean costing significant amounts of money or significant legal exposure to an organization? What about a moral problem that may exist? In any case, there are several ways to determine whether substance use is an important problem for organizations, including prevalence, costs of such behavior, and utility analysis.

Prevalence

Crow and Hartman (1992) argued that drug use was relatively rare in the workplace and therefore was not likely to be a problem, particularly in comparison to other substances such as alcohol, which were more common. In responding to the argument that drug use is too rare to constitute a workplace problem, it is useful to consider the NHSDA 2002 report (which, incidentally, is a self-report measure) that found that among full-time employees aged eighteen to forty-nine years old, 8.1 percent indicated heavy alcohol use in the prior month whereas 7.8 percent reported illegal drug use during the same time frame. It is not surprising that these rates differed by gender (for example, only 3.6 percent of women reported heavy alcohol use compared to 11.4 percent of men), age (for example, only 5.5 percent of workers ages thirty-five to forty-nine reported illegal drug use compared with 14.9 percent of workers between the ages of eighteen and twenty-five), and type of occupation (for example, 12.6 percent of production, craft, and repair workers reported heavy alcohol use compared with 4.9 percent of professional specialty employees). Bahls (1998) cited a report by SmithKline Beecham Clinical Laboratories indicating that the percentage of drug positives declined in the first half of 1997 (5.4 percent) as compared to the same time period in 1996 (5.8 percent). Nevertheless, Bahls suggested that this apparent decline could be explained in a number of ways, including a switch in the type of drugs used (for example, more people abusing prescription drugs) and greater skill on the part of drug users in "beating" the test. Whether such percentages indicate that there is a workplace problem or not might be debated at length without a convincing answer. Nonetheless, illegal drug use among employed workers is not rare. And the rate of illegal drug use is nearly the same as heavy alcohol use. Bear in mind that these findings are based on self-reported information, so the actual figures may really be higher.

Two other, related approaches may be used to determine whether there is a problem: estimating the costs of the behavior and estimating the cost-benefit ratio of the solution.

Costs Associated with the Phenomenon

Although it is not traditionally an approach that has been used in the field of I-O psychology, practitioners addressing substance use have focused heavily on the costs of such behavior (it is noteworthy that this perspective has also been applied with apparent success in the area of turnover as well [Griffeth & Hom, 2001]). The cost estimates tend to be quite high for substance use in the workplace. For example, the U.S. Department of Labor estimates that substance use costs employers as much as $100 billion annually in such things as accidents, health care, and lost work time. Although there have been challenges made as to how accurate these estimates are (Faley, Kleiman, & Wall, 1988; Weiss, 1987), the estimates do suggest that the cost of substance use may be quite high.

Cost-Benefit Analysis of the Solution

In a move that essentially avoids the question of whether there is a problem, focusing on utility analysis considers whether the financial benefits of the intervention or solution outweigh its costs. Harris and Heft (1993) reviewed the extant literature on this topic, focusing on two extensive, well-designed studies (Normand et al., 1990; Zwerling, Ryan, & Orav, 1992) that examined the utility of drug testing. The study by Zwerling et al. showed a stronger effect than the former study. Although they used different formulas for calculating the cost-benefits of their drug testing program and had different samples, both studies concluded that the benefits outweighed the costs. Thus, utility analyses suggest that at least drug testing may have significant utility for an organization, although perhaps not for every organization (Zwerling et al., 1992). The fact that the effect size may be small may be outweighed by other factors in the equation. It should also be noted that some have suggested that drug testing may serve as a deterrent to substance use (link H in Figure 12.1), an effect that may be difficult to detect with traditional cost-benefit analyses (Harris & Trusty, 1997).

Is Drug Testing Fair?

Harris and Trusty (1997) reviewed other criticisms of drug testing, several of which might be included under the broad category of fairness. Arguments posed against drug testing on the basis of fairness appear to fall into three areas. One aspect of fairness is whether substance use is a problem in the workplace that deflects attention away from other, equally or even more pressing, problems. Some have argued, for instance, that lack of sleep or high levels of stress are as likely to cause accidents as substance use. I am not aware of any studies comparing different causes of accidents, but a reasonable response is that there are multiple causes of workplace problems and that implementation of one solution (for example, drug testing) should certainly not be a reason to ignore other solutions.

A second argument revolves around how applicants and employees view drug testing. Specifically, critics question the appropriateness of drug testing under certain circumstances (other interventions, such as EAPs, might be seen as more appropriate or reasonable). The potential relationship between drug testing and reactions is represented by link B in Figure 12.1. Harris and Trusty (1997) described three subarguments in this context. First, drug testing might be viewed as unfair insofar as it violates one's sense of privacy, much like asking an applicant about his or her political views might be seen as an invasion of privacy. In this regard, Harris and Trusty noted that drug use is an illegal behavior, which at least for some jobs (that is, safety related), might be an important factor to consider. One could argue, though, that insofar as an employer might be considered, any illegal activity is grounds for concern. Few appear to object, for example, to an organization asking applicants to list their conviction record on an application form. Moreover, recent surveys indicate that drug testing is perceived to be a good thing to do, suggesting that it is not viewed as an unreasonable violation of one's privacy. For example, a Gallup poll conducted in 1995 showed that 81 percent of respondents approved of drug testing for factory workers, and 92 percent approved of drug testing for health care workers. An astonishingly high percentage of people surveyed in 1997 (95 percent) indicated they would "not object to working for an employer who tests for drugs in the hiring process" and an almost equal proportion (91 percent) would not mind working for an employer who tests randomly for drugs (Fendrich & Kim, 2002). Particularly when examined over time, these results suggest that workplace drug testing is increasingly supported by large segments of the public.

Second, Harris and Trusty (1997) argued that drug testing might be viewed as unfair because it may adversely affect minorities. In response to this criticism, however, Harris and Trusty observed that the little empirical evidence that exists in this regard fails to support the notion that race either moderates or mediates the relationship between drug test results and job outcomes.

Third, one could object to drug testing as being "unfair" in that errors are made sometimes. The response to this argument is that no hiring system is perfectly accurate. Indeed, most people would readily acknowledge that the typical, unstructured interview is susceptible to a plethora of errors and biases. At least drug testing has a known set of problems and concerns. It is entirely unclear, therefore, on what basis the critics object to the "fairness" of drug testing.

In terms of research in the area of fairness, most of the studies have applied organizational justice theory (Konovsky & Cropanzano, 1991), focusing on the specific drug screening procedures used by the organization. Future researchers might wish to examine the privacy construct, which may be an aspect of procedural justice (Bies, 1993), to develop further hypotheses. Although I-O psychologists have widely ignored privacy as a construct, the organizational privacy theory of Stone and Stone (1990) suggests, for example, that the purpose for collecting the information helps determine the degree to which participants perceive it to be unfair. More work on the relationship between privacy and drug testing (and related substance use policies) is in order (Mastrangelo & Popovich, 2000).

A discussion of drug test fairness would not be complete without at least a brief mention of the legal issues surrounding drug and alcohol use in the workplace. In this regard, there are numerous relevant factors that organizations must keep in mind in creating and enforcing drug and alcohol policies and programs, including federal, state, and local laws. Although a comprehensive review of these considerations is beyond the scope of this chapter, some examples follow next.

Beginning first with federal laws, the Americans with Disabilities Act (ADA) clearly allows one to refuse to hire or to fire a current drug user. However, alcoholics and recovered drug addicts are generally protected from discrimination, as long as they can perform the job with or without reasonable accommodation. These laws pose some subtle, and potentially thorny, problems for organizations. For example, although consistently and reasonably applied urine drug tests are unlikely to lead to ADA violations, use of the hair test, which may detect drug use back as much as three or more months, can potentially result in discrimination against a recovered drug addict (Overman, 1999). Treating an applicant or employee as though he or she is an alcoholic or recovered drug addict may also be grounds for a successful ADA lawsuit against the organization. ADA also includes a variety of other restrictions on organizations with regard to alcoholism and related pre-employment inquiries (for example, the type of questions that may be asked about alcohol use).

Some states also have laws regarding drug and alcohol policies, particularly in regard to testing procedures. The State of Minnesota, for example, requires companies to have written guidelines governing their drug and alcohol testing programs and to use a properly certified laboratory. Finally, some cities and local governments have encountered lawsuits in regard to their substance testing program. In a recent decision, the Washington Court of Appeals ruled against the City of Seattle's drug testing program for applicants, asserting that the state's constitutional right to privacy prohibited the city from conducting drug tests except for jobs involving a genuine risk to public safety (*Robinson* v. *City of Seattle,* 2000).

Drug and alcohol testing is potentially subject to other laws and legal principles, including wrongful termination, common law right to privacy, and negligence. At the same time, organizations may be legally bound to conduct such testing based on various industry regulations such as the Department of Transportation's rule 49 CFR part 40. Unlike other areas of I-O psychology, however, employment discrimination lawsuits are far less common in the area of drug and alcohol testing (Overman, 1999).

Is Drug Testing an Effective Tool?

In terms of effectiveness, how does drug testing compare to other tools for predicting workplace problems? There has been no research directly comparing the validity of drug testing to other selection devices. The literature, however, suggests that other tests (for example, integrity; Ones, Viswesvaran, & Schmidt, 1993) may be at least as effective in predicting criteria such as turnover and absenteeism, particularly in light of the fact that the correlation for drug testing may be 0.09 at best. Moreover, the incremental validity of drug testing is likely to be even lower if other predictors that correlate with it are used. Harris and Heft (1993) suggested that from a practical perspective, however, drug testing may be preferred over other predictors due to greater acceptability by unions and concern over claims of adverse impact. Clearly, comparison of drug testing with other selection tools is an important applied question that deserves more research. Practically speaking, however, it may be difficult if not impossible to persuade an organization to conduct a scientifically sound study in which applicants are not selected on the basis of the results of a drug test.

Is the Relationship Between Drug Use and Job Outcomes Moderated by Amount of Use or the Substance Used?

This section focuses on link C in Figure 12.1. One criticism of drug testing is that it picks out even "light," weekend-only users of drugs, even though these employees are not adversely affected by their drug use on the job. From a statistical viewpoint, this would suggest that there is a nonlinear relationship between drug test results and job outcomes. Blank and Fenton (1989) divided their sample into three groups based on the drug test results (light, medium, and heavy users of marijuana) and compared their attrition rates. Not only did they find a significant difference between these three groups, but the light users left the Navy in higher rates (39 percent) than did the drug-negative users (19 percent). Thus, there is no evidence to date of a nonlinear relationship between drug use and job outcomes. Furthermore, even light drug users appear to be adversely affected. Nonetheless, more research on this issue seems in order.

A related question is whether "hard" drug use is more predictive of job outcomes than "soft" drug use. Using the differential validity framework, it seems possible that some drugs might be related to job outcomes whereas others might not be. A comparison of the studies of Normand et al. (1990) and Zwerling et al. (1990) shows that the drug that is more consistently predictive of job outcomes changes from study to study. Thus, there is no clear answer to the question. Whether this is due to base rate differences (for example, marijuana use is more prevalent than cocaine use) or differential effects of different drugs is unclear.

In sum, there is much we do not know about the effect of substance use on job outcomes. Although it seems reasonable to expect a stronger relationship than has been presently found, a number of explanations exist for why it is relatively small. Further research is needed here to determine whether various moderators and mediators will explain more variance in the relationship between substance use and job outcomes. I turn next to research examining workplace antecedents of substance use.

What Is the Effect of the Workplace on Substance Use?

A question of obvious importance is whether in fact the workplace contributes to substance use. If the answer is yes, then changes in the workplace may help ameliorate the problem. Three basic workplace influences on substance use have been identified: alienation and stress, workplace norms, and policy enforcement (Bacharach, Bamberger, & Sonnenstuhl, 2002). These are described in more detail next.

Alienation and Stress

As reflected in link D in Figure 12.1, there is a large literature, primarily from a sociological viewpoint, that has examined the effects of workplace alienation and stress on substance use. Seeman and Anderson (1983) have examined the relationship between alienation and alcohol use and found a significant relationship. However, others have not found such a relationship (Greenberg & Grunberg, 1995). Very similar findings have been reported for stress, a construct that has been widely studied in the I-O psychology literature. Similar to alienation, relationships between stress and substance use have generally been small and often statistically nonsignificant, depending on the sample size (Harris & Heft, 1992).

One potential explanation is that measurement problems, particularly in substance use, affect the magnitude of the relationship. Given the earlier points regarding underreporting when self-reports are used, this possibility deserves more careful investigation. Another option, alluded to above, is that work stress affects the pattern, but not necessarily the amount, of substance used.

Alternatively, some scholars have searched for more complex models that explain the relationship between these two variables. One such model assumes that the relationship between alienation-stress and substance use is mediated or moderated by one's reasons for use. That is, employees who drink alcohol, for example, in order to reduce tension or stress may be more susceptible to using alcohol to solve workplace alienation and stress problems. Several papers, reviewed in Harris and Heft (1992), provided support for this notion, and recent research continues to support this effect. In two separate papers, Greenberg and Grunberg and their colleagues (Greenberg & Grunberg, 1995; Grunberg, Moore, & Greenberg, 1998) examined a series of models relating reasons for drinking, stress, job satisfaction, alcohol use, and negative consequences associated with drinking. Although the data were the same for both studies, one study tested reasons for drinking as a mediator; the second study tested reasons for drinking as a moderator. The dependent variables were amount of alcohol consumed and negative consequences associated with alcohol consumption. In terms of reasons for drinking as a mediator, their posited model held up fairly well and they concluded that stress affects problem drinking through job satisfaction, which in turn affects problem drinking through reasons for drinking.

Conceptually, I believe that reasons for drinking makes more sense as a moderator. The results of the second study showed that reasons for drinking did moderate the stress-negative consequences relationship. However, reasons for drinking did not moderate the stress-alcohol use relationship. Respondents who were most likely to use alcohol for coping reasons demonstrated the largest relationship between stress–job satisfaction and negative consequences. Although all of this research has focused on alcohol consumption, it seems logical to assume similar results might be found for illegal substance use.

In sum, reasons for substance use makes good sense in understanding the relationship between stress and substance use. However, Bacharach et al. (2002) recently reported that the relationship between reasons for drinking and substance use is much more complex. Hence, it seems relevant to consider the next two factors: workplace norms and policy enforcement.

Workplace Norms

As reflected in link E in Figure 12.1, several recent studies have examined the role of workplace norms as they affect substance use. Bennett and Lehman (1998) examined the role of perceived drinking climate, which they operationalized as ratings of coworkers' alcohol use. They found that work group cohesiveness and drinking climate interacted together to affect drinking problems. Specifically, a stronger "drinking climate" led to more work-related problems, but this was moderated by higher group cohesiveness. Even more interesting, individual drinking was less predictive of workplace problems than drinking climate (that is, coworkers' alcohol use).

MacDonald, Wells, and Wild (1999) tested several models of the effects of job security, social isolation at work, and peer pressure to use alcohol and drugs (it is not clear from the article whether this latter scale included only work-related friends or not) on the relationship of alcohol consumption to alcohol problems. Controlling for amount of alcohol consumed, MacDonald et al.

(1999) found that peer pressure and social isolation affected alcohol problems. They also found that peer pressure moderated the relationship between alcohol consumption and alcohol problems. MacDonald et al. suggested that peer pressure may moderate the relationship by encouraging inappropriate patterns of drinking, such as binge drinking.

Finally, in a test of alienation-stress, workplace norms, and policy enforcement (discussed in greater detail below), Bacharach et al. (2002) also found that coworkers' norms played an important role in determining alcohol consumption. Moreover, they concluded that coworkers' norms served as mediators and moderators in their model. Clearly, social norms are important factors in understanding substance use in the workplace.

Policy Enforcement

Aside from Bacharach et al. (2002), there have been no studies regarding the effect of sanctions (link F in Figure 12.1) on substance use. Practically no research has examined the effect of various workplace substance use policies and programs on perceptions of sanctions (link G in the model). Thus, despite Harris and Heft's (1992) observation that the role of sanctions on substance use in the workplace had been almost completely ignored by organizational behavior and human resource management (OB-HRM) scholars and I-O psychologists, there continues to be a lack of research in this regard. There are, however, scattered studies regarding this topic in related areas. In one of the earlier applications to workplace behavior, Hollinger and Clark (1982) examined perceived formal and informal sanctions on workers' property theft (for example, stealing company merchandise) and counterproductive behavior (for example, coming to work late). They measured formal sanctions with a single item concerning the most likely outcome (for example, fire, do nothing) if someone was caught engaged in theft or counterproductive behavior. Informal sanctions were measured with a single item asking what the most common reaction (for example, do nothing, encourage) of coworkers would be. They found that informal sanctions were more closely related to respondents' self-reported counterproductive behavior than formal sanctions. Further analyses indicated that formal sanctions served primarily in an indirect role, by affecting informal sanctions. In turn, this suggests that company policies helped reduce deviance but primarily by increasing the likelihood that one's coworkers would apply punitive sanctions.

Paternoster and Simpson (1996) examined what they termed a "rational choice model" to investigate corporate or white-collar crime, such as price fixing and violation of Environmental Protection Agency emissions standards. In their model, Paternoster and Simpson combined a perceived cost-benefit model with a perceived sanctions approach. Specifically, Paternoster and Simpson tested the following variables:

1. Perceived benefits of the illegal behavior (for example, getting a promotion)
2. Perceived formal sanctions (for example, being arrested)
3. Perceived informal sanctions (for example, losing respect of friends)
4. Self-imposed punishment (feelings of shame)
5. Moral inhibitions

The first four variables were measured for both the individual and the firm (for example, self-imposed punishment was interpreted as loss of prestige for the firm). Each of the formal and informal sanctions was estimated by multiplying the perceived probability of the sanction occurring by the severity of the sanction.

Paternoster and Simpson (1996) found that respondents were more likely to commit the illegal act if they felt they and the firm would benefit from it. Moreover, the risk of informal sanctions and self-imposed punishment were negatively related to intentions to commit the illegal act. Like the findings of Hollinger and Clark (1982), formal sanctions at the individual level were only marginally significant, and their strongest effect was on perceptions of informal sanctions.

Moral inhibitions also played an important role on the behavior. Further analyses revealed that when moral objections to the behavior were high, respondents were not affected by formal and informal sanction threats or by personal gain. Thus, when one finds a particular act morally reprehensible, costs and incentives appear to have little effect on one's decision. However, when "moral obligations weaken, compliance is based on perceived incentives and costs" (Paternoster & Simpson, 1996, p. 579). Indeed, this finding meshes with Kohlberg's theory of moral development (Jennings & Kohlberg, 1983), which posits a stage where individuals make decisions based on rewards and costs. A later stage involves making decisions based on self-chosen ethical principles. Thus, Kohlberg's theory of moral development fits with findings reported by Paternoster and Simpson.

To date, there has been scant writing in OB-HRM, let alone I-O psychology, on morality and its effect on behavior in the workplace. The one area where morality has been considered is in regard to ethical decision making, for which a variety of models have been proposed (Jones, 1991). Although a detailed discussion is beyond the scope of this chapter, morality judgment may best be defined as an assessment of "what is right or wrong" (Trevino, 1986, p. 604).

There are a number of potentially important implications of this research for the study of workplace substance use. First, and I think most interesting, is the importance of moral beliefs in determining future actions. To date, most OB-HRM models of behavior ignore perceptions of morality. Yet as Paternoster and Simpson (1996) found, this may be an important predictor of certain behaviors. Quite a different set of considerations may affect employees faced with a choice they consider to have moral implications. Thus, it is possible that employees first determine whether the behavior at issue involves a moral decision. If it does, they might consider what the morality of the proposed behavior is to determine whether to engage in it or not. If they determine it is not a moral decision, they may proceed to determine whether the potential costs (for example, formal and informal sanctions) outweigh the benefits.

The effect of organizational practices and policies on perceptions of formal sanctions for substance use on the job should be investigated more closely. Recent survey results indicate that the majority of organizations send employees who are caught using drugs for treatment, whereas only about 20 percent take immediate disciplinary action. The importance of informal sanctions by peers points to the need for much more careful investigation of this factor. From a theoretical perspective, these informal sanctions may come from at least two parties: family and friends outside of work, and coworkers. The question of which of these two parties plays a more prominent role, or if they both do, needs to be examined more carefully. Of course, from an organizational perspective, it is likely to be easier to influence workers than to influence peers outside of work.

Despite the importance of informal sanctions, the research summarized above indicates that formal sanctions also play an important, though perhaps indirect, role on inappropriate behavior. To date, there has been almost no research on the role of formal sanctions on substance use in the workplace. Yet the alcohol and drug policy area is a good one to study because many companies have formal, official policies about such behavior. We stand to learn a lot by comparing different organizations with different policies in terms of employee perceptions of the sanctions. For example, does having a more punitive policy (say, immediate termination) versus a more rehabilitative policy (the employee must attend counseling) for substance use affect the perceived severity of being caught? What effects does a random drug testing program have on the probability of being caught or the perceived likelihood of receiving the sanction if substances are used? We really don't know how likely employees believe each sanction is to occur, but it seems logical that the probability of being caught is higher if random testing is conducted by the organization.

Second, as summarized above, prior research suggested that formal sanctions have a direct effect on informal sanctions. We don't know what the effect of such formal sanctions is on informal sanctions in the present context. I suspect that there will be variables that moderate this relationship. For example, it seems likely that the greater the extent to which one's work is affected by other workers, the more likely coworkers would be to condemn and report substance use in the workplace. A cockpit crew is likely to be extremely concerned and to impose severe sanctions on coworkers who are using substances. Thus, we might expect that work interdependence moderates the impact of informal sanctions. Another important moderator is likely to be organizational commitment. Specifically, individuals who identify with and support organizational goals and values are likely to want to enforce company rules and policies. Thus, for employees with high organizational commitment, the higher the formal sanctions, the higher informal sanctions are likely to be.

It is also important to consider possible negative side effects of strong sanctions against substance use. Although strong formal sanctions are likely to increase the probability and severity of being caught using drugs or alcohol, it seems possible that such policies may negatively affect perceptions of procedural fairness. In addition, we should consider the type of employee who is attracted and who remains with organizations that have strong sanctions against substance use. Early research, for example, suggested that job applicants tended to be turned away by punitive drug policies (Harris & Heft, 1993). Thus, the effect of perceived sanctions on other variables, such as procedural fairness and organizational attractiveness, needs to be considered.

In sum, I believe that further research examining the role of informal as well as formal sanctions, particularly when moral considerations are measured, may lead to important insights into substance use in the workplace. Certainly this is a rich area for future researchers.

Methodological Issues

In this section, I review time issues in the study of substance use and advocate a relatively novel methodology called *experience sampling methodology*.

Timing Issues Must Be Specified

In a recent article, Mitchell and James (2001) noted that most longitudinal research in the OB-HRM area fails to accurately specify the role of time in causal relationships. They provided eight possible ways, or configurations, in which time may affect the relationship between two variables (although I use the example of work stress and alcohol consumption, the same arguments apply for drug use and job performance). Aside from the typical, simplistic assumption that variable A (say, work stress) causes variable B (for example, alcohol consumption) in a consistent way, Mitchell and James articulated a number of alternative possibilities, including one in which the effect of variable A on variable B changes over time. For example, the effect of work stress on alcohol use may increase over time, as employees increasingly link work stress and alcohol consumption. Little research in the stress-substance use area has examined these possibilities. As Mitchell and James (2001) asserted, the time and occurrence of lags between the variables may be critical in understanding the relationship. However, as in other literature, the time lags between work stress and substance use are rarely discussed.

Future research on work stress and substance use needs to more carefully determine which of these configurations is most appropriate and then collect data accordingly. The timing of measurements in the work stress-substance use area has far too often been a matter of convenience or past practices rather than based on any theoretical model. The question of when to measure the variables of interest, particularly substance use, is critical. Measuring substance use either too soon after or too long after the independent variable can produce misleading results. In the present context, future researchers should make hypotheses about the onset of substance use after experiencing work stress. It should be noted that this is not just a deficiency in the substance use literature; the research on work stress has done little to examine the onset of reactions to negative experiences.

According to Mitchell and James (2001), incorrect timing may have a major effect on conclusions about the relationship between the variables of interest. They stated that the causal cycle between two variables has three periods:

- An equilibration period (for example, during which time work stress begins to affect substance use and substance use begins to change)
- An equilibrium condition (for example, when substance use stabilizes and is no longer changing)
- An entropic phase (for example, a decline in substance use, perhaps because the effect is wearing off)

It is during the equilibrium phase that substance use should be measured; if the measure is obtained during the first or third phase, one's conclusions may be erroneous. Thus, timing issues must be considered much more deliberately if we are to understand the workplace antecedents and consequences of substance use.

Experience Sampling Methodology as an Approach to Studying Substance Use in the Workplace

Experience sampling methodology (ESM) would be of great value in OB-HRM and I-O psychology research in general and the substance use area specifically. As defined by Alliger and Williams (1993), ESM involves the "in-depth study of everyday experiences and ongoing behavior in their natural environment" (p. 526). The basic approach is to collect data from subjects on a regular basis (that is, repeated measures), thus providing "within subjects" as well as "between subjects" data. Typically, for psychological measures, subjects wear a beeper watch that randomly signals them when to record their reactions to some phenomena. Alliger and Williams (1993) cited several advantages to ESM that are relevant to our topic of interest. First, ESM provides a "better understanding of the temporal and dynamic nature of subjective work experience" (1993, p. 528). Second, ESM minimizes the possible effects of memory. Third, collection of within-person data allows for examination of individual differences that are generally not possible with traditional designs. Williams et al. (1991), for example, used ESM to examine the effects of role juggling on working mothers' task enjoyment and mood. Because measures were gathered throughout the day on a daily basis, Williams et al. were able to examine lag effects of mood across days. They found evidence of a contrast effect for mood, such that a more negative mood on one day was followed by a more positive mood the next day.

Armeli, Tennen, Affleck, and Kranzler (2000) used a similar approach, employing diaries, to examine the relationship among mood, work and nonwork events, desire to drink alcohol, and alcohol consumption. On a daily basis, for a period of numerous weeks, subjects made recordings in a diary. Armeli et al. (2000) used multilevel regression analysis to analyze the within-person and between-person results. Among the results of particular interest here was that participants consumed more alcoholic beverages on days with more negative and positive nonwork events and less alcohol on days with more positive work events. Negative work events were only marginally related to desire to drink. The authors found evidence for a complex relationship between work stress and alcohol use. Specifically, although work stress increased the desire to drink, a common effect of stress was to have less time to drink (that is, a greater work load). Thus, work stress had multiple effects, which tended to cancel each other out in terms of amount of alcohol consumed. Clearly, we need more research that uses such approaches to address substance use in the workplace.

Use of ESM methods will enable researchers to have a more precise understanding of the work stress-substance use relationship, time lags between these phenomena, and individual difference variables. Of course, ESM is not without disadvantages. Alliger and Williams (1993) described a number of limitations to the technique, including potential obtrusiveness, self-selection bias, common method bias, and priming or reactivity effects, among others.

Finally, a somewhat unique factor in terms of timing of measurement is the role of season on alcohol and possibly drug use. Specifically, researchers have widely ignored the potential effects of the calendar on the use of these substances, such as the winter holiday season and popular football games. Researchers must devote more attention to controlling the season in which the study was conducted than is currently the case. A study by Cho, Johnson, and Fendrich (2001) recently provided empirical data to indicate that season affected alcohol consumption.

Conclusion

In closing, there are a few themes that I wish to highlight. First, I would like to declare a moratorium on the exclusive use of cross-sectional, self-reported measures of substance use. There are simply too many potential weaknesses in these measures to rely solely on them. What researchers need to use are longitudinal, multiple measures of substance use. New methodologies, such as ESM, are sorely needed here.

Second, more research is needed on the relationship between substance use and job outcomes that employs more complex theories and distinguishes between different usage patterns. Following Kandel and Chen (2000), future investigators must separately examine such relationships by using a variety of moderators, including the reasons for substance use.

Third, much more research on the role of drug policies and practices, formal and informal sanctions, and social norms on the use of substance use is needed. In other words, there is a great need to incorporate organizational concepts, such as privacy theory, in studying workplace substance use than has heretofore been the case.

Finally, I-O psychologists have played at best a very small role in this area. I predict that in the future I-O psychologists will still not become the leaders here for a variety of reasons. Although workplace drug and alcohol policies and programs will continue to be dominated by safety and health personnel, I would assert that I-O psychologists have much to contribute through our knowledge and experience with methodology, work behavior, work reactions, stress, validity research, and cost-benefit analysis. It is time, therefore, for us to become more involved in this area.

Note

1. Throughout the chapter, I generally avoid the term alcohol and drug *abuse*. Although the term *abuse* is often associated with alcohol and drug consumption, I prefer the less value-laden term *use*, as it may be difficult to precisely distinguish between *use* and *abuse* of these substances.

References

Alliger, G., & Williams, K. J. (1993). Using signal-contingent experience sampling methodology to study work in the field: A discussion and illustration examining task perceptions and mood. *Personnel Psychology, 46*, 525–549.

Armeli, S., Tennen, H., Affleck, G., & Kranzler, H. (2000). Does affect mediate the association between daily events and alcohol use? *Journal of Studies on Alcohol, 61*, 862–871.

Bacharach, S., Bamberger, P., & Sonnenstuhl, W. (2002). Driven to drink: Managerial control, work-related risk factors, and employee problem drinking. *Academy of Management Journal, 45*, 637–658.

Bahls, J. (February, 1998). Drugs in the workplace. *HRMagazine, 43*, 80–87.

Bennett, J., & Lehman, W.E.K. (1998). Workplace drinking climate, stress, and problem indicators: Assessing the influence of teamwork (group cohesion). *Journal of Studies on Alcohol, 59*, 608–618.

Bennett, R., & Robinson, S. (2000). Development of a measure of workplace deviance. *Journal of Applied Psychology,* 85, 349–360.

Bies, R. J. (1993). Privacy and procedural justice in organizations. *Social Justice Research,* 6, 69–86.

Blank, D., & Fenton, J. (1989). Early employment testing for marijuana: Demographic and employee retention patterns. In S. W. Gust & J. M. Walsh (Eds.), *Drugs in the workplace: Research and evaluation data* (pp. 139–150). Rockville MD: National Institute on Drug Abuse.

Bolin, A., & Heatherley, L. (2001). Predictors of employee deviance: The relationship between bad attitudes and bad behavior. *Journal of Business and Psychology,* 15, 405–418.

Cho, Y., Johnson, T., & Fendrich, M. (2001). Monthly variations in self-reports of alcohol consumption. *Journal of Studies on Alcohol,* 62, 268–272.

Cook, R., Bernstein, A., & Andrews, C. (1997). Assessing drug use in the workplace: A comparison of self-report, urinalysis, and hair analysis. In L. Harrison & A. Hughes (Eds.), *Validity of self-reported drug use: Improving the accuracy of survey estimates.* Research Monograph 167, NIH Publication 97–4147 (pp. 200–226). Rockville, MD: National Institute on Drug Abuse.

Crow, S., & Hartman, S. J. (1992). Drugs in the workplace: Overstating the problems and the cures. *Journal of Drug Issues,* 22, 923–937.

Faley, R., Kleiman, L., & Wall, P. (1988). Drug testing in the public and private-sector workplaces: Technical and legal issues. *Journal of Business and Psychology,* 3, 154–186.

Fendrich, M., & Kim, J.Y.S. (2002). The experience and acceptability of drug testing: Poll trends. *Journal of Drug Issues,* 81–96.

Galaif, E., Newcomb, M., & Carmona, J. (2001). Prospective relationships between drug problems and work adjustment in a community sample of adults. *Journal of Applied Psychology,* 86, 337–350.

Gill, A. M., & Michaels, R. J. (1992). Does drug use lower wages? *Industrial and Labor Relations Review,* 45, 419–434.

Griffeth, R., & Hom, P. (2001). *Retaining valued employees.* Thousand Oaks, CA: Sage.

Greenberg, E., & Grunberg, L. (1995). Work alienation and problem alcohol behavior. *Journal of Health and Social Behavior,* 36, 83–102.

Grunberg, L., Moore, S., & Greenberg, E. (1998). Work stress and problem alcohol behavior: A test of the spillover model. *Journal of Organizational Behavior,* 19, 487–502.

Harris, M., & Greising, L. (1998). Alcohol and drug abuse as dysfunctional workplace behaviors. In R. W. Griffin & A. O'Leary-Kelly (Eds.), *Dysfunctional behavior in organizations: Nonviolent dysfunctional behavior* (pp. 21–48). Stamford, CT: JAI Press.

Harris, M., & Heft, L. (1992). Alcohol and drug use in the workplace: Issues, controversies, and directions for future research. *Journal of Management, 18,* 239–266.

Harris, M., & Heft, L. (1993). Preemployment urinalysis drug testing: A critical review of psychometric and legal issues and effects on applicants. *Human Resource Management Review, 3,* 271–291.

Harris, M., & Trusty, M. (1997). Drug and alcohol programs in the workplace: A review of recent literature. In C. L. Cooper & I. T. Robertson (Eds.), *International review of industrial and organizational psychology* (Vol. 12, pp. 289–315). Chichester, England: John Wiley.

Hoffmann, J., & Larison, C. (1999). Drug use, workplace accidents and employee turnover. *Journal of Drug Issues, 29,* 341–364.

Hollinger, R., & Clark, J. (1982). Formal and informal social controls of employee deviance. *Sociological Quarterly, 23,* 333–343.

Jennings, W., & Kohlberg, L. (1983). Effects of a just community programme on the moral development of youthful offenders. *Journal of Moral Education, 12,* 33–50.

Johnson, T. P., Fendrich, M., Shaligram, C., Garcy, A., & Gillespie, S. (2000). An evaluation of the effects of interviewer characteristics in an RDD telephone survey of drug use. *Journal of Drug Issues, 30,* 77–102.

Jones, T. (1991). Ethical decision making by individuals in organizations: An issue-contingent model. *Academy of Management Review, 16,* 366–395.

Kandel, D., & Chen, K. (2000). Types of marijuana users by longitudinal course. *Journal of Studies on Alcohol, 61,* 367–378.

Konovsky, M. A., & Cropanzano, R. (1991). The perceived fairness of employee drug testing as a predictor of employee attitudes and job performance. *Journal of Applied Psychology, 76,* 698–707.

Latack, J. C. (1986). Coping with job stress: Measures and future directions for scale development. *Journal of Applied Psychology, 71,* 377–385.

MacDonald, S., Wells, S., & Wild, T. C. (1999). Occupational risk factors associated with alcohol and drug problems. *American Journal of Drug and Alcohol Abuse, 25,* 351–369.

Mastrangelo, P., & Popovich, P. (2000). Employees' attitudes toward drug testing, perceptions of organizational climate, and withdrawal from the employer. *Journal of Business & Psychology, 15,* 3–18.

Mitchell, T. R., & James, L. R. (2001). Building better theory: Time and the specification of when things happen. *Academy of Management Review, 26,* 530–547.

Normand, J., Salyards, S., & Mahoney, J. (1990). An evaluation of pre-employment drug testing. *Journal of Applied Psychology, 75,* 629–639.

Ones, D., Viswesvaran, C., & Schmidt, F. (1993). Comprehensive meta-analysis of integrity test validities: Findings and implications for personnel selection and theories of job performance. *Journal of Applied Psychology, 78*, 679–703.

Overman, S. (1999). Splitting hairs. *HRMagazine, 44*, August, 42–48.

Parish, D. C. (1989). Relation of the pre-employment drug testing result to employment status: A one-year follow-up. *Journal of General Internal Medicine, 4*, 44–47.

Paternoster, R., & Simpson, S. (1996). Sanction threats and appeals to morality: Testing a rational choice model of corporate crime. *Law & Society Review, 30*, 549–584.

Register, C. A., & Williams, D. R. (1992). Labor market effects of marijuana and cocaine use among young men. *Industrial and Labor Relations Review, 45*, 435–448.

Richter, L., & Johnson, P. (2001). Current methods of assessing substance use: A review of strengths, problems, and developments. *Journal of Drug Issues, 31*, 809–832.

Robinson v. *City of Seattle* (2000). Wash. App. LEXIS 1906.

Seeman, M., & Anderson, C. (1983). Alienation and alcohol: The role of work, mastery, and community in drinking behavior. *American Sociological Review, 48*, 60–77.

Stein, J., Smith, G., Guy, S., & Bentler, P. (1993). Consequences of adolescent drug use on young adult job behavior and job satisfaction. *Journal of Applied Psychology, 78*, 463–474.

Stone, E. F., & Stone, D. L. (1990). Privacy in organizations: Theoretical issues, research findings, and protection mechanisms. *Research in Personnel and Human Resources Management, 8*, 349–411.

Trevino, Linda K. (1986). Ethical decision making in organizations: A person-situation interactionist model. *Academy of Management Review, 11*, 601–617.

Weiss, R. (1987). Writing under the influence: Science versus fiction in the analysis of corporate alcoholism programs. *Personnel Psychology, 40*, 341–356.

Williams, K. J., Suls, J., Alliger, G., Learner, S., & Wan, C. K. (1991). Multiple role juggling and daily mood states in working mothers: An experience sampling study. *Journal of Applied Psychology, 76*, 664–674.

Wish, E., Hoffman, J., & Nemes, S. (1997). The validity of self-reports of drug use at treatment admission and at follow-up: Comparisons of urinalysis and hair assays. In L. Harrison & A. Hughes (Eds.), *Validity of self-reported drug use: Improving the accuracy of survey estimates.* Research Monograph 167, NIH Publication 97-4147 (pp. 200–226). Rockville, MD: National Institute on Drug Abuse.

Zwerling, C., Ryan, J., & Orav, E. (1990). The efficacy of preemployment drug screening for marijuana and cocaine in predicting employment outcome. *Journal of the American Medical Association, 264,* 2639–2643.

Zwerling, C., Ryan, J., & Orav, E. J. (1992). Costs and benefits of preemployment drug screening. *Journal of the American Medical Association, 266,* 91–93.

CHAPTER 13

Broadening Our Understanding of Organizational Retaliatory Behavior

Daniel P. Skarlicki, Robert Folger

Abstract: In this chapter we review previous work on organization-al retaliatory behavior (ORB) and discuss the features that can differentiate ORB from other "dark side" behaviors. We highlight how our previous research provides value for both theory and research. We then introduce *moral retaliation* and explain why individuals other than the victim can also have retaliatory motives. Based upon these considerations, we provide a redefinition of ORB and illustrate some of its goals and character. Last we discuss our work-in-progress in which we attempt to understand the conditions under which individuals might choose reconciliation rather than retaliation as a reaction to workplace wrongdoing.

Research in the organizational sciences has tended to focus on positive discretionary employee behaviors in the workplace—those that contribute to effective organizational functioning, including organizational citizenship behavior (Organ, 1988), prosocial behavior (Brief & Motowidlo, 1986), contextual performance (Borman &

Note: Support for this chapter was provided by a grant to the first author by the Social Sciences and Humanities Research Council of Canada.

Motowidlo, 1993), organizational spontaneity (George & Brief, 1992), and civic virtue (Van Dyne, Cummings, & Parks, 1995). Although this focus is useful, it is also important to understand behaviors that have the potential to detract from organizational effectiveness, including their causes and consequences.

Of all the various types of motivations that people experience, the feeling that rule breakers should be punished is "older, more universal, and socially more significant" than any other justice feeling (Hogan & Emler, 1981). Both victims and nonvictims make fairness judgments, become upset and angry when social rules are violated, and are motivated to take actions in response. Moreover, there is evidence that people's need to "right the wrong" has increased in recent years (Ellsworth & Gross, 1994). Despite this fundamental and most basic motivation, relatively little research has explored individuals' retaliation in the workplace.

In this chapter we begin with a general definition of retaliation. We then briefly describe our earlier research (Skarlicki & Folger, 1997; Skarlicki, Folger, & Tesluk, 1999) and clarify what has been learned by these studies. We step back from this research in order to consider how to guide and develop further the understanding of workplace retaliation—its definition, antecedents, and consequences. We also highlight some of the unique features that our approach to retaliation provides for both theory and research. Second, we introduce and explain *moral retaliation,* in which we point out occasions in which individuals other than the victim have retaliatory motives. Third, based upon considerations raised in our discussion of moral retaliation, we redefine *organizational retaliation behavior* (ORB) and illustrate some of its goals and character. Last we discuss our work-in-progress in which we attempt to understand the conditions under which individuals might choose reconciliation rather than retaliation as a reaction to workplace wrongdoing.

Retaliation Defined

Retaliation refers to a person's orientation and motivation to "make the wrongdoer pay" that is targeted toward a social actor called a transgressor. A transgressor is someone who is accountably associated with a transgression—an event that harms or jeopardizes a victim in some sense meaningful to the perceiver. In organizational settings, transgressors are social actors who can be specific or generic, individual or collective, including an individual person (for example, a supervisor), several persons (for example, the senior management team), a single institutional entity (the company for which one works), or a collective category of persons or institutions (industries considered polluters).

The antecedents of retaliation involve variables that bring about a negative evaluation of the transgressor and his or her behavior. Retaliation involves the perception that a transgressor is somehow culpable and thus held accountable for the transgression. Although many inanimate objects do not logically qualify as culpable actors, people nonetheless often treat personifications such as God and Mother Nature as transgressors and deem them accountable for negative outcomes.

Retaliation also involves accountability and blame for placing in jeopardy certain morally valued states of affairs such as the welfare of another social actor as the victim or the healthy status of the moral order, such as blaming a polluter as transgressor. In terms used by Heider (1958), a positive unit relation of accountable association is imputed between transgressor and transgression. Loosely, we can say this is the condition of the transgressor being considered "answerable" to inquiries, even if only imagined by the perceivers, regarding the transgression and the transgressor's contributing role (compare with "fairness theory," Folger & Cropanzano, 1998, 2001).

Much like fairness, accountability is highly perceptual. A victim, for example, might consider an organization to be a culpable transgressor without knowing the role of specific decision makers. Although some discussion of other possibilities might be useful in the long run (for example, a deed seems evil even though conditions can make it difficult or impossible to identify any given transgressor "candidate" or "suspect" unambiguously as an evildoer), we focus on cases where perceivers have already reached at least a tentative conclusion regarding the transgressor's blameworthiness.

Moreover, retaliation is part of a dynamic and ongoing process. For example, retaliation may begin as a response to a perceived violation that can be followed by a counteraction by the alleged transgressor (for example, imposing sanctions for whistle blowing), which is followed by a further reaction, and so on. We expand on the potential for "reaction to retaliation" later in this chapter.

Our core hypothesis is that a retaliatory motivation involves a state of affairs in which a retaliatory response is deemed justifiable. By "justifiable," we mean that it is based on a belief that the victims or others have the right to impose a negative social sanction on the transgressor because the transgressor has "earned" such an outcome as a "deserved" state. The quality and amount of retaliation can be informed by various principles, including that the punishment should fit the crime (for example, equity theory) or that the punishment itself should avoid being inequitably harsh (U.S. Constitution's prohibition against cruel and unusual punishment), or that the punishment should not only balance accounts but also send a signal to discourage future rule-breaking ("I don't get even, I get one better").

In the following section we briefly describe our previous research and explain its conceptual and empirical bases. We then step back from those studies and explore some of the features associated with this approach.

Organizational Retaliation Behavior

In our earlier research (Skarlicki & Folger, 1997; Skarlicki et al., 1999), we focused on ORB in terms of "adverse reactions to perceived unfairness by disgruntled employees toward their employer" (p. 434). We were interested in understanding the relationship between employees' perceptions of (un)fairness and ways that they attempt to "even the score" or otherwise "get back at" the transgressor. Rather than focusing on events that might be deemed highly illegal or difficult to observe (for example, theft, sabotage), however, we wanted to also capture the many "little" things that represent employee retaliation.

Our original conceptualization of ORB was meant to serve as a counterpart to organizational citizenship behavior. Previous research has shown that employees' perceptions of fair treatment are positively related to their tendency to go above and beyond the call of duty, labeled organizational citizenship behavior (OCB) (Organ, 1988). OCB has been defined as discretionary behavior, not formally recognized or rewarded by the organization but that in the aggregate can contribute to effective organizational functioning. OCB includes the many ways that employees can express their discretionary behavior by doing things such as helping one's coworker or volunteering to serve on a committee. The relationship between fairness and OCB has been explained in terms of social exchange theory (Blau, 1964); when employees perceive that they are being fairly treated, they tend to look for ways to reciprocate. One way to repay fair treatment is by engaging in OCB (Organ, 1988).

ORB in contrast represents an employee's response to perceived *un*fairness by the employer or its leaders. Although ORB can include rather serious actions such as theft and sabotage, analogous to OCB it also includes reactions to fairness (only in this case it is unfairness) in the small ways that might not be observed or recognized by the organization or its agents. Examples of ORB can range from violence and aggression to withdrawing one's efforts. Unlike OCB, which contributes to effective functioning, ORB can be either functional or dysfunctional to an organization's effectiveness—or both, in some mixed degree.

Our measurement strategy was to identify behaviors that could be observed and rated by an employee's coworker. To do this we developed a site-specific list of ORB by using the critical incident technique (Flanagan, 1954). The items generated by this procedure are provided in the list below. When we compared employees' self-reported perceptions of fairness with ratings of the ORB supplied by their coworkers, we found that employees' fairness judgments correlated negatively with their ORB.

Items Depicting Retaliation in Skarlicki and Folger (1997)

- On purpose, damaged equipment or work process
- Took supplies home without permission
- Wasted company materials
- Called in sick when not ill
- Spoke poorly about the company to others
- Refused to work weekends or overtime when asked
- Left a mess unnecessarily (did not clean up)
- Disobeyed a supervisor's instructions
- "Talked back" to his or her boss
- Gossiped about his or her boss
- Spread rumors about coworkers

- Gave a coworker the "silent treatment"
- Failed to give coworker required information
- Tried to look busy while wasting time
- Took an extended coffee or lunch break
- Intentionally worked slower
- Spent time on personal matters while at work

Stepping back from our original studies, we argue that our approach to studying reactions to unfairness via ORB has a number of implications for research. First, our measure of ORB provides variance necessary for most statistical analyses. Previous studies have investigated the relationships among fairness and isolated behaviors such as theft (Greenberg, 1990) and vandalism (DeMore, Fisher, & Baron, 1988) that typically have low correlations with attitude measures and thus limit our ability to predict such behaviors. These low correlations are frequently caused by large amounts of unique variance associated with highly specific and narrowly targeted forms of negative workplace behaviors that have adverse organizational effects. Moreover, because events such as sabotage and violence are low base-rate phenomena, they are difficult to measure with any reliability, thereby precluding any meaningful measurement and statistical analysis. Our perspective of ORB consists of a composite of reactions that can occur with relatively greater frequency because they are "safer" behaviors. In much the same way that individuals may not be formally penalized for failing to engage in OCB, employees will not necessarily lose their jobs for engaging in ORB. These behaviors, however, can also represent the "tip of the iceberg" of other larger reactions that are occurring within the organization.

Second, unlike other types of "dark side" behaviors such as deviance, incivility, or antisocial behavior, ORB can have both functional and dysfunctional implications for individuals and organizations, which we term "the good, the bad, and the ugly." Retaliation can be dysfunctional for the organization because it can involve damage and loss to goods (for example, sabotage) and resources (stealing time). It can also be detrimental to the individual retaliator in terms of feelings of guilt, anxiety, and stress that can be associated with such things as the worry of getting caught for the retaliation. Moreover, a preoccupation with retaliation is likely to have the potential to detract from one's own personal performance.

In contrast to solely dark side behaviors, acts of retaliation can also have potentially functional consequences. Whereas "deviant behavior" presumes wrongful and inherently negative conduct on the part of the employee, some mistreatment makes retaliation more legitimate than deviant. Just as conflict can sometimes be used constructively for change, legitimate retaliation under some circumstances might provoke needed organizational changes and, therefore, would qualify as more constructive than some instances of similar behavior exhibiting mere deviance or antisocial behavior. Examples of functional organizational consequences include keeping employee mistreatment in check and holding managers accountable to moral codes of behavior. Functional consequences for the individual include the psychological restoration of equity. We provide other examples of functional and dysfunctional ORB for both the individual and the organization in Table 13.1.

Third, ORB differs from other "dark side" constructs in an important way: whereas other perspectives label the individual actor

Table 13.1. Typology of Retaliation: Examples of Dysfunctional and Functional Consequences for the Organization and Individual.

	For the Organization	For the Individual
Dysfunctional	Cutting customer service—loss of customers	Negative affect: Guilt Anxiety
	Sabotage—damaged goods and equipment	Regret
	Theft—loss of resources	Rumination Distraction
	Whistle-blowing—loss of reputation and goodwill	
	Low staff morale—performance implications	
Functional	Change and improvement	Restores equity
	Keeps individuals accountable	Relieves one's own sense of moral obligation

as transgressor, ORB activities represent an individual's response to the transgressor. By framing the behavior as a reaction to another person's provocation (or to an offense by the organization as an entity), our approach to ORB provides a potentially interesting benefit for researchers; namely, we believe it increases participants' willingness to discuss their behavior. This is because participants are able to view their reactions as more legitimate than "bad." For instance, in our research we were readily able to get job incumbents to talk about their ORB.

Fourth, some reactions to unfairness are known only by the person who engages in the activity. This can be problematic from a measurement perspective because self-ratings of both the predictor (that is, perceptions of fairness) and the criterion (reactions to [in]justice) can contribute to common method variance in statistical analysis. Moreover, self-reports of negative behavior can be vulnerable to social desirability bias because these behaviors can often result in company sanction. In our research, ORB was developed to circumvent these problems by defining ORB in terms of behavior that is observable by one's peers. Our procedure ensured that our ORB measure was content-valid for our research site and was defined in terms of observable behavior rather than a person's traits (for example, deviant or antisocial). Moreover, because we did not impose on our respondents a preconceived notion of what specific actions "getting even with the organization" might mean, we were able to uncover a variety of subtle responses to perceived injustice that constitute the behavioral repertoire of employees at this company.

A problematic aspect of referring to this behavior as retaliation, however, is that it involves intent, which can never be observed. Moreover, many of these behaviors can occur for reasons other than perceived unfairness. Nonetheless, our measure of retaliation covaried reliably with individuals' perceptions of unfairness. The three dimensions of fairness, namely distributive (the fairness of outcomes), procedural (the fairness of the procedures used to derive one's outcomes), and interactional justice (the fairness of treatment received from one's supervisor) and their interactions accounted for 68 percent of the variance in retaliation. Given that the measures of retaliation were developed via a scientifically based procedure, were content-valid, and demonstrated a significant relation to (un)fairness, we propose that retaliation was indeed motivated by the employees' perceived unfairness.

In summary, our approach to studying retaliation provides certain features that we propose make it distinct from other approaches to the "dark side" of organizational behavior. Having provided an overview of some key definitional issues, we now turn our attention to broadening and clarifying what is subsumed under the heading of retaliation. Before doing so, we consider a form of retaliation that is often overlooked in research but can help us to understand and clarify the nature of retaliation.

Moral Retaliation

By *moral retaliation* we consider that people can make fairness judgments and be motivated to react to mistreatment without being directly and personally victimized or disadvantaged. Moral retaliation refers to moral transgressions and universal impartiality regarding what people "owe to one another" (compare with Scanlon, 1998) as so labeled by any "reasonably moral" person. Also relevant is Rawls's (1971) discussion of entitlement: by reason of their humanity, individuals are entitled to the right to be treated in a way that fosters positive self-regard. Studies show that individuals can become upset when a transgressor shows disrespect, even though they themselves are not involved or negatively affected by the outcome. Cooley's (1902) classic research on queue jumping, for example, shows that although people are more likely to confront a line-intruder who cuts in line ahead of them, they also demonstrate indignation toward someone who cuts in line behind them. The indignation arises from the perceived disrespect the intruder has shown for the system of social rules under which all members of the moral community are expected to live (Miller, 2001).

Moral transgressions might not necessarily be directly experienced or observed by the perceiver, but their awareness must be sufficient to instigate their cognitive appraisal. This can include, for example, employees who are angered by the mistreatment of a coworker, whether they saw it occur first hand or heard about it happening. It can also involve the liability judgments and punitive damages that jurors assign in a court of law when such members of the public are not themselves directly victimized. This category also includes morally offended persons or groups whose own self-interests are not otherwise directly harmed or jeopardized by the specific offense. For example, many Canadian and U.S. citizens feel morally outraged about a company's treatment of employees in a third-world "sweatshop" even though they do not care about the product and do not believe that their own employment or that of their fellow citizens is jeopardized. Thus, rather than focusing on retaliation toward the transgressor by the victim, moral retaliation also involves perceivers other than the victim (for example, third-party observers). In addition, the victim category can include nonpersons (such as when the transgressor harms the environment as a polluter). Moreover, acts of vengeance and retribution can be carried out both personally and by friends and social groups of the victims, and by vaguely self-interested groups such as neighbors.[1]

Considerable empirical evidence suggests that third parties indeed engage in moral retaliation that is related to their fairness perceptions. Skarlicki, Ellard, and Kelln (1998), for example, proposed that observers are motivated to avoid an organization as a way to punish it for being unfair. They found that third parties' perceptions of layoff fairness predicted their consumer and employment application intentions. Crosby (1982) reported that feelings of resentment regarding the working conditions of working women were reported not only by the working women themselves, but also by members of other groups, including employed men. Bies and Greenberg (2002) concluded that the sporting goods giant Nike's unfair labor practices in its third-world factories resulted in a poor company image and a drop in the company's stock price and sales. Leung, Chiu, and Au (1993) showed that observers' fairness concerns were related to their sympathy and support for industrial actions. Goldman (1999) found that in layoff situations, observers (that is, friends, family members, coworkers) had a significant influence on victims' decisions to file legal claims of mistreatment. These studies show that perceptions of unfairness and one's subsequent reactions do not depend solely upon personal experiences—they can be initiated vicariously.

It is also relevant to consider that observers such as potential employees, consumers, and investors make decisions about resource allocations based not only on economic concerns but also on certain fairness rules (Kahneman, Knetsch, & Thaler, 1986). In the current economic environment, competition for staff, customers, and investment capital is increasing. Corporate social performance (that is, corporate policies based on justice principles) has been shown to correlate positively with financial performance (Ruf, Muralidhar, Brown, Janney, & Paul, 2001). Thus, third parties' perceptions of employee mistreatment have the potential to erode a company's goodwill and competitive advantage.

Some research has gone one step further in highlighting the character of moral retaliation. Specifically, moral retaliation may have very little to do with self-interest: in fact, people may be willing to take an economic loss in order to punish transgressors who are deemed unfair (Kahneman et al., 1986). In conjunction with design details we omit here, a study by Turillo, Folger, Lavelle, Umphress, and Gee (2002) systematically ruled out each of the following possible sources of self-interest that failed to emerge as a significant determinant of behavior:

- *Public image.* Remaining anonymous, respondents could not get any credit from anyone else for "doing good for goodness' sake."
- *Public message.* Because no one other than the researchers would see the raw data, respondents were not able to use their punishment as a public message that "crime does not pay," thereby negating an explanation of general deterrence (sending a message to the general public) that might otherwise have been possible.
- *Perpetrator deterrence.* To have any hope that the punishment might deter the perpetrator from committing a similar transgression in the future, the respondent would have to believe that the perpetrator was aware of being punished. But variations in such awareness (present versus absent) had no effect, indicating that self-interested deterrence was not influential.

In short, Turillo et al. (2002) found that third parties not only punished moral misdeeds by strangers despite no actual damage to a victim but also despite any positive consequences for themselves or anyone else. In order to capture the motivations that might not necessarily be based in self-interest and that might occur for both victims and nonvictims, we therefore considered it necessary to broaden the definition of retaliation.

Organizational Retaliation Behavior Revised

In an effort to incorporate the potential contribution of moral retaliation to our understanding of workplace retaliation, we expand our definition of ORB to include retaliation as victims' reactions as well as negative sanctions from third parties. We also expand the antecedents of retaliation beyond injustice, our original focus, to (perceived) *wrongdoing* in general. The concept of wrongdoing, as we define it, entails a *wrongdoer* of necessity. "We do not call anything wrong unless we mean to imply that a person ought to be punished in some way for doing it; if not by law, by the opinion of his fellow creatures; if not by opinion, by the reproaches of his own conscience" (J. S. Mill from Ch. 5 of *Utilitarianism,* as quoted by Scanlon, 1998, p. 152).

Specifically, we redefine retaliation as *reactions by disapproving individuals to organizational misdeeds.* They are behaviors that demonstrate censure toward either the misdeed, the doer, or both. Retaliation can be motivated by the provocation of transgressive (morally offensive) organizational conduct by the company or its agents. Retaliation is intended to somehow restore justice, to right wrongs, or at least react with a negative orientation regarding the wrongdoer as a way to enforce the socially relevant moral dictates (punitive sanctioning, retaliation, or retribution rather than necessarily restitution per se). Our revised definition replaces *disgruntled* with *disapproving* because, given the potential functional aspects of retaliation, it may be a perfectly rational, well-reasoned response even in the absence of disgruntlement. Moreover, at least some forms of retaliation can reflect an "it's a matter of principle" reaction that we can conceptualize as almost inherently positive (even noble) in the following sense: *not* to react negatively at all in response to malfeasance (if without punishment, at least with an inner sense of anger and condemnation) is equivalent to condoning wrong, which in turn constitutes a secondary form of wrong (see the discussion of this type of "jural" obligation in Chapter 8 of Fiske, 1991). Our definition implies that the transgressor is accountable, answerable, or culpable for affairs that could and should have been conducted differently (compare with Folger & Cropanzano, 1998, 2001). The source of the punitive sanctioning could originate from a victim or a third party.

Our definition adopts a catholic, ecumenical viewpoint—an attitude of deliberate pluralism reflecting our own moral stance toward retaliation (for a parallel that criticizes defining aggression as inherently bad, see de Waal, 1992, 1996). Our definition of retaliation makes no a priori judgment about its goodness or badness, rightness or wrongness (qua punishment or negative social sanctioning) per se. Rather we propose that evaluative judgments concerning retaliation will vary with the perceiver and circumstances. Research and theory on reactions to unfair treatment, for example, often note that justice, like beauty, is in the eye of the beholder; the same goes both for wrongdoing and retaliation. On the one hand, citizens everywhere collectively endorse and legitimate punishment by the legal system. On the other hand, "on the books" penalty statutes in that same system do not always go without condemnation themselves (for example, opposition to the death penalty).

Our point is such an exceedingly simple one that we need only state the obvious: Sometimes people retaliate against perceived wrongs that either actually are wrong, or that need to be addressed in light of the knowledge that others consider them wrong. Alternatively, retaliation can bring the transgressor's attention to such an instance in a way that few other means might. In that sense, retaliation can be functional for the transgressor.

Having gotten such caveats out of the way concerning the "bad" and the "ugly" possibilities of retaliation, we turn our major attention to the "good"—in quotation marks and with a slightly tongue-in-cheek quality, as evidenced by our playful reference to the title of a spaghetti Western movie. Again, our definition does not endorse retaliation or imply that it deserves the evaluative judgment of being "good," "right," or "moral." Nonetheless, we think we can avoid being prescriptive and yet garner descriptive usage from insisting that not all retaliation should be viewed in exclusively negative terms.

Last, we point to the meanings, functions, or possible purposes of retaliatory harm to transgressors as "perceived" by victims and nonvictim observers (rather than in terms of the transgressors' intentions). If all harm were automatically bad, and if retaliation is defined as having intended harm as a component, then retaliatory harm toward transgressors might seem wrong or bad by definition.

But if harm under some circumstances can have moral legitimacy as deserved punishment (for example, jail time for criminal offense), the mere fact that the transgressor suffers some negative consequences does not qualify as sufficient grounds for condemning victims and nonvictims for retaliation without considering whether retaliation can have some morally appropriate functions and purposes. We now turn our attention to some of the objectives individuals may want to achieve through retaliation.

Functions of Retaliation

The goals of retaliation can be functional and multifaceted.[2] One objective could be to *restore a material balance* between involved parties. In this regard, both victims and observers might be motivated to fix contranormative departures such as underpaying employees for their labor, breaking contracts, or failing to reciprocate. A second objective might be to *educate the offender*. De Waal (1996) reported that even in the animal world, there is a tendency to "teach a lesson to those who act negatively" (p. 159). Folger and Pugh (2002) argued that people retaliate toward rudeness as a way to signal that it costs nothing to be polite. A third objective might be to *restore the social order* between parties. Bies and Tripp (1995), for example, found that employees who have been the subjects of insults from managers express a sense of injustice and feel that some response is necessary to restore justice. Breaches of status rules often require an apology. If no apology is forthcoming, then retaliation is likely to occur (Ohbuchi, Kameda, & Agarie, 1989). A fourth objective might involve addressing *threats to collective material resources*. For example, people are outraged when public funds are embezzled or public property is vandalized, or natural resources are squandered or ruined. A fifth category focuses on *protecting basic cultural and social values of a society*. Examples include protecting the sanctity of human life, the rights of individuals not to be physically violated, and the rights of children to a stable and nurturing environment. The goal of retaliation in these situations is to restore the validity of violated norms or values and to ensure they are not violated further. Miller and Vidmar (1981), for example, found that people are more concerned about punishing the transgressor than about compensating the victim. Finally, perhaps the noblest possible function of ORB occurs when offended parties (especially third parties) seek to punish malfeasance even when the consequences provide no benefit and instead impose a cost on the punisher (Fehr & Gaechter, 2002; Turillo et al., 2002).

We also stipulate, however, that all aspects of the phenomena in question are *as perceived,* and we consider not only third-party perceivers as retaliators but also third-party perceivers who become aware of retaliation by someone else (either the victim or another third party). Thus, in our revised definition of retaliation, several alternative combinations are possible. For example, (a) the victim might retaliate; (b) the observer might retaliate; (c) the victim might not retaliate because he or she does not perceive the transgressor to be a wrongdoer or (despite viewing the transgressor as a wrongdoer) for other reasons such as fear of repercussions from the transgressor; (d) the third party observer might not retaliate because he or she considers the transgressor to be blameless, in which case the designation of a transgressor would then have to refer to perceptions by the victim or another third party.

The Character of Organizational Retaliatory Behavior

As noted earlier, our original list of ORB (Skarlicki & Folger, 1997) was organization-specific. Our discussion here adds to that list by simply noting examples that "sample the space" of the retaliation domain rather than trying to enumerate exhaustively and exclusively all possible instance types. Retaliatory actions can take on numerous qualities and characteristics.

1. Retaliation can be targeted toward the social actor as an *individual* or the *collective* of individuals (for example, the organization).
2. Reactions can be aimed at the perceived *direct* source of the transgression (an individual transgressor such as supervisor, peer, or subordinate or a collective group-entity such as "the company"). Direct retaliation activities can involve actions such as open rebellion and organizing a union. Homans (1961) argued, however, that when the source of an injustice is more

powerful than the individual, attempts to restore justice will be largely *indirect*—directed at a relatively safer target (for example, "ripping off" a customer), especially when such behavior is viewed as having an adverse impact for the transgressor.

3. Retaliation can range from *active* (for example, deliberate disobedience, confronting one's supervisor, going on strike, boycotting, picketing, attempting to motivate others to retaliate) to *passive* response (withdrawing from work, giving the transgressor the silent treatment).

4. Reactions to mistreatment can be *illegitimate-unlawful* (for example, theft of resources, such as time, goods, money) or *legitimate-lawful* (for example, grievance procedure, litigation). We expect that to the degree that lawful and legitimate approaches to retaliation are deemed accessible, effective, unbiased, and not susceptible to counterretaliation, they will be preferred responses to wrongdoing.

5. Individuals can react *verbally* (for example, indulging in negative gossip, bad-mouthing the supervisor to others, attempting to tarnish the transgressor's reputation) as well as *physically* (for example, causing physical damage, sabotaging, dropping a wrench into machinery).

6. Retaliation can be *attempted* or *completed*. We do not assume that wrongdoing needs to involve actual harm, damage, or the like. Our conception of wrongdoing, in that regard, parallels modern treatments of aggression (and, in fact, we suspect that people view transgressions as being in the same "fuzzy set" as aggression, to which they counteraggress or counterattack punitively). An assassin whose bullet misses its target still qualifies as having acted aggressively—and, under morally condemnable circumstances would also qualify as a transgressor. A dentist who causes actual pain is not necessarily aggressive; similarly, actual harm in and of itself does not necessarily constitute wrongdoing.

7. Retaliation can range from *small and minor* (often the tip of the iceberg) to *large and serious* (violence and aggression).

It is evident from this listing that ORB can vary on several dimensions. The usefulness of each of these dimensions for theory and research warrants empirical examination.

Antecedents of Retaliation

In an effort to understand the variables that predict retaliation, we first consider our earlier studies in which we found that distributive, procedural, and interactional justice interacted to predict ORB (Skarlicki & Folger, 1997; Skarlicki et al., 1999). Specifically, our research found that reasonably fair procedures mitigate an individual's retaliatory tendencies that would otherwise be maximized by the combination of having low levels of both distributive and interactional justice. Similarly, we found that when supervisors show adequate sensitivity and concern toward employees and treat them with dignity and respect, the employees seem somewhat willing to tolerate the combination of an unfair pay distribution and unfair procedures that would otherwise contribute to retaliatory tendencies.

Note that referent cognitions theory (Folger, 1986, 1987) predicts interactions between outcome (distributive) and process (procedural) factors (for a review of confirming evidence, see Brockner & Wiesenfeld, 1996). In this case, however, we found that procedural and interactional justice are capable of functioning as substitutes for each other. The outcome by process interaction was significant only at a low level of interactional justice, which suggests that cues about interpersonal insensitivity provide unique information to individuals when deciding whether to "get back at" the transgressor for low outcomes, thereby punishing an organization or its agents perceived blameworthy because of injustice. Also, distributive and interactional justice interacted only at a low level of procedural justice, which suggests that unfair procedures can set the stage for an increase in the retaliation for unfair outcomes, particularly in the presence of low interpersonal justice. We concluded that statistical models allowing only for the test of main effects and two-way interactions (distributive by procedural justice or distributive by interactional justice) might run the risk of being incorrectly specified.

As was noted earlier, perceived unfair employee treatment results in similar retributive motivations on the part of third-party observers. Skarlicki et al. (1998), for example, found that providing voice and an adequate explanation to the layoff victim predicted the fairness judgments and the retributive behavior of third-party observers. Skarlicki et al. also found that observers were capable of deeming the victim to be responsible for the transgressor's treatment. If the victim is deemed responsible or blameworthy for the mistreatment, then morally valued states of affairs (for example, we need to live in a just world) are not violated and retaliation is not necessary. Thus, one important difference between third-party observers and victims in terms of their retaliation tendencies is that third parties might more often than victims attribute blame for the transgressor's treatment to the victim. The victim, in contrast, is presumably more often less likely to perceive that he or she is deserving of mistreatment. Interesting research by Turillo et al. (2002) shows instances in which third-party observers responded to offensive acts with punishment even when they did not know the victim's feelings.

A second source of variance in ORB can arise from between-person differences. Skarlicki et al. (1999), for example, found that two personality variables, namely, negative affectivity and agreeableness, moderated the relationship between fairness perceptions and retaliation. Specifically, fairness perceptions predicted retaliation more so for people who were higher (versus lower) on negative affectivity, and lower (versus higher) on agreeableness. These two variables accounted for ORB variance over and above the variance explained by fairness perceptions alone. This suggests that not all victims will respond to (mis)treatment in the same way. Research is needed to determine whether personality differences would also influence reactions among third parties.

Other examples of between-person variables that could be potentially relevant to the study of ORB include hostile attribution bias and right-wing authoritarianism. People who score high on hostile attribution bias tend to exhibit a low threshold for inferring disrespect from the actions of others (Dodge & Somberg, 1987). Authoritarians tend to be aggressive and punitive toward various persons when such aggression is seen as sanctioned by legitimate authorities (Altemeyer, 1988). Other studies of individual differences (for example, self-construal, Brockner, Chen, Mannix, Leung, & Skarlicki, 2000) also provide promising avenues for future research.

A third source of variance in retaliation can come from personal and social norms. Norms can provide a context for what is deemed fair and right, and also for what is appropriate in terms of retaliation. Being ridiculed by a superior officer, for example, may be tolerated more in some settings (for example, by someone serving in the military) than others (say, a receptionist in a university) because of differences in the organization's culture. In their normative model of justice, Leung and Tong (2001) argued that to the extent that social justice norms are responsible for justice perception and behavior, justice effects will covary with factors that moderate the effects of these social justice norms. In contrast, the effects of personal norms should be more stable and less affected by contextual factors. Norm salience refers to whether a norm is salient in a given situation. Although this notion has not attracted much attention in the justice literature, Mohiyeddini and Schmitt (1997) showed that individuals reacted differently to injustice depending on their sensitivity toward justice, which is conceptualized as a stable individual disposition. We might also speculate that if one is not sensitive about justice, the relevant justice norms are not salient. Norm salience provides another explanation as to why some individuals do not react strongly to the injustice they experienced.

A fourth source of variance in ORB comes from the social information and cues that often exist in a work environment. For example, employees can learn from one another about an organization's or a leader's reputation for being a fair or unfair employer or a fair or unfair manager. Jones and Skarlicki (in press) found that an authority figure's reputation for fairness significantly affected how individuals reacted to their subsequent (mis)treatment. Participants in this study overheard peers discuss the authority figure's reputation (fair, unfair, or control), and then were subsequently exposed to either fair or unfair treatment by the authority. Unfair treatment led to higher levels of retaliation among those participants who had come to expect the authority to be fair than among participants who were not exposed to any social cues. Thus, a reputation as a fair manager paradoxically might be a liability because he or she may be held to a higher standard due to a recipient's expectations, and thus might risk greater disapproval when treating someone unfairly than an authority whose reputation is either unfair or unknown. In summary, social information accounted for ORB above the variance explained by the actual treatment the victim received. Their study underscores the importance of understanding how individuals' retaliation may be affected by numerous variables, some of which are personally experienced and others that may be experienced vicariously.

Reactions to Retaliation

A critical but underresearched question regarding retaliation concerns how others react to someone who retaliates toward a transgressor. Research on whistle blowing, for example, has shown that attempts to "right the wrong" do not always garner positive consequences for the whistle blower. This research has shown that many whistle blowers are dedicated, long-service employees who were finally unable to reconcile unethical organizational practices with their strong sense of individual responsibility. Many whistle blowers, however, are fired, transferred, demoted, and personally intimidated for their lack of conformity. The degree to which whistle blowing is effective at meeting its goals depends upon the level of managerial support, the seriousness of the retaliation, and whether the whistle blower went outside the organization (Near & Miceli, 1986).

There is considerable room for variance in opinions when it comes to the appropriateness of informal sanctions (that is, not applied by a formally legitimized authority acting in an official capacity). Negative social sanctions administered by private citizens (for example, company employees) do not come with the automatic backing of institutionalized legitimacy, and the dangers seen when vigilantism gets excessive loom darkly in the background. Moreover, ORB is like OCB in that it tends to be spontaneous and to lie outside the normal confines of routines. Because it can lie outside the legal system, retaliation does not come neatly categorized in a systematized way that links a known range of specific penalties with a predefined set of categories for wrongdoing (for example, differentiations such as between manslaughter and murder). This "on the fly" inventiveness and spontaneity almost ensures a less-than-perfect fit between the "punishment" and the "crime." When "water-cooler gossip" elicits some bad-mouthing of a supervisor by someone feeling victimized by that person's conduct, for example, various aspects of the conversation itself (specific content and context, who is present, and so forth) could easily overshadow the exact nature of the offense in determining the magnitude of the retaliation expressed by making negative remarks about the supervisor. Indeed, the role of gossip as retaliation constitutes an underresearched area much in need of clarifying investigations. The larger question of how others react to retaliation clearly warrants research attention.

Evolutionary Roots of Moral Emotions

In this section we introduce, as a work-in-progress, a new perspective on understanding when individuals (that is, victims or observers) who become cognizant of a wrongdoing are likely to choose a path of retaliation versus reconciliation. We do so by introducing the broadly generic concept of *deonance,* defined as moral emotions underlying reactions to mistreatment. Deonance is based on the Greek word *deon,* most commonly translated as referring to duty and obligation but also serving as the root for a modifier, *deontic,* often treated as virtually synonymous with morality. We stipulate specific features for three emotions in particular: deontic anger, deontic guilt, and deontic shame.

We propose a highly speculative working hypothesis about interpersonal behavior surrounding moral transgression that involves the evolutionary roots of emotional impulses that can influence retaliatory behavior. In particular, we argue that from the standpoint of "hot" versus "cool" systems (see Ayduk, Mischel, & Downey, 2002; Metcalfe & Mischel, 1999), the "hot" emotional reactions to transgression and its aftermath have their roots in visceral orientations associated with fight-flight arousal. Briefly stated, *deontic anger* refers to the visceral reactions preparatory to a fight or contest. The physical changes that the viscera undergo presume a context that calls for efforts to defeat opposition—that is, to engage in effortful activity to overcome or dominate an opposing force. *Deontic guilt,* however, implies a humble or deferential orientation not unlike surrender or submissiveness. *Deontic shame* is more complex in that its primary orientation involves defensive avoidance (compare with flight), but if confrontations occur and create feelings like being "cornered," these can also elicit defensive hostility to protect threatened self-esteem.

Deontic anger refers to outrage about an offender's transgression. The violation in question is characterized by dominance against the victim (comparable to a "put-down") as well as arrogance of power associated with not accepting a higher authority of moral standard. The latter is the ultimate display of a power-based attempt at dominance in that it signifies acting as though "above the law." For this reason, employees frequently attribute "stepping over the line" to those who have power they can exercise (for example, management), whereas those in power often view its use as legitimate. Note that the same can apply, however, to coworkers as bullies acting "uppity" by transgressing codes of conduct that peers endorse.

We deliberately limit our discussion to emotion rather than behavior. Just as attitudes correlate imperfectly with behaviors because the latter are subject to additional determinants, ours is a partial analysis that examines emotional arousal as a key contributor to the directions in which behavioral tendencies start to be aimed. Such proclivities translate into actual behavior, however, in conjunction with a myriad of other determinants requiring further analysis. People often exercise self-control and pursue the deliberative reflection of "cool" cognition. Such impulses, however, often get subordinated in ways that allow actions with a degree of disregard for contingent consequences and repercussions. Of course, a fully developed model would ultimately need to address, as well, instances in which people undertake thoughtfully orchestrated courses of action with probable consequences in mind—yet are motivated for the sake of congruence with a "hot" impulse (for example, carefully planned revenge based on feeling outraged).

Retaliation Versus Reconciliation

Retaliation, and just how much retaliation to apply, are only a subset of the possible responses to perceived wrongdoing. Tangney (1996) proposed that shame and guilt are emotions likewise relevant in conjunction with an offense—in this case, of course, felt by the offender. We consider them here as separate mediators of subsequent reactions by victims and third parties. In particular, we believe that indications of an offender's guilt as a deontic emotion (that is, in the eyes of victims or third parties) help encourage reconciliation, whereas an offender's shame instead tends to maintain conflictual relations. Shame is connected to a more global assessment of the self, whereas guilt is more concerned with specific behaviors than the whole person. People who experience shame feel less control over their situation and tend to engage in withdrawal behaviors (sometimes mixed with defensive hostility), whereas people experiencing guilt feel they have relatively more control over the situation and are more likely to engage in reparation behaviors.

The basic prediction is simple and familiar (for example, witness apparent signs of the offender's contrition). Victims and third-party observers will increase their reconciliation-facilitating tendencies—that is, will feel appeased—to the extent that they perceive deontic guilt on the part of the offender. Deontic guilt refers to the transgressor demonstrating any of the "four R's" of reconciling apologies: the transgressor accepts *responsibility* for the offense, expresses or manifests *remorse* or a willingness to *repair* or make *restitution* for at least some of the damage, and expresses or manifests *repentance,* indicating a disinclination to offend similarly in the future. Unapologetic transgressors are viewed as committing intentional violations, which provoke greater deontic anger and more retaliation than unintentional acts of harm (Dyck & Rule, 1978). Expressions of remorse take the sting out of an offense because they affirm the status of the victim and acknowledge that the victim has been treated unjustly. Crucial to this construct is that an apology per se is not always so important to reconciliation between the parties as, say, the offender's apologetic manner or sincere intent to change, as *perceived by* the victim or observer.

Whereas complete reconciliation represents one pole of the continuum, continued antagonism and retaliation—fueled by the offender's deontic shame—is the other extreme. Borrowing loosely from Tangney (1996), we see the distinction between deontic guilt and deontic shame as a difference in *approach.* Though either process can be initiated from a single event or offense (and mixtures of both emotions often occur together), deontic guilt describes the reconciliatory movement of the transgressor toward the victim or observer. Deontic shame, in contrast, refers to the transgressor's avoidance of the victim or observer and thus to any of a variety of factors inhibiting or causing movement "away from reconciliation."

Tangney (1996) described shame as concentrating negatively on the self, rather than attending to the victim and such things as the harm or suffering the victim has experienced. Shame turns any victim-related thoughts into "bad self" themes rather than "poor victim" themes. Deontic shame makes the offender want to "crawl under the table," to run and hide or cover up the shameful act. These consequences correspond to the "distancing" behaviors that have been observed in earlier research (Folger & Skarlicki, 1998) in which we interpreted the indication of reduced amounts of time set aside for meeting with a laid-off employee (to deliver the news, for example) as evidence of a desire to avoid contact with the victim. In fact, the role-playing students in those studies indicated distancing tendencies even if the vignette informed them that someone else—their boss, the CEO—might be considered the "true" offender because the boss was the one who had actually made the decision. Hence, it appears that transgressors are not the only individuals who can feel deontic shame. "Guilt by association" can have its counterpart in "shame by association."

A shame-rage syndrome or shame-rage cycles also fall into the category of deontic shame. In effect, when an offender cannot escape accusatory, condemning confrontations that arouse or exacerbate shame, he or she becomes more likely to behave defensively and, hence, often with some degree of hostility. Consider, for example, the spouse or lover who has wronged a partner. Even if the offender initially orients contritely, his or her tendencies to become defensive can be aroused if the other person "won't let go," or continues a diatribe on every aspect of the offender's shameful behavior. Again, these behaviors have power-force and dominance-submission themes at their core (compare with Folger & Butz, in press).

Deontic anger is often associated with the perception that the transgressor has acted in a disrespectful way, as if to signal that the transgressor is dominant to the victim. Intentionality is a key component in determining the amount of deontic anger associated with disrespectful acts. For instance, even actions that do not produce harm can arouse deontic anger if the victim or observer believes that harm was the intended goal of the transgressor's actions (Batson, Bowers, Leonard, & Smith, 2000).

The "perception" of a dominance-like characteristic as central to moral violation, however, may not be salient at the level of full consciousness. Just as people are unlikely to monitor increased levels of hormones in their bloodstream consciously when they are angry, it might be even less likely that we register with full awareness our tacit or implicit coding of an offense along power-force-dominance lines. People might agree, if asked, that a moral violation strikes them as similar to an act of "bullying," but such language might not occur to them without this suggestion. We believe, however, that some type of inner representation of power-force-dominance, when combined with the element of the aversive state, does help to distinguish actions as being offensive in the first place. The aversiveness element and the power-coercion elements go hand in hand, as a display of "might" rather than "right."

In sum, we propose that deontic shame on the part of the transgressor is likely to contribute to greater distancing or defensive hostility by the transgressor as well as a greater likelihood that victims and third-party observers will retaliate for the offense (or at least harbor some ill-will toward the transgressor). In contrast, when the transgressor appears to demonstrate deontic guilt for having committed the offense (for example, apologizing, displaying contrition), there is a greater likelihood that victim and observers will choose the path of reconciliation.

Conclusions

Our earlier research on retaliation (Skarlicki & Folger, 1997; Skarlicki et al., 1999) focused on gaining an understanding of how people react to perceived unfairness in the workplace. We developed a site-specific measure and found that retaliation can be observed, measured, and ultimately understood within a justice framework. Although our definition and approach to measurement has several unique contributions to theory and research, our earlier research was not intended as a treatise on the full scope of retaliation. Our goal in this chapter was to revisit our earlier research and provide a more comprehensive understanding of organizational retaliation by employees.

In this chapter we introduced and used moral retaliation as a way to explicate why individuals other than victims can become upset by mistreatment and be motivated toward retaliation. We noted that the actions involved in retaliation can take on numerous qualities and characteristics ranging, for example, from verbal to physical, from attempted to completed, from small and minor to large and serious. Moreover, we argued that retaliation can take on forms that are functional or dysfunctional to the organization as well as to the retaliator. We proposed that antecedents of retaliation can include situational, personality, and contextual variables, and that models of retaliation may need to consider the interaction of all three. Last, we attempted to understand conditions under which retaliation might be replaced by reconciliation. We proposed that if retaliation and reconciliation lie on two ends of a continuum of reactions to mistreatment, an important future research direction lies in understanding the conditions when retaliation is more versus less likely. We proposed that deontic shame on the part of the transgressor, on the one hand, is likely to lead him or her to avoid the victim of a mistreatment (and sometimes to become defensively hostile), which might increase retaliation tendencies among victims and observers. Deontic guilt, on the other hand, has a greater potential for influencing the transgressor to approach the victim remorsefully, which we proposed will facilitate greater opportunities for reconciliation and forgiveness. This analysis thus reveals prospects for further theorizing and research on ORB that extend considerably beyond the scope of the efforts associated with the introduction of the concept.

Notes

1. Although the term *retaliation* typically has connotations of "getting back at someone who harmed you," in this chapter we broaden the term to include the third parties' perspective (that is, "getting back at someone for having violated a moral or social norm"). We also refer to retaliation rather than punishment, for example, because not all punishment is motivated by retaliation.

2. Although we refer to the goals and functions of retaliation, we do not preclude that at least some retaliators might view their reactions as ends-in-themselves rather than as actions taken as the means for achieving further ends. For a related philosophical discussion of this point, see Metz (2000).

References

Altemeyer, B. (1988). *Enemies of freedom: Understanding right-wing authoritarianism.* San Francisco: Jossey-Bass.

Ayduk, O., Mischel, W., & Downey, G. (2002). Attentional mechanisms linking rejection to hostile reactivity: The role of "hot" versus "cool" focus. *Psychological Science, 13,* 443–448.

Batson, C. D., Bowers, M. J., Leonard, E. A., & Smith, E. C. (2000). Does personal morality exacerbate or restrain retaliation after being harmed? *Personality and Social Psychology Bulletin, 26,* 35–45.

Bies, R., & Greenberg, J. (2002). Justice, culture, and corporate image: The swoosh, the sweatshops, and the sway of public opinion. In M. Gannon & K. Newman (Eds.), *The Blackwell handbook of cross-cultural management* (pp. 320–334). Oxford, UK: Blackwell.

Bies, R. J., & Tripp, T. M. (1995). The use and abuse of power: Justice as social control. In R. Cropanzano & M. Kacmar (Eds.), *Organizational politics, justice, and support: Managing social climate at work* (pp. 131–145). New York: Quorum Press.

Blau, P. M. (1964). *Exchange and power in social life.* New York: Wiley.

Borman, W. C., & Motowidlo, S. J. (1993). Expanding the criterion domain to include elements of contextual behavior. In N. Schmitt, W. Borman, & Associates (Eds.), *Personnel selection in organizations.* San Francisco: Jossey-Bass.

Brief, A. P., & Motowidlo, S. J. (1986). Prosocial organizational behaviors. *Academy of Management Review, 11,* 710–725.

Brockner, J., Chen, Y. R., Mannix, E. A., Leung, K., & Skarlicki, D. P. (2000). Culture and procedural fairness: When the effects of what you do depend on how you do it. *Administrative Science Quarterly, 45,* 138–159.

Brockner, J., & Wiesenfeld, B. M. (1996). An integrative framework for explaining reactions to decisions: Interactive effects of outcomes and procedures. *Psychological Bulletin, 120,* 189–208.

Cooley, C. H. (1902). *Human nature and the social order.* New York: Scribner's.

Crosby, F. J. (1982). *Relative deprivation and working women.* New York: Oxford.

DeMore, S. W., Fisher, J. D., & Baron, R. M. (1988). The equity-control model as a predictor of vandalism among college students. *Journal of Applied Social Psychology, 18,* 80–91.

de Waal, F.B.M. (1992). Aggression as a well-integrated part of primate social relationships: A critique of the Seville statement on violence. In J. Silverberg & J. P. Gray (Eds.), *Aggression and peacefulness in humans and other primates* (pp. 37–56). New York: Oxford University Press.

de Waal, F.B.M. (1996). *Good natured: The origins of right and wrong in humans and other animals.* Cambridge, MA: Harvard University Press.

Dodge, K. A., & Somberg, D. R. (1987). Hostile attributional biases among aggressive boys are exacerbated under conditions of threats to the self. *Child Development, 58,* 213–224.

Dyck, R. J., & Rule, B. G. (1978). Effect on retaliation of causal attributions concerning attack. *Journal of Personality and Social Psychology,* 36, 521–529.

Ellsworth, P. C., & Gross, S. R. (1994). Hardening of the attitudes: Americans' views on the death penalty. *Journal of Social Issues,* 50, 19–52.

Fehr, E., & Gaechter, S. (2002). Altruistic punishment in humans. *Nature,* 415 (6868), 137–140.

Fiske, A. P. (1991). *Structures of social life: The four elementary forms of human relations: Communal sharing, authority ranking, equality matching, market pricing.* New York: Free Press.

Flanagan, J. C. (1954). The critical incident technique. *Psychological Bulletin,* 51, 327–358.

Folger, R. (1986). Rethinking equity theory: A referent cognitions model. In H. W. Bierhoff, R. L. Cohen, & J. Greenberg (Eds.), *Justice in social relations* (pp. 145–162). New York: Plenum Press.

Folger, R. (1987). Reformulating the preconditions of resentment: A referent cognitions model. In J. C. Masters & W. P. Smith (Eds.), *Social comparison, social justice, and relative deprivation: Theoretical, empirical, and policy perspectives* (pp. 183–215). Hillsdale, NJ: Erlbaum.

Folger, R., & Butz, R. (in press). Relational models, "deonance," and moral antipathy toward the powerfully unjust. In N. Haslam (Ed.), *Relational models theory: Advances and prospects.* Mahwah, NJ: Erlbaum.

Folger, R., & Cropanzano, R. (1998). *Organizational justice and human resource management.* Thousand Oaks, CA: Sage.

Folger, R., & Cropanzano, R. (2001). Fairness theory: Justice as accountability. In J. Greenberg & R. Cropanzano (Eds.), *Advances in organizational justice* (pp. 1–55). Stanford, CA: Stanford University Press.

Folger, R., & Pugh, S. D. (2002). The just world and Winston Churchill: An approach/avoidance conflict about psychological distance when harming victims. In M. Ross & D. T. Miller (Eds.), *The justice motive in everyday life* (pp. 168–186). New York: Cambridge University Press.

Folger, R., & Skarlicki, D. P. (1998). When tough times make tough bosses: Managerial distancing as a function of layoff blame. *Academy of Management Journal,* 41, 79–87.

George, J. M., & Brief, A. P. (1992). Feeling good/doing good: A conceptual analysis of the mood at work/organizational spontaneity relationship. *Psychological Bulletin,* 112, 310–329.

Goldman, B. M. (1999). Toward an understanding of employment discrimination claiming: An integration of organizational justice and social information processing theories. *Personnel Psychology,* 54, 361–386.

Greenberg, J. (1990). Employee theft as a reaction to underpayment inequity: The hidden costs of pay cuts. *Journal of Applied Psychology,* 75, 561–568.

Heider, F. (1958). *The psychology of interpersonal relations.* New York: Wiley.

Hogan, R., & Emler, N. P. (1981). Retributive justice. In M. J. Lerner & S. C. Lerner (Eds.), *The justice motive in social behavior: Adapting to times of scarcity and change* (pp. 125–143). New York: Plenum Press.

Homans, G. C. (1961). *Social behavior: Its elementary forms.* New York: Harcourt, Brace & World.

Jones, D., & Skarlicki, D. P. (in press). The effects of overhearing peers discuss an authority's reputation for fairness on reactions to subsequent treatment. *Journal of Applied Psychology.*

Kahneman, D., Knetsch, J. L., & Thaler, R. H. (1986). Fairness and the assumptions of economics. *Journal of Business,* 59, S285–300.

Leung, K., Chiu, W. H., & Au, Y. F. (1993). Sympathy and support for industrial actions: A justice analysis. *Journal of Applied Psychology,* 78, 781–787.

Leung K., & Tong, K. (2001, August). *Toward a normative model of justice.* Paper presented at the International Round Table on Innovations in Organizational Justice, Vancouver, British Columbia.

Metcalfe, J., & Mischel, W. (1999). A hot/cool system analysis of delay of gratification: Dynamics of willpower. *Psychological Review,* 106, 3–19.

Metz, T. (2000). Censure theory and intuitions about punishment. *Law and Philosophy,* 19, 491–512.

Miller, D. T. (2001). Disrespect and the experience of injustice. *Annual Review of Psychology,* 52, 527–553.

Miller, D. T., & Vidmar, N. (1981). The role of justice in punishment reactions: A social psychological analysis. In M. J. Lerner & S. Lerner (Eds.), *The justice motive in social behavior: Adapting to times of scarcity and change* (pp. 145–172). New York: Plenum Press.

Mohiyeddini, C., & Schmitt, M. J. (1997). Sensitivity to befallen injustice and reactions to unfair treatment in a laboratory situation. *Social Justice Research,* 10, 333–353.

Near, J., & Miceli, M. P. (1986). Retaliation against whistleblowing: Predictors and effects. *Journal of Applied Psychology,* 71, 137–145.

Ohbuchi, K. I., Kameda, M., & Agarie, N. (1989). Apology as aggression control: Its role in mediating appraisal of and response to harm. *Journal of Personality and Social Psychology,* 56, 219–227.

Organ, D. W. (1988). *Organizational citizenship behavior: The good soldier syndrome.* Lexington, MA: Lexington Books.

Rawls, J. (1971). *A theory of justice.* Cambridge, MA: Harvard University Press.

Ruf, B., Muralidhar, K., Brown, R. M., Janney, J. J., & Paul, K. (2001). An empirical investigation of the relationship between change in corporate social performance and financial performance: A stakeholder theory perspective. *Journal of Business Ethics, 32,* 143–156.

Scanlon, T. M. (1998). *What we owe to each other.* Cambridge, MA: Harvard University Press.

Skarlicki, D. P., Ellard, J. H., & Kellen, B.R.C. (1998). Third-party perceptions of a layoff: Procedural, derogation, and retributive aspects of justice. *Journal of Applied Psychology, 83,* 119–127.

Skarlicki, D. P., & Folger, R. (1997). Retaliation in the workplace: The roles of distributive, procedural, and interactional justice. *Journal of Applied Psychology, 82,* 434–443.

Skarlicki, D. P., Folger, R., & Tesluk, P. (1999). Personality as a moderator in the relationship between fairness and retaliation. *Academy of Management Journal, 42,* 100–108.

Tangney, J. P. (1996). Conceptual and methodological issues in the assessment of shame and guilt. *Behavior Research and Therapy, 34,* 741–754.

Turillo, C. J., Folger, R., Lavelle, J. J., Umphress, E. E., & Gee, J. O. (2002). Is virtue its own reward? Self-sacrificial decisions for the sake of fairness. *Organizational Behavior and Human Decision Processes, 89,* 839–865.

Van Dyne, L., Cummings, L. L., & Parks, J. M. (1995). Extra-role behaviors: In pursuit of construct and definitional clarity: A bridge over muddied waters. *Research in Organizational Behavior, 17,* 215–285.

CHAPTER 14

On Incivility, Its Impact, and Directions for Future Research

Christine M. Pearson, Christine L. Porath

He was being unfair, unprofessional. In meetings he'd roll his eyes if he didn't agree with a point being made, or he disliked the individual making it. Or he'd turn his back and start to do something else while someone was still talking. It seemed like he lacked respect and disregarded others' feelings and opinions. (Manager)

Until the incident occurred, I looked up to this man, he was a leader in our company. But he was so nasty to me and for no reason. All I could do was replay in my mind what had happened, trying to figure out why. . . . I could actually feel myself disconnecting at work and it seemed like the right thing to do. (Manager)

We know it when we see it. Our greeting is ignored by a colleague we pass in the hall; we're inconvenienced by teammates because they have let deadlines slip; no one bothers to introduce us to a newcomer when we join a group of coworkers in the lunchroom; we find that the copy machine we're about to use has been left empty . . . again. From the receiving side, when workplace incivility occurs, others have disregarded our feelings and behaved rudely or uncaringly toward us. Certainly, uncivil behavior reflects a lack of common courtesy in the workplace. But does incivility really matter? Are these low-grade dark side behaviors worthy of organizational attention?

For more than six years, we have been studying the antecedents, characteristics, and consequences of workplace incivility. We have interviewed and conducted focus groups with more than six hundred employees, managers, and professionals in varying industries across the United States. We have collected survey data from an additional sample of more than 1,200 employees, managers, and professionals representing all industrial categories in the United States and Canada. The grand conclusion: incivility does matter. Whether its costs are borne by targets, their colleagues, their organizations, their families, their friends outside work, their customers, witnesses to the interactions, or even the instigators themselves, there is a price to be paid for uncivil encounters among coworkers.

We define workplace incivility as *low-intensity deviant (rude, discourteous) behavior with ambiguous intent to harm the target in violation of workplace norms for mutual respect* (Andersson & Pearson, 1999). This definition sets incivility apart from many other types of deviant behavior at work. Empirical distinctions between incivility and other forms of deviance have been confirmed (Pearson, Andersson, & Porath, 2000; Pearson, Andersson, & Wegner, 2001).

However, because there has been a rapid proliferation of concepts and constructs that subsume negative or deviant workplace behavior (O'Leary-Kelly, Duffy, & Griffin, 2000a), we highlight how incivility varies from other forms of "dark side" organizational behavior. Workplace deviance concepts differ in terms of the motivation for the act, the target of the act (for example, individual, organization, or both), and the breadth of behaviors comprised (Duffy, Ganster, & Pagon, 2002; O'Leary-Kelly et al., 2000a). We briefly explain how workplace incivility varies from several related concepts by using the dimensions suggested by O'Leary-Kelly and colleagues (2000a).

Incivility and Employee Deviance

Employee deviance is behavior that violates institutionalized norms and, in doing so, threatens the well-being of the organization, its members, or both (Robinson & Bennett, 1995). Several differences between incivility and workplace deviance exist. First, whereas employee deviance comprises behaviors against individuals, it also includes behaviors aimed at the organization. Incivility, however, includes only behaviors directed at another individual. Second, whereas employee deviance includes more serious forms of deviance such as aggression and violence, incivility includes only minor forms of interpersonal deviance (for example, avoiding, insulting).

Incivility, Violence, and Workplace Aggression

Whereas violence is an intense form of deviant behavior and includes physical aggression (Averill, 1983; Baron & Neuman, 1996; Dietz, Robinson, Folger, Baron, & Schulz, 2003; Neuman & Baron, 1998; Tedeschi & Felson, 1994), incivility is less intense and excludes any forms of physical contact. Unlike other, less intense forms of aggression, the intent to harm or injure someone is ambiguous in the case of incivility. That is, one may behave uncivilly with the intent to do harm, or one may behave uncivilly out of ignorance or oversight.

Incivility and Other Individual Behaviors in Organizations

Similarities and differences also exist between incivility and other individual behaviors in organizations, such as petty tyranny (Ashforth, 1994), abusive supervision (Tepper, 2000), and interactional injustice (Bies & Moag, 1986). For example, incivility is similar to petty tyranny and abusive supervision. Both constitute lack of consideration toward others and self-aggrandizement on the part of the instigator, and they feature a similar level of intensity. However, incivility need not be committed top-down as in the case of petty tyranny (Ashforth, 1994). Rather, incivility can occur from superior to subordinate, from subordinate to superior, or between peers.

Incivility has also been compared with interactional injustice, since both constructs include perceptions of unfairness or mistreatment. However, although interactional injustice identifies behaviors of decision makers that are associated with unfair treatment during the enactment of specific organizational procedures (Bies & Moag, 1986), incivility can occur between any members of an organization. Moreover, incivility can occur outside the procedural context.

Although the disrespectful words and behaviors that comprise incivility are not dramatic, they occur with regularity at work (Cortina, Magley, Williams, & Langhout, 2001; Ehrlich & Larcom, 1994; Graydon, Kasta, & Khan, 1994; Pearson & Porath, 2002). Ten percent of the people we surveyed witness incivility daily within their workplaces. Approximately 20 percent claim that they are the direct targets of incivility at work at least once per week (Pearson & Porath, 2002). In another recent study, 71 percent of employees reported experiencing incivility in the past five years (Cortina et al., 2001). Also, many people seem to believe that incivility, in general, is on the rise. In a poll of more than two thousand respondents conducted by Public Agenda, an American research firm, nearly four out of five believe that lack of respect and courtesy is a serious problem. Three out of five believe things have gotten worse recently (Remington & Darden, 2002).

Given the prevalence of workplace incivility and the problems associated with its occurrence, we believe that it is important to continue exploring the phenomenon and its impact. In this chapter, we begin by discussing the antecedents of incivility. We follow with details on the nature of uncivil interactions, including information about the targets and instigators, as well as the context of the interaction, as based on a growing stream of research. Then we highlight the impact of incivility on a number of stakeholders within the organization: the target, the instigator, witnesses, and the organization at large. Also, we discuss the secondary impact of incivility, that is, the impact on those outside the immediate encounter, including customers, as well as the target's family and friends. The detrimental impact on so many stakeholders underscores a need for careful attention by managers and further study by scholars. Therefore, we conclude by considering recommendations for organizations as well as directions for future research.

Antecedents to Uncivil Behavior: Responding to Social and Organizational Trends

Social critics offer up various causes and culprits that foster incivility from the infiltration of technology to ineffectual education systems to absentee parenting to media exploitation of life's dark side to the general decline of interest and investment in the "common good." In the quest for individual rights, some contend that we have become a society driven by social isolation, self-expression, and disdain for authority and norms. Putnam (2000) is convinced that a rudeness epidemic has taken root in our desires to be social isolates. Bellah and colleagues (1985) decry the creeping erosion of a sense of community that was once the strength of America. Carter (1999) and Howard (2002) contend that self-indulgence, the "Slapjack" assertion of individual rights, and the disabling of authority are upending our abilities to cooperate and share the values of "civilized" behavior.

Certainly, changes in the nature of work affect civility, or the lack thereof (Andersson & Pearson, 1999; Pearson, Andersson, & Porath, forthcoming). Employees we have encountered at all levels in the course of our research claim that the corporate drive for "lean and mean" has developed in seemingly perverse ways: leanness and meanness have turned inward. Intense pressures to succeed turn colleague against colleague. In interviews and focus groups, executives and leaders tell us that corporate schemes to rearrange, recast, or reduce the workforce often make long-standing norms and values irrelevant. Part-timers, subcontractors, temporary workers, as well as long-term employees disenfranchised by budget cuts and downsizing, seem to have little need or desire to adhere to former organizational expectations for building civility. With an eye focused squarely on survival in the short-term, why would a worker invest in relationships with individuals or an organization that may be severed at any time?

For nearly half of our questionnaire respondents, work and life stresses such as time pressure have constrained their ability and desire to invest in or maintain relationships. As we have been told repeatedly in focus groups, workers are challenged by managing dual careers, single-parenting, and working across multiple time zones. These trends absorb time and attention, making the maintenance of casual relationships a luxury and, for some, civility just one more sponge.

Across industries, we have heard that an organizational focus on individual, short-term contributions and outcomes may also foster incivility. According to our respondents, there are a number of reasons for this focus. Respondents at various levels of their organizational hierarchies have conjectured that it is easier for an organization to track and evaluate an individual employee's singular contribution than to track how that individual, over time, contributes to or depletes group or organizational outcomes. Furthermore, dollars gained or output delivered are easily transferable and, therefore, appealing for the individual's balance sheets: they can quantify these credits to demonstrate value added within or outside the organization. Credits that can be counted may help buffer workplace instability. Viewed from this field perspective, it is not surprising that some individuals look out for themselves at work and, in so doing, focus on short-term contributions above all. Such actions reap the immediate payoffs in many organizations. In such settings where how much you do obscures how you do it, civility may seem superfluous.

The push for individual productivity may displace civility. Many of us find ourselves in a frenzied state at work, constantly pressed for time. According to 42 percent of workers whom we surveyed, this type of time pressure fuels uncivil behavior. As some told us, it simply takes too long to be nice. For those time-pressured workers who believe this line of thinking, civility is irrational.

As work environments have gone casual, some long-standing cues about respect and politeness may have vanished, as well (Andersson & Pearson, 1999; Gonthier, 2002; Martin, 1996). To be sure, our data do not suggest that wearing Dockers to work breeds incivility. But smart aleck remarks and careless bantering may erode authority and strain relationships, and accommodations for antisocial conduct can pave the way to uncivil behavior.

The Nature of Uncivil Interaction: Key Players and Organizational Context

Civility has little to do with adhering to stringent parameters of etiquette. Rather, it is a demonstration of common courtesy that comprises sensibility and respectful treatment of others (Carter, 1999; Elias, 1982; Morris, 1996; Wilson, 1993). Whereas civility helps build relationships through empathy and regard, incivility can erode relationships and cause interpersonal alienation. Overt aggression, direct threats, sexual harassment, and physical contact exceed the bounds of incivility: no such behaviors fall within the construct, nor are they included in our research. Instead, as we have noted, incivility is a low-intensity social interaction between two or more parties at work, to which one takes some degree of offense. Generally, incivility begins between a nuclear dyad of "target" and "instigator."

The Target and the Instigator

Being the target of incivility is an equal opportunity role. Across our data, we have found that men are just as likely to be on the receiving end of workplace incivility as are women. However, when it comes to doling out incivility, men take the lead. According to the experiences of our questionnaire respondents, an instigator is more than twice as likely to be male. Also, for 60 percent of our respondents, instigators held positions of higher organizational status than their targets. When both of these demographics are considered, our findings suggest that men are seven times as likely to instigate uncivil words or deeds on someone of lower status than on someone of higher status. By contrast, our data demonstrate that female instigators are equally likely to behave uncivilly toward their superiors as toward their subordinates, but less likely to be uncivil to their peers (Pearson et al., 2000; Porath & Pearson, 2000).

As to preferences, our data show that both male and female instigators prefer targets of their own sex slightly. Instigators, on average, tend to be six years older than their targets. And those who behave uncivilly tend to have spent two more years in their organization than their targets have, although neither role tends to be that of a newcomer (Pearson et al., 2000; Porath & Pearson, 2000). According to our data, targets averaged thirty-five years of age, whereas instigators averaged forty-one years.

The Organizational Setting

Our data confirm that incivility occurs in all types of industries, in organizations ranging in size from two to more than 100,000 employees. In the organizations where incivility occurred, employees were generally polite to one another, treated one another with respect, and showed understanding for one another. The vast majority of our respondents believed that their organizations were responsive to sexual harassment, overt threats, and physical attacks among employees. If such deeds were to occur where they worked, more than four out of five questionnaire respondents reported that perpetrators would be reprimanded or career constraints would be levied against them. However, in the case of workplace incivility, less than half of targets believed that instigators would face any type of a reprimand.

The Reach of Workplace Incivility

> Incivility reinforces isolation and reduces responses and choices. It shuts people down. They go into a shell and don't come out. You lose the benefit of others' ideas, creativity, and participation. (Manager)

Think of a time when a colleague treated you uncivilly. Chances are, the impact affected other people, as well, both directly and indirectly. There may have been witnesses to the encounter who watched or listened to see how the situation would evolve. Also, witnesses may have come to your rescue or reassured you afterwards, or they may have modeled the behavior, experimenting with their own versions of incivility on other unsuspecting employees. We have found that if you're a man, chances are that you spread the word among colleagues and attempted to build a supportive coalition among your subordinates; if you're a woman, you probably solicited support from family members or friends outside work (Porath & Pearson, 2000). If sufficiently troubled, you may have reported the situation also to your boss, your company's human resources expert, or even your attorney.

When someone is disrespectful, rude, or insensitive toward others at work, the impact is felt not only by the target, but also by other internal and external stakeholders, as depicted in Figure 14.1. We have found that virtually all targets (94 percent) describe the encounters to someone (Pearson et al., 2000; Pearson & Porath, 2002). Sixty-nine percent tell family members about what has happened. Half tell friends outside work. For targets who spread the word within the organization, two out of three people describe the situation to peers, half tell their superiors, and about one in five tell their subordinates. All of these reports cause a cascade of harm. As a result, coalitions can emerge in defense of the

Figure 14.1. The Reach of Workplace Incivility.

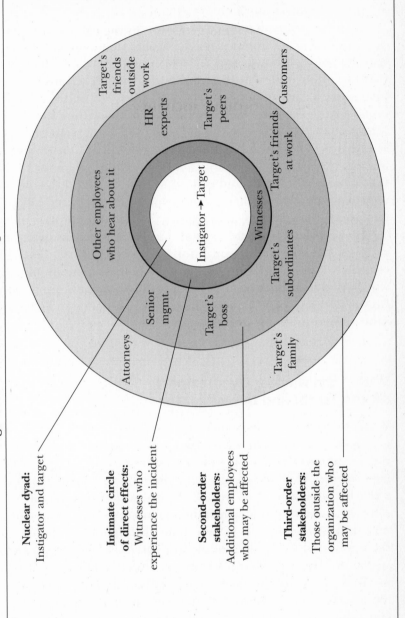

Nuclear dyad:
Instigator and target

Intimate circle of direct effects:
Witnesses who experience the incident

Second-order stakeholders:
Additional employees who may be affected

Third-order stakeholders:
Those outside the organization who may be affected

Instigator → Target

Witnesses

Other employees who hear about it

Attorneys

Senior mgmt.

HR experts

Target's peers

Target's boss

Target's subordinates

Target's friends at work

Target's family

Target's friends outside work

Customers

target and the instigator's reputation can be tarnished far beyond the bounds of those within the intimate circle of direct effects, who are present during the uncivil event.

Incivility can lead to words and deeds that are harmful to the organization in additional ways. According to our data, more than half of the targets waste work time worrying about the incident or planning how to deal with or avert future interactions with the instigator. Nearly 40 percent reduced their commitment to the organization; 20 percent told us that they reduced their work effort intentionally as a result of the incivility, and 10 percent of targets said that they deliberately cut back the amount of time they spent at work (Pearson et al., 2000). In a study of more than four thousand attorneys, Cortina and colleagues (2002) found that people who experienced incivility at work experienced reduced job satisfaction, increased stress, and a desire to leave their profession.

Incivility may also lead to more indirect effects on the organization. Others in the organization may model uncivil behavior, especially if such behavior goes unpunished. At a minimum, incivility tends to damage organizational culture in subtle, and harmful ways. At its worst, incivility bleeds over to many stakeholders inside and outside the organization.

Within the Nuclear Dyad: Impact on the Target and the Instigator

When workers experience incivility, most lose respect for the instigators. Also, more than a third find that their commitment to the organization diminishes as a direct result of the incivility that they experienced. Half told us that they contemplated changing jobs as a result of the encounter. Less than one-fourth of the targets were satisfied with the ways in which their companies handled the situation, and as a result, fully 12 percent actually left their jobs to avoid the low-intensity incivilities of the instigator (Pearson et al., 2000).

Some targets of incivility respond directly against the instigator. In overt forms, they may engage in rounds of tit-for-tat behavior, sometimes escalating each round as the incivilities mount: you learn that your colleague has left your name off of an important report that you contributed to, you respond by ignoring his requests for information; he "neglects" to tell you about an important deadline, you barge into his office and insult his competence; he shoves you out the door. In this case, incivility has escalated to violence in several quick rounds. In more covert forms, the target may try to avoid or ignore the instigator. Although this behavior is subtler and may seem harmless to the instigator, it can have long-term negative impact. By "disappearing" herself (Fletcher, 1998, 1999), the target may make it more difficult for the instigator to obtain resources or to link into informal communication lines. As a result, even when the target holds less formal power than the instigator, it may be more difficult for the instigator to get work done or to hear important information in a timely manner.

The target can also respond indirectly by undermining the instigator's reputation as he describes the situation within or outside the organization. Or the target can act in ways detrimental to the organization. In some extreme cases, targets damage or steal property belonging to the instigator or the organization in an effort to even the score (Pearson et al., 2000).

Our research (Pearson & Porath, 2002; Porath & Pearson, 2000) suggests that instigators who are uncivil to males should expect to enter into a cycle of incivility, "duking" it out. Male targets tend to respond by reciprocity, whether in aggressive or passive ways, especially when they are treated uncivilly by male instigators. Female targets, however, are more likely to respond by avoiding their instigators.

Impact on Second-Order Stakeholders

Incivility not only affects the target, the instigator, and the organization, but also can have ripple effects on a second order or a third order of stakeholders. When we refer to second- or third-order stakeholders, we do not mean to imply that the effects are less intense for these individuals. Rather, these designations suggest the stakeholders' proximity to organizational effects. By these labels, we wish to indicate the distance that the rippling must travel. Regarding the "intimate circle," stakeholders experience the interaction personally. "Second-order" stakeholders are affected more directly because they are members of the organization in which the incivility occurs. "Third-order" stakeholders are affected by their affiliation with the nuclear dyad, those in the intimate circle, or those of second-order status.

Incivility can tarnish the satisfaction, motivation, and organizational commitment of employees outside the nuclear dyad as well as those employees outside the intimate circle. When employees see or hear about uncivil behavior, they report that they lose work time avoiding or worrying about the event (or how they may become the instigator's next targets). Similarly, productivity may wane among these employees, either purposefully or unknowingly. The responses of witnesses and others who hear about the incident may be similar to the target's responses. Whether actions are intended to support a colleague, "do what's right," or displace their own frustrations about the incivility, there is potential for the initial uncivil interaction to cascade into secondary reactions from second-order respondents.

Impact on Third-Order Stakeholders

In addition to inciting second-order spillover from those within the organization, there is an additional wave of outsiders who may feel the effects of incivility. As discussed above, many targets involve family and friends by telling them about the interaction. These external, third-order stakeholders may be called upon for support, whether emotional (as in the case of family and friends) or legal (as in the case of attorneys). They may even empathize with the target, sharing common sentiments of frustration and anger.

Although admitted only infrequently by questionnaire respondents, incivility can also spew over to customers when they encounter targets, witnesses, or other second-order stakeholders who are annoyed, upset, or distracted about what has happened. In extreme cases, instead of experiencing friendly service, customers may find disgruntled employees anxious to spread their disregard for the company.

What Can Be Done to Curtail Workplace Incivility?

For organizational members who are concerned about the impact of incivility, there are many options for action. This is especially true for those at the top, who have a strong hand in establishing norms and modeling behavior. In the course of our research, many targets have indicated that they hold organizational leaders at fault for avoiding their responsibilities to curtail the phenomenon before serious harm occurs. We offer a variety of actions for organizations that take seriously the negative repercussions of workplace incivility.

Set Expectations and Adhere to Them at the Top

The first step in curtailing incivility is for senior management to determine what they see as appropriate standards of conduct. In many organizations, expectations about civility are documented in the mission statement or employee policy manuals. Simple examples abound: "Treat each other with respect" (Boeing); "Trust and respect the [employee]" (Saturn); "We treat each other with respect and dignity" (AT&T). By setting expectations, the organization has provided guidance for employees, as well as establishing a minimal acceptable type of behavior against which transgressions can be measured.

Of course, the impact of leadership does not stop here. Among the most troubling comments we have heard across industries are descriptions of situations where incivility is not only condoned, but also modeled by senior management. In fact, one-fourth of respondents report that they have modeled uncivil behavior after witnessing the incivilities of their leaders. Where incivility is condoned, employees throughout the company learn quickly that incivility is acceptable. In the worst cases, they come to believe that it is the way to assert power and ascend to the top. If executives are serious about curtailing incivility, their own behaviors toward colleagues and among themselves must be civil.

In one setting in which we were observers, it was not uncommon for the two leaders of the organization to air their disagreements in shouting matches in public hallways. In this particular case, although most workers did not model the behavior themselves, the uncivil words and deeds of the few often left their targets in tears. And when eruptions occurred, there was nowhere for targets to find organizational support. Some exited the organization and some "shut down" (as we were told repeatedly). After all, these targets had witnessed or heard about blatant disrespect at the very top. Why would they assume their situations would be given any credence? Employee respect for authority was, at best, intertwined with confusion regarding the behaviors of the individual leaders themselves.

Recruit and Select Civil Employees

Like any other change in organizational norms, it is extremely difficult to turn an uncivil environment into a civil one. But to the extent that management values civility among employees, it is important to consider this issue even as early in the employment life cycle as selection. Many managers and human resources personnel tell us that they are able to obtain only "name, rank, and social security number" when following up on references. However, in organizations that are serious about civility among employees, we hear different results. Every effort is made to tap into personal contacts in order to get a deeper sense of the top job candidates' characteristics as colleagues. Sometimes this requires spending additional time and thought tapping into personal and professional networks across an array of organizational employees before hiring an individual.

In one of the worst cases we have heard, all reference checks for a perspective organizational leader were conducted by the placement service that had been commissioned to fill the position. Sadly, it took little time after he was hired for this instigator's typical workplace behaviors to surface. Almost as soon as he was hired, his uncivil behaviors began to seep into the organization. The unsettling nature of this normative shift was intensified when incumbent senior managers realized that they had been but a phone call away from professional colleagues elsewhere who could have told them precisely what it was like to work with this individual.

Encourage and Listen to Feedback, and Take Action as Needed

If an organization strives to maintain civility, infractions must be dealt with swiftly. Occasionally, some employees will displace stress or disappointment on fellow workers as an exceptional occurrence. Even in these cases, when disrespect and disregard result, the behavior should not go unnoticed by management. When unacceptable actions are not corrected, they may be deemed appropriate. In the case of repeat instigators, it is imperative to curtail the behaviors if a respectful environment is to thrive. When someone repeatedly treats colleagues, subordinates, or superiors badly, she must be held accountable for her actions. Ignoring such behavior can foster multiple forms of cascading or spillover (as we have noted above) that can taint the entire workplace.

Many employees complain that they have become careless about their own behaviors because, in many of their organizations, nobody seems to care how people treat one another (Pearson & Porath, 2002). A typical scenario we have heard repeatedly is that of an instigator who is moved from one department to another because his incivility is loathsome, but his managers are not willing to stand up to him. In some cases, we have heard that the special talents or connections of the instigator seem to protect him. In others, a blind eye of management has been attributed to an unwillingness to confront "messy" interpersonal issues. In any case, the phenomenon of incivility is worthy of additional organizational attention.

Directions for Future Research

Incivility is a new construct in organizational research that promises relevance to other streams of deviance research, as well as resonance for employees, managers, and organizations. Studies have emerged from the perspective of the target primarily (Cortina et al., 2001, 2002; Pearson et al., 2000, 2001). Most research has addressed the behavioral responses of targets as related to their instigators and their organizations (Cortina et al., 2001; Pearson et al., 2000; Zauderer, 2002). Additional interesting issues and questions abound. We review several promising directions next.

Within the Nuclear Dyad: The Instigator's Perspective

To understand the full scope of incivility, lingering critical questions concern the instigator's view: why do people behave uncivilly toward coworkers? What organizational or individual characteristics are antecedents to the instigator's uncivil behavior? At what point, if ever, are instigators aware of the impact of their words and deeds as they affect their targets, witnesses, and themselves? Recent work on moral disengagement and its link to antisocial behavior (Duffy, Tepper, & O'Leary-Kelly, 2003) may provide interesting intersections for learning more about the instigator's actions. We acknowledge that social desirability may affect data collection, especially from the instigator's view. For those interested in conducting such research, however, understanding the instigator's perspective could inform individual and organizational means of addressing incivility in fundamental ways.

Within the Intimate Circle of Direct Effects: The Witness's Perspective

Those who study incivility have alluded to the affects on additional stakeholders. But to our knowledge, no empirical findings have been reported yet. Based on extensive anecdotal data (Pearson et al., 2001), witnesses seem to play a role in the escalation and cascading of incivility. Related research by Duffy and colleagues (2003) found that employees who witness supervisors displaying undermining behaviors led the witnesses to disengage their own sanctions against antisocial behavior, for example. What are the contingencies under which witnesses intensify versus mitigate an instigator's actions? Most targets characterize their instigators as cunning (Pearson et al., 2000). If their characterizations are accurate, does this imply that instigators are mindful about their audiences? For example, do the witnesses of incivility (like those who are targeted) tend to be of lower organizational power than the instigator? Does incivility occur only in front of people who have insufficient power to wield an immediate formal retribution?

Effects on Second-Order Stakeholders

We know little about the effect of incivility beyond the intimate circle encompassing instigator, target, and witnesses. To our knowledge, no one has examined the effects on the target's boss or subordinates or on other employees who simply hear about incivility. Our data from the target's perspective suggest that other employees are affected behaviorally and emotionally. Future research might track organizational conditions or individual characteristics that affect the tendencies of these stakeholders to support the target during and after the incivility. We have also theorized that incivility spills through the organization when rudeness seems to be acceptable behavior (Andersson & Pearson, 1999). Research by Robinson and O'Leary-Kelly (1996) lends further credence to this theorizing. They found that people who work in groups that display high levels of aggressive actions are more likely to display aggressive actions themselves. But under what circumstances do second-order stakeholders in incivility model the behavior? In what ways are their behaviors affected by a subtle deviance that occurs at a distance?

Effects on Third-Order Stakeholders

We know that many targets describe their situations to family and friends outside work. But as yet there are no findings about how these third-order stakeholders react when someone they care about has been disregarded. From a somewhat different perspective, it would also be interesting to determine whether the incivility experienced at work is displaced by the target on family or friends outside work. Does workplace incivility lead to domestic incivility?

Linking the behavior of targets to their subsequent attitudes and actions toward customers could be important to scholars and managers. A better understanding of the back-of-the-house treatment of employees could enrich the emerging stream of research regarding the employee-customer interface. Ultimately, does the customer lose when employee-to-employee incivility occurs? When they come in contact with a customer, what individual attributes or organizational conditions lead employees to control or displace their responses to being the target of a coworker's incivility? And how does this form of emotion management (Hochschild, 1983) affect the target and the organization in the long run?

The Power of Organizational Norms

The issue of "norms" raises a wide variety of questions that are worthy of future investigation. Since norms provide guidelines for individuals about the appropriateness of an activity (Ashford, Rothbard,

Piderit, & Dutton 1998; Jackson, 1965), organizational norms should also influence the appropriateness of politically deviant behaviors (O'Leary-Kelly, Griffin, & Glew, 1996; Pearson, 1998). Employees may perceive the appropriateness of such behaviors when they see role models engaging in deviance or when organizational authorities fail to discipline deviant behavior (Pearson, 1998). Similarly, O'Leary-Kelly and colleagues (1996) have theorized that interpersonally deviant behaviors are sensitive to reinforcement (Bandura, 1973; Krebs & Miller, 1985) and, therefore, should be anticipated when organizational norms encourage them.

Data suggest that organizational norms may influence incivility. For example, Robinson and O'Leary-Kelly (1998) found that group norms for antisocial behavior predicted the extent to which coworkers engaged in antisocial behavior. Also, findings demonstrate that social norms influence workplace aggression (Greenberg & Alge, 1998) and theft (Greenberg, 1998).

Incivility has been defined, in part, as a transgression against typical workplace norms (Andersson & Pearson, 1999). Norms are somewhat fluid: they may vary by context or culture and they tend to shift over time (Schein, 1990, 1992). We know that in the workplace, values develop and are enacted in subcultures in patterns that may match, parallel, or oppose overall organizational norms (Martin, 1992; Robinson & O'Leary-Kelly, 1998). It would be fruitful to study how incivility affects and is affected by subcultural (for example, workgroup or plant) and organizational norms or by transfer through emotional contagion (Barsade, in press). This focus could be particularly compelling if studies were conducted in organizational subcultures where behavioral expectations about employee-to-employee interactions were not just incongruous but also in dramatic opposition. Do employees adjust their levels of civility as they move from one environment to another? When it comes to the subtleties of incivility, how do individuals and the organizations reconcile these differing expectations and behaviors?

The Interface with Globalization

The effect of cultural differences as related to workplace incivility raises important questions related to globalization. Research illustrates that expectations (among team members) vary across cultures (Gibson & Zellmer-Bruhn, 2001). However, we know nothing about how organizations adapt expectations about civility as they venture into new cultural arenas, despite the probability that norms of varying settings will collide. Do definitive boundaries between what is civil and what is not reflect the expectations of the home office or the regional outpost? To what extent are organizations cognizant of these challenges when they expand globally? Earley and Erez (1997) detail challenges faced when (transplanted) managers learn new expectations in new contexts. However, we know little about how transplanted employees learn to alter behavior in alignment with shifts in expectations so that they do not behave uncivilly. We might expect that inadvertent incivility is greatest when employees enter new terrain, but is there a "honeymoon" period of adjustment during which rude behavior from newcomers is tolerated?

Incivility and Diversification

On a broader reach, those interested in studying processes and consequences of diversification might examine how and where incivility seeps into a diverse environment. How does diversification affect incivility? As employees who reflect new worldviews join the workforce, do the parameters of incivility become more elastic or more brittle? Do organizational attempts to integrate those who are "different" (for example, through initiatives such as sensitivity training or policy setting) increase or reduce the occurrences and intensities of incivility? Will a civil work environment smooth diversification? Does better understanding lessen our tendency to be uncivil, or does it enhance our ability to target rudeness subtly?

Calculating Financial Costs

No empirical research of which we are aware has traced specific financial costs attributable to incivility. Certainly, this information would be useful to research and practice. We know that the subtleties of incivility take a toll from targets, witnesses, instigators, and their organizations, but what is a reasonable bottom-line estimate for such transgressions? We are intrigued by a smattering of responses to our research that indicates that "being nice" makes workers "soft" and that incivility is an efficient means of sorting out workplace "wimps." Through financial analyses, it would be fascinating to determine whether there are settings in which incivility actually contributes to profitability.

Concluding Thoughts

As a new construct, incivility offers challenging and rewarding opportunities. For those drawn to the "dark side" via the complexities of interpersonal interaction, incivility is intriguing. Extending what (little) is known about the phenomenon cannot only build scholarly understanding of this form of workplace deviance but can also make an impact on the subtleties of daily interactions among workers and managers.

References

Andersson, L. M., & Pearson, C. M. (1999). Tit-for-tat? The spiraling effect of incivility in the workplace. *Academy of Management Review,* 24(3), 452–471.

Ashford, S. J., Rothbard, N. P., Piderit, S. K., & Dutton, J. E. (1998). Out on a limb: The role of context and impression management in selling gender-equity issues. *Administrative Science Quarterly,* 43, 23–57.

Ashforth, B. E. (1994). Petty tyranny in organizations. *Human Relations,* 47, 755–778.

Averill, J. R. (1983). Studies on anger and aggression: Implications for theories of emotion. *American Psychologist,* 38, 1145–1160.

Bandura, A. (1973). *Aggression: A social learning analysis.* Englewood Cliffs, NJ: Prentice-Hall.

Baron, R. A., & Neuman, J. H. (1996). Workplace violence as a workplace aggression: Evidence on their relative frequency and causes. *Aggressive Behavior,* 22, 161–173.

Barsade, S. G. (in press). The ripple effect: Emotional contagion and its influence on group behavior. *Administrative Science Quarterly.*

Bellah, R. N., Madsen, R., Sullivan, W. M., Swidler, A., & Tipton, S. M. (1985). *Habits of the heart: Individualism and commitment in American life.* Berkeley: University of California Press.

Bies, R. J., & Moag, J. S. (1986). Interactional injustice: Communications criteria of fairness. In R. Lewicki & B. Sheppard (Eds.), *Research on negotiation in organizations* (Vol. 1, pp. 43–55). Greenwich, CT: JAI Press.

Carter, S. L. (1999). *Civility: Manner, morals and the etiquette of democracy.* New York: Basic Books.

Cortina, L. M., Magley, V. J., & Lim, S.G.P. (2002). *Individual differences in response to incivility in the workplace.* Paper presented at the Annual Meeting of the Academy of Management, Denver.

Cortina, L. M., Magley, V. J., Williams, J. H., & Langhout, R. D. (2001). Incivility in the workplace: Incidence and impact. *Journal of Occupational Health Psychology, 6,* 64–80.

Dietz, J., Robinson, S. L., Folger, R., Baron, R. A., & Schulz, M. (2003). The impact of community violence and an organization's procedural justice climate on workplace aggression. *Academy of Management Journal, 46*(3), 317–326.

Duffy, M. K., Ganster, D. C., & Pagon, M. (2002). Social undermining at work. *Academy of Management Journal, 45,* 331–351.

Duffy, M. K., Tepper, B. J., & O'Leary-Kelly, A. M. (2003). *The role of moral disengagement in antisocial work behaviors.* Working paper, University of Kentucky, Gatton College of Business and Economics.

Earley, C., & Erez, M. (1997). *The transplanted executive: Why you need to understand how workers in other countries see the world differently.* New York: Oxford University Press.

Ehrlich, H. J., & Larcom, B.E.K. (1994). *Ethnoviolence in the workplace.* Baltimore: Center for the Applied Study of Ethnoviolence.

Elias, N. (1982). *The history of manners.* New York: Pantheon.

Fletcher, J. K. (1998). Relational practice: A feminist reconstruction of work. *Journal of Management Inquiry, 7,* 163–186.

Fletcher, J. K. (1999). *Disappearing acts: Gender, power and relational practice at work.* Cambridge: MIT Press.

Gibson, C., & Zellmer-Bruhn, M. (2001). Metaphors and meaning: An intercultural analysis of the concept of teamwork. *Administrative Science Quarterly, 46,* 274–303.

Gonthier, G. (2002). *Rude awakenings: Overcoming the civility crisis in the workplace.* Chicago: Dearborn Trade Publishing.

Graydon, J., Kasta, W., & Khan, P. (1994). Verbal and physical abuse of nurses. *Canadian Journal of Nursing Administration,* Nov-Dec., 70–89.

Greenberg, J. (1998). The cognitive geometry of employee theft: Negotiating "The Line" between taking and stealing. Dysfunctional behavior in organizations: Non-violent dysfunctional behavior. In R. W. Griffin, A. O'Leary-Kelly, & J. M. Collins (Eds.), *Monographs in organizational behavior and industrial relations* (Vol. 23B, pp. 147–193). Stanford, CT: JAI Press.

Greenberg, J., & Alge, B. (1998). Aggressive reactions to workplace injustice. In R. W. Griffin, A. O'Leary-Kelly, & J. Collins (Eds.), *Dysfunctional behavior in organizations,* Vol.1: *Violent behavior in organizations* (pp. 119–145). Greenwich, CT: JAI Press.

Hochschild, A. R. (1983). *The managed heart: Commercialization of human feeling.* Berkeley: University of California Press.

Howard, P. K. (2002). *The collapse of the common good.* New York: Ballantine Books.

Jackson, J. (1965). Structural characteristics of norms. In I. D. Steiner & M. Fishbein (Eds.), *Current studies in social psychology* (pp. 301–308). New York: Holt, Reinhart and Winston.

Krebs, D. L., & Miller, D. T. (1985). Altruism and aggression. *Handbook of social psychology* (pp. 1–71). New York: Random House.

Martin, J. (1992). *Cultures in organizations: Three perspectives.* New York: Oxford University Press.

Martin, J. (1996). *Miss Manners rescues civilization.* New York: Crown Publishers.

Morris, J. (1996). Democracy beguiled. *The Wilson Quarterly,* Autumn, 24–35.

Neuman, J. H., & Baron, R. A. (1998). Workplace violence and workplace aggression: Evidence concerning specific forms, potential causes, and preferred targets. *Journal of Management,* 24, 391–419.

O'Leary-Kelly, A. M., Duffy, M. K., & Griffin, R. W. (2000a). Construct confusion in the study of antisocial work behavior. In G. R. Ferris (Ed.), *Research in Personnel and Human Resource Management* (Vol. 18, pp. 275–303). Stamford, CT: JAI Press.

O'Leary-Kelly, A. M., Griffin, R., & Glew, D. (1996). Organization-motivated aggression: A research framework. *Academy of Management Review,* 21, 225–253.

O'Leary-Kelly, A. M., Paetzold, R. L., & Griffin, R. (2000b). Sexual harassment as aggressive behavior: An actor-based perspective. *Academy of Management Review,* 25, 372–388.

Pearson, C. M. (1998). Organizations as targets and triggers of aggression and violence: Framing rational explanations for dramatic organizational deviance. *Research in Sociology of Organizations,* 15, 197–223.

Pearson, C. M., Andersson, L. A., & Porath, C. L. (in press). Workplace incivility. In P. Spector & S. Fox (Eds.), *Counterproductive workplace behavior.* Washington, D.C.: American Psychological Association.

Pearson, C. M., Andersson, L. A., & Porath, C. L. (2000). Assessing and attacking workplace incivility. *Organizational Dynamics,* 123–137.

Pearson, C. M., Andersson, L. A., & Wegner, J. A. (2001). When workers flout convention: A preliminary study of workplace incivility. *Human Relations,* 54, 1387–1420.

Pearson, C. M., & Porath, C. L. (2002). *Rude awakening: Detecting and curtailing workplace incivility.* London, Ontario: Richard Ivey School of Business, University of Western Ontario.

Porath, C. L., & Pearson, C. M. (2000). *Gender differences and the behavior of targets of workplace incivility: He 'dukes' it out, she 'disappears' herself.* Paper presented at the Annual Meeting of the Academy of Management, Toronto, Ontario, Canada.

Putnam, R. D. (2000). *Bowling alone: The collapse and revival of American community.* New York: Simon & Schuster.

Remington, R., & Darden, M. (2002). *Aggravating circumstances: A status report on rudeness in America.* New York: Public Agenda.

Robinson, S. L., & Bennett, R. J. (1995). A typology of deviant workplace behaviors: A multidimensional scaling study. *Academy of Management Journal, 38,* 555–572.

Robinson, S. L., & O'Leary-Kelly, A. (1998). Monkey see, monkey do: The role of role models in predicting workplace aggression. *Proceedings of the Academy of Management,* 288–292.

Schein, E. (1990). Organizational culture. *American Psychologist,* February, 109–119.

Schein, E. H. (1992). *Organizational culture and leadership,* 2nd ed. San Francisco: Jossey-Bass.

Tedeschi, J. T., & Felson, R. B. (1994). *Violence, aggression and coercive actions.* Washington, D.C.: American Psychological Association.

Tepper, B. (2000). Consequences of abusive supervision. *Academy of Management Journal, 43,* 178–190.

Wilson, J. Q. (1993). *The moral sense.* New York: Free Press.

Zauderer, D. G. (2002). Workplace incivility and the management of human capital. *Public Manager, 31*(1), 36–43.

CHAPTER 15

The Methodological Evolution of Employee Theft Research

The DATA Cycle

Jerald Greenberg and Edward C. Tomlinson

Enron, GlobalCrossing, WorldCom, and Adelphia Communications are more than just four companies whose bankruptcies captured headlines in 2002. They have become icons of the greediness that has plagued the executive suite in recent years. Their respective chief executives, Kenneth Lay, Gary Winnick, Bernard Ebbers, and John Rigas, were forced to resign in disgrace amidst allegations of epic accounting scandals that enabled them to line their pockets with hundreds of millions of dollars at the expense of shareholders, creditors, and employees (Dwyer, 2002).

Such episodes of "white collar crime," as it is commonly known, often are elusive because they are masterminded by high-ranking officials whose allegiance to the company typically goes unchallenged (Podgor & Israel, 1997). Moreover, because "cooking the books" and then selling one's stock at artificially inflated prices is essentially an indirect form of profiting, it tends not to be considered in the same class as the common thief who takes home a few extra dollars from the cash drawer. Of course, the impressive scale of grand theft makes it special—and its sheer boldness makes it the stuff of headlines. Yet when all is said and done, both are engaging in "unauthorized appropriation of company property," behaving in ways consistent with the definition of employee theft (Greenberg, 1995, p. 154).

In this chapter our primary focus is on the less dramatic, yet equally compelling, form of employee theft commonly referred to as petty theft or pilferage. Petty theft is characterized by "taking items in small quantities and/or items of limited value" (Greenberg & Scott, 1996, p. 118). The actions of petty thieves take an enormous bite out of the bottom lines of the companies that employ them. In fact, it has been claimed that petty thieves account for more business losses than grand theft committed by white collar criminals (Emshwiller, 1993; Lipman & McGraw, 1988). Thus, although the factory worker who takes home some tools for his personal use or the office worker who takes home a few pencils for her kids are unlikely to be the subject of newspaper stories, their actions constitute theft and, as a whole, are a formidable source of corporate loss. Although employee theft occurs at all levels in all types of businesses, it is especially problematic in the retail sector, where U.S. retailers lost over $15.24 billion from employee theft in 2001 alone, making it the most costly form of larceny (Hollinger & Davis, 2002).

Because of its social and business significance, it is not surprising that both scientists and practitioners in many different disciplines have paid considerable attention to the issue of petty theft. Among clinical psychologists, for example, efforts to understand employee theft have been framed as a matter of deviant personality (for example, Wolman, 1999); industrial psychologists see it as a problem resulting from ineffective selection procedures (Sackett, 1994); criminologists consider it as stemming from vices, such as gambling and substance abuse (Robin, 1969); and specialists in workplace security see it as the inevitable result of inadequate auditing, monitoring, and control procedures (Jaspan, 1974). More recently, organizational scientists (for example, Greenberg, 1997a, 1997b, 1998; Greenberg & Scott, 1996) have drawn on their knowledge of interpersonal and managerial dynamics in conceiving of employee theft as a form of social behavior (for related efforts focusing on other forms of workplace deviance, see Murphy, 1993; Robinson & Greenberg, 1998).

As one might suspect, this diversity of professional focus and purpose has left us with a broad array of conclusions about employee theft based on an even broader array of research investigations—data-gathering efforts ranging from highly rigorous and carefully controlled studies to ones that rely on the most casual of observations by observers. Consequently, we are blessed with a wealth of findings from an unusually broad array of research methods, thereby creating an opportunity to assess the extent to which research findings regarding employee theft flow in a logically consistent manner. The purpose of this chapter is to describe the evolution of research methods that have been used to examine the antecedents of employee theft, and to assess the state of the science. This analysis gives us an opportunity to describe the manner in which research on employee theft has evolved over the years, and to glean insight from this evolution that can be used to advance our understanding of other counterproductive (and hence, difficult to study) behaviors in the workplace. Our intent is not to identify and describe all research on employee theft in a comprehensive manner. Instead, we have focused on major representative studies that reflect the primary issues addressed and the principal research methods used to elucidate them.

Our vehicle for organizing these efforts will be a framework in which we identify four primary purposes for conducting research on employee theft and various methods with which each primarily tends to be associated. We begin by presenting this framework.

The DATA Cycle

Our analysis of the research literature on employee theft leads us to recognize that studies of employee theft have been conducted with each of four loosely linked research objectives in mind. These include research conducted for descriptive purposes, analytical purposes, theoretical purposes, and applied purposes. These may be described as follows:

- *Descriptive studies.* The most basic research investigations are those conducted for descriptive purposes—that is, to describe the phenomenon of interest. These studies seek to paint a picture of the overall nature and extent of the phenomenon of employee theft and to identify its major parameters.
- *Analytical studies.* Research investigations in the analytical category are conducted for purposes of identifying the inter-

relationships between variables likely to affect theft behavior. They build upon and extend knowledge derived from descriptive studies.

- *Theoretical studies.* Research considered theory-based is designed to test theoretical propositions about the antecedents of employee theft likely to be derived from analytical studies. Theoretical studies usually are based on one or more underlying theoretical conceptualizations.

- *Applied studies.* Research also is conducted for purposes of assessing the effectiveness of various techniques of curtailing employee theft. The most rigorous of such applied studies are based upon interventions suggested by theoretical studies.

Potentially—and at least to some extent, in reality—these four research purposes are linked in cyclical fashion. In other words, descriptive studies aid in the conduct of analytical studies, which in turn, facilitate theoretical studies, which are closely in service to applied studies. We envision these types of research as phases in a cycle of research conducted over the years. Drawing on the initials of each of these four phases—descriptive, analytical, theoretical, and applied—we refer to this as the DATA cycle. (For a graphic summary, see Figure 15.1.)

By presenting employee theft research in terms of systematic efforts designed with specific purposes in mind, we highlight the

Figure 15.1. The DATA Cycle.

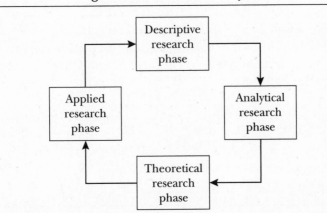

tendency for research within each phase to be characterized by the use of specific methods. This is not surprising insofar as certain research techniques are better suited to some purposes than others. In each of the next four sections of this chapter we will identify the major types of research conducted within each of the four research phases. (For an outline of what follows, see Table 15.1.)

Descriptive Research Phase

The earliest investigations of employee theft were purely descriptive in nature. That is, they were performed for purposes of gaining insight into employee theft by "getting into the heads" of those who commit it. Appropriately, the research was exploratory in nature insofar as it was not guided by carefully developed theoretical notions—or by any preconceived conceptualizations at all, for that matter. Research of this type represents a logical launching point for investigating employee theft (or most any other phenomenon, for that matter) insofar as it provides an opportunity to identify some of the key variables involved and the parameters within which they operate. Given this purpose, it is not surprising that the earliest studies of employee theft were qualitative in nature (specifically, involving open-ended interviews, observations, and

Table 15.1. Phases of the DATA Cycle
and Associated Predominant Research Methods.

Primary Research Purpose	Associated Predominant Research Methods
Descriptive research	Observations
	Open-ended and semi-structured interviews
Analytical research	Interviews
	Questionnaires
Theoretical research	Lab experiments
	Field experiments and quasi-experiments
	Questionnaires
Applied research	Intervention experiments

combinations thereof) research methods that lend themselves to the exploratory nature of descriptive research.

Open-Ended and Semi-Structured Interviews

One of the first investigations of employee theft was conducted by the criminologist Cressey (1953), as reported in his book *Other People's Money*. Cressey's objective was to discover what made embezzlers different from those who don't embezzle—specifically, what led people who were entrusted with other people's money to violate that trust, and how they operated. With this in mind, he conducted open-ended interviews with 133 convicted embezzlers who were incarcerated in three prisons. Some of the interviews were recorded verbatim in writing, whereas in some other cases notes were not taken at all, thus casting doubt on the accuracy of data reporting. Problems also exist in this research with respect to sampling insofar as Cressey included only felons who were cooperative, thereby raising questions about the generalizability of his findings. Probably the most serious indictment, however, is that Cressey did not include a control group against which to compare the responses of the embezzlers, thereby making it impossible to achieve his stated objective.

Notwithstanding these limitations, which are typical of descriptive studies, the purely descriptive function of the investigation was well-served. Cressey reported several findings that identify the underlying motives of embezzlers. Specifically of interest to criminologists, he discovered that embezzlers suffered serious financial problems and had opportunities to resolve them by engaging in embezzlement. These findings predate more scientifically respectable criminological evidence of the same phenomenon by three decades (for example, Hollinger & Clark, 1983). Cressey also reported results that offered important psychological insight into the criminal mind. Specifically, none of the embezzlers considered themselves as having done anything wrong! They used complex rationalizations to maintain their self-images as trustworthy individuals, findings in keeping with the cognitive and intrapersonal dynamics of employee theft further noted and elaborated upon almost a half-century later (Dabney, 1995; Greenberg, 1999). Notably, they reported taking company property in response to unfair treatment, but given that they perceived what they did as readily justifiable, they did not regard themselves as crooks, but considered themselves to be wrongfully imprisoned. For example, Cressey interviewed a hotel clerk who explicitly noted that stealing was his way of redressing a complaint against his company: "I had this fancy grievance against the company, and the owner was not straightening it out fast enough. . . . You might say it [my theft] was in the spirit of retaliation" (p. 59).

Insight into the rationalizations used to neutralize ostensibly criminal behavior also was provided by Gouldner's (1954) interview study of gypsum factory workers. Notably, Gouldner reported an "indulgency pattern" in which supervision was so lax that foremen regularly permitted factory workers to take home company-owned tools and raw materials for their personal use. Indeed, because this behavior was permitted by supervisors, employees had no reason to regard it as inappropriate. Still, it is clear that supervisors were a party to employee theft by condoning such behavior.

Although also descriptive in intent, a more sophisticated interview study was undertaken by Horning (1970) almost two decades after Cressey's (1953) and Gouldner's (1954) seminal work. Horning (1970) conducted semi-structured interviews with 106 unionized male, blue collar employees of an electronics assembly plant. These were workers from different departments within the company who had different degrees of access to items that were most likely to be stolen. The interviews focused on employees' attitudes toward property ownership, toward theft in general, and their awareness of group norms regarding theft. To get a high response rate (over 88 percent), the researcher courted the assistance of the most influential employees, who served as "informal emissaries" by encouraging their colleagues to participate. And to ensure that participants would not be afraid to share their feelings about the taboo topic under investigation, interviews were conducted off the worksite—at the workers' homes, in fact.

Horning (1970) found that theft by employees was, by and large, a solitary activity rather than a group activity. It was tolerated only insofar as the items taken were of "uncertain ownership" and to the extent that their absence failed to draw supervisory attention. Furthermore, strict norms existed regarding precisely what items could be taken and the acceptable quantities (for example, it was considered acceptable to take home some power tools so long as their absence failed to slow down production). Organizational stories were widely used to communicate messages about the limits on employee theft that existed within the organization's culture. For example, tales often were told about certain workers who were chastised for stealing so much that work suffered, thereby sending the message that there are strict limits on the amount of theft that was accepted. Likewise, it was communicated clearly that limits were imposed on the nature of the property that could be taken. For example, norms permitted only the taking of small items considered to have little value to anyone, such as unused hardware (for example, screws, nuts, and bolts) and scrap parts. Norms strongly prohibited the taking of property that clearly belonged either to other employees or to the company.

Similar norms were found to exist among garment factory workers interviewed by Sieh (1987). In this case, work groups strongly regulated the parameters of theft. Taking items of negligible worth (zippers, pins, old patterns, and fabric scraps) was considered acceptable, as was the practice of throwing an extra garment or two out the window to be picked up later. However, selling these items to a competitor or flaunting the theft by wearing stolen items to a company function was strictly prohibited. These findings are in keeping with the findings of other interview studies that also reported the existence of norms regulating the nature and extent of theft in other industries (for example, norms regulating what food items are considered acceptable for waiters to take from their restaurants; Hawkins, 1984).

Observation Studies

Several investigations have been conducted in which researchers infiltrated work groups, making various observations and gathering information from the workers they befriended. One study using this technique is Mars's (1974) classic investigation of crews of British dock workers—twenty-six men with whom he interacted closely over an eighteen-month period. Although Mars neither worked with the men nor directly observed theft, he was told a great deal about theft practices by his informants. His major conclusion was that over time, normal work roles are adjusted to serve widespread norms of theft that develop within crews. In other words, theft among employees becomes institutionalized. For example, it was considered part of crane operators' jobs to stack crates sufficiently high as to conceal their nefarious activities from management. Others whose vantage points gave them good visual access over the docks were expected to stand watch against management and to send a warning signal when necessary. Mars (1974) learned that the dock crews developed careful rules regarding theft that were designed to sustain their enterprise. Among other rules, the so-called "taxing" of ships only could be done in proportion to the size of the delivery. Taking too much merchandise from any one ship, it was feared, would raise questions that they preferred not to answer.

Also noteworthy is Ditton's (1977) ethnographic research, in which he worked undercover at a bread bakery in England. This allowed him to conduct impromptu unstructured interviews by disguising them as casual conversation among coworkers. Ditton's most interesting finding was that theft of small amounts of bread was so prevalent among employees that the company was forced to raise production levels to meet the demand. Typically, theft took the form of delivery drivers shorting orders to their various accounts so they could take home some loaves for themselves. In some instances, drivers routinely shorted so many deliveries that they were able to set up their own private businesses by selling stolen loaves to other stores. This practice was so widespread that it came to be considered appropriate. In fact, although management officials did not condone this practice, they did nothing to stop it from occurring. After all, they reasoned, this practice represented a relatively inexpensive way of promoting workers' morale by supplementing their wages.

Multiple-Method Studies

Several descriptive studies were conducted that relied on multiple research methods. The most ambitious of these is Dalton's (1959) decade-long qualitative investigation of theft among employees of three factories and a department store. The data in this study came from interviews with employee-informants, work diaries, direct observation, and information gathered by informally socializing with employees. Although the research was not conducted to test any preconceived conceptual ideas, data collection focused on the informal social norms that condone or encourage employee theft. Dalton's major conclusion was that management officials were involved widely in helping their employees engage in theft of company property. In many cases, taking company property was viewed as a legitimate form of informal payment and was not regarded as inappropriate. In fact, the taking of company property was regarded as "side payments" that managers could use to supplement the far less flexible, formal wage system. At one of the factories studied, foremen went so far as to manufacture items for employees to take. Within the department store Dalton studied, it was commonplace for items to be intentionally damaged in a superficial manner so that they could be sold to employees at drastically reduced prices. Theft was so widespread, in fact, that networks of reciprocal arrangements developed within the store: employees in one department regularly helped those in other departments take merchandise in exchange for like assistance granted at some other time.

Conclusions Drawn from Descriptive Studies

Despite the fact that the early interview studies, observation studies, and multiple-method studies were plagued with sampling problems and considerable potential for bias, there can be no doubt that they served a valuable descriptive function in the research literature on employee theft. They not only identified some dynamics that later were tested in more sophisticated research, but they also went a long way toward inspiring later, more rigorous scientific investigations. Indeed, these are precisely the kind of "launching-pad functions" that descriptive research studies are expected to serve. Specifically, two major themes consistently emerge from descriptive studies:

- That employee theft is governed by informal social processes experienced at work
- That employee theft results from perceptions of unfair treatment on the job

Although the scientists conducting these descriptive studies may not have acknowledged explicitly that the "merely descriptive" nature of their findings would pave the way for more systematic investigations, it is clear that their work did precisely this. In other words, these descriptive studies inspired later researchers to perform more analytical investigations. We now will examine the methods and conclusions of this phase of research.

Analytical Research Phase

With a broad base of descriptive accounts from which to seek inspiration, employee theft researchers had a useful basis for moving to the next step—analyzing the interconnections between variables related to employee theft. As in many descriptive studies, researchers taking a more analytical approach also relied upon the use of interviews. However, as we will indicate, these were more highly focused and designed to assess relationships between variables associated with theft. Given the narrowed focus of analytical research compared to the broader based, descriptive research, it makes sense that investigations falling into this category also make use of questionnaires—the ubiquitous tool of the modern social scientist. Our description of analytical research on employee theft will distinguish between investigations relying on the use of interviews and those relying on the use of questionnaires. Within each research method, our discussion will differentiate between investigations focusing primarily on informal social processes and those focusing primarily on unfair treatment by employers.

Interview Studies

Here we will demonstrate how interview studies have been used to move from the descriptive research phase to the analytical research phase. This analysis will examine separately research bearing on both of the general conclusions drawn from descriptive research.

Informal Social Processes

Building on Cressey's (1953) descriptive accounts of the role of group norms in employee theft, Altheide, Adler, Adler, and Altheide (1978) thoroughly interviewed eight informants in different occupations over a ten-year span. Despite the small number of participants in the Altheide et al. (1978) investigation, their findings are noteworthy. They found that social norms not only accounted for theft among employees, but also that these norms governed a wide range of behavior among employees and that adherence to them influenced the degree to which people were accepted by others.

For example, among department store workers, Altheide et al. found that the employees who were held in highest esteem by their coworkers were those who displayed the results of their theft efforts. In other words, theft was not only condoned among one's peers (as Horning, 1970, reported in his purely descriptive account), but Altheide et al. took this a step further by demonstrating that employees regularly shared information about their theft with their colleagues as a means of cultivating a positive image of themselves among them. For example, one of Altheide et al.'s informants who worked at a large department store admitted that he took several books after he was chastised by his manager. Feeling belittled, he showed the books to his coworkers in an effort to demean the manager in the eyes of his coworkers. This made the employee feel better not only because he got to reciprocate the belittlement (albeit only vicariously given that the manager did not know of his actions), but also because it raised his esteem among his coworkers.

Interview studies of an analytical nature also have contributed to our knowledge of the complex nature of the way theft is regulated by employees. We see this, for example, in Mars's (1982) systematic interviews with employee-informants who worked in offices. Like Dalton (1959), Mars also reported that theft was widespread and deeply entrenched into organizational culture, "woven into the fabric of people's lives" (p. 17), as he put it. In fact, theft was considered such an essential aspect of life in many organizations that it was considered a regular part of people's incomes—so much so, in fact, that in many jobs, informants told Mars that it was considered abnormal for them not to steal. The analytical research by Mars took things beyond simple description. Within some work groups, he found that theft was carefully coordinated among employees according to closely regulated social norms. Notably, the more employees contributed to the practice of theft, the more they were rewarded by their colleagues with opportunities to engage in forms of theft that were regulated by the work group as a whole, such as making personal long-distance phone calls. The more a worker aided and abetted theft by one's colleagues, the higher status he or she was accorded, and the more time that individual was allotted in unauthorized phone usage. In fact, the most helpful employee thieves received the greatest reward—impunity while making expensive international calls.

Analytical interview studies also have extended earlier descriptive research (for example, Gouldner, 1954) that show that norms involving the appropriateness of theft sometimes involve supervisors who condone such acts. Whereas the earliest descriptive studies found that supervisors sometimes permitted—or even encouraged—acts of theft, follow-up analytical studies have painted a far more complex picture of the dynamics involved. For example, Liebow (1967) reported that there is a high level of duplicity in this practice: "The employer knowingly provides the conditions which entice (force) the employee to steal the unpaid value of his labor, but at the same time, he punishes him for theft if he catches him doing it" (pp. 38–39). In a fascinating analysis, Altheide et al. (1978) note the complex socio-linguistic mechanisms involved in this process. Whereas the primary public injunction is verbal in nature (for example, "don't steal"), it often is accompanied by a metaphoric secondary injunction that is nonverbal, such as "the wink"—a gesture that contradicts the verbal statement, sending the message, "I have to tell you that you can't steal, but of course you can." For example, an employee may be told that he can purchase products at "give away" (wink) prices. At the same time, any attempt to open the closed meaning of the wink by directly questioning its interpretation is sure to meet with denial (for example, "Of course you cannot steal; I didn't say you could"). Noting the complexities of meta-communicative tactics of this sort is one of the key contributions of analytical studies.

Unfair Treatment

Another interesting extension of purely descriptive accounts of employee theft may be seen in several interview studies showing that employee theft was not indiscriminate. Rather, it often occurred among employees who felt that they were denied something that was coming to them. In other words, several interview studies alert us to a connection between theft and feelings of injustice. For example, Zeitlin (1971) interviewed a clothing store employee, who said, "I feel I deserved to get something additional for my work since I was not getting paid enough" (p. 26). Similarly, a copper miner who was complaining about the dangerous conditions under which he worked told Altheide et al. (1978), "I'll take this wrench; I mean, they owe it to me" (p. 105). Likewise, Analoui and Kakabadse (1991) interviewed a British barmaid who confessed to stealing money (by pocketing cash given to her to pay for a round of drinks) because the restaurant manager refused to compensate her for the taxi fare she needed to get home after working late. Although she usually was quite honest, on this occasion the woman felt completely entitled to take the money, saying, "I'll get a taxi and he'll pay for it" (p. 52).

Analytical studies reported not only that people steal in an effort to restore feelings of justice, but also that their willingness to do so is affected by the nature of the social treatment they received from their employers. As an illustration, consider the comments of a young woman interviewed by Altheide et al. (1978) who worked in two record stores at which she was paid identical wages for doing the same work. At one store she felt mistreated by her boss, and said, "I stole there all the time . . . because I didn't like him at all" (p. 105). In contrast, she felt very well treated by the manager of the other store, noting that there, "you just didn't want to steal; there was no reason to . . . you liked to work there" (pp. 105–106). Together, these findings are important insofar as they establish a link between fairness and theft that subsequently was examined in more rigorous theory-based experiments we will discuss later (for example, Greenberg, 1990, 1993a, 2002). Specifically, they suggest that inequitable outcomes lead people to steal but so, too, does poor interpersonal treatment (which researchers consider another form of injustice; Greenberg, 1993a).

Questionnaire Studies

Having demonstrated that interview studies have been used to move employee theft from the descriptive research phase to the analytical research phase, we now will do the same for questionnaire studies. Here, too, we will examine separately research bearing on both of the general conclusions drawn from descriptive research.

Informal Social Processes

Some of the most extensive investigations of employee theft involved giving questionnaires to employees for purposes of analyzing social dynamics uncovered in earlier descriptive studies. For example, Horning (1970) described theft among factory workers as being primarily solitary in nature. However, subsequent questionnaire studies found that solitary theft also occurred among other groups of employees, including those working in convenience stores (Terris & Jones, 1982) and in department stores (Robin, 1969). Further questionnaire research also has examined the conditions under which theft is likely to be performed by individuals acting alone as opposed to a group effort. Specifically, Hollinger and Clark (1982) revealed that acts of theft tend to be solo in retail and manufacturing facilities because within those industries people tend to work alone as opposed to working in small groups (or at least that was the case at the time the research was conducted). However, among people who usually work in small groups, theft activities tended to reflect the coordinated theft of group members. For example, in his descriptive study, Mars (1974) described how groups of dock workers cooperated with one another in a fashion that made it possible for them to steal cargo from ships. However, later analytical research by Mars (1982) revealed that whether theft occurred alone or in groups depended on the nature of the jobs. Because employees in some types of jobs (for example, teams of miners, trash collection crews, and airline flight crews) work in concert with others naturally, theft among people in these professions tends to occur in groups as well. In fact, Mars (1982) refers to these employees as "wolves" because they generally "steal in packs" (p. 32). In one extreme case, the entire staff of parking meter collectors in San Francisco coordinated their efforts so carefully and maintained such strong norms promoting theft that they managed to steal $3 million over a six-year period (Bullard & Resnick, 1983).

Analytical questionnaire research also sheds new light on the rather broad idea suggested by descriptive studies that group norms support deviant behavior (Gouldner, 1954). For example, in a mail survey of over nine thousand employees selected randomly from three industries in three metropolitan areas of the United States, Hollinger and Clark (1982) asked respondents to rate the extent to which various formal sanctions (for example, dismissal) and informal sanctions (for example, ostracism by coworkers) would be effective in deterring theft. The results were clear: respondents claimed to be more strongly influenced by informal, social sanctions than by formal, organizational sanctions.

At least, in part, this appears to be the result of the tendency for informal sources of control used by colleagues to be immediate in nature (that is, coworkers give immediate feedback when informal norms regarding theft are broken insofar as such actions may threaten their own opportunities to engage in theft). By contrast, the threat of formal sanctions may be a less compelling source of control because in most cases, theft acts have to be extreme before action is likely to be taken—if it is even taken at all (Snyder, Broome, Kehoe, McIntyre, & Blair, 1991). And inaction in response to theft reinforces it by sending the message that such activity may be considered acceptable (Carter, 1987). Indeed, a survey of retail employees reported that over half reported taking merchandise but that only about 16 percent admitted feeling any guilt for these actions (Tatham, 1974). This is in keeping with further studies showing that justifications for engaging in theft are the result of a collective rationalization process (Backman, 1985). Commenting on his own questionnaire findings, for example, Hollinger (1989) said, "Justifications for theft are passed from the experienced employees to the newly hired. When substantial numbers of the work force have a reservoir of easily invoked excuses for their dishonesty, we can see how theft can quickly become widespread in an organization" (p. 26).

Unfair Treatment

Predicated on the assumption that employees steal as an expression of dissatisfaction with their jobs, some of the most thorough and influential questionnaire studies are the analytical investigations focusing on the relationship between employee theft and job satisfaction. For example, Mangione and Quinn (1975) surveyed a broad-based sample of over 1,300 American workers about their level of job satisfaction and also obtained self-reports of the frequency with which they stole from their employers. Despite the use of a crude one-item measure of satisfaction and the obvious limitations of trusting self-reports about taboo subjects (Lee, 1993), the results were interesting. Although theft was negatively correlated with job satisfaction among men over thirty years old, no such association was found among younger men or women of any age, suggesting that the relationship is not straightforward and that it may be moderated by demographic variables.

Extending these findings and using more sophisticated, multidimensional measures of job satisfaction, Hollinger and Clark (1983) surveyed almost five thousand employees who worked in retail stores, manufacturing plants, and hospitals. They also included self-reports of theft that focused on specific items that were available to be taken by respondents in each of the business sectors (for example, merchandise, tools, and drugs, respectively). The researchers found significant negative correlations between employee theft and most dimensions of job satisfaction for employees in the retail and hospital sectors but a nonsignificant relationship among factory workers. Hollinger and Clark interpreted these findings as evidence that factory workers had available to them fewer desirable items to steal than those who worked in retail stores or hospitals.

Although this may be so, it is inconsistent with the possibility that employees stole because they wanted to "even the score" with employers who harmed them in some fashion (Greenberg, 1997a, 1997b). After all, even a factory worker who feels aggrieved may be expected to steal from the company, if only to strike back at it, thereby retaliating against the entity that treated him or her unfairly (Kemper, 1966). Indeed, several items assessing perceived fairness were included in Hollinger and Clark's measures of job satisfaction, and these were strongly correlated in the negative direction with reports of employee theft: the more unfairly employees reported feeling about their jobs, the more frequently they reported engaging in theft from their companies. In fact, feelings of unfair treatment were among the strongest predictors of employee theft: "When employees felt exploited by the company . . . these workers were more involved in acts against the organization as a mechanism to correct perceptions of inequity or injustice" (Hollinger & Clark, 1983, p. 142). This is in keeping with evidence showing that another costly form of deviant work behavior—vandalism—occurs as a response to feelings of injustice (DeMore, Fisher, & Baron, 1988). Indeed, stealing appears to be one of several forms of deviant behavior that occurs in response to unfair treatment, such as bringing lawsuits against former employers (Lind, Greenberg, Scott, & Welchans, 2000) and acting aggressively toward others (Greenberg & Alge, 1998).

Theoretical Research

With analytical research conducted to help scientists understand the complex relationships between variables involved in employee theft, the stage is set for additional studies to be conducted that structure these findings by imposing theoretical ideas. Thus, whereas the analytical studies may be thought of as being conducted for theory-development purposes (at least some of them), the research we will describe here was conducted for purposes of testing theories. They are not theories of employee theft, per se. Instead, they are broader social science theories that are being tested in the context of employee theft. Such efforts are important not only because they provide ecologically valid ways to test existing theories, but also because they promise to provide important new insight into our understanding of the phenomenon of employee theft.

It is noteworthy that although investigations of employee theft have been going on for many years, work marking the theoretical research phase has been far more recent. What's more, only a small number of studies of employee theft fall into this category. It is not surprising, given the need to carefully control extraneous factors in tests of theory, that most theory-testing studies have relied upon the use of experiments—the research method best suited to this purpose. This includes research conducted both in the laboratory and in the field. We now will describe these efforts as they bear on the two foci we have been tracing: informal social processes and unfair treatment.

Informal Social Processes

One of the key findings of descriptive and analytical studies is that social approval is a central factor in influencing employee theft: stealing is a way to gain and maintain the approval of key others in the workplace (Greenberg, 1998). The underlying conceptual notion is found in reinforcement theory (Keller, 1969)—the approval of others is a desirable outcome, so behavior that leads to it is strengthened. For obvious ethical reasons, experimental research has focused not on the use of social reinforcements to encourage theft but to discourage it. For example, in field experiments comparing the effectiveness of various rewards to discourage employee theft, it was found that small rewards in the form of lottery tickets were effective in reducing cash shortages in retail stores (Gaetani & Merle, 1983) and that punishment in the form of making cashiers pay for shortages out of their own pockets (Marholin & Gray, 1976) also decreased the frequency of stealing. Although it has been tested in only a limited fashion in the context of employee theft, there is good reason to believe that reinforcement theory can be a useful approach for understanding this phenomenon.

In addition to noting the benefits of financial reinforcements, Gaetani and Merle (1983) also found that praise from supervisors was highly effective in reducing shortages from cash drawers. By simply telling cashiers how pleased they were with cashiers' maintaining a balanced cash drawer, managers of retail beverage stores were able to make considerable progress in reducing shortages. In other words, this experimental study found that social rewards reinforced not stealing, thereby supplementing descriptive and analytical studies that show that social rewards also reinforced stealing. We note, however, that a serious confounding makes these results difficult to interpret. Specifically, we cannot tell whether the theft reduction occurred as a result of the praise itself or because the giving of praise regarding shortages sent the message that shortages were being more carefully monitored than usual. As such, although reinforcement theory appears to be useful for understanding theft behavior, its ultimate benefits have yet to be realized, particularly with respect to social reinforcements.

A closely related approach that has received attention among sociologists is social bonding theory (Hirschi, 1969), which specifies that certain factors will encourage or discourage conformity with deviant behavior witnessed in the workplace. Among these is commitment to a group. The more someone is committed to conforming to groups, the less he or she will be involved in breaking its rules. This notion was tested by Hollinger (1986) using the same dataset reported in his earlier large-scale survey (Hollinger & Clark, 1982). Specifically, Hollinger (1986) found that the more employees were committed to their organizations (as assessed in terms of their interest in seeking employment elsewhere), the less they admitted stealing from their companies. Employees who were planning on leaving were less committed and therefore less strongly affected by normative constraints against stealing.

Further research has extended these findings in two ways. First, it has been found that theft rates are about one-third higher among part-time and temporary employees than among full-time and permanent employees ("Study Shows," 1995), insofar as part-timers and temps are predisposed to have only little commitment to their organizations (Moorman & Harland, 2002). Second, it has been demonstrated that commitment to an organization diminishes in strength the closer in time an employee comes to leaving it, thereby weakening constraints against theft (Boye, 1991; Thoms, Wolper, Scott, & Jones, 2001). The weakened bonds against conforming to antitheft norms among employees approaching the end of their tenure with a company may lead them not only to risk getting fired (since it was a less costly outcome) but also to take advantage of their limited remaining time by taking what they believe they deserved from employers toward whom they may be exacting revenge and desire to even the score (Greenberg, 1998). This is in keeping with research on equity and organizational justice (for a review, see Colquitt & Greenberg, 2003) that also has been used to explain employee theft (Greenberg & Lind, 2000). We now turn to this line of theory-based research.

Unfair Treatment

Underpayment as a motive for theft has been a major theme of the descriptive and analytical studies reviewed here. In recent years, Greenberg (1990, 1993a, 2002) has shed conceptual light on this work in his experimental research applying equity theory (Adams, 1965) and conceptualizations of interactional justice (for a review, see Bies, 2001) to employee theft.

The idea that underpaid employees will be inclined to steal from their employers follows from equity theory's (Adams, 1965) claim that people will experience distress when they are inadequately compensated for the work they perform. One way to alleviate this distress is by taking steps to raise the rewards received—which, despite its dubious propriety—can be accomplished by taking company property. Greenberg (1990) first demonstrated that this occurs in a quasi-experiment conducted in three manufacturing plants. In two of these locations a financial crisis led company officials to impose a 15 percent pay cut over a ten-week period for all employees. In the third factory, which served as a control group, no changes were made to the pay received. As predicted by equity theory, employees who experienced pay cuts expressed feelings of underpayment, and the rates of theft in the plants in which they worked were significantly higher than the corresponding rate in the control group. These findings confirm the notion that employees stole company property as a means of compensating themselves for their lost wages.

Greenberg (1990) also found that the manner in which the pay cut was explained to the employees made a dramatic difference in theft. Employees in one randomly selected plant received an elaborate explanation regarding the reason for the pay cut that was presented in a socially sensitive and concerned manner (the adequate explanation condition). In contrast, employees in the other plant received only limited information about the reason for the pay cut that was presented in a more businesslike and unsympathetic fashion (the inadequate explanation condition). This proved to make a dramatic difference: although theft rates for both underpaid groups rose during the pay-cut period, they grew only half as much in the plant whose workers received the adequate explanation. These findings are important insofar as they demonstrate that interpersonal treatment moderates employees' reactions to unfair payment. Moreover, they are in keeping with research and theory on interactional justice demonstrating that fairness demands treating people with dignity and respect and that failing to do so weakens restraints against expressing feelings of inequity in inappropriate ways (Bies, 2001; Greenberg, 1993b; Greenberg & Alge, 1998).

Acknowledging that the explanation adequacy manipulation confounded the quality of information and the manner in which it was presented, Greenberg (1993a) followed up this experiment with a laboratory study in which these variables were disentangled and manipulated independently. Participants were students performing a task for which they were given a motive to steal (by being paid less than the promised amount) and an opportunity to steal (by confronting them with money and leading them to believe that the experimenter would not be able to tell how much money they took). It was found that both the quality of information and the sensitivity with which it was presented affected employee theft. Higher degrees of each limited subjects' tendencies to take more than they were entitled. Moreover, these effects were additive, such that high levels of both together had the greatest mitigating effects on theft. Recently, Greenberg (2002) extended these findings further by demonstrating that workers were not equally inclined to steal in response to underpayment on a task. Theft was significantly less likely to occur among employees whose companies had an ethics program in place that provided clear guidelines about taking company property, especially when they were less inclined to steal by virtue of their stage of moral development (Kohlberg, 1984).

Applied Research

Over the years, a large and growing body of applied research has developed on the use of integrity testing as a means of filtering potential employee thieves out of the selection process (Ones, Viswevaran, & Schmidt, 1993). Although some studies have reported lower rates of theft in companies that use these tests than those that do not (Jones, Slora, & Boye, 1990), several practitioners and psychometricians have contended that these instruments are far from perfect (Miner & Capps, 1996; Sackett, 1994). Insofar as this work is not predicated on the foundations laid in this chapter and because it falls beyond the chapter's scope, we have elected to exclude it from the present discussion. Still, we felt compelled to remind the reader of this important line of applied research.

More relevant to the present discussion is work focusing on efforts to deter theft founded on the various interpersonal and intrapersonal dynamics we have been discussing. Practitioners from many disciplines long have been dispensing advice about how to curtail employee theft (Weiner, 1998) based on assumptions about human behavior, although remarkably little of their advice follows directly from carefully conducted research studies designed to test theory. Although we are not claiming that all such advice is necessarily inaccurate, its basis may be questionable, leading us to advocate advice based on applied research that follows carefully from tests of theory. In this regard, we acknowledge one of the authors' earlier articles in which the importance of basing application on theory has been spelled out in detail (Greenberg & Lind, 2000). Specifically, it was argued that research findings should be used as the basis for developing interventions and that the results of these interventions should be used as the basis for revising theories as necessary. We can point to some evidence showing that this is occurring in the case of employee theft.

Informal Social Processes

Respondents in several of the descriptive and analytical studies we reviewed earlier explicitly noted that a key reason that they stole is that doing so was a source of fun for them. For example, a worker interviewed by Mars (1982) referred to stealing as fun, "a pleasurable departure from routine and an implicit challenge to authority" (p. 35). Zeitlin (1971) also expressed the idea that employees enjoy "beating the system," and has gone so far as to advise employers to allow their employees to steal as a potential way to enhance job satisfaction. Although we are not aware of any companies that promote employee theft as a motivational tool (nor do we advocate this practice ourselves), Latham (2001) offers sound theoretical reason to believe that the thrill associated with employee theft is one of the major reasons it is committed.

Drawing from the vast research on goal setting theory (for a review, see Locke & Latham, 2002), Latham (2001) notes that people are motivated to seek goals they believe they have a chance of meeting (that is, outcome expectancy is high) insofar as they believe they have a chance of mastering the skills that lead them to those goals (that is, self-efficacy is high). Based on this, Latham (2001) argues that to get workers to strive toward a goal, it is necessary for them to believe that they have a chance of attaining desired outcomes. Interviews with 1,200 employees of a forest products company revealed that many employees had high outcome expectancies with respect to employee theft. Workers who stole were confident that they could do it without getting caught. As one worker put it, "We are so good we could steal a head-rig [a piece of equipment weighing one ton] from a sawmill" (p. 712). They also used the word "thrill" to describe their feelings of accomplishment. By contrast, workers who didn't steal did not believe they could get away with it and did not think that stealing would be a source of enjoyment for them.

With this in mind, Latham introduced an intervention designed to reduce theft at the mill, which was costing the company about $1 million each year. The goal of the intervention was to reduce that number to less than $1,000. The idea was straightforward: If people steal because it brings them a thrill, then reduce the thrill expected by stealing. To accomplish this, Latham introduced a "library system" that permitted employees to borrow legally the very items that previously were stolen. They also introduced "amnesty days" in which previously stolen items could be returned with no questions asked. Not only was company property "returned by the truckload," as Latham (2001, p. 714) put it, but impressively, "Theft dropped to near zero immediately and has remained inconsequential by company accounting methods for 3 years subsequent to the intervention" (p. 714). By removing the excitement of stealing, employees had little reason to do so, thereby eliminating it. Although impressive, it is important to caution (as Latham does himself) that these findings may be generalizable only to companies in which employees steal primarily out of a sense of boredom. Still, we believe that the rationale underlying Latham's intervention (that is, reducing a source of outcome expectancy) may be applied successfully in other organizations.

Unfair Treatment

It is not only boredom that motivates employee theft, but also, as we have chronicled, the desire to redress unfair treatment. Clearly, financial constraints and organizational policies make it difficult, if not impossible, always to pay employees amounts they believe are fair. However, Greenberg's experiments (1990, 1993a) found that the degree to which underpayment promotes theft is mitigated by the manner in which the conditions of underpayment are explained to employees. With this in mind, Greenberg (1999) conducted an intervention study designed to reduce theft by promoting fairness. The setting was three discount stores from the same chain that were experiencing exceptionally high levels of internal shrinkage (that is, theft from storerooms, where only employees, but not customers, could go). A preexperimental survey revealed that the employees were dissatisfied with their jobs, felt underpaid, and depicted their managers as being disrespectful, uncaring, and insensitive. They also reported that supervisory personnel tended to explain very little to them about key organizational decisions. In short, they were treated similarly to those receiving low levels of information and social sensitivity in Greenberg's (1990, 1993a) experiments.

The intervention was designed to change the behavior of managers in one of the three store locations selected at random. This consisted of training managers in interpersonal justice training (IJT): techniques of delegation, supportive communication, and related topics that correspond to the variable shown by Greenberg (1990, 1993a) to mitigate theft reactions to underpayment. The training occurred for two hours per week over an eight-week period. It consisted of using various exercises and case studies that enhanced understanding of the need to be forthcoming with information in a sympathetic fashion. To avoid biasing the results, nothing was said about the goal of reducing employee theft. Managers at another store received training in an unrelated topic (customer service) and those at the third location received no training at all. These two stores constituted control groups.

The results were impressive. IJT was effective at improving employees' attitudes after the training was completed relative to the pretraining period and also relative to those groups that did not receive this training. Of greater interest, theft was reduced by half (from a rate of about 8 percent to a rate of about 4 percent) in the group that received IJT. This effect first emerged two weeks after training was completed and remained stable for six months afterwards. By comparison, there was no change in theft within either of the control groups. It is noteworthy that theft reductions occurred not as a result of direct training in loss control methods (the more typical direct route; Tilley, Dafoe, & Putsey, 1999), but rather, training in how to treat employees fairly. This study reflects a useful new direction for organizational justice researchers to take, one that builds upon existing theories and uses them as the basis for creating useful interventions for improving organizational conditions.

Extracting Value from the DATA Cycle

The DATA cycle presented here is a cogent organizing framework for the employee theft literature. Accordingly, we present this framework as a valuable tool for researchers on two grounds: descriptive and prescriptive.

Beyond identifying an ideal approach to organizing the logical ordering of various approaches to research, our discussion suggests that the DATA cycle does a good job of describing the historical evolution of research on employee theft. As such, it may be considered a descriptive approach to research (for a summary of conclusions about employee theft that have traced through the DATA cycle, see Table 15.2).

The framework provides a systematic means of assessing the state of the extant literature on employee theft and readily can identify gaps from earlier phases that should be addressed in subsequent phases. As such, the DATA cycle also can be characterized

Table 15.2. Tracing the Development of Research Findings with the DATA Cycle.

Major Theme of Descriptive Research	Developed Further in Analytical Research	Tested in Research Designed to Test Theories	Theory-Based Intervention Tested in Applied Research
Informal social norms govern employee theft	Conformity to theft norms is a source of group acceptance	Social reinforcement predicts theft	Eliminating the social rewards of stealing reduces theft
People who feel unfairly treated steal from their employers	Theft as a response to unfair treatment is believed to be justified	Theft occurs in response to underpayment inequity and interactional injustices	Interventions promoting fair treatment of workers among managers reduces theft among workers

as a prescriptive approach to research insofar as it identifies an ideal order for conducting studies of different types. That is, descriptive studies represent a useful starting point for understanding a phenomenon. Then, building on these descriptions, analytical studies can be performed that set the stage for theories concerning the phenomenon to be tested. These theories, in turn, identify various forms of application studies that can be conducted (a link described in detail by Greenberg & Lind, 2000). Finally, based on these applications, researchers stand to be alerted to new descriptive foci for a second generation of the cycle.

In support of this contention, we highlight two particular prescriptive benefits for employee theft research that emerge from this framework. The first benefit is concerned with the use of varied methods to study employee theft. Researchers are routinely faced with a host of decisions (for example, research design, data analysis techniques) that involve fundamental tradeoffs and thus critically affect the inferences that can be drawn from their studies (Scandura & Williams, 2000). To the extent that this impairment constrains the ability of researchers to design a flawless study, it becomes necessary to rely on triangulation, a process whereby multiple methods are employed with hopes of producing converging evidence with regard to a phenomenon of interest (McGrath, 1982). For example, we reviewed several studies that have suggested that employees steal as a result of social norms, yet this conclusion could be challenged on the grounds that the chosen research method compelled the subjects to justify their theft to the researcher rather than admit some personal shortcoming (for example, greed). Findings that are robust across different methods (for example, using an analytical, self-report, anonymous questionnaire to verify findings from earlier descriptive research) build our confidence in the effect we discovered while suppressing criticisms that an effect was merely an artifact of a particular design.

The second prescriptive benefit for employee theft research is that later phases of the framework are ideally suited to answer questions raised by earlier phases. As an example, we point to the issue of causality in the job satisfaction-theft relationship (Greenberg & Scott, 1996). Although earlier descriptive and analytical work has suggested that dissatisfaction with one's job may motivate employee theft, this does not rule out the possibility that theft may result in job dissatisfaction out of a need to justify such deviant behavior. Another possibility is that both theft and job dissatisfaction may be the result of a third variable, such as job commitment (Snyder et al., 1991) or substance abuse (Mangione & Quinn, 1975). Theoretical studies (Greenberg, 1990, 1993a) and applied studies (Greenberg, 1999) have provided more carefully controlled studies that have yielded additional evidence of the job dissatisfaction-theft causal relationship.

Moreover, beyond the benefits the DATA cycle offers for the employee theft literature, we contend that our framework may be applied fruitfully to many other research areas within organizational behavior, and is particularly well-suited for a variety of "dark side" phenomena. Counterproductive behaviors within organizations are often considered "taboo" topics—implicitly acknowledged by organizational members but seldom flushed out into the open in a manner that readily facilitates scientific study. Examples include domestic violence that spills over into the workplace, instances of sexual harassment, and covert discrimination against gay and lesbian employees. To maximize the development of these emerging research literatures, it is vital to harness the ability of early phases to capture grounded conceptualization and operationalization of relevant variables, so that later phases have a solid foundation upon which to build. Specifically, in the case of employee theft, we discovered a variety of contaminated dependent variable operationalizations of employee theft, such as a "theft suspicion score" of employees completed by the manager (Jones & Terris, 1983) and cash register shortages (Bernardin & Cooke, 1993). These measures can be criticized on the grounds that they are not "pure" measures of theft, have dubious construct validity, and as a result may produce flawed conclusions.

Ushering in the Second Revolution of the DATA Cycle

The DATA Cycle has completed one revolution and now is beginning a second generation. As evidence of this, we look to a new generation of descriptive studies. The earliest descriptive studies of employee theft sought to describe the phenomenon by observing and interviewing employees in organizations. Although crude, these studies led to analytical studies, which led to theoretical studies, and then finally, applied studies. Now that we know about effective ways of curtailing employee theft, the stage is set once again to describe the nature and extent to which theft occurs in organizations. Doing so is especially important as a means of assessing the effectiveness of implementations.

Illustrative of second-generation descriptive studies are those conducted by Dalton and his associates by using various masked-response techniques. Specifically, Wimbush and Dalton (1997) advocated the measurement of sensitive behavior, such as attaining admissions of employee theft, by using two techniques: the unmatched count technique (UCT; Dalton, Wimbush, & Daily, 1994), and the randomized response technique (RRT; Dalton, Wimbush, & Daily, 1996). These techniques represent an advancement over standard self-report questionnaires (for example, as used by Boye & Slora, 1993), insofar as they are likely to result in more honest (hence, valid) responses. They also are an improvement over the informant studies reported here insofar as they make it possible to survey large numbers of respondents while preserving their anonymity.

In the UCT, two groups of respondents read a list of statements and then are asked to identify how many of them are true with respect to themselves. One group is given a completely innocuous set of items (for example, "I usually take a vitamin supplement almost every day"). The other group is given the same set plus one additional, target item (for example, "I am involved in the theft from my employer of cash, supplies, or merchandise worth more than $5.00 in the course of a month"). By comparing the means of the two groups, the researchers can determine how many participants admit to the target item (that is, the number of items with which people agree when the target item is included compared to the corresponding number when the target item is excluded).

The RRT relies on similar logic. In this technique respondents are asked to mark a statement admitting a deviant act (such as theft) as being true either if it actually is true with respect to them, or if a coin they toss lands heads-side up. Given that the probability of the coin landing on heads is 50–50, proportions of agreement above 0.50 may be attributed to admission of the act.

Comparisons between these matched-response techniques and conventional questionnaires proved informative (Wimbush &

Dalton, 1997). Using conventional self-report measures, admissions of monthly theft were 12.9 percent when asked about theft in excess of $50 per month. However, the corresponding figures were significantly higher among similar respondents using the UCT (57.9 percent) and the RRT (59.2 percent). Wimbush and Dalton (1997) take their findings as evidence that people tend to under-report theft behavior on conventional questionnaires insofar as they may be afraid of being identified (and subsequently punished) for their actions.

Because the use of masked-response techniques is new, their appropriateness needs to be assessed in future research. Thus far, they appear to be useful. With respect to tapping admissions of theft over $5, Ahart and Sackett (2001) found that the UCT yielded significantly higher admission rates than standard questionnaires only among participants to whom the UCT was explained and who were told in advance that they would be using it, thereby potentially cueing a pro-honesty response set. In another domain, LaBrie and Earleywine (2000) found that the UCT yielded higher admission rates with respect to engaging in sexually risky behavior.

Assuming that the UCT and the RRT more accurately identify the base rates of employee theft than conventional research techniques, it becomes clear that we are describing a behavior that is not infrequent in nature but, rather, quite common. We envision that the UCT and the RRT may be used further to assess the relationships between variables in the manner of earlier analytical studies, and that measures of theft using these techniques may serve as research variables in future theoretical—and applied—efforts. We note also that other researchers have tried to overcome self-report survey limitations by measuring counterproductive behaviors indirectly by using peer reports of observed theft (Skarlicki & Folger, 1997). Researchers should continue to explore the relative efficacy of different operationalizations of employee theft.

Conclusion

Although recent events have served as a poignant reminder of the egregious nature of theft within organizations, we are fortunate to have a vast historical anthology of research that provides insight into the phenomenon of employee theft, the motives that give rise to this behavior, and the interventions that eradicate or mitigate it. Our review of this literature highlights the iterative and evolving objectives captured by the DATA cycle. In so doing, we have attempted to demonstrate how a wide array of research methodologies has converged on the recurring themes of informal social processes and perceptions of unfair treatment. Further, we believe the DATA cycle provides unique perspective on how the vast and disparate literature on employee theft has matured into a coherent and integrated whole, as the findings from earlier phases form the launching pad of subsequent phases. Indeed, we believe this model also has the potential to serve as an exemplar for researchers in other fields.

References

Adams, J. S. (1965). Inequity in social exchange. In L. Berkowitz (Ed.), *Advances in experimental social psychology* (Vol. 2, pp. 269–299). New York: Academic Press.

Ahart, A. M., & Sackett, P. R. (2001, April). *Evaluating the unmatched count technique as a measure of counterproductivity.* Paper presented at the meeting of the Society for Industrial and Organizational Psychology, Toronto, Ontario, Canada.

Altheide, D. L., Adler, P. A., Adler, P., & Altheide, D. A. (1978). The social meanings of employee theft. In J. M. Johnson & J. D. Douglas (Eds.), *Crime at the top.* Philadelphia: Lippincott.

Analoui, F., & Kakabadse, A. (1991). *Sabotage.* London: Mercury.

Backman, C. W. (1985). Identity, self-presentation, and the resolution of moral dilemmas: Toward a social psychological theory of moral behavior. In B. R. Schlenker (Ed.), *The self and social life* (pp. 261–289). New York: McGraw Hill.

Bernardin, H. J., & Cooke, D. K. (1993). Validity of an honesty test in predicting theft among convenience store employees. *Academy of Management Journal, 36,* 1097–1108.

Bies, R. J. (2001). Interactional (in)justice: The sacred and the profane. In J. Greenberg & R. Cropanzano (Eds.), *Advances in organizational justice* (pp. 89–118.). Stanford, CA: Stanford University Press.

Boye, M. W. (1991). *Self-reported employee theft and counterproductivity as a function of employee turnover antecedents.* Unpublished doctoral dissertation, DePaul University, Chicago.

Boye, M. W., & Slora, K. B. (1993). The severity and prevalence of deviant employee activity within supermarkets. *Journal of Business and Psychology*, 8, 245–253.

Bullard, P. D., & Resnick, A. J. (1983). SMR forum: Too many hands in the corporate cookie jar. *Sloan Management Review*, 24(3), 51–56.

Carter, R. (1987, July). Employee theft often appears legitimate. *Accountancy*, pp. 75–77.

Colquitt, J. A., & Greenberg, J. (2003). Organizational justice: A fair assessment of the state of the literature. In J. Greenberg (Ed.), *Organizational behavior: The state of the science* (2nd ed.). Mahwah, NJ: Erlbaum.

Cressey, D. (1953). *Other people's money: A study in the social psychology of embezzlement*. Belmont, CA: Wadsworth.

Dabney, D. (1995). Neutralization and deviance in the workplace: Theft of supplies and medicines by hospital nurses. *Deviant Behavior*, 16, 313–331.

Dalton, D. R., Wimbush, J. C., & Daily, C. M. (1994). Using the unmatched count technique to estimate base rates for sensitive behavior. *Personnel Psychology*, 47, 817–828.

Dalton, D. R., Wimbush, J. C., & Daily, C. M. (1996). Candor, privacy, and "legal immunity" in business ethics research: An empirical assessment of the randomized response technique. *Business Ethics Quarterly*, 6, 87–99.

Dalton, M. (1959). *Men who manage*. New York: John Wiley.

DeMore, S. W., Fisher, J. D., & Baron, R. M. (1988). The equity-control model as a predictor of vandalism among college students. *Journal of Applied Psychology*, 18, 80–91.

Ditton, J. (1977). *Part-time crime: An ethnography of fiddling and pilferage*. London: Macmillan.

Dwyer, P. (2002, October 14). Nowhere to run, nowhere to hide. *Business Week*, pp. 44–45.

Emshwiller, J. R. (1993, December 3). Corruption in the bankruptcy system injures firms in need. *The Wall Street Journal*, p. B1.

Gaetani, J. J., & Merle, J. C. (1983). The effect of data plotting, praise, and state lottery tickets on decreasing cash shortages in a retail beverage chain. *Journal of Organizational Behavior Management*, 5, 5–15.

Gouldner, A. W. (1954). *Wildcat strike: A study in worker-management relationships*. New York: Harper and Row.

Greenberg, J. (1990). Employee theft as a reaction to underpayment inequity: The hidden cost of pay cuts. *Journal of Applied Psychology*, 75, 561–568.

Greenberg, J. (1993a). Stealing in the name of justice: Informational and interpersonal moderators of theft reactions to underpayment inequity. *Organizational Behavior and Human Decision Processes*, 54, 81–103.

Greenberg, J. (1993b). The social side of fairness: Interpersonal and informational classes of organizational justice. In R. Cropanzano (Ed.), *Justice in the workplace: Approaching fairness in human resource management* (pp. 79–103). Hillsdale, NJ: Erlbaum.

Greenberg, J. (1995). Employee theft. In N. Nicholson (Ed.), *The Blackwell encyclopedic dictionary of organizational behavior.* Oxford, England: Blackwell.

Greenberg, J. (1997a). The STEAL motive: Managing the social determinants of employee theft. In R. Giacalone & J. Greenberg (Eds.). *Antisocial behavior in organizations* (pp. 85–108). Thousand Oaks, CA: Sage.

Greenberg, J. (1997b). A social influence model of employee theft: Beyond the fraud triangle. In R. J. Lewicki, B. H. Sheppard, & R. J. Bies (Eds.), *Research on negotiation in organizations* (Vol. 5, pp. 22–49). Greenwich, CT: JAI Press.

Greenberg, J. (1998). The cognitive geometry of employee theft: Negotiating "the line" between taking and theft. In R. W. Griffin, A. O'Leary-Kelly, & J. Collins (Eds.), *Dysfunctional behavior in organizations,* Vol. 2: *Nonviolent behaviors in organizations* (pp. 147–193). Greenwich, CT: JAI.

Greenberg, J. (1999). *Interpersonal justice training (IJT) for reducing employee theft: Some preliminary results.* Unpublished data, The Ohio State University, Columbus.

Greenberg, J. (2002). Who stole the money, and when? Individual and situational determinants of employee theft. *Organizational Behavior and Human Decision Processes,* 89, 985–1003.

Greenberg, J., & Alge, B. (1998). Aggressive reactions to workplace injustice. In R. W. Griffin, A. O'Leary-Kelly, & J. Collins (Eds.), *Dysfunctional behavior in organizations,* Vol. 1: *Violent behaviors in organizations* (pp. 119–145). Greenwich, CT: JAI.

Greenberg, J., & Lind, E. A. (2000). The pursuit of organizational justice: From conceptualization to implication to application. In C. L. Cooper & E. A. Locke (Eds.), *I/O psychology: What we know about theory and practice* (pp. 72–105). Oxford, England: Blackwell.

Greenberg, J., & Scott, K. S. (1996). Why do workers bite the hands that feed them? Employee theft as a social exchange process. In B. M. Staw & L. L. Cummings (Eds.), *Research in organizational behavior* (Vol. 18, pp. 111–155). Greenwich, CT: JAI Press.

Hawkins, R. (1984). Employee theft in the restaurant trade: Forms of ripping off by waiters at work. *Deviant Behavior,* 5, 47–69.

Hirschi, T. (1969). *Causes of delinquency.* Berkeley: University of California Press.

Hollinger, R. C. (1986). Acts against the workplace: Social bonding and employee deviance. *Deviant Behavior,* 7, 53–75.

Hollinger, R. C. (1989). *Dishonesty in the workplace: A manager's guide to preventing employee theft.* Park Ridge, IL: London House.

Hollinger, R. C., & Clark, J. P. (1982). Formal and informal social controls of employee deviance. *The Sociological Quarterly,* 23, 333–343.

Hollinger, R. C., & Clark, J. P. (1983). *Theft by employees.* Lexington, MA: Lexington Books.

Hollinger, R. C., & Davis, J. L. (2002). *2001 national retail security survey: Final report.* Gainesville, FL: Center for Studies in Criminology and Law.

Horning, D.N.M. (1970). Blue-collar theft: Conceptions of property, attitudes toward pilfering, and work group norms in a modern industrial plant. In E. O. Smigel & H. L. Ross (Eds.), *Crimes against bureaucracy.* New York: Van Nostrand Reinhold.

Jaspan, N. (1974). *Mind your own business.* Englewood Cliffs, NJ: Prentice-Hall.

Jones, J. W., Slora, K. B., & Boye, M. W. (1990). Theft reduction through personnel selection: A control group design in the supermarket industry. *Journal of Business and Psychology,* 5, 275–279.

Jones, J. W., & Terris, W. (1983). Predicting employees' theft in home improvement centers. *Psychological Reports,* 52, 187–201.

Keller, F. S. (1969). *Learning: Reinforcement theory* (2nd ed.). New York: Random House.

Kemper, T. D. (1966). Representative roles and the legitimation of deviance. *Social Problems,* 13, 288–298.

Kohlberg, L. (1984). *The philosophy of moral development: Moral stages and the idea of justice.* New York: HarperCollins.

LaBrie, J. W., & Earleywine, M. (2000). Sexual risk behaviors and alcohol: Higher base rates revealed using the Unmatched-Count Technique. *Journal of Sex Research,* 7, 321–326.

Latham, G. P. (2001). The importance of understanding and changing employee outcome expectancies for gaining commitment to an organizational goal. *Personnel Psychology,* 54, 707–716.

Lee, R. M. (1993). *Doing research on sensitive topics.* Newbury Park, CA: Sage.

Liebow, F. (1967). *Tally's corner.* Boston: Little, Brown.

Lind, E. A., Greenberg, J., Scott, K. S., & Welchans, T. D. (2000). The winding road from employee to complainant: Situational and psychological determinants of wrongful termination claims. *Administrative Science Quarterly,* 45, 557–590.

Lipman, M., & McGraw, W. R. (1988). Employee theft: A $40 billion industry. *Annals of the American Academy of Political and Social Science,* 498, 51–59.

Locke, E. A., & Latham, G. P. (2002). Building a practically useful theory of goal setting and task motivation. *American Psychologist,* 57, 705–717.

Mangione, T. W., & Quinn, R. P. (1975). Job satisfaction, counterproductive behavior, and drug use at work. *Journal of Applied Psychology,* 60, 114–116.

Marholin, D., & Gray, D. (1976). Effects of group response-cost procedures on cash shortages in a small business. *Journal of Applied Behavior Analysis,* 9, 25–30.

Mars, G. (1974). Dock pilferage: A case study in occupational theft. In P. Rock & M. McIntosh (Eds.), *Deviance and social control.* London: Tavistock.

Mars, G. (1982). *Cheats at work: An anthropology of workplace crime.* Boston: G. Allen and Unwin.

McGrath, J. (1982). Dilemmatics: The study of research choices and dilemmas. In J. E. McGrath, J. Martin, & R. A. Kulka (Eds.), *Judgment calls in research* (pp. 69–102). Newbury Park, CA: Sage.

Miner, J. B., & Capps, M. H. (1996). *How honesty testing works.* Westport, CT: Quorum Books.

Moorman, R. H., & Harland, L. K. (2002). Temporary employees as good citizens: Factors affecting their OCB performance. *Journal of Business and Psychology,* 17, 171–187.

Murphy, K. R. (1993). *Honesty in the workplace.* Pacific Grove, CA: Brooks/ Cole.

Ones, D. S., Viswevaran, C., & Schmidt, F. L. (1993). Comprehensive meta-analysis of integrity test validities: Findings and implications for personnel selection and theories of job performance. *Journal of Applied Psychology,* 78, 679–703.

Podgor, E. S., & Israel, J. H. (1997). *White collar crime in a nutshell* (2nd ed.). Belmont, CA: West Wadsworth.

Robin, G. D. (1969). Employees as offenders. *Journal of Research on Crime and Delinquency,* 6, 17–33.

Robinson, S. L., & Greenberg, J. (1998). Employees behaving badly: Dimensions, determinants and dilemmas in the study of workplace deviance. In D. M. Rousseau & C. Cooper (Eds.), *Trends in organizational behavior* (Vol. 5, pp. 1–23). New York: John Wiley.

Sackett, P. R. (1994). Integrity testing for personnel selection. *Current Directions in Psychological Science,* 3, 73–76.

Scandura, T. A., & Williams, E. A. (2000). Research methodology in management: Current practices, trends, and implications for future research. *Academy of Management Journal,* 43, 1248–1264.

Skarlicki, D. P., & Folger, R. (1997). Retaliation in the workplace: The roles of distributive, procedural, and interactional justice. *Journal of Applied Psychology*, 82, 434–443.

Sieh, E. W. (1987). Garment workers: Perceptions of inequity and employee theft. *British Journal of Criminology*, 27, 174–190.

Snyder, N. H., Broome, O. W., Jr., Kehoe, W. J., McIntyre, J. T., Jr., & Blair, K. E. (1991). *Reducing employee theft: A guide to financial and organizational controls.* New York: Quorum Books.

Study shows part-timers commit more thefts than full-timers. (1995, March). *Management Solutions*, 40(3), 4.

Tatham, R. L. (1974). Employee views on theft in retailing. *Journal of Retailing*, 50, 49–56.

Terris, W., & Jones, J. (1982). Psychological factors related to employees' theft in the convenience store industry. *Psychological Reports*, 51, 1219–1238.

Thoms, P., Wolper, P., Scott, K. S., & Jones, D. (2001). The relationship between immediate turnover and employee theft in the restaurant industry. *Journal of Business and Psychology*, 15, 561–577.

Tilley, B., Dafoe, R., & Putsey, L. (1999). *Positive loss prevention.* Uxbridge, Ontario, Canada: Bob Tilley.

Weiner, A. N. (1998). *How to reduce business losses from employee theft and customer fraud.* Vestal, NY: Almar Press.

Wimbush, J. C., & Dalton, D. R. (1997). Base rate for employee theft: Convergence of multiple methods. *Journal of Applied Psychology*, 82, 756–763.

Wolman, B. B. (1999). *Antisocial behavior: Personality disorders from hostility to homicide.* Amherst, NY: Prometheus Books.

Zeitlin, L. R. (1971). A little larceny can do a lot for employee morale. *Psychology Today*, June, 22, 24, 26, 64.

CHAPTER 16

Dark Side Issues

Concluding Observations and Directions for Future Research

Anne M. O'Leary-Kelly, Ricky W. Griffin

It is the fortunate prerogative of editors to have the last word in volumes such as this. In this closing chapter, we happily indulge in this prerogative, sharing our reactions to this thought-provoking set of chapters. We note that our intention is not to review individual chapters, but rather to share thoughts regarding what these chapters have to say when considered together. Because of the diversity in topics discussed in this volume, we believe that much can be learned by considering these topics in the context of each other.

More specifically, we focus here on three key issues mentioned in our introductory chapter. First, we discuss the general nature of dark side behaviors, as depicted in these chapters, and identify what we regard as some important similarities and distinctions between them. Second, we share several observations regarding the costs and consequences of these negative workplace behaviors. Finally, we present ideas for future research by describing how perspectives used in research on one dark side behavior might be informative to research on other negative work behaviors.

The Nature of Dark Side Behaviors

We suggested in our introductory chapter that most dark side behaviors are latecomers to the discipline of organizational behavior. Once these phenomena were recognized, though, research proceeded quite rapidly. Perhaps in an effort to make up for lost time, researchers enthusiastically developed research agendas and frameworks, and accumulated research findings. More recently, however, a few cautionary notes about the direction of this research have been sounded. Specifically, some authors have argued that we must pay more attention to the nature of these behaviors and their similarities and differences (O'Leary-Kelly, Duffy, & Griffin, 2000; Robinson & Greenberg, 1998). Because we have made such cautionary statements ourselves (in our 2000 paper just cited), we feel compelled to share some observations regarding the nature of the dark side behaviors explored in this volume.

First, we are struck by the diversity of conduct described here. Each of the chapters explore at least ten forms of conduct. We suggest ten (as opposed to a full fourteen) because some of the chapters address more specific forms of conduct that are described generally in another chapter. For example, the discussion of discrimination against gay, lesbian, and bisexual (GLB) employees (in the Deitch, Butz, and Brief chapter) is a more specific form of discrimination generally (discussed in the Dipboye and Halverson chapter). Similarly, excessive careerism (the chapter authored by Bratton and Kacmar) examines a specific type of negative political behavior (discussed in the more general form in the chapters by Hall, Hochwarter, and Ferris, and Bowen). Finally, two chapters (those authored by Baron and Neuman) explore the same general type of conduct—workplace aggression.

Considering these ten forms of dark side conduct, it is interesting to note that the behaviors described are each quite distinct. That is, most chapters describe actions that are unlikely to be confused with those described in another chapter—for example, incivility, workplace drug and alcohol abuse, psychological contract violation, the formation of idiosyncratic contracts, intimate partner violence. Although there certainly may be instances of these individual behaviors occurring together (for example, alcohol abuse and intimate partner violence), it is not difficult to distinguish between these in a measurement sense. This is of note because recent papers (including ours) have raised the concern that an unacceptable level of construct overlap exists in the research on dark side behaviors. For example, we (and others) have suggested that it is necessary to pay close attention to construct validity issues in distinguishing conduct such as workplace aggression, organization-motivated aggression, and deviance. Although we continue to agree with this argument, we are compelled to acknowledge that this type of overlap does not exist in the conduct described in most of our chapters. That is, it is quite likely that there will be strong discriminant validity between constructs such as psychological contract violation, alcohol and drug abuse, and discrimination against GLB employees. It seems important, then, to counterbalance our earlier criticism with the recognition that many dark side behaviors (such as those described in this volume) are less susceptible to the methodological concerns raised earlier. Perhaps, as we suggested in our earlier paper (O'Leary-Kelly et al., 2000), this issue comes down to one of specificity. When dark side behaviors are categorized and described at an aggregate (general) level (for example, as with categories such as "workplace aggression" or "organizational deviance"), it may become difficult to distinguish between them empirically. However, when dark side behaviors are described at the more specific, detailed level, concerns regarding overlap appear to be less justified. In any event, there is a promising trend (evident in some chapters in this book) of researchers discussing how the dark side behavior of concern to them may differ from other forms of negative actions. We suggest that this trend is promising because it signals an awareness of these construct validation concerns and a maturing of this general research area.

We also want to share observations about some ways in which the behaviors in this volume are similar and different, not from the standpoint of measurement, but conceptually. First, it strikes us that some behaviors discussed here are inevitably a part of organizational life while others are far from preordained. Beginning with the former, it seems impossible for an organization to prevent actions such as political behavior and careerism, because these are so fundamentally a part of organizational life and human behavior. Alternatively, other dark side behaviors described here do not (and do not have to) exist in *all* organizations (for example, illegal discrimination, aggression, sexual harassment, workplace alcohol and drug abuse). In addition, there are behaviors that fall in a category somewhere in between the two poles on the inevitability continuum—behaviors that are not inevitable but that seem highly likely to occur given the complexities inherent to coordinating human behavior within a goal-oriented setting (that is, organizational life). For example, we would regard dark side actions such as psychological contract violation, incivility, and idiosyncratic contracts to fall in this "in between" category; these actions are not preordained, but it seems likely that over time they will occur in most organizations.

These distinctions are, we believe, important to recognize because they have fundamental implications for how organizations control dark side behaviors. When negative actions are inevitable (or seemingly inevitable), an organization's control efforts should emphasize *containment* and *buffering*. That is, managers should work to minimize the frequency or severity of these actions and to alleviate the breadth of negative consequences that result from these actions. For example, we expect that at least some employees in large organizations will perceive a psychological contract breach. Rather than fight the inevitable, then, managers should accept that this outcome *will* occur, but then concentrate their effort on (1) ensuring that it does not occur for the aspects of the contract that are most fundamental to employees, and (2) ensuring that the negative consequences from a broken contract for one employee do not spread to other employees. In regard to the first point, recent research cited in the Robinson and Brown chapter (Farmer & Fedor, 1999) suggests that the breach of relational aspects of a contract (for example, job security) is more fundamental and leads to more severe reactions than does a breach of transactional (for example, benefits) aspects of the employment contract. This suggests that a containment strategy in which great effort is given to protection of relational elements may minimize the negative effects of psychological contract violation. In regard to the second point (the spillover effects from a broken contract), we suspect that social accounts, which appear to minimize negative effects of contract breach for the employee who is affected (discussed in the Robinson and Brown chapter), also may be important for ensuring that other employees do not become disillusioned as a result of the treatment of a coworker. That is, social accounts can be used to justify the contract breach to the offended employees, and also to minimize the negative contagious effects on other employees.

A second, related observation regarding the nature of dark side behaviors is that some of these behaviors are inherently negative (for example, aggression, alcohol and drug abuse, discrimination, sexual harassment, intimate partner violence, incivility), whereas others become "dark side" only if they reach a threshold level of intensity or prevalence (for example, careerism, political behaviors, idiosyncratic deals). In their chapter, Skarlicki and Folger even argue that organizational retaliatory behavior, if not too severe, can have positive consequences for the firm, such as restoring equity and prompting organizational change. This point is interesting, we think, in that it shifts the emphasis from outright organizational *control* of some behaviors to the issue of *monitoring*. Control and monitoring are two fundamentally different goals, requiring quite different forms of management intervention. Therefore, solutions that apply to one form of negative behavior (for example, a zero tolerance policy related to alcohol and drug abuse) may not be feasible when applied to other organizational behaviors (for example, careerism). Although this point may appear obvious, its implication is that organizations must develop prevention systems separately for each of the dark side behaviors they face, rather than adopting one general approach (for example, zero tolerance) and force-fitting this as a prevention device for all negative conduct.

A third key distinction between the behaviors described here relates to who is typically identified as the initiator. Some actions are generally regarded (by researchers) as enacted by individual employees (for example, organizational retaliatory behavior, alcohol and drug abuse, intimate partner violence, political behavior, incivility), whereas others typically are recognized as organizationally enacted (for example, psychological contract breach, idiosyncratic contracts). It is interesting to consider which perspective has been used in research to date and how a change in this perspective might influence future research. For example, it is intriguing to consider the *organizational* equivalent of actions typically regarded as *individually* enacted (such as organizational retaliatory behavior and political behavior). In regard to retaliatory behavior, although equal employment case law contains many instances of organizations engaging in retaliatory actions against their employees, research on retaliation by employers is rare. In similar vein, the ways that organizations engage in political behavior (internal impression management attempts by the organization, downward—as opposed to upward—influence efforts) are underresearched compared to the literature on employee-initiated politicking. Similarly, some actions seem underresearched from the *individual* perspective. Perhaps most obviously, research on employees initiating a violation of the psychological contract with their employers (instead of the reverse), the effects of this on the organization (for example, lowered trust, more rigid employment contracts) and on other employees (for example, perceived inequity) seem particularly interesting.

Finally, it is interesting to note that research traditions differ in their emphasis on target perceptions. For some dark side behaviors (sexual harassment, psychological contract violation, for example), a major focus of research is on how *targets* interpret the negative behavior as opposed to why the *actors* initiate them. In other areas (for example, workplace aggression, organizational retaliatory behavior), however, research has placed greater emphasis on the factors that motivate an actor's negative behavior than on target perceptions of that behavior. This distinction is interesting because it emphasizes opportunities for future research. That is, research that traditionally has considered target perceptions might emphasize actor motives, and vice versa. For example, Paetzold argues in her chapter that research that examines harasser motives is only beginning to emerge but is very important to emphasize in future research on sexual harassment. Similarly, research that explores how targets of workplace aggression react (that is, how they now perceive, feel about, and act toward their employing organization and toward the aggressive actor) would make significant contributions.

Costs and Consequences of Dark Side Behaviors

Employers are unlikely to develop interventions around conduct they regard as irrelevant or benign. If employers do not recognize conduct as problematic, they will not explore whether it has costs for the organization. Some of the dark side behaviors in this volume are only now being recognized as organizationally relevant. Perhaps the best example of this is evident in the chapter on intimate partner violence (IPV) by Carol Reeves. In that chapter, she argues that traditional divides between work and home (between the professional and the personal) make it difficult for many organizations to accept the very real consequences and costs that they incur as a result of IPV. In fact, few organizations have even explored the issue of how IPV might influence their employees, their operations, or their bottom line. In cases like this, dark side behaviors are essentially "invisible" problems whose costs are unacknowledged and unknown.

Other dark side behaviors considered in this volume appear to reside in a murky limbo in which organizations may acknowledge that the behavior is problematic, but they are relatively ignorant to the real costs that the action incurs for them. For example, most employers do not welcome uncivil conduct, yet they may not recognize it as severe or costly enough to warrant prevention efforts. However, an awareness of the costs of incivility (in their chapter, Pearson and Porath argue that there are direct effects, second-order effects, and even third-order effects from incivility) seems likely to lead a firm to acknowledge this issue as one worthy of attention. Similarly, although many managers might acknowledge an awareness of discrimination against gay, lesbian, and bisexual (GLB) employees, they may not regard this as problematic (for example, because they believe there are relatively few GLB individuals in their firm, because they believe the discrimination in their firm is not severe compared to that in other firms or in society generally, because there typically is no legal requirement to protect these employees against discrimination).

These assessments and evaluations by firms are essentially socially constructed events. What is regarded as relevant and problematic shifts over time with societal and organizational events and norms. We argued above that few employers regard IPV as an organizationally relevant issue. Not long ago, sexual harassment was regarded in a remarkably similar light—for example, as private conduct between two people that did not involve the organization. Fortunately, these perceptions are becoming more socially unacceptable and many/most firms recognize that sexual harassment is an issue with real costs for the organization and its employees. It seems likely that a similar shift in attitudes and societal norms may influence the seriousness with which issues such as IPV and GLB discrimination are viewed. For example, as societal (and organizational) norms move away from conceptualizing GLB individuals as "out of the norm" or "different," and toward regarding them as valued human resources whose lowered productivity or turnover has a negative impact on the organization, then it becomes difficult to regard GLB discrimination as benign or as having few costs for the organization.

Our key point, then, is that employers are likely to develop interventions only around conduct they regard as costly, yet the recognition of costs is a social phenomenon. The degree to which employers regard a dark side behavior as costly is not an objective fact but a shifting perception that is influenced by societal thinking. This suggests that organizational researchers have an opportunity to influence these shifting perceptions through research that documents the costs that dark side behaviors have for work organizations. If firms can be convinced that conduct such as intimate partner violence or GLB discrimination has real, bottom-line consequences, prevention efforts are a rational response.

Future Research on Dark Side Behaviors

Given these general observations regarding dark side behaviors and their costs, we turn to a discussion of future research. Before we share our thoughts, it is important to remind readers that authors of most chapters have shared their own ideas for how research in their area of interest should proceed. We do not wish to repeat these suggestions but, rather, to share some additional thoughts that come from examining all of these chapters together. More specifically, we focus on how perspectives on antecedents (motivating factors) for one form of dark side conduct might be instructive to research on other forms of conduct.

In order to accomplish this objective, we first must identify the antecedent factors that have been identified in research described in each of the chapters. The first column in Table 16.1 contains our summary of the primary antecedents/motivators that are discussed within the chapters included here. We caution the reader that we were not able to include *all* antecedent factors named in each chapter, but emphasize those that were particularly prominent. This list, then, represents motivating factors that have been considered as precursors to various forms of dark side behavior. It should be noted that individual difference antecedents are not discussed here (because of the great variety of specific individual difference variables) but were named in most of the chapters in this book.

Table 16.1. Future Research on Dark Side Behaviors.

Antecedent Factors	WPA	IPV	Discrimination	SH	ORB	Incivility	Alcohol and Drug Abuse	Psychological Contract Violation	Excess Careerism	Idiosyncratic Contracts	Negative Political Behavior
Accountability/sanctions		✓									
Injustice							✓		✓		✓
Organizational performance pressure										✓	
Work stress		✓									
Work alienation	✓					✓					
Economic factors									✓	✓	
Organizational change								✓			
Ambiguous environment			✓					✓	✓		✓
Organizational attachment				✓							
Displacement		✓				✓					
Modeling							✓			✓	
Environmental conditions					✓	✓					
Stimulus cues			✓	✓							
Economic dependence			✓		✓		✓	✓			
Group norms	✓		✓	✓							
Self-presentation	✓		✓	✓	✓						

A brief explanation of each of these antecedent factors and their source is in order. Beginning with *accountability and workplace sanctions*, research on several dark side behaviors has emphasized their importance. For example, work place sanctions were identified in the Harris chapter as important to the prevention of alcohol and drug abuse and in the Bratton and Kacmar chapter as important to the occurrence of excessive careerism. Similarly, the chapter (by Skarlicki and Folger) on organizational retaliatory behaviors suggests that these behaviors are most likely to occur if the aggrieved individual believes that the organization is accountable for his or her injury. *Injustice* involves an individual's belief that he or she has been treated unfairly (we note that a close cousin of perceived injustice is the perception of goal interference). This factor is pervasive in research on workplace aggression (Baron chapter, Neuman chapter), organizational retaliatory behavior (Skarlicki and Folger chapter), and incivility (Pearson and Porath chapter); research in these chapters indicates that perceived injustice may lead to each of these negative behavioral responses.

Some research posits *organizational performance pressure* as a motivating factor for dark side behavior. For example, the Pearson and Porath chapter suggests that incivility will occur when the organization has an intense desire to perform well and puts similar pressure on its employees. Similarly, pressure to succeed may lead organizations to enact idiosyncratic employment contracts (Rousseau chapter). *Stress* is named as an antecedent factor in several of the chapters, including that by Neuman (on workplace aggression), Reeves (on intimate partner violence), and Pearson and Porath (on incivility). These chapters argue that when employees experience work stress, their likelihood of engaging in workplace aggression, intimate partner violence, and uncivil conduct is enhanced.

Work alienation also has been examined as a precursor to dark side behaviors. Specifically, in his chapter Harris suggests that one trigger for workplace alcohol and drug abuse is employees' isolation from their work. Some research (discussed in the chapters by Reeves on intimate partner violence, and by Robinson and Brown on psychological contract violation) has identified *economic factors* (for example, an economic downturn, individual poverty) as precursors. That is, intimate partner violence is expected to occur more often under negative economic conditions (poverty, for instance), and psychological contract breach is expected to be perceived more often during times of economic downturn. Further, *organizational change* and *ambiguous organizational environments* (in which employees are uncertain about fundamental issues such as how their behavior will be evaluated) have been identified as contributing conditions to actions such as incivility and excessive careerism.

Another factor, weak *organizational attachment* (specifically, issues such as low organizational commitment, job satisfaction, and motivation), has been proposed as an antecedent to excessive careerism (in the chapter by Bratton and Kacmar). Some research has posited *displacement* (versus direct provocation) as a contributing factor in dark side conduct. Specifically, the chapter by Baron suggests that workplace aggression may occur when individuals who have been provoked by one object or agent displace their aggression onto another object or agent. Also evident in the workplace aggression literature is a focus on *modeling* as an antecedent factor, with the suggestion that individuals who have models for negative conduct become more likely to enact this conduct. *Environmental conditions* (for example, noise, temperature, crowding) also have been proposed as antecedents to workplace aggression (see the Baron chapter). Further, as discussed in the Baron chapter, *stimulus cues* (objects that cue up aggressive conduct, such as the presence of a weapon) have been important in predicting general aggression and are expected to be important in workplace aggression.

The *economic dependence* of targets has also been proposed as a contributing factor in some dark side behaviors. For example, Reeves suggests this as a motivating factor in intimate partner violence. Other research (see the Skarlicki and Folger chapter, the Harris chapter, the Dipboye and Halverson chapter) has emphasized *group or other social norms* as an important influence on organizational retaliatory behavior, workplace alcohol and drug abuse, and illegal discrimination. Finally, some research (see the chapter by Paetzold on sexual harassment) has recognized that an individual's desire to cultivate a valued reputation or identity (that is, *self-presentation issues*) sometimes may lead to negative work conduct.

Given this brief introduction to each of the antecedent factors, we now ask how research on each of the dark side behaviors considered in this volume (depicted in the column headings in Table 16.1) might be informed by these antecedent factors. Although we believe that research on each of the dark side behaviors is robust and interesting, we also believe that there is a tendency for research traditions to develop around a particular topic and for alternative perspectives to become invisible. For example, we argued earlier that much more research on sexual harassment has considered target perceptions (that is, what factors lead targets to regard an event as sexual harassment) than harasser motives (that is, what factors lead harassers to enact sexual harassment). Because early research on this topic focused on target perceptions, researchers became interested in this issue and their ideas for future research developed around this perspective. Although this is certainly appropriate in that it facilitates the methodical development of knowledge regarding one aspect of this phenomenon, it also encourages researchers to overlook that there are other interesting aspects to be explored (for example, harasser motives).

The matrix in Table 16.1 presents, we believe, a way for researchers to determine how antecedents of other dark side behaviors might be relevant to their topic of interest. Specifically, we suggest that new research ideas may come from filling in each of the cells in the matrix. We found that thinking about how a particular antecedent factor might be relevant to a research topic encouraged us to get outside of existing research traditions and to think about new directions—directions that already have theoretical and empirical foundations in related research areas.

In the remainder of our concluding chapter, we will discuss the "Future Research Matrix" that is presented in Table 16.1. Because we do not have the space (and we suspect readers would not have the patience!) to discuss all cells in this table, we highlight three cells for each of the dark side behaviors discussed in this volume (the appropriate cells are identified in Table 16.1 with a check mark). These three cells are chosen based on our personal interests; that is, we emphasize future research approaches that we find to be particularly interesting. We invite all readers to conduct their own similar analyses.

Workplace Aggression (WPA)

Within the organizational literature, the primary antecedent of workplace aggression has been perceived injustice (see the chapters by Baron and Neuman). However, perusing the list of antecedents in

Table 16.1, we find many other variables that may play a significant role in prompting this form of negative conduct. We are particularly struck by the fact that little research has considered workplace aggression from a group-level perspective. Particularly with less severe forms of aggression (for example, verbal versus physical, passive versus active), it seems likely that *work group norms* may shape the occurrence and expression of these actions. For example, work group norms may develop around the appropriateness of making verbal threats or the acceptability of statements that ridicule others. Similarly, work group norms can influence an individual's perceptions regarding how instrumental aggression will be to achieving valued outcomes. Because workplace aggression occurs within a social context, the norms of that context are important to a full understanding of the behavior. To date, we are aware of few studies that explore workplace aggression at the group level. One such study (Robinson & O'Leary-Kelly, 1998), though, provided preliminary evidence that the work group *did* influence group members' likelihood of engaging in less severe forms of aggressive conduct.

A second interesting area for future research involves the possible effects of *work alienation*. Many accounts of specific incidents of severe workplace aggression (for example, homicide) depict the perpetrator as a lonely, isolated person who essentially gives up on himself and other people. This suggests that alienation may play a key role in severe workplace aggression. It also is likely that even less severe forms of conduct may be related to alienation. For example, it is plausible that individuals who feel alienated from their work or employment setting are more likely to steal, engage in sabotage, or regard negative actions toward coworkers as of little consequence. Research on this issue might even occur at the organizational level. That is, researchers might examine the relationship between general levels of alienation in a firm and levels of negative outcomes such as sabotage or employee theft.

Finally, we are intrigued by the potential impact of *self-presentation issues* on workplace aggression. Although there is a tradition of examining these issues in relation to general aggression (for example, Tedeschi & Felson, 1994) in this case, this perspective does not appear to have had much impact on the study of workplace aggression. However, it seems likely that the decision to behave aggressively will be affected by beliefs about how this action will be viewed by individuals in the social environment. At times, aggressive actions may actually help an individual obtain or maintain a valued social identity. For example, in some workplaces, employees who try to "beat the system" by stealing from the employer or engaging in covert acts of sabotage may be regarded as heroic figures by coworkers who are bored or otherwise alienated. The contributing effect that such self-presentational issues may have on workplace aggression has received virtually no research attention, but such research could build on the strong foundation existing in social psychology (for example, Tedeschi & Felson, 1994).

Intimate Partner Violence (IPV)

There are many aspects of intimate partner violence that might be examined in research, and virtually none of these have yet been explored. In other words, there are a wealth of connections that might be made between the antecedent factors listed in Table 16.1 and this form of dark side conduct. However, we must confine ourselves to discussing only three of these that we find to be particularly noteworthy.

First, we are interested in the effects of *work stress* as a contributing factor to intimate partner violence. One interesting question is whether the work stress of the victim/target may influence the likelihood and setting of domestic violence. Because control of the intimate partner is a primary goal of batterers, and because work stress may make the intimate partner less available to the batterer (because she is distracted, because she has less energy for domestic endeavors), this may be a factor that triggers domestic violence. Further, because the workplace is a causal factor, it seems plausible that the batterer will enact violence in a way that punishes both the victim and the organization that is regarded as partly to blame (that is, he may enact violence on work premises). The recognition of these types of connections between work and home will be, we believe, critical to understanding when and why intimate violence spills over to the workplace.

Second, it is interesting to consider whether *workplace sanctions or accountability* for intimate partner violence will have any effect on an employee's likelihood of enacting it. Organizations often impose negative sanctions against employees who engage in other forms of criminal behavior, but we suspect that many employers know of employees who are domestic violence perpetrators but take no disciplinary action. If organizations took disciplinary action against such employees, is the incidence of intimate partner violence likely to decrease (because the perpetrator is fearful of losing his job) or increase (because the perpetrator blames the victim for the punishment)? Virtually nothing is known about how organizational actions might help or harm in regard to intimate partner violence, so this seems a particularly critical area of research.

Third, the issue of *displacement* is interesting. To what extent is intimate partner violence triggered by work-related frustration or negative affect? Are there direct connections between perpetrators experiencing negative outcomes at work and their enactment of violence at home? Stated another way, is intimate partner violence sometimes a form of organizational retaliatory behavior, in which frustration toward the organization is released through violence toward an intimate? While we suspect that this is often the case, again there is little research that explores these types of work-family interfaces and conflicts.

Discrimination

One promising area for future research on workplace discrimination involves the contributing role played by *ambiguous environments*. When norms, values, and/or expectations are unclear in a work setting, the likelihood of employees engaging in negative conduct is heightened. Essentially, the lack of clear expectations and standards allows individuals to define the social environment according to their own rules. If we assume that individuals are self-interested and that much discrimination (for example, racial, sexual) is caused by one individual putting personal interests above those of someone else, then discrimination seems a likely outcome of such loosely structured work environments. More specifically, discrimination against individuals who are regarded as "easy marks" (that is, those who are marginalized in society) seems especially likely. Therefore, the impact of ambiguous environments may be particularly strong in regard to discrimination against gay, lesbian, and bisexual employees, who clearly are marginalized in American society.

Second, the potential impact of *stimulus cues* is interesting here. In many cases of workplace discrimination there are reports of objects being used as part of the discriminatory conduct. For example, cartoons depicting racial minorities in a negative or inhuman light might be displayed on work premises. There is very little research on the impact of these displays and their contributing role in discriminatory conduct. It would be interesting for research to explore this phenomenon, perhaps by conceptualizing these displays as stimuli that not only trigger negative thoughts regarding specific groups but also convey the message that expression of such negative thoughts (for example, through racial harassment) is acceptable within this social environment.

Third, *self-presentation* issues seem highly relevant to discriminatory conduct. The very notion of hostile environments, which represent one aspect of discriminatory conduct, implies that discriminatory conduct can be a social phenomenon. More specifically, it seems likely that employees often may engage in discrimination as a way of establishing their own reputation in the social group. For example, individuals may make derogatory comments regarding coworkers of color as a way of gaining favor in an all-white work group, or they may withhold job opportunities from older employees as a way of gaining favor with a young management team. It seems highly plausible that these types of issues influence discriminatory behavior, but research has been slow to examine their impact.

Sexual Harassment (SH)

The *stimulus cues* mentioned above in our discussion of general discriminatory behavior are also very interesting in regard to sexual harassment, a more specific form of sex-based discrimination. There is little research in sexual harassment on the effects of stimuli that frame one gender in a negative light. However, it seems very likely that both overtly negative stimuli (for example, public posting of pornography, sexually explicit graffiti) and more subtle stimuli (for example, calling female employees by their first names and male managers by titles and surnames, asking female managers to take on secretarial duties in a meeting) may act as prompts for sex-based discrimination or even harassment.

Second, as mentioned above, *self-presentational* issues are interesting. Particularly in traditionally male work environments, or in environments that reward attributes that traditionally have been regarded as male (for example, physical strength, courage), there may be strong pressure to maintain the cohesion of the group by distancing oneself from female attributes or individuals. This may explain why, historically, some especially egregious instances of harassment have occurred in settings such as police stations, fire stations, the military, and shop floors. Explanation of the role that self-presentation motives play in these types of incidents would be most beneficial.

Finally, we mentioned earlier (as does Paetzold in her chapter) that there is little research that focuses on perpetrators of sexual harassment. The little research that does exist tends to approach this from an individual differences perspective—that is, determining the "type of person" who might enact harassment. What also is interesting, however, is research that explores the type of employee-employer relationship that might facilitate harassing actions. Because harassment has negative consequences not only for the target but also for the organization, perhaps harassers are more likely to enact this conduct when they have low regard for their employer (low *organizational attachment*). Indeed, a person who is strongly identified with an organization and who takes the organization's best interests to heart seems less likely to engage in harassing conduct than someone who has little attachment to the employer. The role that factors such as organizational identification and commitment, as well as psychological contract type (for example, relational versus instrumental), might play in decisions to harass represents another interesting, viable research question.

Organizational Retaliatory Behavior (ORB)

Most research on organizational retaliatory behavior has examined justice as a precursor (see the chapter by Skarlicki and Folger). Another interesting, but underresearched, antecedent factor is *environmental conditions*. The extent to which an individual encounters uncomfortable levels of temperature, noise, or crowding may both serve as a main and a moderator effect. In regard to the former, employees who regularly operate in these uncomfortable conditions may take action against the organization *because of* these conditions (for example, they might sabotage noisy equipment).

In regard to the latter, employees who are contemplating ORB (perhaps because of some perceived injustice by the organization) may be more likely to enact this when they also are frustrated by uncomfortable environmental conditions (that is, the environmental conditions trigger the expression of ORB in a particular time and place). Both of these effects are worthy of additional research attention.

A second area of future research involves the impact of *economic dependence* on ORB. Because ORB is a behavior that directly targets the organization, punishment by the organization for such actions (if they are discovered) may be particularly severe. If so, this may discourage those employees who are most economically dependent on the organization from even contemplating such actions. If true, this implies that ORB involves a conscious, rational decision-making process, as opposed to an anger-driven, "lashing-out" type of reaction. It also suggests that some individuals have the "freedom" to enact revenge or retaliation whereas others feel too economically vulnerable to take this action. Exploration of the effects of economic dependence on decision-making processes and on self-control of ORB would be most interesting.

Finally, we believe that *self-presentation* issues also have relevance to ORB. In some (albeit dysfunctional) work environments, retaliation against the employer may be a socially valued act. If employees gain reputationally for "getting even" with the employer, then this behavior becomes very difficult to control. In addition, employees who are rewarded for ORB by coworkers may begin to lower their injustice threshold. Perhaps organizational actions that did not lead to injustice perceptions in the past will begin to be reframed as unjust, because such framing allows for opportunities to retaliate and thereby enhance reputation. Research on these types of interplays between self-presentational issues and the need for retaliation and the likelihood of retaliation would be intriguing.

Incivility

Two antecedent factors that seem highly relevant to the occurrence of workplace incivility are *work alienation* and negative *environmental conditions*. Both of these antecedent factors involve disconnection from fundamental aspects of the workplace (the work itself, the physical setting) and may lead employees to behave in rude, discourteous ways. Specifically, employees who feel alienated from the work that they do are likely to experience negative affect around this alienation. It seems likely that this disaffection will surface in interpersonal encounters with others, particularly in those encounters that are directly connected to the work that causes the alienation. Similarly, employees who experience uncomfortable environments may express their discomfort through discourtesies toward others. Indeed, environmental conditions may even create the *perception* of incivility when it is not intended. Recently, one of us had a conversation with a manager who supervised employees who worked in a particularly noisy environment. This manager believed that many of the interpersonal conflicts in her workplace were explained by the fact that employees had to stand close to each other and shout in order to be heard. She suggested that these violations of traditional communication norms (for example, violation of personal space, loud tones that sound angry) led to conduct being interpreted as impolite or even aggressive. It is fascinating to consider that employees may know intellectually that their coworkers must shout at them to be heard, but that they still may interpret this conduct as uncivil and may react accordingly.

It also is interesting to consider *displacement* in regard to incivility. In the same way that we suggested earlier that acts of aggression such as intimate partner violence may involve displaced aggression, we wonder whether incivility is often triggered by negative affect or frustration generated elsewhere. That is, how often does incivility involve anger or dislike for the target, and how often is it just a function of the individual's general mood or frustration with some other person or object? Although there is no empirical answer to this question, our hunch is that the latter may be closer to the truth.

Workplace Alcohol and Drug Abuse

In regard to alcohol and drug abuse, it would be interesting to explore what role the organizational setting plays in these phenomena. For example, when employees perceive unjust treatment (*injustice*) by the organization, does this trigger drug or alcohol abuse at work? More specifically, is a particular form of injustice (distributive, procedural, or interactional) more likely to be associated with this negative conduct? For example, because drug and alcohol abuse is a self-destructive act, is interactional injustice (which conveys a sense that the employee is not worthy of respect) more likely to trigger substance abuse? A better understanding of the role that fair treatment by the employer plays in this conduct would be beneficial.

Second, we return to the notion of *environmental conditions* as an antecedent factor. If substance abuse is prompted by a desire to "escape from reality," then negative work conditions may be a reality that employees are particularly interested in escaping. For example, are employees who work in crowded environments more likely to abuse substances at work, or does the physical closeness of coworkers discourage them from doing so? These types of research questions, which consider the influence of an employee's physical comfort at work on workplace substance abuse, seem worthy of study.

Finally, *economic dependence* issues are noteworthy. From a completely rational perspective, we would predict that employees who are highly dependent on their jobs (for example, who have low skill levels and therefore have few employment alternatives; who live in areas where there are few employment opportunities) will be less likely to abuse drugs and alcohol at work, because such behavior puts their jobs in jeopardy. However, this "rational" prediction ignores the despondency that individuals with few job opportunities might experience and the possibility that despondency itself triggers alcohol and drug abuse. A better understanding of how these types of factors interact to encourage or discourage workplace substance abuse would be valuable.

Psychological Contract Breach and Violation (PCV)

To this point, we have focused our discussion around antecedents that have not been explored in research on the dark side behavior of interest. We stray from this general approach in our discussion of the effects of *organizational change* on psychological contract breach and violation. In their chapter, Robinson and Brown do mention organizational change as a possible precursor to perceptions of psychological contract violation. However, their discussion of this antecedent is as a *possible* factor only—there is no empirical evidence that organizational changes are associated with strong perceptions of psychological contract violation. However, we agree with these authors that this is a factor that seems likely to influence perceptions of broken promises, therefore we highlight it here as in need of future research attention.

Similarly, we would be interested in seeing research that explores the effects of *ambiguous environments* on perceptions of psychological contract breach and violation. When employees operate in settings that are unclear regarding normative behavior, values, and role expectations, the chance for psychological contract breach to occur seems heightened. In addition, when breach occurs in these types of environments, employees may react more negatively (that is, breach may be more likely to lead to violation) because they attribute more blame to employers. Although these speculations seem plausible, research is needed.

Finally, the *economic dependence* of employees is interesting in regard to psychological contracts. Are employees who are more dependent on the organization less likely to perceive contract breaches, because this creates cognitive dissonance that they may be unable to resolve? When employees are more economically dependent on organizations, is there greater occurrence of contract breaches by the organization because management knows that employees' violation perceptions are less likely to be associated with turnover? Answers to these research questions would provide new insights into the perceptions of employees and the actions of organizations around contract breach.

Excessive Careerism

Essentially, employees who engage in excessive careerism are those who enact extremely self-interested behavior around their career success and progress. An interesting question, then, is what might lead such individuals to perceive a need for this type of behavior. One possible answer is that employees who feel unfairly treated by the organization may believe that they must now look out for themselves and not for the interests of the organization. That is, perceived *injustice* may at times encourage excessive careerism; affected employees may shift their career orientation from one that is more "local" (organization-based) to one that is more "cosmopolitan" (pursuing career advancement and success beyond the boundaries of their organization). Research that explores the viability of this prediction would be interesting.

In addition, we are intrigued by the question of whether environmental changes could trigger excessive careerism. If individuals are operating within a shifting environment (either due to *economic factors* such as a downturn in the economy or *organizational change* factors such as restructuring or downsizing), it seems likely that protective instincts will kick in and self-interested behavior may increase. Because careerism is self-interested behavior around an individual's *career,* this may be a particularly relevant way to enact self-interest when the work environment is changing.

Idiosyncratic Employment Contracts

Research on idiosyncratic contracts is quite new, so as with intimate partner violence there are many research opportunities. One particularly interesting question is when these contracts are most likely to occur, and several antecedent factors from Table 16.1 provide insight into this question. First, it seems likely that such contracts will be present when an organization faces significant *performance pressure* (that is, it operates in a turbulent environment, it operates in a competitive industry). Under these conditions, organizations may be willing to upset their internal equity and offer idiosyncratic contracts in order to address these performance-related concerns. Similarly, it seems probable that *economic factors* may play a role. During times of recession, when individuals have more trouble finding jobs, organizations may be less likely to use idiosyncratic contracts (because they are less necessary to successful recruitment). But if their competitors regularly engage in idiosyncratic contracts, firms may blindly follow the lead (*modeling*) even if employees could have been recruited and retained with more traditional contracts. Also interesting is the question of whether these conditions (that is, performance pressure, economic factors, modeling by other organizations) lead employees to be more accepting of idiosyncratic contracts—that is, do employees regard these conditions as appropriate justifications for atypical employment contracts? Are some of these justifications by the organization (for example, "We face significant performance pressure") more likely to be associated with positive employee reactions compared to others (for example, "Other firms are doing it")?

Negative Politics

As with excessive careerism, we are interested in the causal role that *injustice* might play in political behavior. There is a sense in the research described in the Hall, Hochwarter, Ferris, and Bowen chapter that political behavior is driven by an individual's desire to manipulate—to create some outcome. Less obvious is the notion that political behavior may involve a *reaction*. That is, perhaps negative political behavior sometimes is triggered by a perception that one has been unfairly treated. The political conduct, then, may involve efforts to restore justice or to retaliate against those who caused the injustice. This would be an interesting perspective to explore in future research.

Second, we are interested in the contributing role that *organizational change* plays in political behavior. Does political behavior occur more often, and is it more dramatic, during times of change? Although we expect the answer to this question to be "yes," empirical verification is needed. Similarly, is political behavior perceived differently during times of organizational change? That is, are the same behaviors regarded by coworkers as more negative or manipulative when enacted during unsettling times?

Finally, *modeling* seems highly relevant to the emergence of political behavior. Such behavior probably is learned by watching others, so the presence of models in the work group or workplace should be investigated as a possible antecedent. In essence, modeling could become a tool for either building a highly political organizational culture (if the models are rewarded for their actions) or for discouraging a political culture (if the models are punished for their actions).

Thoughts on Research Methods

To this point, one chapter in this volume (the one by Greenberg and Tomlinson) has received little attention in our conclusion. We address this chapter separately because it serves a somewhat different purpose than other chapters in the book. The chapter by Greenberg and Tomlinson is a treatise on the development of a specific research area (employee theft). They explore the different approaches to research that have been taken historically (termed the DATA cycle), and discuss their strengths and weaknesses. This provides a nice framework for thinking about research within each of the topic areas described in other chapters. Although space limitations prevent us from exploring the status of each dark side behavior in relation to the DATA cycle, we invite readers to take this step. To us, this chapter is an important reminder that it is not just *what* we study, but also *how* we study it that is critical to our ability to build knowledge.

Concluding Thoughts

There are two approaches to reading this book. First, one might read each chapter separately, taking note of what is known regarding the dark side behavior described in the individual chapters. We hope that this approach represents your "first read" of this book. The second approach is to integrate these chapters, looking at what each implies about the other and how research in one area informs that in others. This latter approach, we believe, represents the true strength of volumes such as this. It is our hope that you will take the time for this "second read" and consider each dark side behavior in context of the others. Even the second time through, we can promise you a great journey.

References

Farmer, S. M., & Fedor, D. B. (1999). Volunteer participation and withdrawal: A psychological contract perspective on the role of expectation and organizational support. *Nonprofit Management and Leadership, 9*, 349–367.

O'Leary-Kelly, A. M., Duffy, M. K., & Griffin, R. W. (2000). Construct confusion in the study of antisocial work behavior. In G. R. Ferris (Ed.), *Research in personnel and human resources management* (Vol. 18, pp. 275–303). Stamford, CT: JAI Press.

Robinson, S. L., & Greenberg, J. (1998). Employees behaving badly: Dimensions, determinants and dilemmas in the study of workplace deviance. In C. L. Cooper & D. M. Rousseau (Eds.), *Trends in organizational behavior* (Vol. 5, pp. 1–30). Chichester, England: John Wiley.

Robinson, S. L., & O'Leary-Kelly, A. M. (1998). Monkey see, monkey do: The influence of work groups on the antisocial behavior of employees. *Academy of Management Journal, 41,* 658–672.

Tedeschi, J. T., & Felson, R. B. (1994). *Violence, aggression, and coercive actions.* Washington, DC: American Psychological Association.

Name Index

Subject Index

Outcomes: examining moderators of breach, 319–325; impact of negative impression management, 304–305; internal locus of control over, 301; negative IM and nature of, 299–300

OWCP (Office of Workers' Compensation Practices), 81

P

PA (positive affect), 250

Pan American World Airways, Inc., Diaz *v.*, 147–148

Passive harasser models of sexual harassment, 166–168

Perceptions of politics, 302–303

Person-specific employment arrangements: blurry boundaries among, 273*fig*; dilemma of relative standing, 275–276; facets of, 265*t*; idiosyncratic, 265, 270–274, 281–284; organizational practice of, 284–285; preferential, 264–269; slippery slope to the dark side in, 274; unauthorized, 265, 269–270

Personal determinants of aggression, 45–48

Personal response sexual harassment response, 171

Physical violence. *See* Violence

PO (person-organization) approach, 152–153

Political behaviors: accountability as key influence on, 299; cognitive and affective processes of, 247–250; comparing citizenship behavior and, 247–248; destructive, 15–16; forms of social influence and, 243–244; Future Research Matrix on negative, 470*t*, 484; hypothesis/study on beneficial, 242–243; negative impression management and propensity for, 300–303; role of emotions/emotional labor in, 249–250; role

of political skills in, 248–249. *See also* Dark side perspective of politics; Organizational politics

Political skills: deficiency in, 248–249; organization-specific, 266; role in political behaviors, 248–249

POPS (Perceptions of Organizational Politics scale), 246, 253, 267

POS (Perceived Organizational Support), 267

Power: extreme careerism in pursuit of, 291; IPV (intimate partner violence) and role of, 106–107, 118; as necessary to individual success, 242; negative regard of development/use of, 241–242

Power structure sexual harassment response, 171

Preattribution, 51

Preferential employment arrangements, 264–269

Proactive reciprocity motivation, 271

Procedural justice, 69, 279–280

Professional mediation sexual harassment response, 171

Provocation, 38–41

Psychological contract breach: additional directions for future research on, 330–331; antecedents of, 313–315; conceptual/definitional issues of, 310–311; consequences of, 315–319; described, 309; Future Research Matrix on, 470*t*, 481–482; key characteristics of, 311–313; methodological challenges of, 328–330; moderators of the breach-outcome relationships, 319–325; practical implications of, 325–327

Psychological contract breach consequences: attitudinal, 316–317; behavioral, 317–319; studies on, 315–316